1962

The Supreme Court Review

1962
The

"Judges as persons, or courts as institutions, are entitled to no greater immunity from criticism than other persons or institutions. . . . [J]udges must be kept mindful of their limitations and of their ultimate public responsibility by a vigorous stream of criticism expressed with candor however blunt."
—*Felix Frankfurter*

". . . while it is proper that people should find fault when their judges fail, it is only reasonable that they should recognize the difficulties. . . . Let them be severely brought to book, when they go wrong, but by those who will take the trouble to understand them."
—*Learned Hand*

THE LAW SCHOOL
THE UNIVERSITY OF CHICAGO

Supreme Court Review

EDITED BY
PHILIP B. KURLAND

THE UNIVERSITY OF CHICAGO PRESS

LIBRARY OF CONGRESS CATALOG CARD NUMBER: 60-14353

THE UNIVERSITY OF CHICAGO PRESS, CHICAGO & LONDON
THE UNIVERSITY OF TORONTO PRESS, TORONTO 5, CANADA

COMPOSED AND PRINTED BY THE UNIVERSITY OF CHICAGO PRESS
CHICAGO, ILLINOIS, U.S.A.

TO

MR. JUSTICE FELIX FRANKFURTER

"... a truly civilized man ...
confiden[t] in the strength and security
derived from the inquiring mind ...
unafraid of the uncertitudes."

CONTENTS

PHILIP B. KURLAND

THE REGENTS' PRAYER CASE: "FULL OF SOUND AND FURY, SIGNIFYING..."

I. Engel v. Vitale

The two decisions of the 1961 Term that aroused the greatest public interest were *Baker v. Carr*[1] and *Engel v. Vitale*.[2] The first opened the federal courts for review of State legislative apportionment by accepting jurisdiction over a challenge to Tennessee's failure to redistrict in accordance with the terms of its own constitution. The second invalidated the use in New York's public schools of a prayer composed by the Board of Regents. "The Tennessee decision and its aftermath have, predictably, brought protests from rural forces. But the criticism has been relatively mild, and there has been strong support for the court from many quarters. It is ironic that a case with so much less potential for real change in the country's social and political structure—the prayer case—has provoked so much greater outcry."[3]

Philip B. Kurland is Professor of Law, The University of Chicago.

1 369 U.S. 186 (1962).

2 370 U.S. 421 (1962). See Neal, *Baker v. Carr: Politics in Search of Law*, [1962] Supreme Court Review, *infra*.

3 Anthony Lewis, New York Times, July 2, 1962, p. 12, col. 4.

A. INJUDICIOUS OPINIONS

The immediate reaction to *Vitale* certainly was gross. The press was divided.[4] The divines were also divided, in part along denominational lines. The Catholic hierarchy and its spokesmen were almost unanimous in condemnation of the Court in most vehement terms.[5] Most of the Jewish clergy approved the decision.[6] The Protestant ministry was in greater conflict.[7]

---

[4] "[E]ven worse was the sight of so many otherwise responsible newspapers getting completely swept off their feet by the tide of emotionalism." New York Herald Tribune, July 5, 1962, p. 18, col. 3. The press was divided pretty much as one would have anticipated, as shown by the following examples:

In defense of the Court: New York Times, New York Herald Tribune, New York Post, Pittsburgh Post-Gazette, Hartford Courant, Chicago Sun-Times, Milwaukee Journal, St. Louis Post-Dispatch, Louisville Courier-Journal, Washington Post.

Attacking the Court: New York Journal (all Hearst papers), New York News, Baltimore Sun, Boston Globe, Chicago Tribune, Kansas City Star, Los Angeles Times, San Francisco News-Call Bulletin, Washington Star.

[5] Cardinal Spellman's statement was not untypical: "I am shocked and frightened that the Supreme Court has declared unconstitutional a simple and voluntary declaration of belief in God by public school children. The decision strikes at the very heart of the Godly tradition in which America's children have for so long been raised." The Brooklyn *Tablet* labeled the decision "preposterous." The *Catholic News,* the archdiocesan paper for New York, found the "implications . . . appalling." The Jesuit weekly *America* used the adjectives: "asinine," "stupid," "doctrinaire," and "unrealistic." The Catholic spokesmen frequently spoke, nonetheless, of the profit that might be garnered by utilizing the opinion to prove the need for parochial schools to be supported by public funds.

The Vatican also contributed its views, if somewhat belatedly. *Osservatore Romano* expressed doubts about the opinion but, becomingly, in more moderate tones. It stated "regrets" at the "disconcerting" action of the Justices "whatever [their] motivation." *La Civilta Catolica* said: "The possible implications are such as to give rise to certain preoccupations."

[6] The rabbinate was not as unanimous as the Catholic clergy. Most were in accord with the declarations of praise from the New York Board of Rabbis, the Rabbinical Assembly of America, and the Commission of Social Action of Reform Judaism. But there were voices, like that of a Rabbi Kelman of Brooklyn, asserting that: "It is regrettable from the point of view of Judaism that this prayer was banned."

[7] The Reverend Billy Graham thundered, paralogically, against the decision: "God pity our country when we can no longer appeal to God for help." And James A. Pike, Episcopal Bishop of San Francisco, announced that "the Supreme Court has just deconsecrated the nation." More common among those who spoke out for Protestantism was the attitude of Harold E. Fey, editor of the *Christian Century,* and a distinguished group of theologians who joined him: "The Court's decision protects the integrity of the religious conscience and the proper function of religious and governmental institutions."

The politicians were politicians; most of them who spoke to the question seemed to see an opportunity to make political capital by coming out in favor of God. Representative Andrews was typical of the southern reaction: "They put the Negroes in to the schools and now they have driven God out of them." Representative Rooney of New York, a leader in the fight to secure public money for Catholic schools, labeled the decision as "asinine," and, with others, saw it as Communistic in substance if not in inspiration. Former Presidents Hoover and Eisenhower both were shocked by the Court's action. President Kennedy and Governor Rockefeller—neither of whom seemed to have any liking for the result—were outstanding for their moderate reaction. The latter was alone among all the governors of the United States in opposing a resolution calling for a constitutional amendment to reverse the judgment: "Until the whole question can be considered in terms of the fundamental precept of freedom of religion, which was the basis for the constitutional provision upon which the Supreme Court based its opinion, I shall abstain from the endorsement of any hasty action by the Governors relating to amendment of the Constitution of the United States." President Kennedy's statement came in response to a question at his regular press conference:

> The Supreme Court has made its judgment, and a good many people obviously will disagree with it. Others will agree with it. But I think it is important for us if we are going to maintain our constitutional principle that we support the Supreme Court decisions even when we may not agree with them. . . . I would hope that [the people] will support the Constitution and the responsibility of the Supreme Court in interpreting it, which is theirs, and given to them by the Constitution.

"We start down a rough road," said Mr. Justice Jackson in his dissent in *Zorach*,[8] "when we begin to mix compulsory public education with compulsory godliness." The road was not made any smoother by the Court's original journey over it, as the immediate reaction to *Vitale* so readily demonstrated. The attack on the Court when it condemned Illinois' released-time program[9] was not unlike

---

8 Zorach v. Clauson, 343 U.S. 306, 325 (1952).

9 McCollum v. Board of Education, 333 U.S. 203 (1948). See KURLAND, RELIGION AND THE LAW 86–90 (1962) (hereinafter RELIGION).

the vituperative assault following the Regents' prayer case.[10] The success of these storm tactics is attested by the Court's retreat in *Zorach*, where Mr. Justice Douglas, writing for the Court, sustained the New York released-time program, distinguishing *McCollum* on gossamer-thin grounds. This past success can only encourage further efforts to drive the Court back down that rocky road. But one weapon should be removed from the arsenal of attackers if possible: that is the weapon of hyperbole. Misconstruction and misrepresentation of the Court's action in *Vitale* should not be permitted to bring about its downfall as misrepresentation and misconstruction of *McCollum* destroyed that case, at least temporarily. It is the function of this essay, therefore, to attempt an accurate report of the issues and judicial history of *Vitale* and only then to offer a critical evaluation.

B. THE FACTS

In 1951, the New York Board of Regents became

> aware of the dire need, in these days of concentrated attacks by an atheistic way of life upon our world and in these times of rising juvenile delinquency, of crime increasing both numerically and in gravity of offense, with an ever-swelling number of criminals being counted in the younger age groups, of finding ways to pass on America's Moral and Spiritual Heritage to our youth through the public school system.[11]

Among the antidotes to the deterioration of "our youth" and, presumably, as its contribution to the success of the United States effort in the cold war, the Board concocted a prayer to be utilized at the opening of classes each day in conjunction with the salute to the flag. The prayer: "Almighty God, we acknowledge our dependence upon Thee, and we beg Thy blessings upon us, our parents, our teachers and our country."

The special competence of the Board to establish the proper form for expressing devotion to God was never revealed. It was revealed, however, that the Board "counted five attorneys among its [thir-

---

10 See, *e.g.*, Statement by Catholic Bishops Attacking Secularism as an Evil, New York Times, Nov. 21, 1948, § 1, p. 63, col. 1; O'NEILL, RELIGION AND EDUCATION UNDER THE CONSTITUTION 219–53, 254–72 (1949).

11 Brief for the Board of Regents of the University of the State of New York as *Amicus Curiae*, p. 14. (Capitalization in original.)

teen] members" and had experienced legal counsel as well. Because of the legal advice available, it was suggested that no ruling that the Board promulgated could run afoul of the First Amendment. "[I]t is apodictic[12] that the Board of Regents at the times here involved was, as it now is, fully aware of and conversant with the doctrine of separation of Church and State."[13]

However one may evaluate other contested facts in the record, it is quite clear that the intention of the Board in recommending the use of this prayer was to inculcate in the school children "the belief in a Supreme Being."[14] At the same time, in achieving this goal, the Board wished to avoid giving offense to any of the country's three major religious faiths: Protestant, Catholic, Jewish. To avoid infringing on the rights of any who might not accept the orthodoxy of any of these religions, the Board provided for voluntary abstention from participation for those who chose not to number themselves among "all men and women of good will" who would "subscribe" to the Board's "program."[15]

In July of 1958, the Board of Education for a school district in New Hyde Park, New York, provided by resolution "that the regents prayer be said daily in our schools."[16] It ordered the district principal to see "that this be instituted as a daily procedure to follow the Salute to the flag."[17] Accordingly, the practice was adopted in New Hyde Park schools. The prayer was said aloud at the beginning of classes each day, led by the teacher or a student singled out by the teacher for this purpose.[18] Possibly before,[19] but certainly after, the order of the trial court in this litigation,[20] teachers were instructed to abstain from encouraging participation by unwilling children, who were to be excused from participation or permitted to absent themselves from the classroom on written requests of their parents or guardians.

---

12 For non-pedants among the readers of this essay, it must be noted that "apodictic" is defined thus: "Of clear demonstration; established by incontrovertible evidence. (By Kant applied to a proposition enouncing a necessary and hence *absolute* truth.)" 1 OXFORD ENGLISH DICTIONARY 327 (1933).

13 Brief, *supra* note 11.

14 *Id.* at 15; Record, pp. 28–39.

15 Record, p. 29.

16 *Id.* at p. 40.

17 *Ibid.*

18 *Id.* at 14, 24–27, 66.

19 *Id.* at 27, 66.

20 *Id.* at 170–73.

In January, 1959 five parents of children attending schools in New Hyde Park, all citizens of the United States and of New York, all taxpayers of the school district,[21] removed themselves from the Regents' category of "men and women of good will" by seeking an order in the nature of mandamus from the trial court of general jurisdiction to compel the discontinuance of the Regents' prayer ceremony in the schools of the district. The objections asserted were that "the saying of the said prayer and the manner and setting in which it is said . . . violate the prohibition against laws respecting an establishment of religion [and] laws prohibiting the free exercise of religion. . . ."[22]

C. JUDICIAL OPINIONS

1. *Supreme Court of Nassau County.* Justice Meyer of the Supreme Court of Nassau County wrote an exhaustive and erudite opinion[23] in which he ordered the New Hyde Park Board of Education to issue regulations clarifying the rights of students to abstain from participation but ruled that with this safeguard there was no violation of either the separation or the freedom clause of the First Amendment:[24]

> [I]t is concluded that the "establishment" clause of the Constitution does not prohibit the noncompulsory saying of the Regents' prayer in the public schools, but that the "free exercise" clause requires that respondent board take affirmative steps to protect the rights of those who, for whatever reason, choose not to participate.

---

[21] *Id.* at 11–12.

[22] *Id.* at 15–17. More specifically, they asserted that the ceremony was unconstitutional because it: (1) "entails the use of the public school system . . . the time and efforts of the teachers and the staff . . ."; (2) "constitute[s] the teaching of religion and religious practices in a form, manner and setting which is contrary to the religion and religious practices of [four of] . . . the petitioners . . . and . . . their children" and others in the district; (3) is "contrary to the beliefs concerning such matters" of the non-religious "petitioner and his children" and others in the district; (4) has "necessarily resulted in the exercise of coercion upon the children . . . to engage, against their will, in the saying of a religious prayer . . ."; (5) is "sectarian and denominational" and "favor[s] one or more religions and religious practices over others"; (6) "favor[s] the belief in religion over non-belief therein"; and (7) has "necessarily resulted in divisiveness among the students . . . and among their parents. . . ." *Ibid.*

[23] 18 N.Y. Misc. 2d 659 (Sup. Ct. Nass. Co. 1959).

[24] *Id.* at 662.

Recognizing the extrinsic difficulties of deciding the case, Meyer quickly rejected the notion that "emotionalism" or "in terrorem" contentions should play any part:[25]

> [T]he thesis that the present rate of juvenile delinquency evidences the need for prayer in the schools is a matter of policy and of no weight in determining what the constitutional provisions framed in 1789 and 1865 mean.[26] So also while it may validly be argued that the appointment of chaplains by the Congress in 1791 represents a practical construction by the Congress responsible for the First Amendment of its meaning, the fact that the appropriation acts covering the pay of Congressional chaplains has never been held invalid is of no weight, since no citizen has standing to bring an action to prevent such a payment. Again, Franklin's suggestion to the Constitutional Convention of daily prayer as a means of breaking its deadlock assumes lesser proportion when it is realized that the suggestion, though seconded, was not adopted by the convention. Similarly, to be rejected, in view of the essentially different nature of prayer on the one hand from the study of historical fact on the other, is the specter of "Godless" schools in which, if the prayer here involved is not sanctioned, references to God in the Constitution and the Declaration of Independence will not be permitted. In sum, the constitutional line to be drawn can only be determined by an analysis of the fact situation involved, the history of the constitutional provisions, and the holdings (together with but distinct from the language used in stating those holdings) of judicial decisions construing the constitutional provisions (or provisions essentially similar).

After extensive examination of the history of the constitutional provisions, he reached the conclusion that neither at the time of the adoption of the First Amendment nor at the time of the adoption of the Fourteenth was it believed that these constitutional provisions invoked any ban on the use of prayer to open the school day. Even if this conclusion was an accurate one, the question remains whether

---

[25] *Id.* at 669.

[26] "More in point would be the fact that Patrick Henry made the same argument in 1784 in support of the Bill Establishing a Provision for Teachers of the Christian Religion (Brant, James Madison, The Nationalist [1948] 344), that the initial passage of the bill by the Virginia Legislature provoked Madison's famous Memorial and Remonstrance, and that, as a result, the assessment plan which the bill would have imposed was killed by the next session of the Legislature." *Id.* at 669, n. 34.

it was material.[27] Nevertheless it provided one of the two pillars on which the judgment of the trial court rested. For the court, on the basis of this history, reached the rather strange conclusion that if "the purpose [of the prayer] is to inculcate in pupils a love of God, then . . . it would constitute religious instruction in violation of the 'establishment' clause."[28] The reason the "establishment" clause is not breached is because "prayer in the schools is permissible not as a means of teaching 'spiritual values' but because traditionally, and particularly at the time of the adoption of the First and Fourteenth Amendments, this was the accepted practice."[29] Apparently this is saying that if the actions commanded by the State had any meaning they would be invalid as engagement in religious proselyting, but that they were sustainable because they were meaningless or, perhaps, because they were the kind of State aid to religion that was indulged in the past and must, therefore, be condoned in the present and the future.

Zorach v. Clauson[30] was the second foundation on which the judgment of the Supreme Court of Nassau County rested:[31]

> The *Zorach* case holds that the Constitution does not require separation in every and all respects and, as we have seen, constitutional history confirms a tradition of prayer, including prayer in the schools. Even without the constitutional history, some form of prayer would appear to fall within the realm of permissible accommodation. Despite the board's "spiritual heritage" argument, the prayer under consideration cannot be deemed religious instruction. It is recited during opening exercises rather than as a part of any instructional period. It is phrased in traditional prayer form rather than in any form normal for instructional materials. Essentially, it is devotional and, as such, is designed to be repeated daily, without change, over a 12-year school course. Twenty-two words in length, and thus taking substantially less than one minute to recite and a good deal less time for recitation than does the legislative

---

[27] See Bickel, *The Original Understanding and the Segregation Decision*, 69 Harv. L. Rev. 1 (1955).

[28] 18 Misc. 2d at 673. The court conditioned this statement on the compulsory nature of the prayer. But while compulsion would clearly affect the problem of "freedom," if that is a separable question, it is difficult to see how the "establishment" conclusion can turn on this factor.

[29] *Ibid.*

[30] 343 U.S. 306 (1952).

[31] 18 Misc. 2d at 693–94.

> prayer deemed by *Zorach* to be within permissible constitutional degree, the instant prayer, at least when its recitation is limited to daily exercises at the opening of school, must be classified as outside *McCollum's* proscription of religious instruction and within *Zorach's* sanction as an accommodation.

Unless the court really believed that the labels "instruction" and "accommodation" solved the problem, reliance on *Zorach* failed to assay the weakness of that authority. That it was basically inconsistent with *McCollum*[32] (whose vitality has since been reaffirmed[33]), that *Zorach* had, in effect, been largely discounted by its author,[34] and that it rested primarily on the notion that the activities in question did not take place on the school premises were all matters that Meyer apparently preferred to ignore.

2. *Appellate Division.* The Appellate Division for the Second Department, Justices Nolan, Beldock, Christ, Pette, and Brennan, affirmed the trial court's judgment in a per curiam opinion in which all joined except Beldock:[35] "We agree with the views expressed in the opinion [below]." Beldock agreed with the conclusion but not with the reasons offered by the trial court. For him the case was much more simple of solution. His rationale, however, rested on a distinction more apparent to him than it may be to others:[36]

> My sole reason for sustaining the "Regents' Prayer" is that, in my opinion, the prayer here involved *does not constitute religious teaching.* The recital of this prayer does nothing more than acknowledge the existence of God and dependence upon him. It gives no training or instruction of any religious nature whatever. There can be no constitutional objection to a prayer which is said without rites or ceremony or doctrinal teaching, and which serves at the beginning of each day to give each student who believes in God "a brief moment with eternity" and a feeling of "humility before the Supreme Power" (*Doremus* v. *Board of Educ.*, 5 N.J. 435, 452, appeal dismissed [for want of jurisdiction] 342 U.S. 429). Such a prayer merely affirms and reaffirms "that this is a religious nation"; it recognizes (as do the Federal Constitution, every State Constitution and every colonial grant and charter beginning with

32 McCollum v. Board of Education, 333 U.S. 203 (1948).

33 See Torcaso v. United States, 367 U.S. 488, 493 (1961).

34 See Douglas, J., in McGowan v. Maryland, 366 U.S. 420, 563–64 (1961).

35 11 N.Y. App. Div. 2d 340, 341 (1960).

36 *Id.* at 343. (Emphasis in original.)

> the one to Christopher Columbus) "a profound reverence for religion and an assumption that its influence in all human affairs is essential to the well being of the community" (*Holy Trinity Church* v. *United States,* 143 U.S. 457, 468, 470).

This "sole reason" was buttressed by seven more pages essentially relying on *Zorach v. Clauson.* However Beldock may have felt about the opinion of the trial court, the reasons he asserted did not differ essentially from that court's reasoning.

3. *Court of Appeals.* The unanimity of judicial opinion theretofore apparent was shattered when the case reached the New York Court of Appeals.[37] Chief Judge Desmond, for the court, quickly disposed of the "freedom-of-religion" issue:[38] "The order here appealed from contains adequate provisions to insure that no pupil need take part in or be present during the act of reverence, so any question of 'compulsion' or 'free exercise' is out of the case (see *Zorach v. Clauson,* 343 U.S. 306)." The separation problem took more words but was as easily disposed of. By switching the issue from that of a prescribed prayer to the right of the majority to express its beliefs, he was able to rest on the following appeal to "natural law" as an integral part of our legal and constitutional system:[39]

> The "universally accepted tradition" referred to by Justice Beldock has been maintained without break from the days of the Founding Fathers, all of whom believed in the existence of God (see Cousins, In God We Trust), to the day of the inauguration of President Kennedy. It is an indisputable and historically provable fact that belief and trust in a Creator has always been regarded as an integral and inseparable part of the fabric of our fundamental institutions. It is not a matter of majority power or minority protection. Belief in a Supreme Being is as essential and permanent a feature of the American governmental system as is freedom of worship, equality under the law and due process of law. Like them it is an American absolute, an application of the natural law beliefs on which the Republic was founded and which in turn presupposes an Omnipotent Being.

It might be suggested that at least one difference exists between "natural law beliefs" and "freedom of worship, equality under the law and due process of law." The latter are specified as within the protection of the Constitution, the former are not.

---

[37] 10 N.Y. 2d 174 (1961).

[38] *Id.* at 179–80.

[39] *Id.* at 181–82.

Aside from the reference to *Zorach*, the only Supreme Court statement thought relevant was the dictum in *Holy Trinity v. United States*,[40] on which *Zorach* had also relied.

There were short concurring opinions by Judges Froessel and Burke. Froessel rested on *Zorach* and distinguished *McCollum*:[41] "Here no partiality is shown, nor are classrooms being turned over to religious instructors. . . ." Burke agreed with Desmond and Froessel because the alternative demanded "the interpolation of a Marxist concept that mandates a prescribed ethic" that "force[s] on the children a culture that is founded upon secularist dogma."[42]

Judge Dye wrote the dissenting opinion, in which Judge Fuld concurred. He refused to be trapped by slogans: "No one doubts for a moment that we are a religious people."[43] He suggested that one of the reasons that the people's religiosity had been sustained was because of the protections afforded by the First Amendment. "[O]ur State is free to function without interference by or dictation from an organized church. This mutual forbearance in spirit and in practice has eliminated divisiveness in a most sensitive area, created mutual respect for both church and State and has unified our people in a way that no other force could do."[44]

The dissent then asserted that the decisions of the Supreme Court of the United States were appropriate guides to a conclusion. Starting with Black's statement of principle in *Everson*,[45] the opinion turned to *McCollum* and distinguished *Zorach*, largely in reliance on Douglas' statement in *McGowan v. Maryland* and the Court's opinion in *Torcaso*.[46] The applicable principle derived by the dissenters was stated this way:[47]

> Running through the fabric of these definitive decisions, like the pattern of a tree of life in an intricate tapestry, is a clearly defined line of demarcation between church and State, which may not be overstepped in the slightest degree in favor of either the church or the State. In such light, a board of education

---

40 143 U.S. 457 (1892). See Religion 26–27.

41 10 N.Y. 2d at 183.

42 *Id.* at 184.

43 *Id.* at 185.

44 *Id.* at 186.

45 *Id.* at 186–87; Everson v. Board of Education, 330 U.S. 1, 15–16 (1947); see Religion 80–85.

46 See *supra* notes 33 and 34.

47 10 N.Y. 2d at 189–90.

> may not require the saying of the Regents prayer as a daily school procedure. It is a form of State-sponsored religious education; in fact, according to the Regents, its purpose is "teaching our children, as set forth in the Declaration of Independence, that Almighty God is their Creator" (1951 Statement of Belief) and "will give to the student an understanding and appreciation of his role as an individual endowed by his Creator . . . and of reverence for Almighty God." It would thus "fulfill its [the school's] high function of supplementing the training of the home." . . . This requirement falls squarely within the categories of disability accounting for the decisions in *Everson* and *McCollum* (*supra*): use of public school classrooms during regular school hours, limitation of participation to those children whose parents consent and, in addition, being led by a teacher or by a person designated by the teacher. Under such announced purpose and method of performance, it cannot be less than instruction contrary to the establishment and freedom clauses, nor can the requirement be excused on the theory that the saying of the prayer—although conducted in the presence of the student body in the assembly hall of [sic] the classroom—is nonetheless a voluntary act, since no child is "required or encouraged to join in said prayer against his or her wishes" . . . , or on the theory that during the saying the child may remain silent, leave the room or report late. This is no answer, for it contains the very elements the prayer is supposed to eliminate: divisiveness, a type of compulsion, exerting as it does a pressure which an immature child is unable to resist because of his inherent desire to conform, and constituting a subtle interference by the State with the religious freedom guaranteed by the First Amendment. . . .

Their conclusion:[48]

> The inculcation of religion is a matter for the family and the church. In sponsoring a religious program, the State enters a field which it has been thought best to leave to the church alone. However salutary the underlying purpose of the requirement may be, it nonetheless gives to the State a direct supervision and influence that overstep the line marking the division between church and State and cannot help but lead to a gradual erosion of the mighty bulwark erected by the First Amendment. This does not mean that the State is or should be hostile to religion—merely that the State should not invade an area where the constitutionally protected freedom is absolute and not open to the vicissitudes of legislative or judicial balancing.

---

[48] *Id.* at 191–92.

4. *The Supreme Court Opinions.* By the time the case was presented to the Supreme Court for decision, the arguments had been reduced to a small number and the issues were made in extremely general terms. Although the petition for certiorari had kept open the possibility of urging violation of the freedom clause in accordance with the position taken by the dissenters in the Court of Appeals,[49] by the time the brief on the merits was presented, only the establishment issue was argued.[50] The primary authority relied upon by the petitioners was *McCollum.* The respondents rested largely on the long-continued existence of the practice of prayer in public places and on *Zorach.* Under the circumstances one might have anticipated that the Court would be required, at least, to reconcile the *McCollum* and *Zorach* cases. But the Court's opinions were as broad and general as the arguments and the opinions in the lower courts. The only thing left clear by the opinions is that, if the decisions of the past had failed to produce a governing principle, no remedy of that defect was to be found in *Vitale.*

Mr. Justice Black's opinion for the Court was joined by the Chief Justice, and Justices Clark, Harlan, and Brennan. Mr. Justice Douglas wrote a concurring opinion and Mr. Justice Stewart wrote a dissent. The reader gets an impression of the Justices of the majority walking on eggs and of the two minority Justices stamping after them.

The majority reached its conclusion without the citation of a single prior Supreme Court judgment, except for a reference to the history of the First Amendment contained in *Everson.*[51] History purported to be the main reliance of the Court. Black started with the proposition that the ceremony commanded by the Board of Education was a religious one. "There can, of course, be no doubt that New York's program of daily classroom invocation of God's blessings as prescribed in the Regents' prayer is a religious activity. It is a solemn avowal of divine faith and supplication for the blessings of the Almighty."[52] He relied on a recitation of history to show that once government enters the business of prescribing prayers it invites the exercise of pressures from various groups within the

---

49 *Id.* at 187.

50 Petition for certiorari, p. 4; Brief for Petitioners, p. 3.

51 370 U.S. at 428–29, n. 11.

52 *Id.* at 424.

community as to the content of such prayers. This kind of activity has been proved by history to be destructive of the public peace. And, like Father John Courtney Murray,[53] Black thought it was for the preservation of the public peace by the avoidance of such contests that the First Amendment was framed. To prevent this evil, the Constitution forbade the coincidence of governmental and religious authority.

> By the time of the adoption of the Constitution, our history shows that there was a widespread awareness among many Americans of the dangers of a union of Church and State. . . . The First Amendment was added to the Constitution to stand as a guarantee that neither the power nor the prestige of the Federal Government would be used to control, support or influence the kinds of prayer the American people can say—that the people's religions must not be subjected to the pressures of government for change each time a new political administration is elected to office.[54]

The Court rejected the notion that the absence of "compulsion" eliminated the problem:[55]

> The Establishment Clause, unlike the Free Exercise Clause, does not depend upon any showing of direct governmental compulsion and is violated by the enactment of laws which establish an official religion whether those laws operate directly to coerce nonobserving individuals or not. This is not to say, of course, that laws officially prescribing a particular form of religious worship do not involve coercion of such individuals. When the power, prestige and financial support of government is placed behind a particular religious belief, the indirect coercive pressure upon religious minorities to conform to the prevailing officially approved religion is plain. But the purposes underlying the Establishment Clause go much further than that. Its first and most immediate purpose rested on the belief that a union of government and religion tends to destroy government and to degrade religion. . . . The Establishment Clause thus stands as an expression of principle on the part of the Founders of our Constitution that religion is too personal, too sacred, too holy, to permit its "unhallowed perversion" by a civil magistrate.

---

[53] MURRAY, WE HOLD THESE TRUTHS (1958).

[54] 370 U.S. at 429–30.

[55] *Id.* at 430–32.

The Court also rejected the proposition that this required separation of church and State exhibited a hostility to religion:[56]

> It has been argued that to apply the Constitution in such a way as to prohibit state laws respecting an establishment of religious services in public schools is to indicate a hostility toward religion or toward prayer. Nothing, of course, could be more wrong. . . . [The authors of the Bill of Rights] knew that the First Amendment, which tried to put an end to governmental control of religion and of prayer, was not written to destroy either. . . . It is neither sacrilegious nor antireligious to say that each separate government in this country should stay out of the business of writing or sanctioning official prayers and leave that purely religious function to the people themselves and to those the people choose to look to for religious guidance.

The *de minimus* notion was similarly treated by reference to Madison's *Memorial and Remonstrance against Religious Assessments*.[57] And the parade of horribles that suggested that the use of the word "God" in public activities was within the ban stated in the opinion was disposed of by a footnote:[58] "Such patriotic or ceremonial occasions bear no true resemblance to the unquestioned religious exercise that the State of New York has sponsored in this instance."

The majority opinion thus dealt with every argument raised by respondents or by the courts below in support of the Regents' prayer ceremony except that which rested on *Zorach*. As to the relevance or vitality of that case, the Court was completely silent.

The holding of the Court was, indeed, a narrow one:[59] "[T]he constitutional prohibition against laws respecting an establishment of religion must at least mean that in this country it is no part of the business of government to compose official prayers for any group of the American people to recite as a part of a religious program carried on by government." It was the concurring and dissenting opinions that read into the Court's judgment a breadth and effect that the Court specifically disavowed. And it was this reading that was accepted by the divines as an appropriate target for criticism.[60]

Mr. Justice Douglas' concurring opinion gave new meaning to

---

56 *Id.* at 433–35.

57 *Id.* at 436.

58 *Id.* at 435, n. 21.

59 *Id.* at 425.

60 See *supra*, text at notes 5–7.

the proposition: "Millions for defense but not one cent for tribute." As he not infrequently does in other complex cases, he found the problem simple of statement and equally simple of solution:[61] "The point for decision is whether the Government can constitutionally finance a religious exercise. Our system at the federal and state levels is presently honeycombed with such financing." Unlike Black, he found "no element of compulsion or coercion in New York's regulation. . . ."[62] This was consistent with the opinion he wrote for the Court in *Zorach*, but *Zorach* was not used to bolster this conclusion. Nor was it distinguished in any way. *Zorach* was cited only for its famed, troublemaking, and essentially meaningless statement: "We are a religious people whose institutions presuppose a Supreme Being."[63] He did distinguish *McCollum* on this score. For in that case "the influence of the teaching staff was . . . brought to bear on the student body, to support the instilling of religious principles."[64] Indeed, the only case that he thought to stand in the way of his conclusion was *Everson*, "which allowed taxpayers' money to be used to pay 'the bus fares of parochial school pupils as a part of a general program under which' the fares of pupils attending public and other schools were also paid."[65] This statement of the facts of *Everson* is erroneous, for there was no such "general program" involved in *Everson*,[66] but the error is unimportant to Douglas' thesis. The appropriate principle that he stated in a footnote is not inconsistent with anything that Black said. "The First Amendment . . . prevented secular sanction to any religious ceremony, dogma, or rite."[67] But the guiding principle of his opinion is both narrower and broader: not one cent of the taxpayers' money may be used for or given to any religion-connected activity or institution. This comes closer to non-judicial statements by Douglas than to any principle or judgment enunciated by the Court, except that in the dissenting opinion of Mr. Justice Rutledge in the *Everson* case which Douglas quoted in his *Vitale* opinion.[68] Douglas, like some of

---

[61] 370 U.S. at 437.

[62] *Id.* at 438.

[63] 343 U.S. at 313, quoted at 370 U.S. 442.

[64] 370 U.S. at 439.

[65] *Id.* at 443.

[66] See RELIGION 80–85.

[67] 370 U.S. at 442, n. 7.

[68] *Id.* at 443–44. It is interesting to note that Douglas found this proposition unconvincing in *Everson* in which he was a member of the majority.

the Court's critics, would seem to have been more concerned with the problem of federal aid to parochial education than with the facts of the case immediately before him. His extra-judicial conclusion, stated in terms not dissimilar to his language in *Vitale*, was that any such aid would be unconstitutional.[69]

Mr. Justice Stewart's dissent rested on the proposition that the Court's judgment infringed the rights of the majority: "to deny the wish of these school children to join in reciting this prayer is to deny them the opportunity of sharing in the spiritual heritage of our Nation."[70] He thus attributed to the Court the decision of a much harder case than that with which it was presented. His proposition assumed that the prayer ceremony was initiated by the children or their parents rather than being imposed by the Board of Education.[71] In any event, reading the opinion of the Court as broadly as did Douglas, Stewart found it inconsistent with the quotation from *Zorach*, which means all things to all men, and to Stewart a justification for state-sponsored religious ceremonies.

II. An Evaluation

Despite the wide-eyed surprise with which *Vitale* was greeted by its detractors, serious students of the subject hardly found it startling. Indeed, many of them, not classifiable even by the Court's most vehement critics as "secularists," not only anticipated the result but seemed to think it the proper one. Thus, in 1953, Professor Wilbur Katz wrote:[72]

> As to public schools, the problem of neutrality may be stated as a problem of keeping the schools secular (*i.e.*, ruling out

---

69 See Hutchins, Two Faces of Federalism 58–60 (1961).

70 370 U.S. at 445.

71 The distinction was recognized even by the New York American Legion. At its 1962 State convention, it passed a resolution stating: "It is manifestly clear that a prayer chosen by the pupils or their parents and voluntarily recited by them at the beginning of each school day is not a procedure coming within the prohibition of [the Court's] decision or the First Amendment to the Constitution." Certainly it is not "manifestly clear." But it presents a different problem than that resolved by the Court in *Vitale*.

72 Katz, *Freedom of Religion and State Neutrality*, 20 U. Chi. L. Rev. 426, 438 (1953). (Emphasis added.) *Cf.* Kauper, Civil Liberties and the Constitution 39–41 (1962); Sutherland, *Due Process and Disestablishment*, 62 Harv. L. Rev. 1306, 1338–39 (1949).

> any attempt to inculcate religious belief) and yet avoiding inculcation of secularism (*i.e.*, a philosophy of life which leaves no place for religion). Such neutrality is not easy to achieve.
>
> Except in the released time and flag salute cases, the Supreme Court has not yet been required to decide questions concerning public school programs. The problem of Bible reading was recently before the Court, but the case was dismissed without a decision. *Devotional exercises in public schools, however simple and nonsectarian, are difficult to reconcile with a rule of neutrality.* Such exercises present a problem quite different from that presented by incidental inclusion of religious material in literary and social studies. Occasionally, advocates of strict church-state separation demand careful exclusion of all references to religion. Handling of such material on a basis of neutrality may not always be easy, but consistently to exclude it is to abandon neutrality at the outset.

Moreover, however novel the issue of school-prayer problems may have been for the Supreme Court, it and its analogue, Bible reading, have been the subject of litigation in State courts for many years.[73] And if it is true that the majority of the State courts—prior to the Supreme Court's application of the religion clauses to the States—have sustained the validity of such activities, that has been largely due to the fact that "Protestantism has been the dominant religious force in helping to shape the pattern of American life and the content of American culture."[74] The State court decisions have not been unanimous. Illinois, for example, has long since banned devotional exercises in its public schools, for reasons very much like those suggested in the *Vitale* opinion, without the resultant destruction of religious life that the critics of *Vitale* so dolefully predict. And it is not insignificant that the successful attack in Illinois was made by Catholic interests, not by the "secular" evildoers that

[73] The cases are collected in Harrison, *The Bible, the Constitution and Public Education,* 29 TENN. L. REV. 363, 380–90 (1962).

[74] KAUPER, *op. cit. supra* note 72, at 4. "The public school system as it first developed and as it has continued in some parts of the country to this day was essentially a Protestant school system, and it is not surprising that despite the Protestant emphasis on separation of church and state, the reading of the King James version of the Bible as a devotional exercise was not uncommonly an accepted part of the public school program. And the idea that no public funds should go to support competing schools, notably parochial or religious schools, has revealed another distinctive aspect of Protestant thinking." *Id.* at 4–5.

the Catholic hierarchy singled out for criticism in its comments on the Regents' prayer decision.[75] In *People ex rel. Ring v. Board of Education*,[76] Catholic parents secured an order of mandamus forbidding the reading of the King James Bible, the singing of hymns, and recital of the Lord's Prayer in the public schools. The Illinois courts held these devotional activities invalid despite the fact that the school had excused from compliance the Catholic children whose parents brought the suit:[77]

> The exclusion of a pupil from this part of the school exercises in which the rest of the school joins, separates him from his fellows, puts him in a class by himself, deprives him of his equality with the other pupils, subjects him to a religious stigma and places him at a disadvantage in the school, which the law never contemplated. All this is because of his religious belief. If the instruction or exercise is such that certain of the pupils must be excused from it because it is hostile to their or their parents' religious beliefs, then such instruction or exercise is sectarian and forbidden by the constitution.

In disposing of the *Vitale* problem, the Court was faced with the ordinary problems of the legal process;[78] evolution not revolution was the effect of its judgment.

A. THE STANDING-TO-SUE ISSUE: PREGNANT SILENCE

Mr. Justice Stone warned that "inferences from silence should be cautiously drawn."[79] He went on: "the weight to be given to silence is for the tribunal conducting the trial."[80] More ancient authority has it that "in an instrument well drawn, as in a poem well composed, silence is sometimes most expressive."[81] The silence of the Court in *Vitale* on the question of the right of petitioners to raise the question of separation is certainly somewhat enigmatic. Only

---

75 See *supra* note 5.

76 245 Ill. 334 (1910). See also Herold v. Parish Board of Educ., 136 La. 1034 (1915); State ex rel. Weiss v. District Board, 76 Wisc. 177 (1890); State ex rel. Freeman v. Scheve, 65 Neb. 853 (1902); State ex rel. Finger v. Weedman, 55 S.D. 343 (1929).

77 *Id.* at 351.

78 See Levi, Introduction to Legal Reasoning (1st Phoenix ed. 1961).

79 United States ex rel. Vajtauer v. Commissioner of Immigration, 273 U.S. 103, 112 (1927).

80 *Ibid.*

81 Wilson, J., in Chisholm v. Georgia, 2 Dall. 419, 454 (1792).

future action of the Court will prove how meaningful it is. In the meantime, speculation seems not inappropriate.

One reason contributing to silence, perhaps, was the failure of the respondents to raise the standing issue. Although they had asserted a procedural defect of no merit,[82] and had been made aware of the issue by the trial court,[83] respondents abstained from putting the issue to the Court. On this score, the Court indulged them.

The question remains, however: On what is the petitioners' standing predicated? In the lower courts, and so long as the imposition on the children's freedom was in issue, there could be no doubt of their right to complain of that infringement through their parents. But that issue was abandoned in the Supreme Court and the Court's opinion rests exclusively on the separation issue.[84]

The question of proper standing in the separation cases has wound its way over a tortuous path. In *McCollum*, the first released-time case, the right of the mother of a school child to maintain the suit was challenged. Mr. Justice Black, for the majority, quickly disposed of the issue:[85] "A second ground for the motion to dismiss is that the appellant lacks standing to maintain the action, a ground which is also without merit. *Coleman v. Miller*, 307 U.S. 433, 443, 445, 464." The reference to *Miller* hardly clarifies the basis for the holding. At the first place cited, *Miller* stated: "[W]here the claim of a complainant that a state officer be restrained from enforcing a state statute because of constitutional invalidity is sustained by the state court, the statute enables the state officer to seek a reversal by this Court of that decision."[86] Of course, no such issue was presented by *McCollum*. On the second dictum page referred to, the Hughes opinion for the Court in *Miller* asserted: "[T]he Court has sustained the more immediate and sub-

---

[82] Respondents contended that the case should have been brought up by appeal rather than by certiorari. Joint Brief of Respondents and Intervenors-Respondents Opposing Certiorari, pp. 2–3. Citing impeccable authority, ROBERTSON & KIRKHAM, JURISDICTION OF THE SUPREME COURT OF THE UNITED STATES § 10 (1951 ed.), petitioners quickly disposed of this argument. Reply Brief of Petitioners in Support of Certiorari, p. 5.

[83] "Petitioners' standing to sue is established by the Zorach case as a matter of both New York and Federal law." 18 N.Y. Misc. 2d at 666.

[84] See text *supra*, at note 50.

[85] 333 U.S. at 206.

[86] 307 U.S. at 443.

stantial right of a resident taxpayer to invoke the interposition of a court of equity to enjoin an illegal use of moneys by a municipal corporation."[87] But, as Mr. Justice Jackson asserted in his concurring opinion, there was no showing of monetary expenditure in *McCollum.* The third reference was to Mr. Justice Frankfurter's opinion, in which Justices Roberts, Black, and Douglas joined. But this provides no greater assistance. The principle there stated was:[88] "No matter how seriously infringement of the Constitution may be called into question, this is not the tribunal for its challenge except by those who have some specialized concern which belongs to all."

The so-called "pocketbook" rationale was the justification for jurisdiction in *Everson:* "It is true that this Court found a justiciable controversy in *Everson.* . . . But *Everson* showed a measurable appropriation or disbursement of school-district funds occasioned solely by the activities complained of."[89] In *Doremus,* an appeal from a State-court judgment sustaining Bible reading in New Jersey public schools, the Court disclaimed jurisdiction on the ground that the pupil whose parent sued had been graduated and the taxpayer could not show any expenditure for the activity in question on which to predicate his standing to sue. The language of the majority opinion suggested that even had the pupil not been graduated there would still be no standing:[90]

> In support of the parent-and-school-child relationship . . . there is no assertion that she was injured or even offended [by the Bible reading] or that she was compelled to accept, approve or confess agreement with any dogma or creed or even to listen when the Scriptures were read.

When the released-time program was again in question in *Zorach,* the Court acknowledged an absence of "expenditure of public funds"[91] but sustained jurisdiction and distinguished *Doremus* because the petitioners were "parents of children currently attending schools subject to the released time program."[92] *Doremus* still lived when the Court sustained jurisdiction in 1961 in the Maryland Sunday closing-law case, on the ground that appellants "con-

---

[87] *Id.* at 445.

[88] *Id.* at 464.

[89] Doremus v. Board of Education, 342 U.S. 429, 434 (1952).

[90] *Id.* at 432.

[91] 343 U.S. at 308–09.

[92] *Id.* at 309, n. 4.

cededly have suffered direct economic injury."[93] This economic interest was suggested as the basis for distinguishing the rule in *Doremus*, "where complainants failed to show direct and particular economic detriment."[94]

In *Vitale*, all the defects of allegation noted by the Court in *Doremus* were avoided.[95] But the complaint alleged conclusions only; there were no facts showing any economic costs to any plaintiff. The rule seems to have developed, however, that, where the alleged violation of the separation clause has occurred by reason of activities within the public school, a parent of a child attending the school has standing to raise the issue in the federal courts without showing any compulsion exerted on his child to comply with or to participate in the activities about which complaint is made. The result is perhaps desirable, for it permits a very limited class to exert the powers of a watchdog to keep the schools, the most vulnerable area, free from the imposition of religious indoctrination. It is hard to see, however, why the parents are a better group to exercise this power of surveillance than other citizens. Their interest in school activities is greater. But so, too, is their vulnerability to the pressures of the community in which they and their children live. Perhaps the Court is starting down the road toward justification of the "public action" that Professor Jaffe has advocated,[96] but is typically moving by short steps. If so, however, that goal is more likely to be reached if the Court would attempt to achieve it by fuller explanation of what it is doing. To state a requirement of direct, individual, economic interest and, nevertheless, to sustain jurisdiction where no such interest is shown is to forswear a major function of judicial opinions: to enlighten the litigants and those who may follow them about the rules that the Court is applying.

B. THE HISTORICAL ARGUMENTS

History is a useful tool to help find an answer; it is seldom an answer in itself. That it may be used in different ways to justify different conclusions is demonstrated by the several opinions in *Vitale*.

---

93 McGowan v. Maryland, 366 U.S. 420, 430 (1961).

94 *Id.* at 430, n. 8.

95 See *supra* note 22.

96 Jaffe, *Standing to Secure Judicial Review: Public Actions*, 74 HARV. L. REV. 1265 (1961).

The trial court based its conclusion of validity on its reading of history; the Supreme Court relied on history to invalidate the use of the Regents' prayer. In each instance, however, the history revealed was used to measure different things. The trial court sought to demonstrate that the kind of activity prescribed by the New Hyde Park Board of Education was engaged in at the time of the adoption of the First and Fourteenth Amendments and continued thereafter. From this it derived the conclusion that these Amendments could not have created a ban on these practices. The Supreme Court examined the history to discover the evils that the First Amendment was framed to inhibit. From its examination it concluded that the removal of the State from the function of specifying methods of worship was a primary objective of the Amendment. It concluded, therefore, that the Regents' prayer fell under the interdict of the Amendment.

The weaknesses of the trial court's approach are apparent. The first is the questionable authority of the history proffered. Certainly it is inconsistent, at least in part, with that described by Mr. Justice Frankfurter in his concurring opinion in *McCollum,* which substantiated his conclusion:[97] "[L]ong before the Fourteenth Amendment subjected the States to new limitations, the prohibition of furtherance by the State of religious instruction became the guiding principle, in law and feeling, of the American people." The second flaw in the trial court's argument is that it assumes identity between behavior and Constitutional mandate. The defect was noted in these terms by Lord Bryce:[98]

> It is accepted as an axiom by all Americans that the civil powers ought to be not only neutral and impartial as between different forms of faith, but ought to leave these matters entirely on one side, regarding them no more than it regards the artistic or literary pursuits of the citizen. . . . Just because these questions have been long since disposed of, and excite no present passion, and perhaps also because the Americans are more practically easy-going than pedantically exact, the National government and the State governments do give to Christianity a species of recognition inconsistent with the view that civil government should be absolutely neutral in religious matters.

97 333 U.S. at 215.

98 2 Bryce, American Commonwealth 698, 701 (3d ed. 1906).

In more specific terms, this kind of historical equation would mean that the Eighteenth Amendment did not purport to prohibit the sale of alcoholic beverages because sale and consumption continued at so high a rate throughout its short-lived existence.[99] On this theory, the comparatively few convictions for violation of the Volstead Act were invalid. Or, in more contemporary terms, the concept would justify the objection of Negro enfranchisement so clearly stated by the Sheriff of Terrell County, Georgia:[100] "We want our colored people to go on living like they have for the last hundred years." Finally, this use of history is weakened by the unsoundness of the base on which it rests: that the meaning of "due process" is static and does not change with the development of the country. Although this position has been espoused even by a few scholars,[101] it has usually been rejected by the Court.[102] And the clearest demonstration of this proposition is that for most of the period during which the events cited by the trial court occurred, the First Amendment was not held to be applicable to the actions of the States. Certainly, not until *Hamilton v. Board of Regents*[103] did the Court seriously consider the application of the religion clauses to the States and not until *Cantwell v. Connecticut*,[104] in 1940, was State action held invalid as violative of the religion clauses.

Nor was the Supreme Court's reliance on history dispositive of the issues of the case. For, again as said by Frankfurter in *McCollum*,[105] "the mere formulation of a relevant Constitutional principle is the beginning of the solution of a problem, not its answer." At best, all that Black's history provided was "a relevant Constitutional principle." That the abstraction derived from the recited history does not itself solve the *Vitale* problem is probably revealed by the fact that there has been little quarrel with the opinion's statement of history, however much there has been with its conclusion. That it

---

99 See SINCLAIR, PROHIBITION: ERA OF EXCESS (1962).

100 See Sitton, Sheriff Harasses Negroes at Voting Rally in Georgia, New York Times, July 27, 1962, p. 1, col. 2. (Sitton merits a Pulitzer Prize for this story.)

101 See, *e.g.*, CROSSKEY, POLITICS AND THE CONSTITUTION (1953).

102 See, generally, GOVERNMENT UNDER LAW, SUTHERLAND ed. (1956); Bickel, *supra* note 27.

103 293 U.S. 245 (1934). See RELIGION 38–41.

104 310 U.S. 296 (1940). See RELIGION 51–54.

105 333 U.S. at 212.

was an essential ingredient in the judgment, however, is not to be gainsaid.

C. MC COLLUM AND ZORACH

The arguments presented to the Court in terms of its own precedents centered on *McCollum v. Board of Education*[106] and *Zorach v. Clauson*,[107] for it was in these cases that the Court had been asked to pass upon the use of public-school systems to provide religious training for their students. The "released-time" programs involved in the two cases were similar but not identical. In each, students were "released" from their obligations to attend classes in secular education in order to receive religious training. In each, only students whose parents had elected to have them receive such education received it. In each, students not taking these religious-education courses were required to attend to assignments given to them, and to them alone, by the public schools. In *McCollum* the religious education was conducted on the school premises. In *Zorach* this training was given off the school property. In neither was the religious education offered by the public-school teachers. In *McCollum* the plan was held unconstitutional; in *Zorach* the program was sustained.

Mr. Justice Black wrote the opinion for the Court in *McCollum.* Of the nine Justices, only Mr. Justice Reed dissented from the judgment. The Court's opinion rested primarily on the statements of principle to be found both in the majority and minority positions in *Everson:*[108]

> The . . . facts . . . show the use of tax-supported property for religious instruction and the close cooperation between the school authorities and the religious council in promoting religious education. The operation of the State's compulsory education system thus assists and is integrated with the program of religious instruction carried on by separate religious sects. Pupils compelled by law to go to school for secular education are released in part from their legal duty upon the condition that they attend the religious classes. This is beyond all question a utilization of the tax-established and tax-supported public school system to aid religious groups to spread their faith.

---

106 333 U.S. 203 (1948).

107 343 U.S. 306 (1952).

108 333 U.S. at 209–10, 212. (Emphasis added.)

> And it falls squarely under the ban of the First Amendment (made applicable to the States by the Fourteenth) as we interpreted it in *Everson*. . . .
>
> Here not only are the State's tax-supported public school buildings used for the dissemination of religious doctrines. *The State also affords sectarian groups an invaluable aid in that it helps to provide pupils for their religious classes through use of the State's compulsory public school machinery. This is not separation of Church and State.*

The opinion in no way relied on any notion of compulsion exerted on the nonconforming children to attend religious classes. In *McCollum*, no less than in *Vitale*, the students who chose not to receive religious indoctrination were free to avoid it. Frankfurter's lengthy concurring opinion,[109] joined by Jackson, Rutledge, and Burton, did not overlook the nature of the compulsion involved, any more than did Black in *Vitale*.[110] For the concurring Justices:[111]

> The fact that this power has not been used to discriminate is beside the point. Separation is a requirement to abstain from fusing functions of Government and of religious sects, not merely to treat them all equally. That a child is offered an alternative may reduce the constraint; it does not eliminate the operation of influence by the school in matters sacred to conscience and outside the school's domain. The law of imitation operates, and non-conformity is not an outstanding characteristic of children. The result is an obvious pressure upon children to attend. . . . The children belonging to these non-participating sects will thus have inculcated in them a feeling of separatism when the school should be the training ground for habits of community, or they will have religious instruction in a faith which is not that of their parents. As a result, the public school system of Champaign actively furthers inculcation in the religious tenets of some faiths, and in the process sharpens the consciousness of religious differences at least among some of the children committed to its care. These are consequences not amenable to statistics. But they are precisely the consequences against which the Constitution was directed when it prohibited the Government common to all from becoming embroiled, however innocently, in the destructive religious conflicts of which the history of even this country records some dark pages.

---

109 *Id*. at 212–32.

110 See text *supra*, at note 55.

111 333 U.S. at 227–28.

If *McCollum* were to provide the guide, therefore, *Vitale* was clearly correctly decided. *Vitale* had all the elements of *McCollum* plus teacher supervision. If *McCollum* had been the last prior word on the subject, *Vitale* could reasonably have rested on that decision. But *McCollum* was followed, not only by a furor like that accompanying *Vitale*, but by *Zorach* as well.

The distinction on which *Zorach* rested, however, would itself give little help to those asserting the validity of the Regents' prayer:[112]

> In the *McCollum* case the classrooms were used for religious instruction and the force of the public school was used to promote that instruction. Here, as we have said, the public schools do no more than accommodate their schedules to a program of outside religious instruction. We follow the *McCollum* case. But we cannot expand it to cover the present released time program unless separation of Church and State means that public institutions can make no adjustments of their schedules to accommodate the religious needs of the people. We cannot read into the Bill of Rights such a philosophy of hostility to religion.

That the distinction was a tenuous one at best was clearly revealed by the dissents of Justices Black,[113] who had written *McCollum*, Frankfurter,[114] and Jackson.[115] That distinction does not help the lower-court judgments in *Vitale* because the religious exercises in *Vitale* took place in the public-school classrooms.

The dragon's teeth sown by the *Zorach* case did not derive from its holding, but rather from its dicta. For it was here that Douglas, writing for the Court, suggested that co-operation, not neutrality, was the function of government in the area of religion:[116]

> The First Amendment . . . does not say that in every and all respects there shall be a separation of Church and State. Rather, it studiously defines the manner, the specific ways, in which there shall be no concert or union or dependency one on the other. That is the common sense of the matter. Otherwise the state and religion would be aliens to each other—hostile, suspicious, and even unfriendly. Churches could not

---

112 343 U.S. at 315.

113 *Id. at* 316, 317, 320.

114 *Id.* at 320–23.

115 *Id.* at 342, 345.

116 *Id.* at 312–13, 313–14.

> be required to pay even property taxes. Municipalities would not be permitted to render police or fire protection to religious groups. Policemen who helped parishioners into their places of worship would violate the Constitution. Prayers in our legislative halls; the appeals to the Almighty in the messages of the Chief Executive; the proclamations making Thanksgiving Day a holiday; "so help me God" in our courtroom oaths—these and all other references to the Almighty that run through our laws, our public rituals, our ceremonies would be flouting the First Amendment. A fastidious atheist or agnostic could even object to the supplication with which the Court opens each session: "God save the United States and this Honorable Court."
>
> We would have to press the concept of separation of Church and State to these extremes to condemn the present law on constitutional grounds. . . .
>
> We are a religious people whose institutions presuppose a Supreme Being. . . . When the state encourages religious instruction or cooperates with religious authorities by adjusting the schedule of public events to sectarian needs, it follows the best of our traditions. For it then respects the religious nature of our people and accommodates the public service to their spiritual needs. . . .

The language just quoted would surprise those who had read only Douglas' concurring opinion in *Vitale*. For the very things he cited as proof of the validity of the New York released-time program, he put forth as unconstitutional in *Vitale*:[117] "What New York does on the opening of its public schools is what we do when we open court. . . . What New York does on the opening of its public schools is what each House of Congress does at the opening of each day's business. . . ." And in his footnotes, presumably demonstrating further violation of the First Amendment, he referred to military chaplains, the flag salute, the national coinage, the national anthem, Christmas trees, etc.[118] "The fact that taxpayers do not have standing in the federal courts to raise the issue . . . is of course no justification for drawing a line between what is done in New York on one hand and on the other what we do and what Congress does in this matter of prayer."[119]

Mr. Justice Douglas, nonetheless, found nothing in *Zorach* in-

---

117 370 U.S. at 439–40.

118 *Id*. at 438, n. 2; 440, n. 5; 442, n. 8.

119 *Id*. at 441, n. 6.

consistent with his conclusion that the Regents' prayer was unconstitutional. And it is true that there is other language in *Zorach* to sustain Douglas' concurrence in *Vitale*. For he also said there:[120] "Government may not . . . undertake religious instruction. . . . It may not make a religious observance compulsory." But it should be noted that Douglas, unlike the majority, in *Vitale*, found that "there is no element of compulsion or coercion in New York's regulation requiring that public schools be opened each day with the [Regents'] prayer. . . ."[121] Thus, *Zorach* solely on its holding and its distinction of *McCollum* is not inconsistent with *Vitale*. If meaning is to be given to the language of the Court in *Zorach*, on which the lower courts in fact relied, there is much there to sustain the validity of the Regents' prayer. But there is clear indication from later opinions of the Court that it is *McCollum* that has survived and not *Zorach*. Douglas, himself, concurred specially in *Cammarano v. United States*,[122] saying:

> that proposition savors of the notion that First Amendment rights are somehow not fully realized unless they are subsidized by the State. Such a notion runs counter to our decisions . . . and may indeed conflict with the underlying premise that a complete hands-off policy on the part of government is at times the only course consistent with First Amendment rights. See . . . *McCollum*. . . .

The Sunday closing-law cases and the Maryland oath case of the 1960 Term removed any doubt that *McCollum* has prevailed.[123]

Despite the fact that the Court, in its opinion failed to refer to any of its prior judgments as authority, it would seem clear that the results it reached in *Vitale* were consistent with them and a different conclusion would have contradicted the Court's earlier professions of a doctrine of neutrality.

D. THE ISSUE OF COERCION

The issue of coercion has been thought peculiar to the freedom clause rather than to the separation clause of the Constitution. It thus disappeared from argument when petitioners in *Vitale* abandoned the freedom issue in the Supreme Court. Neither *Vitale* nor

---

120 343 U.S. at 314.

121 370 U.S. at 438.

122 358 U.S. 498, 515 (1959).

123 See RELIGION 97–108.

McCollum rests on the proposition that the nonconformist children were coerced into attendance at religious ceremonies or indoctrination. The factor of coercion is difficult of measurement and more difficult of evaluation in terms of the appropriate effect to be given specific excuse from the obligation of participation. Is it relevant to the "establishment" issue? Despite frequent disclaimers of reliance, it is clear that the notion of coercion has played an important part in the decision-making process. Most of the Justices who would invalidate the procedures utilized in the released-time and prayer-reading cases seem to have found that coercion did exist,[124] and some of these would explicitly utilize this factor, among others, in reaching their conclusion.[125]

Failure to utilize the element of coercion in reaching judgment avoids a difficult problem, for coercion short of physical compulsion is an elusive concept. At the same time, if this failure to announce that coercion is relevant amounts to concealment of a real and important component of judgment, it makes harder the task in future litigation of defining the content of the separation-clause decisions. Is it possible, for example, that the availability of religious ceremonies to members of the armed forces, with freedom to abstain from attendance, would be distinguished from *Vitale* because the element of coercion is thought to be either eliminated or reduced by the fact that the military participants are of an age at which their freedom of choice can really be exercised? This is not to suggest that the answer should be different from that reached in *Vitale*, but only that the Court's judgments can serve their function of stare decisis only when the grounds for the judgment are adequately revealed.[126] And the question remains whether they have been adequately revealed when the element of coercion is constantly referred to but not specifically relied on.

E. DEISM AS A NATIONAL RELIGION

One of the arguments suggested by the defenders of the Regents' prayer was that its validity should be sustained because its contents

---

124 See, *e.g.*, Black, J., quoted in text *supra*, at note 55.

125 See, *e.g.*, Frankfurter, J., dissenting in *Zorach*, 343 U.S. at 227–28; quoted in text *supra*, at note 111.

126 See Bickel & Wellington, *Legislative Purpose and the Judicial Process*, 71 Harv. L. Rev. 1 (1957).

reflect the common denominator of all religious groups in the United States: the belief in the existence of God. It was this theme that was picked up by the Court's critics who assumed, because they chose to do so, that the rejection of this argument was a rejection of the proposition that God exists. The Court made clear that it was doing nothing of the sort. It did no more than recognize the incompetence of government to pass on such a question. But it is somewhat strange to discover the appeal of Horace Mann's old proposition that the schools should promulgate a "common core" of American religion. For the culmination of such action, more clearly than any that has yet come before the Court, is suggestive of the establishment of a State religion, separate and distinct from existing sects and cults. As the American Council on Education noted some time ago:[127]

> The notion of a common core suggests a watering down of the several faiths to the point where common essentials appear. This might easily lead to a new sect—a public school sect—which would take its place alongside the existing faiths and compete with them.

More recently Father Gustave Weigel suggested a similar conclusion:[128] "The moral code held by each separate religious community can reductively be unified, but the consistent particular believer wants no such reduction." And the official magazine of the United Presbyterian Church has reached the same conclusion:[129] "If you have faith-in-general, you have no Faith to speak of. Faith has to be something-in-particular. A nondenominational prayer is doomed to be limited and circumscribed. If prayer starts soaring, it starts to be controversial, which is the one thing a nondenominational prayer dares not be."

F. THE IMPLICATIONS OF VITALE

The necessary effect of *Vitale* is neither so broad nor so narrow as some of its detractors and supporters would have it. Its holding is limited: "[I]t is no part of the business of government to compose

---

127 Quoted in Harrison, *supra* note 73, at 417.

128 Weigel, *The Church and the Public Conscience*, 210 ATLANTIC 116, 117 (August 1962).

129 PRESBYTERIAN LIFE, Aug. 15, 1962.

official prayers for any group of the American people to recite as a part of a religious program carried on by government."[130] That it also extends to prayers not composed but simply prescribed by government would also seem to be clear: "[G]overnment in this country, be it state or federal, is without power to prescribe by law any particular form of prayer which is to be used as an official prayer in carrying on any program of governmentally sponsored religious activity."[131] This may be proved at the next Term of Court,[132] unless some specious distinction, like that used to differentiate *Zorach* from *McCollum*, should result from the invidious pressures being exerted on the Court, or, if discretion proves again to be the better part of valor, the Court will manage to avoid decision in the Bible-reading cases. That *Vitale* also casts further doubts on the vitality of *Zorach* and, therefore, on the proposed "shared-time" programs[133] must be conceded. But these are the limits of the Regents' prayer case at this time. For it is clear, despite the concurring and dissenting opinions, that *Vitale* was concerned only with "unquestioned religious exercise" and is not intended to cast doubts on various "patriotic or ceremonial occasions" such as "singing" the national anthem or "reciting . . . the Declaration of Independence" or the "many manifestations in our public life of belief in God."[134]

III. Conclusion

If, as has already been suggested, no over-all doctrine refining the meaning to be given to the religion clauses of the First Amendment was forthcoming from the Court prior to *Vitale*, that omission is yet to be repaired. At the same time, it seems clear that the *Vitale* case, in its result if not in its language or method, is compatible with the thesis expressed in *Religion and the Law*:[135] "The freedom and separation clauses should be read as stating a single precept: that government cannot utilize religion as a standard for ac-

---

130 370 U.S. at 425.

131 *Id.* at 420.

132 Schempp v. School District of Arlington Township, 201 F. Supp. 815 (E.D. Pa. 1962), appeal filed May 24, 1962; Murray v. Curlett, 228 Md. 239 (1962), petition for certiorari filed May 15, 1962.

133 See Cassels, A Way Out of Our Parochial-Public School Conflict, Look 54 (Aug. 28, 1962).

134 370 U.S. at 435, n. 21.

135 Religion 18, 112.

tion or inaction . . . these clauses, read together as they should be, prohibit classification in terms of religion either to confer a benefit or to impose a burden." The Court has, of course, shown no readiness to treat the freedom and separation clauses other than as distinct commands of the Constitution. *Vitale* has suggested a shorter rationalization, at least for the separation clause, that may differ only in language rather than content from that quoted above: religion "is no part of the business of government."

It is hard to believe that many who now find this notion unpalatable will not soon, or eventually, be applauding it. A contrary result in *Vitale*, for example, could easily have authorized the reading in school ceremony of a version of the New Testament that is anathema to some students, whenever those students were free to abstain from participation. Not least appreciative may be the Catholic hierarchy for the Court's contribution to the restriction on the Protestant emphasis in the public schools.[136] Equally grateful may be the Protestant community whose fear of Catholic domination demands separation of governmental power from clerical authority.[137] Indeed, when time gives the opportunity for thoughtful evaluation rather than emotional reaction, *Vitale* may come to be recognized as one of the bulwarks of America's freedom from the ills that continue to plague those countries where "toleration" rather than "freedom" and "separation" are the guides to government action.[138]

---

136 "The public school system as it first developed and as it has continued in some parts of this country to this day was essentially a Protestant school system. . . ." KAUPER, *op. cit. supra* note 72, at 4.

137 "The view is prevalent that Catholics do not accept, or accept grudgingly, the implications of the First Amendment to the Constitution. While many Americans can speak with deep feeling about the separation of church and state, the impression is that Catholics would prefer some form of union of church and state." Lally, *Points of Abrasion*, 210 ATLANTIC 78 (August 1962).

138 *Cf. On Second Thought . . .*, TIME 40 (Aug. 24, 1962).

ROBERT G. McCLOSKEY

ECONOMIC DUE PROCESS AND THE SUPREME COURT: AN EXHUMATION AND REBURIAL

I. The Problem

American political life has often been marked by a tendency to adopt policies today and to think about them in some remote tomorrow, if at all. This national habit of mind is presumably rooted in our famous pragmatic temperament. Much can be—and has been—said for it. But the attribute, like most attributes, has the defects of its merits. If Jack builds a house without thinking the plan through in advance, he may then justly congratulate himself that he is at least sheltered from the elements while his more deliberative neighbor still shivers. But he should not be surprised if it turns out that the corners are a little awry or that the second bedroom impinges on what he hoped would be an ample living room. He must accommodate himself to the fact that the *ad hoc* decisions of the past may set unforeseen limits on his way of life in the future.

These general reflections about American propensities and their consequences are also applicable to the modern history of America's peculiar institution, the Supreme Court of the United States. Since about 1937, the Court has been rebuilding its constitutional dwelling place, knocking down a wall here, constructing a new corridor

---

Robert G. McCloskey is Professor of Government, Harvard University.

there, in response to a bewildering succession of conflicting impulses. If these impulses are united by some commonly shared understanding about the form and extent of the ultimate structure, the Justices have been remarkably taciturn about revealing it. Vast new areas of constitutional supervision have been opened in such decisions as *Palko v. Connecticut*,[1] *Burstyn v. Wilson*,[2] and *Brown v. Board of Education*,[3] to name only three among many. Other regions, once significant, have been closed off to judicial intervention: the fields of the national commerce power and of economic due process are the standard examples.[4] Still others have been temporarily opened, then more or less firmly shut again—or vice versa. One thinks of picketing as free speech,[5] on the one hand, and the flag-salute issue, on the other.[6] Each of these developments has been accompanied by one or more Court opinions offering a particularized justification: it would be nice to have that extra living room; or, no house really needs a separate dining room these days. But little attempt has been made to reckon with their effect on each other or on the over-all structure that was taking shape.

The purpose of this paper is to trace one such development in the disorderly constitutional flux of the past twenty-five years: the decline and virtual demise of "economic due process." Such a survey might seem to be mere bootless antiquarianism. But the story of the senescence of this once-robust doctrine may provide us with hints about several live questions that concern students of the Supreme Court. What is the character of the process which the Court goes through when it reaches a radical turning point in its doctrinal history? Why does this process take the form it does? More specifically, why did the Court abandon the cause of economic rights, and why so completely? Can the abandonment be fully justified in the light of any consistent view of the rights themselves or of the

---

1 302 U.S. 319 (1937).

2 343 U.S. 495 (1952).

3 347 U.S. 483 (1954).

4 See Stern, *The Problems of Yesteryear—Commerce and Due Process*, 4 VAND. L. REV. 446 (1951).

5 See Cox, *Strikes, Picketing and the Constitution*, 4 VAND. L. REV. 574 (1951).

6 Minersville School Dist. v. Gobitis, 310 U.S. 586 (1940); West Virginia Bd. of Educ. v. Barnette, 319 U.S. 624 (1943); see MANWARING, RENDER UNTO CAESAR (1962); KURLAND, RELIGION AND THE LAW 41–47 (1962).

Court's role in our political system? If not, is it either likely or desirable that the law should retrace its steps in this field, or has the possibility of a second guess been foreclosed by the general drift of judicial history?

II. The Demise of a Doctrine: The Method

The judicial reaction against economic due process after 1937 is unique in the history of the Supreme Court. There have been gradual shifts from negativism to permissiveness, as in the antitrust field during the decades after *E. C. Knight*;[7] there have been abrupt departures from salient negative doctrines as in *Nebbia*[8] or in *Graves v. New York*.[9] But it is hard to think of another instance when the Court so thoroughly and quickly demolished a constitutional doctrine of such far-reaching significance. The concomitant destruction of "dual federalism" in the commerce field is doubtless the closest analogue. But there the negative standard had rested in fact on a comparatively scanty handful of precedents, and the Court in *United States v. Darby*[10] could draw on a line of contrary pronouncements beginning with Marshall. On the other hand, the judicial power to strike down an economic statute on the ground that it was "arbitrary, capricious, or unreasonable" had been frequently exercised and seemed to stand on a solid base. Most of the Court's critics and some of its friends might have hoped in the early 1930's that the "rational basis" standard would be applied more leniently. But only a singularly prescient observer could have dreamed that the Court would soon abandon the concept altogether.

Yet that is what happened. There is no need to retell the familiar story in detail,[11] but a few high points are worth repeating. *West Coast Hotel v. Parrish*[12] is commonly and rightly thought of as the

---

7 United States v. E. C. Knight Co., 156 U.S. 1 (1895).

8 Nebbia v. New York, 291 U.S. 502 (1934).

9 Graves v. New York ex rel. O'Keefe, 306 U.S. 466 (1939).

10 312 U.S. 100 (1941).

11 See Stern, *supra* note 4; Rodes, *Due Process and Social Legislation in the Supreme Court—a Post Mortem*, 33 Notre Dame Law. 5 (1957); Hetherington, *State Economic Regulation and Substantive Due Process of Law*, 53 Nw. U. L. Rev. 13, 226 (1958); Wood, Due Process of Law 1932–1949 (1951).

12 300 U.S. 379 (1937), overruling Adkins v. Children's Hospital, 261 U.S. 525 (1923).

watershed case. We know that it was because of what occurred thereafter. But the actual words of Chief Justice Hughes in that case did not suggest very plainly that the whole doctrine of substantive due process was scheduled for destruction. He spoke of the wage regulation as "reasonable," citing a 1911 decision,[13] and he even invoked in defense of the present law the distinction made in 1908 between men and women as parties to a labor contract.[14] It was still possible to believe, then, that the Court was merely overruling *Adkins*, but maintaining its power to strike down other economic legislation that might fail the reasonableness test. *Senn v. Tile Layers Protective Union*,[15] a little later in the Term, suggested that the range of allowable legislative judgment was growing but not that it was unlimited. In *United States v. Carolene Products*,[16] a year later, Justice Stone for the majority went a little further, declaring that regulatory legislation is valid unless the facts "*preclude* the assumption that it rests upon some rational basis." But he still assumed "for present purposes" that an economic statute could be attacked by disproving the facts that were supposed to provide the law with its rational base, and his approval of the law seemed to rest in part on his judicial knowledge that there were facts to support a legislative ukase against "filled milk."

But by 1941, in *Olsen v. Nebraska*,[17] the Court was ready to take another long stride away from the pre-1937 doctrine. The subject matter of this case evoked fond memories of those bygone days, for it concerned regulation of employment-agency rates, and such regulation had been roundly condemned by the old Court in *Ribnik v. McBride*.[18] But now Mr. Justice Douglas, for a unanimous Court, not only repudiated *Ribnik* and its famous doctrine of "business affected with a public interest," but came close to announcing that the issue of economic regulation was no longer of judicial concern. There is no requirement, he said, that the State make out a case for the needfulness or appropriateness of the law. "Differences of opinion on that score suggest a choice which 'should be left where

13 Chicago, B. & Q. R.R. v. McGuire, 219 U.S. 549 (1911), cited 300 U.S. at 392.

14 Muller v. Oregon, 208 U.S. 412 (1908), cited 300 U.S. at 394.

15 301 U.S. 468 (1937).

16 304 U.S. 144, 152 (1938). (Emphasis added.)

17 313 U.S. 236.

18 277 U.S. 350 (1928).

. . . it was left by the Constitution—to the states and to Congress.' "[19] There was no suggestion here, as there was in *West Coast Hotel* and *Carolene Products*, that the State must point to facts which might reasonably justify the regulation. The presumption of constitutionality was no longer debatable. *Olsen* suggested, as a contemporary comment put it, that there was then "a complete lack of constitutional foundation for the assertion of private right under the due process clause where contractual or proprietary interests are involved."[20]

In case the business community and its legal minions might have missed the point in 1941, the Court made it pellucid in later decisions. Everyone has his favorites among these, but a reference to *Day-Brite Lighting v. Missouri*[21] and *Williamson v. Lee Optical Co.*[22] should suffice. In the first, the Court, again via Mr. Justice Douglas, declared that it was not the business of the Court to decide whether legislation "offends the public welfare"[23] and that "debatable issues as respects business, economic, and social affairs" were for legislative decision.[24] In the second, the same Justice upheld a law requiring a prescription from an optometrist or ophthalmologist before an optician could even fit old lenses into a new frame. Though the law may exact a "needless, wasteful requirement in many cases," the legislature "might have concluded" that the waste was justified in order to achieve the objective of protecting health.[25] When these cases were taken together with a companion series in which the Equal Protection Clause was given a similarly permissive scope,[26] there could be little doubt as to the practical result: no claim of substantive economic rights would now be sustained by the Supreme Court. The judiciary had abdicated the field.

This was the result. But it is of some interest to note how the result had been achieved. Obviously two paths lay open. One was that which seemed to be suggested by Mr. Justice Black's dissent in

---

19 313 U.S. at 246.

20 40 MICH. L. REV. 743, 745–46 (1942).

21 342 U.S. 421 (1952).

22 348 U.S. 483 (1955).

23 342 U.S. at 423.

24 *Id.* at 425.

25 348 U.S. at 487.

26 See, *e.g.*, Railway Express Agency, Inc. v. New York, 336 U.S. 106 (1949); Queenside Hills Realty Co. v. Saxl, 328 U.S. 80 (1946).

Connecticut General Life Insurance Co. v. Johnson,[27] *i.e.*, to repudiate in explicit and unmistakable terms the very bases for the Court's jurisdiction over economic questions. Such a course was at least imaginable. The Justices might have reconsidered not only the corporation-as-person doctrine, as Black proposed, but the very idea of substantive due process in the economic field. They might, that is, have held in so many words that economic legislation was no longer subject to judicial review on the question whether it had a "rational basis." This possibility may have been in Stone's mind (though never, one suspects, in his plans) when in *Carolene Products* he only assumed "for present purposes" that the rational basis test was still relevant; it may partly explain Black's disavowal of that portion of Stone's opinion.[28] Certainly Douglas came close to it in *Olsen*. A few years later, in the *Lincoln Union* case,[29] Black came even closer when he implied that the only constitutional limits in the economic field were the specific prohibitions of the Constitution.

The other possibility was to retain the rhetoric of the rational basis standard, but to apply it so tolerantly that no law was ever likely to violate it. This was the course ultimately chosen, one more consonant with Stone's view that such issues were better dealt with "gradually and by intimation."[30] Even Douglas seems to have accepted the rational basis concept for these rhetorical purposes.[31]

This was perhaps the "judicial" way to bring the result about. It preserved some shreds of the idea of continuity, and that idea, myth or not, is important to the constitutional tradition. It enabled the Justices to feel their way along toward a policy whose contours were probably not yet clear in their own minds. It may have helped to maintain unanimity: it is hard enough to understand how Justice Roberts could have accepted the *Olsen* opinion; it is even harder to envision him concurring in an explicit renunciation of all judicial authority to protect property holders.

---

27 303 U.S. 77, 83 (1938).

28 304 U.S. at 155.

29 Lincoln Federal Labor Union v. Northwestern Iron & Metal Co., 335 U.S. 525 (1949).

30 MASON, HARLAN FISKE STONE: PILLAR OF THE LAW 469 (1956); see also Dunham, *Mr. Chief Justice Stone*, in DUNHAM & KURLAND, MR. JUSTICE 47 (1956).

31 See DOUGLAS, WE THE JUDGES (1956).

So much at least can be said for the approach chosen, leaving aside for the moment the question whether the result itself was desirable. But the matter has another aspect. When policies are established "gradually and by intimation," when the question of their existence is partially obscured by preservation of the old rhetoric, there is always a chance that the destruction of those policies will not be recognized. A flat decision to discard substantive due process root-and-branch would have compelled the Justices to explain themselves, to examine the basis for their abnegation. In the actual event they have never fully done so, at least in public, and this leaves, to say the least, a large gap in the rationale that underlies the structure of modern constitutional law.

The reticence of the Court does, however, provide the non-judicial observer with an opportunity. It leaves him free to speculate about the explanations and justifications that the Justices have neglected to provide. And the speculation at least seems desirable: one of the cardinal doctrines of American constitutional history should not be denied the modest rite of a funeral oration.

III. Action and Reaction

What then was the explanation of this extraordinary shift in judicial values? It must be emphasized that this is not merely the question why the Court took leave of the unyielding negativism represented by such judgments as *Adair v. United States*[32] or *Coppage v. Kansas*[33] or by the anti–New Deal dogmatics of 1934–1936. That question may not be an easy one, for historical questions seldom are, but its mysteries are not unfathomable. An answer would have to begin with the specific enigma of Justice Roberts; after that the road is comparatively clear. His shift in 1937 created a majority opposed to the extreme version of constitutional laissez faire, and it was to be expected that that majority would be strengthened as new appointments were made in the following years. The shift from *Morehead v. New York ex rel. Tipaldo*[34] to *West Coast Hotel*, startling though it was as a specific event, was not beyond prediction: the basis for it had been well laid in the recent past by both judges and scholars.

The harder question is: Why did the Court move all the way from

---

[32] 208 U.S. 161 (1908). [33] 236 U.S. 1 (1915). [34] 298 U.S. 587 (1936).

the inflexible negativism of the old majority to the all-out tolerance of the new? Why did it not establish a halfway house between the extremes, retaining a measure of control over economic legislation but exercising that control with discrimination and self-restraint?

Precisely such a halfway house had frequently been described in judicial opinions of the past, so there is little chance that the post-1937 Justices had overlooked its conceptual existence. Justice Brandeis in *New State Ice Co. v. Liebmann*[35] had admonished the Court against erecting its prejudices into legal principles but had still conceded that "the reasonableness of every regulation is dependent on the relevant facts."[36] Indeed, he conducted an exhaustive examination of those facts in his opinion. Justice Stone had himself carefully adumbrated such a position, saying in *Ribnik* that price regulation is within the States' power when "any combination of circumstances seriously curtails the regulative force of competition, so that buyers or sellers are placed at such a disadvantage in the bargaining struggle that a legislature might reasonably anticipate serious consequences to the community as a whole."[37] To be sure, Justice Holmes had, in *Tyson & Brother v. Banton*,[38] laid down a standard comparable in its permissiveness to the *Olsen* doctrine:[39] "The truth seems to me to be that, subject to compensation when compensation is due, the legislature may forbid or restrict any business when it has a sufficient force of public opinion behind it." This is the *de facto* policy of the modern Court. But Stone, as has been said, filed a separate dissent in *Tyson*, and even Holmes in other opinions had conceded that the supposed rational basis of economic statutes is subject to judicial scrutiny.[40] As a result of such scrutiny, the Court would not strike down an arguably rational law, but it would require some showing by the State that there was a basis for believing it to be rational and would consider evidence to the contrary presented by the affected business. Laws like those involved in the *Lee Optical* case[41] and in *Daniel v. Family Security Life Ins.*

35 285 U.S. 262, 311 (1932).

36 *Id.* at 301–02.

37 277 U.S. at 360 (dissenting opinion).

38 273 U.S. 418, 445 (1927) (dissenting opinion).

39 *Id.* at 446.

40 See, *e.g.*, Adkins v. Children's Hospital, 261 U.S. 525, 567 (1923) (dissenting opinion).

41 Note 22 *supra*.

Co.[42] might be invalidated, or at any rate more sharply queried.

Assuming then that this standard—this modest residue of the old economic supervision—was consciously and purposefully rejected, what explains the rejection? And, to make the difficulty a little more acute, what accounts for the fact that such survivors of the old Court as Stone and Roberts concurred in the choice, that the *Olsen* opinion was unanimous? A couple of "behavioral" or psychological explanations come to mind as possibilities. They are put forward diffidently, for motive is hard to ascertain with respect to only one man; when a group of nine highly sophisticated individuals is involved, the complexities become awesome.

For one thing, it may be that Stone and Roberts joined in the movement so as to preserve the rhetoric of supervision and thus some faint shadow of doctrinal continuity. Black, as his biographer says, wanted to "reject utterly and completely the doctrine . . . that the due-process clause gives to courts the power to determine the reasonableness of regulations."[43] Considering his well-known enthusiasm for calling a spade a spade,[44] we can well believe that Black would have liked to spell this out in an explicit abdication speech. We cannot tell how many of his brethren would have joined him then. But by the spring of 1941, there were, besides himself, four Roosevelt appointees on the Court, and further appointments were obviously pending. The veterans may have felt that the most they could hope for was the fictional survival of the rational basis test.

A second possible explanation may be more fruitful, since it relates, not only to the question why the veterans were willing to retreat so far, but also why the newer Justices seemed resolved to do so. It is that extremism had bred extremism in thinking about the role of the Supreme Court. Between 1923 and 1937, a conservative majority had, from time to time, embraced a policy of adamant resistance to economic experiment, and this obstructionist spirit had reached its zenith in the judicial reaction against the New Deal.

---

42 336 U.S. 220 (1949). The statute prohibited life insurance companies and their employees from operating undertaking businesses, and undertakers from serving as agents for life insurance companies.

43 Frank, Mr. Justice Black: The Man and His Opinions 111 (1949).

44 See Mendelson, Justices Black and Frankfurter: Conflict in the Court (1961).

What the Chief Justice himself had said in the *Railroad Retirement* case[45] was true of the conservative majority in most of the great anti–New Deal decisions. That majority had raised a barrier, not only against particular features of the law, but "against all legislative action of this nature by declaring that the subject matter itself lies beyond the reach" of governmental authority.[46] This intransigence had tended to discredit the whole concept of judicial supervision in the minds of those who felt that government must have reasonable leeway to experiment with the economic order. The result was that the two wings of the Court (and of the country) had almost ceased to communicate with each other. The dissenting opinions of Stone in *United States v. Butler*[47] and Sutherland in *West Coast Hotel*[48] are not a dialogue between men who share a common ground but disagree about its implications. The opinions represent wholly different realms of discourse. If the position of the conservatives had been less extreme, there might have been in 1937 the basis for a viable, moderate doctrine of economic supervision. It is almost touching to observe Sutherland, in *Carmichael v. Southern Coal & Coke Co.*,[49] after the "revolution" of 1937, urging that the State law could be cured of its constitutional infirmities and that, if it were, the objective of relieving unemployment could be attained despite the Due Process Clause. This language of sweet reason had not been conspicuous in the negative decisions of previous years. Now it came too late. The extreme of the past had generated the extreme of the present. The Court which had claimed the full loaf was winding up without even the half. Such a result is not surprising when dogmatism has been substituted for discussion.

Factors like these may help to explain the impulse to discard the old due process doctrine, bag and baggage. Yet one would like to think that a more thoughtful process was going on somewhere below the surface, that the policy of virtual abdication was not merely a reflex against the excesses of the past but a considered and justified decision about the proper scope of judicial review. The written

45 Railroad Retirement Board v. Alton R.R., 295 U.S. 330, 374 (1935) (dissenting opinion).

46 *Id.* at 375.

47 297 U.S. 1, 78 (1936).

48 300 U.S. at 401.

49 301 U.S. 495, 527 (1937) (dissenting opinion).

record to support such a supposition is not, alas, very convincing.[50] Scattered remarks in decisions cited above, and in others, assailed the dead horse of "the Allgeyer-Lochner-Adair-Coppage" doctrine,[51] *i.e.*, the Justices argued against "social dogma" and for "increased deference to the legislative judgment"[52] in the economic field. But they did not explain why the abuses of power in those earlier decisions justified abandonment of the power itself, nor why the deference to the legislature should be carried to the point of complete submission. The nearest thing to an explanation is perhaps to be found in Mr. Justice Frankfurter's concurrence in *American Federation of Labor v. American Sash & Door Co.*, where he argued that "the judiciary is prone to misconceive the public good" and that matters of policy, depending as they do on imponderable value issues, are best left to the people and their representatives.[53] This is a coherent and not unconvincing viewpoint, but the trouble with it has always been that it implied similar judicial withdrawal, not only from the economic field, but from other areas that pose questions of policy, such as freedom of expression. Well aware of this difficulty, Frankfurter tried to meet it in this opinion by declaring that matters like press censorship and separation of church and state are different, because "history, through the Constitution, speaks so decisively as to forbid legislative experimentation" with them.[54] Scholarship has since provided reason to doubt that history speaks so plainly after all, even on these subjects,[55] and without a strong historical rationale the argument falters badly, for the arguments against judicial intervention in economic affairs become arguments against intervention in the policy sphere generally. Learned

[50] FREUND, ON UNDERSTANDING THE SUPREME COURT 11 (1949); Learned Hand said in 1946: "Just why property itself was not a 'personal right' nobody took the time to explain." HAND, THE SPIRIT OF LIBERTY 206 (1960). Nobody, so far as I am aware, has yet taken that time.

[51] Lincoln Federal Labor Union v. Northwestern Iron & Metal Co., 335 U.S. 525, 535 (1949).

[52] A. F. of L. v. American Sash & Door Co., 335 U.S. 538, 544 (1949) (concurring opinion).

[53] *Id.* at 556.

[54] *Id.* at 550.

[55] LEVY, LEGACY OF SUPPRESSION (1960); Brief for Appellees, McCollum v. Board of Educ., 333 U.S. 203 (1948).

Hand of course was ready to accept this implication[56] and Frankfurter himself has come very near to it. But it is certainly not the dominant doctrine of the modern Court, which has fairly consistently held to the "dual standard" enunciated by Stone in the *Carolene Products* case.[57] So we are left with a judicial policy which rejects supervision over economic matters and asserts supervision over "personal rights"; and with a rationale, so far as the written opinions go, that might support withdrawal from both fields but does not adequately justify the discrimination between them.

IV. The Doubtful Distinction between Economic and Civil Rights

Although no such rationale can be detected in the written opinions, however, the possibility of its existence cannot be entirely dismissed. The Supreme Court has sometimes preferred to leave ultimate arguments unexpressed, to let justification for a course of conduct, as well as the course itself, emerge "gradually and by intimation." And this may be the case with the great retreat from economic supervision. Perhaps there is a coherent apologia for that retreat; perhaps this apologia was in the Justices' minds when they shaped the modern constitutional policy. The second "perhaps" can never be transmuted into certainty unless the art of judicial psychoanalysis reaches unforeseen heights. But its plausibility may increase if it appears that there is a rationale which *might* have formed the basis of the policy.

The arguments for demoting economic rights to their modern lowly constitutional status—lowly when compared wtih "personal rights"—fall into two categories. First, there is a group of arguments based on judgments about the nature and relative importance of the rights concerned. For example, it is sometimes argued that laws limiting freedom of expression impinge on the human personality more grievously than do laws curbing mere economic liberty, and that the Court is therefore justified in protecting the former more zealously than the latter.[58] The individual has, *qua* individual, "the

56 Hand, The Bill of Rights (1958).

57 Freund, *op. cit. supra* note 50.

58 Hastie, *Judicial Method in Due Process Inquiry*, in Government under Law 326 (Sutherland ed. 1956). He makes an exception of subsistence.

right to be let alone."[59] The right to free choice in the intellectual and spiritual realm is particularly precious to him. A major difficulty with this formulation is that there is the smell of the lamp about it: it may reflect the tastes of the judges and dons who advance it, rather than the real preferences of the commonality of mortals. Judges and professors are talkers both by profession and avocation. It is not surprising that they would view freedom of expression as primary to the free play of their personalities. But most men would probably feel that an economic right, such as freedom of occupation, was at least as vital to them as the right to speak their minds. Mark Twain would surely have felt constrained in the most fundamental sense, if his youthful aspiration to be a river-boat pilot had been frustrated by a State-ordained system of nepotism.[60] Needless to say, no disparagement of freedom of expression is here intended. But its inarguable importance to the human spirit, on the one hand, does not furnish an adequate ground for downgrading all economic rights, on the other.

So much for a purely individual-centered justification for the disparity between economic rights and other civil liberties. Another suggested rationale looks toward the community rather than the separate individuals within it. Progress, it is said, "is to a considerable extent the displacement of error which once held sway as official truth by beliefs which in turn have yielded to other beliefs."[61] To encourage societal progress, it is important then to protect "those liberties of the individual which history has attested as the indispensable conditions of an open as against a closed society,"[62] *e.g.*, freedom of expression.

Presumably this "open society" argument would be relevant no matter how the political system was organized—even a benevolent autocracy must tolerate freedom of expression or risk stagnation. But Alexander Meiklejohn has contended that the point takes on an extra dimension when applied to popular government, to democracy as the West understands that term. In any political system, so the argument runs, the ruler must be fully informed if he is to govern

---

59 Brandeis, J., dissenting, in Olmstead v. United States, 277 U.S. 438, 478 (1928).

60 Kotch v. Pilot Commissioners, 330 U.S. 552 (1947).

61 Frankfurter, J., concurring, in Kovacs v. Cooper, 336 U.S. 77 at 95.

62 *Ibid.*

well, and he cannot be fully informed when someone else is deciding what ideas he shall be allowed to hear. In a democracy the people are sovereign, and it follows that they and no one else must decide what and whom they will listen to. And it further follows that the Constitution must protect any freedoms that help the people to acquire "the intelligence, integrity, sensitivity, and generous devotion to the general welfare that, in theory, casting a ballot is assumed to express."[63] In short, the special importance of certain civil rights derives from their special relationship to the process of self-government. Other rights, including the economic, can be abridged when the legislature deems abridgment desirable.

Some such reasoning probably underlies the related point implied by Mr. Justice Stone in the first paragraph of his famous "footnote four"[64] and by Mr. Justice Frankfurter in the concluding words of the first flag-salute opinion[65] (though neither would of course have followed Professor Meiklejohn in the absolutist conclusions he drew). Stone suggested that judicial scrutiny would be especially exacting when legislation restricted "those political processes which can ordinarily be expected to bring about repeal of undesirable legislation,"[66] and Frankfurter intimated that the crucial question is whether "all the effective means of inducing political changes are left free from interference."[67] These pronouncements may rest partly on Professor Meiklejohn's point that the governors must be fully informed; but they also seem to involve a separable idea: that a majoritarian system must, in the name of both justice and progress, preserve the right of a present minority to make its views the views of the majority. A businessman's price may be controlled by the mandate of a popularly elected legislature, but, if his right to work politically for repeal of the control law is untrammeled, the fundamentals of a just democratic polity are still maintained and so is the fluidity of the sociopolitical order.

The whole "open society" line of argument in its various forms is convincing enough as a justification for protecting the free trade

---

[63] Meiklejohn, *The First Amendment Is an Absolute,* [1961] SUPREME COURT REVIEW 245, 255.

[64] United States v. Carolene Products Co., 304 U.S. 144, 152 (1938).

[65] Minersville School Dist. v. Gobitis, 310 U.S. 586, 600 (1940).

[66] 304 U.S. at 152.

[67] 310 U.S. at 600.

in ideas. If one feels the need to explain why the free speech guarantees are important, these explanations will do pretty well for a start. But they are rather less satisfactory as the basis for a policy of *not* protecting economic freedom, of regarding it as unimportant in a democratic system. For one thing, it is not entirely clear why liberty of economic choice is less indispensable to the "openness" of a society than freedom of expression. Few historians would deny that the growth of entrepreneurial and occupational freedom helped to promote material progress in England in the eighteenth and nineteenth centuries and in America after the Civil War (although they might of course argue that the price paid for this progress was unconscionably high). It is one thing to argue that economic liberty must be subject to rational control in the "public interest"; it is quite another to say in effect that it is not liberty at all and that the proponent of the "open society" can therefore regard it as irrelevant to progress.

As for the "political process" subthemes of the open-society argument—the Meiklejohn-Stone-Frankfurter rationales just described—they too must be queried insofar as they purport to justify a downgrading of economic rights. In fact, their basic difficulty is that, in exalting the freedoms bearing on the political process, they bypass the question of other freedoms altogether. Meiklejohn's arguments for protecting liberty of expression are cogent, but they do not on their face explain why other, "private," rights should be neglected. A decision to protect Peter does not necessarily involve the decision to abandon Paul. In Meiklejohn's own formulation there is indeed a hint that the political is primary, that a right associated with the governing process somehow, because of that association, matters more than any other. This might be so in some imaginary democratic city-state where the political and the social were identical, but it is more dubious when applied to the United States where the sphere of private value can make high claims of its own. One may agree that it is necessary for popular government to protect the political process. But it does not follow that all concern for rights comes to an end when that protection has been provided. Moreover, there is some evidence that Meiklejohn's categories refuse to stand still, even in his own mind. He is not content to define the governing-process freedoms narrowly. He rightly says that "voting is merely the external expression of a wide and diverse number of activities by means of which citizens attempt to meet the responsibilities of making judgments";[68] and this enables him to bring literature and the arts within the concept, since they "lead the way toward sensitive and informed appreciation and response to the values out of which the riches of the general welfare are created."[69] We can refuse to swallow whole the dogmas of nineteenth-century rugged individualism and can still believe that some freedom of occupation and economic choice is also instrumental to the development of this self-determining and sensitive citizen-governor.

If Meiklejohn's argument contains the unexamined assumption that the political is primary and almost exclusive, the "Stone-Frankfurter"[70] point described above contains this and an assumption of its own as well: the majoritarian idea in a peculiarly unqualified form. The notion seems to be that the citizen can have nothing really fundamental to complain about in a law if a free majority has enacted it and if he is protected in his right to agitate for its repeal. But this view ascribes a preponderance to the majority will that has certainly not been acknowledged by the American political tradition. In that tradition, it is not assumed that an unjust law becomes just by virtue of majority approval, not even if the victim has the theoretical right to persuade the majority to change its mind. The denial of that right would aggravate the injustice, but the granting of the right does not dispel it. As Justice Jackson said in the flag-salute dialogue,[71] the very purpose of a Bill of Rights was to place certain fundamental rights beyond the reach of majorities.[72] Of course, it may be argued that economic freedom in its various forms can never be so fundamental a right, but that shifts the discussion to a quite different level.

Furthermore this argument overlooks a difficulty partly recognized by Stone himself in the *Carolene Products* footnote[73] and in-

68 Meiklejohn, *supra* note 63.

69 *Id.* at 257.

70 This term is used only for the purposes of expositional convenience. It does not imply that the particular point referred to represents the full position of either of the two Justices on this question or that their views on the question were identical.

71 West Virginia Bd. of Educ. v. Barnette, 319 U.S. 624 (1943).

72 *Id.* at 638.

73 304 U.S. at 152, n. 4.

voked by him in the first flag-salute case, the problem of "discrete and insular minorities,"[74] *i.e.*, those who have no realistic chance of influencing the majority to rescind the law that does them harm. Stone was speaking specifically of religious, national, or racial minorities, and his suggestion was that prejudice against them might curtail the political processes that would ordinarily be expected to protect their rights. Prejudice against Jehovah's Witnesses for their "queerness" makes repressive governmental action more probable, and precisely because of their queerness they are not likely to be numerous enough or influential enough in any given community so that their weight will be felt in the city council. To speak of their power to defend themselves through political action is to sacrifice their civil rights in the name of an amiable fiction. Yet it is not clear why the thrust of this point should be restricted to ethnic and religious minorities. Perhaps it is true that a prosperous corporation can effectively plead its case at the bar of legislative judgment by resort to publicity and direct lobbying. Economic power may be an adequate surrogate for numerical power; no tears need be shed for helpless General Electric. But the scattered individuals who are denied access to an occupation by State-enforced barriers are about as impotent a minority as can be imagined. The would-be barmaids of Michigan[75] or the would-be plumbers of Illinois[76] have no more chance against the entrenched influence of the established bartenders and master plumbers than the Jehovah's Witnesses had against the prejudices of Minersville School District. In fact the Witnesses may enjoy an advantage, for they are at least cohesive; and other "discrete" minorities, such as racial groups, have occasionally displayed respectable capacities to exert political leverage by virtue of their very discreteness. Not so the isolated economic man who belongs to no identifiable group at all.

V. Judicial Capacity in the Realm of Economic Regulation

For one reason or another then, none of these justifications of the Court's modern hands-off policy in the economic field quite

---

[74] Stone, J., dissenting, 310 U.S. at 606.

[75] Goesaert v. Cleary, 335 U.S. 464 (1948).

[76] People v. Brown, 407 Ill. 565 (1951). See Gellhorn, Individual Freedom and Governmental Restraints 123–24 (1956).

stands up. The distinctions they rely on, between economic rights on the one hand and personal rights on the other, tend to blur when we examine them. And, even if it were thought that the distinctions were tenable, the case would remain incomplete. It might, squeezing it hard, justify a difference in the kind and degree of protection afforded economic rights; but it would not warrant a policy of no protection at all.

Although the policy of abdication cannot be justified in terms of an analysis of the nature and relative unimportance of the rights concerned, there is a second line of thought that merits consideration. Perhaps the decision to leave economic rights to the tender mercy of the legislative power is based on the idea that the Supreme Court is peculiarly ill-equipped to deal with this subject. No one would argue that the right enshrined in Article IV, the guarantee of a republican form of government, is unimportant. Yet the Court has refused to protect it, because of well-founded doubts about judicial competence to make effective judgments in this field. It may be that similar doubts underlie the policy of abdication in the area of economic affairs.

At first blush, this argument seems highly persuasive, at least in broad terms. Anyone familiar with the entanglements resulting from *Smyth v. Ames*[77] will be alive to its merits. Probably no court was really equipped to make the intricate and imponderable economic judgments that the doctrine of that case entailed. And those who remember the Court's crusades against the rise of the welfare state may be dubious about judicial competence on somewhat different grounds. They may feel that economic policy is not only beyond the reach of the Court's expertise, but beyond the reach of its practical power. Whether the nation shall have a minimum-wage law; whether the government shall control prices; whether social security shall be publicly guaranteed—these are questions so "high"[78] and so basic that no court could determine them even if it should. They involve in a word the momentous issue of the welfare state itself, and that issue will be determined by "dominant opinion" with or without judicial approval.

There are, of course, economic subjects so recondite that judicial surveillance of them would be anomalous. The choice between

[77] 169 U.S. 466 (1898).

[78] Finkelstein, *Judicial Self-Limitation*, 37 HARV. L. REV. 338, 345 (1924).

"historical cost" and "replacement cost" as a basis for rate making must be made by the legislature, not because it will always choose well, but because the judiciary lacks the knowledge and expertise for distinguishing good from bad in this area. But this point will carry only as far as its logic will bring it, and there are fields of economic regulation less intricate than the problem of public utility rates. To be sure, even the problems raised in these fields may not be simple. A fair evaluation of Oklahoma's need for its anti-optician law would require the Court to make judgments about a complex matter. But this can be said about most questions that reach the Supreme Court in any field. Our problem is not to identify the issues that present difficulties and then to discard them as improper subjects for judicial review. That would be to abandon judicial review in most of the fields where it is now exercised. Our problem is to determine whether economic statutes always or usually involve such extraordinary difficulties that a modest judiciary must eschew them, even though that same judiciary does claim the competence to judge other, more difficult, issues.

Is it easier for example for the Court to appraise a law empowering a board of censors to ban an "immoral" movie[79] than a law empowering a real estate licensing board to deny a license unless the applicant is of "good moral character"?[80] The two standards would seem to be equally vague and the possibility of arbitrary administrative action would seem to be as menacing in one situation as in the other. Is it plainly easier to balance New Hampshire's need to get information against Paul Sweezy's right to withhold it,[81] than it is to balance South Carolina's need to stamp out the funeral insurance business against the right of an agent of the Family Security Life Insurance Company to make a living selling such insurance?[82] The "public need" in both cases was all but invisible. Is it easier to see that the State corporate registration law in *N.A.A.C.P. v. Alabama*[83] was being used to facilitate private reprisals against Association members than it is to see that State boards of plumbers, barbers, and morticians sometimes use their publicly granted powers to pro-

[79] Kingsley International Pictures Corp. v. Regents, 360 U.S. 684 (1959).

[80] GELLHORN, *op. cit. supra* note 76, at 121.

[81] Sweezy v. New Hampshire, 354 U.S. 234 (1957).

[82] Daniel v. Family Security Life Ins. Co., 336 U.S. 220 (1949).

[83] 357 U.S. 449 (1958).

tect the private financial interests of present guild members to the disadvantage of non-members?[84]

The point is not that the cited cases should necessarily have been decided differently, but rather that the issues they present stand on a common level of difficulty and that judicial scrutiny seems as feasible (or unfeasible) for one issue as for the other. And the further, related, point is that there are kinds and kinds of economic subjects and that it is difficult to fashion a generalization that applies to all. Some subjects may be so inscrutable that judicial review cannot fruitfully cope with them; but this is not a justification for avoiding other economic subjects which are no more opaque than the "personal rights" issues that are the standard coinage of judicial discourse these days.

This point likewise applies to the suggestion that the Court, as the relatively weak and non-political branch, simply lacks the power to dictate the economic order, however otherwise competent its members may be. No doubt the Court was presumptuous to imagine, before 1937, that it could hold back such waves as the wage-control movement or the demand for social security. The tide of the welfare state was flowing, and no court could have reversed it. But neither does the judiciary have the practical power to halt any major social developments backed by insistent popular demand. And this would be so whether the development involved economic questions or questions of "personal rights." It was the dimension of the issues in the anti–New Deal cases that made them incongruous for judicial decision, not the mere fact that they were economic in character. No such judicial delusions of grandeur would be implied by enforcement of the requirement that an occupational qualification must be rationally based, or by similar modest applications of substantive due process. The awful will of the sovereign people is not likely to be aroused because the Court has told the morticians of Winnemac that they cannot use State power to maintain a monopoly—or at least no more than it is aroused by other constitutional decisions that issue almost weekly during each Term. In short, while doubts about judicial expertise and power may warrant withdrawal from some economic questions, they cannot justify withdrawal from all such questions, unless the doubter is willing to go

[84] See Grant, *The Gild Returns to America,* 4 J. Pol. 303 (1942).

the full distance with Learned Hand and give up most of the residue of modern judicial review.

VI. The Disappearing Double Standard

In the light of the inadequacies that seem to afflict all of the arguments for judicial abdication of the field of economic rights, we are perhaps justified in concluding that the policy of abstention was never really thought through. It seems to have been a kind of reflex, arising out of indignation against the excesses of the Old Court, and resting on the vague, uncritical idea that "personal rights" are "O.K." but economic rights are "Not O.K." Thus are fashioned the decisions about the shape of our constitutional polity.

This conclusion gains strength when we note from time to time certain signs of uneasiness with the "double standard." The most familiar such manifestation appears in the judicial and extra-judicial remarks of jurists like Learned Hand, Robert Jackson,[85] and Felix Frankfurter. Their misgivings center around the problem of justifying judicial activism in any field where the Court's only guideposts are the inexplicit "moral adjurations"[86] of the Bill of Rights. They have doubts about a judge's capacity to enforce such adjurations in the economic realm, and their modesty is not altogether dissipated when they turn to the field of personal rights; for they are unsatisfied by easy phrases like "preferred position." Hand, as has been said, carried his doubts somewhat further than the others, perhaps because he was speaking *non ex cathedra* in semiretirement. Jackson and Frankfurter have expressed themselves more restrainedly and therefore less clearly, but the broad drift of their qualms has been plain enough. They would partly resolve the dilemma of the double standard by adopting a modest approach to both economic rights and personal rights, though still retaining perhaps some distinction between them.

The other possibility of course would be, not to protect both kinds of rights less, but to protect both equally, *i.e.*, to reassert the Court's power to disallow economic legislation that lacks a rational basis. It would be too much to say that such a development is por-

---

85 Jackson, The Supreme Court in the American System of Government 57–58 (1955).

86 Hand, *op. cit. supra* note 50, at 163.

tended by a few sporadic judicial pronouncements in recent years, but they may indicate a measure of disquiet with the prevailing dichotomy. From the first the modern Court has been troubled by a recurring problem: how does the dichotomy stand up when economic matters and personal rights are involved in a single governmental action? Examples abound: statutes that strike at picketing, which may be both free speech and an economic activity;[87] State-supported professional dues-paying requirements, such as that involved in *Lathrop v. Donohue;*[88] labor regulations that impinge on freedom of religion;[89] license requirements, and other restrictions with a secular purpose, that nevertheless impose burdens on religious practice,[90] to name only a few. It is no help to the judge faced by these hybrid problems to tell him that the economic order is Caesar's affair while personal rights are the Constitution's affair, for the twain have met and he must decide between one or the other. One solution is to hold that a law primarily "secular" in purpose must stand even if it operates incidentally to infringe personal rights; that the law or an application of it will fall only if it was aimed at or discriminates against personal rights as such.[91] Leaving aside the very real difficulty of determining what a law's primary purpose is, the trouble with this formula is that it does permit the state to impose *de facto* burdens on the exercise of personal rights, and this has disturbed some of the Justices. A Court that has resolved to protect personal rights because of their indispensability to democracy is not likely to be content with a doctrine that allows them to be frittered away, even though an otherwise legitimate secular purpose can be descried. Another imaginable solution is to filter out the personal-rights elements in the law and insist on their protection; the economic-rights residue being left, as usual, to the chance of legislative judgment. But this can involve very nettling problems of discrimination and remedy, as is demonstrated by the

87 Thornhill v. Alabama, 310 U.S. 88 (1940).

88 367 U.S. 820 (1961).

89 Prince v. Massachusetts, 321 U.S. 158 (1944).

90 Murdock v. Pennsylvania, 319 U.S. 105 (1943); and cases cited in note 91 *infra.*

91 Braunfeld v. Brown, 366 U.S. 599 (1961); Gallagher v. Crown Kosher Super Market, 366 U.S. 617 (1961); McGowan v. Maryland 366 U.S. 420 (1961); Two Guys from Harrison-Allentown, Inc. v. McGinley, 366 U.S. 582 (1961).

arguments in such recent decisions as *Lathrop v. Donohue*[92] and the Sunday Law cases.[93]

Moreover this last solution is likely to strain the logic of the Court's position more than it can perhaps bear. In the situation presented by the *Lathrop* case, for example, the Court would have to say that a lawyer has a "right" to practice his profession free from the kinds of restrictions to which the First Amendment refers, that he has under these circumstances a constitutional "right to work," but that the right somehow vanishes when the statute is cured of its First Amendment defects. The State can be as arbitrary as it likes in regulating my occupational freedom just so long as the regulations do not touch on my speech (or religion, or race, or perhaps national origin[94]). The logical strain inherent in such a position has been suggested above. The Court's dilemma is reminiscent of the 1920's, when constitutional history was moving in the opposite direction. A Court that had enshrined economic liberty in the Constitution under the due-process rubric found it increasingly difficult to maintain that the Due Process Clause did not protect other liberties that men might deem important. In spite of the flat statement to the contrary in 1922,[95] within three years thereafter freedom of expression was acknowledged as a constitutional right enforceable against State action.[96]

Perhaps an analogous restlessness helps account for hints about economic freedom, especially the right to work, that have turned up here and there in recent years. In *Barsky v. Board of Regents*[97] in 1954, the Court sustained the suspension of a physician's license against a charge of unreasonableness. The majority was willing to allow the license-revoking authority virtually unlimited discretion and would not conclude that whim and caprice had guided the authority's decision even though the evidence to that effect seemed fairly strong. This is the standard, extreme presumption of validity, that has effectively barred judicial review in the economic field. But the dissenters used language that may point in a rather different

---

[92] Note 88 *supra*.

[93] Note 91 *supra*.

[94] But see State of Ohio ex rel. Clarke v. Deckebach, 274 U.S. 392 (1927).

[95] Prudential Insurance Co. v. Cheek, 259 U.S. 530 (1922).

[96] Gitlow v. New York, 268 U.S. 652 (1925).

[97] 347 U.S. 442.

direction. Mr. Justice Frankfurter, while conceding that the Court must presume the validity of the State agency's action in the absence of evidence to the contrary, nevertheless argued that such evidence should be considered if it does appear on the record. And, in considering it, the Court should ask whether the revocation has "some rational relation to the qualifications required of a practitioner" in the profession. "If a State licensing agency lays bare its arbitrary action, or if the State law explicitly allows it to act arbitrarily, that is precisely the kind of State action which the Due Process Clause forbids."[98] True, the case involved the possibility that the agency here had been influenced by the appellant's supposed left-wing connections, so that this might be regarded as merely another example of special judicial sensitivity when personal rights and economic rights are mixed. But Frankfurter's words do not suggest that he would be any less hostile to an irrelevant standard because it lacked First Amendment undertones. And Douglas, also dissenting, described the right to work in terms that hardly suggest a niggardly interpretation of its range:[99]

> The right to work, I had assumed, was the most precious liberty that man possesses. Man has indeed as much right to work as he has to live, to be free, to own property. . . . To work means to eat. It also means to live. For many it would be better to work in jail, than to sit idle on the curb. The great values of freedom are in the opportunities afforded man to press to new horizons, to pit his strength against the forces of nature, to match skills with his fellow man.

It would be a little hard to laud a right so fully in one breath and in the next to say that judicial review has no concern with it except insofar as another right like freedom of speech is also involved.

In view of such pronouncements it is not surprising that the Court a few years later struck down such a restraint on occupational freedom. In *Schware v. Board of Bar Examiners*,[100] petitioner had been refused permission to take the State bar examination on the ground that he lacked "good moral character." Again First Amendment problems were mingled with the right-to-work issue, but again the language of the Justices suggested a standard that

---

98 *Id.* at 470 (dissenting opinion).

99 *Id.* at 472.

100 353 U.S. 232 (1957).

would forbid arbitrary determinations in general. Mr. Justice Black for the Court declared that State-imposed qualifications "must have a rational connection with the applicant's fitness or capacity" to practice the occupation, and continued: "Even in applying permissible standards, officers of a State cannot exclude an applicant when there is no basis for their finding that he fails to meet these standards, or when their action is invidiously discriminatory."[101] This language is potentially far-reaching, for its suggests (as does the body of the opinion) that the Court is prepared to review and evaluate the administration of licensing requirements in the professions and trades in general. If its potentiality were realized, it would mean that licensing boards were now constitutionally required to show that their findings had a basis in evidence, and that would go far to bring economic rights back under the shelter of the Constitution.

This is probably too much to wring from the decision, although it is easy to believe that Black would be quite prepared to carry it thus far. Mr. Justice Frankfurter's concurring opinion for himself and two others was much more careful. He would, as in his *Barsky* opinion, allow the Board wide discretion in judging "moral character" and would not question individual determinations simply because they involve intuitions, impressions, and other "subjective factors," rather than hard, objective evidence. But even he would overthrow a determination based on "*avowed* considerations" that were inadmissible under appropriate doctrines of due process.[102] This in itself would establish a modest but significant degree of judicial surveillance in the economic field. Nor is there anything in a trio of 1961 "right-to-work" decisions[103] to suggest that the Court was backtracking on this point. To be sure the majority found in each case that the State restriction was rationally justified. But Mr. Justice Harlan, who spoke for the Court in all three, went to considerable lengths to find and evaluate that rational basis. However unsatisfactory his conclusions were to the dissenters, the process of reaching them did not have the perfunctory quality of cases like

---

101 *Id.* at 239.

102 *Id.* at 249. (Emphasis added.)

103 Cohen v. Hurley, 366 U.S. 117; In re Anastaplo, 366 U.S. 82; Konigsberg v. State Bar, 366 U.S. 36.

Olsen[104] and *Queenside Realty*,[105] where the rational-basis terminology seemed to be recited for rhetorical purposes only. Here, on the contrary, a real inquiry was being made.

VII. Requiescat in Pace

It appears then that the Court has at least taken the preliminary steps for re-establishing judicial review of laws infringing occupational freedom. Whether the operative doctrine should be the rather strict one suggested by Mr. Justice Black in *Schware*[106] or the more tolerant one implied in Mr. Justice Frankfurter's concurrence,[107] the fact is that some genuine review of laws in this field does seem plausible. The doctrinal road is open. Of course, the opening of that road with respect to the right to work does not necessarily clear the way for review of other governmental inroads on economic freedom. As has been intimated, there may be special reasons for protecting the right to work: the primacy of the right to the affected individual, the difficulty of protecting it through ordinary political processes. Indeed, there is no assurance that the apparently new attitude toward occupational freedom will itself be translated into the actuality of constitutional limitation. The Court's present position is somewhat similar to the position of 1925–1930 when a doctrinal basis had been laid for protecting speech against State action, but no State law had actually been struck down. Only the Justices themselves could tell us whether the guilds are going to have their comfortable world disturbed by the *deus ex machina* of the Constitution. And perhaps even they could not enlighten us, for there is little in the preceding survey to suggest that they are prone to think a course of action out before embarking on it.

Nevertheless it is legitimate, and perhaps timely, for an observer of the Court's work to ask whether constitutional law *should* move down that road again, whether the Court should reassert its claim to examine the reasonableness of economic legislation. To reiterate a point that has perhaps already been sufficiently made, this is not a question whether the Justices should return to the dogmatics

---

104 Olsen v. Nebraska, 313 U.S. 236 (1941).

105 Queenside Hills Realty Co. v. Saxl, 328 U.S. 80 (1946).

106 Note 100 *supra*.

107 *Id.* at 247.

of *Adkins*[108] and *Ribnik*,[109] or to the delusions of grandeur that prompted the judicial crusade against the New Deal, or to the tangled thickets of *Smyth v. Ames*.[110] The Court could not re-establish "laissez faire" even if it wanted to; some economic matters are too big for the Court to handle and some are too intricate. The question is simply whether the Court should begin to apply a modest but real version of the rational-basis standard in economic fields that are not intrinsically inaccessible to the judicial power.

As has been argued earlier, none of the usual justifications for saying "no" to this question will quite do. Some of the rights involved, such as occupational freedom, are not unimportant, nor are they necessarily any more beyond the reach of judicial capacity than other rights which the Justices have chosen to protect. If this were 1937, if the Court were poised on the brink of the modern constitutional era, the case for retaining some constitutional limits in the economic field might be strong. Those who planned the course of future events might well feel that the objective of a just society would be best served by a judicial policy in which economic rights held a respected place. But the year is not 1937, it is 1962; and modern constitutional policy has developed, not by plan but by impulse, not as a coherent body of doctrine but as a congeries of *ad hoc* responses. These circumstances raise a point that takes us back to the opening paragraphs of this essay. They may constitute in themselves a compelling reason for leaving economic due process in repose.

The reason has to do with what might be called judicial economy. The Court's personal-rights decisions in the past twenty-five years have involved constitutional law in some of the most difficult and emotion-charged issues that modern American government faces. The problem of defining and defending the legal rights of Negroes, in a society that has long shamefully neglected their rights, is alone formidable enough to tax the intellectual and power resources of a single tribunal. Yet this is only the beginning of the lofty assignments the Justices have set for themselves. They have undertaken to evaluate governmental encroachments on political and artistic expression, to supervise, in increasing degree, State administration of criminal law. And each of these major personal-

108 Adkins v. Children's Hospital, 261 U.S. 525 (1923).

109 Ribnik v. McBride, 277 U.S. 350 (1928).

110 169 U.S. 466 (1898).

rights categories is replete with subcategories, each of which poses ample problems of its own. Nor is there any sign that the rate of accretion is slowing down. In 1962, the Court, in one opinion, brought the jungle of electoral apportionment under judicial scrutiny[111] and, in another, reasserted its willingness to act as a national school board in the field of church-state relationships.[112]

Even if there were no practical, political limitations on the range of Court power, this multitude of self-imposed tasks would be intimidating. The lines between liberty and authority, between justice and injustice, between the necessary and the intolerable, are not easy to draw in a single field: to lay them down in such a variety of fields requires a whole series of painstaking evaluations in which not only intuition, but hard, searching analysis must play its part. It is a common and just complaint that the modern Court has so far failed to develop reasoned formulations for many of its judgments in the personal-rights area.[113] This means that important work is left undone each time the Court gathers to itself a new subject for review. Having spent the last twenty-five years assuming new tasks, the Justices could easily spend the next twenty-five working out the problem of how those tasks should be done. These considerations in themselves might argue against taking on any further assignments for the time being, leaving the question of practical power out of account.

In the long run, however, that issue cannot be left out of account. The Supreme Court is an agency of government and, like other agencies of government, must work within the limits of political possibility. It has been suggested above that a revival of economic due process in connection with a subject like occupational freedom would not by itself overstrain the Court's power. But when the prospect of such a development is considered against the background of other recent assumptions of authority, the calculus may be very different. Various personal-rights decisions during that period have taxed not only the "time-chart"[114] and the reasoning

111 Baker v. Carr, 369 U.S. 186 (1962). See Neal, *Baker v. Carr: Politics in Search of Law*, [1962] SUPREME COURT REVIEW, *infra.*

112 Engel v. Vitale, 370 U.S. 421 (1962). See Kurland, *The Regents' Prayer Case: "Full of Sound and Fury, Signifying . . ."* [1962] SUPREME COURT REVIEW 1, *supra.*

113 See Wechsler, *Toward Neutral Principles of Constitutional Law*, 73 HARV. L. REV. 1 (1959); KURLAND, *op. cit. supra* note 6.

114 See Hart, *Foreword: The Time Chart of the Justices*, 73 HARV. L. REV. 84 (1959).

power of the Justices but their effective prestige as well. In the summer of 1958, an accumulation of political resentment led to one of the most serious—and most nearly successful—congressional counterattacks in judicial history.[115] No one yet knows whether *Baker v. Carr* will make more friends for the Court than it makes enemies, but there seems at this writing to be little question about *Engel v. Vitale* on this score.[116] Doubtless it is regrettable that factors like these must be brought into an assessment of judicial capacities. A world in which the ethical-legal mandates of the Court were accepted without question by those affected would be a comfortable world for the Justices and perhaps not a bad one for the United States as a whole. But it is not, and never has been, the world the Court lives in; and in the real world a friend of the Court quails at the thought of seeing it assume still another politically delicate task.

All things considered, then, it seems best that the cause of economic rights be left by the Supreme Court to lie in its uneasy grave. This need not mean that the legislatures of the nation are warranted in ignoring them, nor that the State courts, applying their own constitutions, should be indifferent to plausible due-process claims.[117] These rights, or some of them, do have a bearing on the justness of a society and on the happiness and well-being of the people who live in it. If the Supreme Court of today had a free hand in choosing the subjects of judicial review, there might well be an argument for choosing the right to work over some of the other subjects that engage Court attention. But it does not have a free hand; its liberty of choice has been considerably foreclosed by the episodic course of constitutional law since 1937. The Supreme Court, like the American political system of which it is a part, proceeds by impulse rather than by design, pragmatically rather than foresightedly. Like the United States, the Court derives advantages from this approach; but like the United States, the Court, too, is bound by its limitations.

---

115 See MURPHY, CONGRESS AND THE COURT (1962).

116 See Lewis, *Supreme Court's Term Viewed As One of Most Significant in Its History*, N.Y. Times, July 2, 1962, p. 12; *The Court Decision—and the School Prayer Furor*, 60 NEWSWEEK 43 (July 9, 1962); Kurland, *supra* note 112.

117 But see Hoskins & Katz, *Substantive Due Process in the States Revisited*, 18 OHIO ST. L. J. 384 (1952).

ALLISON DUNHAM

GRIGGS v. ALLEGHENY COUNTY IN PERSPECTIVE: THIRTY YEARS OF SUPREME COURT EXPROPRIATION LAW

In 1962, the Supreme Court rendered its judgment in *Griggs v. Allegheny County*,[1] holding that the county had to compensate the plaintiff because the noise, vibration, and danger resulting from airplane use of the new county airport constituted a taking of an air easement over the plaintiff's property. This was one of a long series of judgments that appear to make up a crazy-quilt pattern of Supreme Court doctrine on the law of expropriation. To describe one square of the pattern, as was the original plan for this paper, seemed to be a futile effort, for the place and role of the square in which *Griggs* is located can make sense, if at all, only in terms of the entire pattern. Each square of the quilt has either been created or redone within the past thirty years and the decisions of the Court for this period provide the subject matter for the article. The purpose of the essay is to discover whether the Court's judgments in

---

Allison Dunham is Professor of Law, The University of Chicago.

1 369 U.S. 84 (1962). The case is considered in detail in the text *infra*, at notes 58 *et seq.*

this area reveal a rational plan or only a haphazard accumulation of rules.

I. Some Relevant Statistics

A brief statistical analysis before the doctrinal review may be of interest. Eighty-nine cases in thirty years[2] reveal that condemnation law does not constitute a large portion of the Court's business: in no year did condemnation cases constitute more than 3 per cent of the cases with opinion.

Table 1 shows a breakdown of the eighty-nine cases by category of problem or event which gave rise to condemnation. Some of the cases appear in more than one category.

---

[2] Of the eighty-nine cases examined, the following are not otherwise referred to in this article: Wilbur v. United States, 288 U.S. 97 (1933); United States v. Acme Operating Corp., 288 U.S. 243 (1933); Harrisonville v. Dickey Clay Co., 289 U.S. 334 (1933); Jacobs v. United States, 290 U.S. 13 (1933); Nashville, C. & St. L. Ry. v. Walters, 294 U.S. 405 (1935); United States v. Creek Nation, 295 U.S. 103 (1935); McCandless v. United States, 298 U.S. 342 (1936); Shoshone Tribe v. United States, 299 U.S. 476 (1937); Creek Nation v. United States, 302 U.S. 620 (1938); Hinderlider v. LaPlata Co., 304 U.S. 92 (1938); United States v. Shoshone Tribe of Indians, 304 U.S. 111 (1938); United States v. Klamath & Moadoc Tribes, 304 U.S. 119 (1938); Patterson v. Stanolind Oil & Gas Co., 305 U.S. 376 (1939); Minnesota v. United States, 305 U.S. 382 (1939); Chippewa Indians v. United States, 305 U.S. 479 (1939); United States v. Powers, 305 U.S. 527 (1939); Chesebro v. Los Angeles County Dist., 306 U.S. 459 (1939); United States v. Sponenbarger, 308 U.S. 256 (1939); Danforth v. United States, 308 U.S. 271 (1939); Paramino Lumber Co. v. Marshall, 309 U.S. 370 (1940); United States v. Appalachian Power Co., 311 U.S. 377 (1940); United States v. Chicago, M., St. P. & P. R.R., 312 U.S. 592 (1941); Oklahoma v. Atkinson Co., 313 U.S. 508 (1941); Cleveland v. United States, 323 U.S. 329 (1945); Catlin v. United States, 324 U.S. 215 (1945); United States v. Commodore Park, 324 U.S. 386 (1945); Bailey v. Anderson, 326 U.S. 203 (1945); North American Co. v. S.E.C., 327 U.S. 686 (1946); Albrecht v. United States, 329 U.S. 599 (1947); Silesian-American Corp. v. Clark, 332 U.S. 469 (1947); Grand River Dam Authority v. Grand Hydro, 335 U.S. 359 (1948); United States v. Toronto, Hamilton & Buffalo Navigation Co., 338 U.S. 396 (1949); United States v. Kansas City Life Ins. Co., 339 U.S. 799 (1950); United States v. Gerlach Livestock Co., 339 U.S. 725 (1950); United States v. Peewee Coal Co., 341 U.S. 114 (1951); United States v. Wheelock Bros., Inc., 341 U.S. 319 (1951); United States v. Certain Parcels of Land, 345 U.S. 344 (1953); F.P.C. v. Niagara Mohawk Power Corp., 347 U.S. 239 (1954); Tee-Hit-Ton Indians v. United States, 348 U.S. 272 (1955); General Box Co. v. United States, 351 U.S. 159 (1956); Walker v. City of Hutchinson, 352 U.S. 112 (1956); Soriano v. United States, 352 U.S. 270 (1957); United States v. Dow, 357 U.S. 17 (1958); Ivanhoe Irrigation District v. McCracken, 357 U.S. 275 (1958); County of Allegheny v. Mashuda Co., 360 U.S. 185 (1959); United States v. 93.970 Acres of Land, 360 U.S. 328 (1959); United States v. Grand River Dam Authority, 363 U.S. 229 (1960); Benz v. New York State Highway Authority, 369 U.S. 147 (1962).

TABLE 1

Subject	Number of Cases	Percentage of Total Condemnation Cases
Public purpose	5	5.6
Police power v. eminent domain	15	16.8
What is compensable	24	27.0
What does market value include	19	21.3
Required procedure in eminent domain	14	15.7
State condemnation cases	15	16.8
Arising out of World Wars I and II	16	18.0
Navigable waters, including power, irrigation, and flood control	29	32.6
Indian lands	10	11.2

II. Judicial Control of Eminent Domain—the Public Purpose Doctrine

Despite the enormous expansion of governmental activity in the last thirty years, the striking fact is that Supreme Court litigation has not often involved a claim that Congress has no power to condemn private property for some particular purpose. Only five of the eighty-nine eminent-domain cases have involved an asserted constitutional limitation on federal or State power of eminent domain.

The literature and earlier cases are replete with statements that compulsory taking must be for a public purpose or use and that the question whether there is a public purpose is a judicial question as to which the legislature cannot bind the courts.[3] Two cases have all but swept away this old learning. In *United States ex rel. T.V.A. v. Welch*,[4] Mr. Justice Black said for the Court that when Congress has spoken, authorizing a condemnation, "its decision is entitled to deference until it is shown to involve an impossibility." Perhaps because Mr. Justice Reed, in a concurring opinion, criticized Black for having gone too far in eliminating judicial review of

3 For a bibliography, see McDougal & Mueller, *Public Purpose in Public Housing: An Anachronism Reburied*, 52 Yale L.J. 42 (1942); Kratovil & Harrison, *Eminent Domain—Policy and Concept*, 42 Calif. L. Rev. 596 (1954); Note, *The Public Use Limitation on Eminent Domain: An Advance Requiem*, 58 Yale L.J. 599 (1949) (particularly the cases and articles cited at nn. 1, 2).

4 327 U.S. 546, 552 (1946).

"public purpose,"[5] Mr. Justice Douglas, in *Berman v. Parker*, was a little more cautious in limiting judicial review:[6] "Subject to specific constitutional limitations, when the legislature has spoken, the public interest has been declared in terms well-nigh conclusive."

While the phrase in the Fifth Amendment dealing with condemnation could be read as imposing only one limitation on the legislative power—to pay just compensation if private property is taken—neither Black nor Douglas was willing to limit judicial review to the matter of compensation. Both of the statements quoted above assume that there may be situations where the private owner can refuse the compensation offered and obtain judicial intervention to prevent the government from taking his property.

The statements in *Welch* and *Berman*, however, serve as a guide only in a negative sense: a death blow has been dealt to tests once widely used. At one time it was stated that private land could be acquired by compulsion only if it were to be used by an appreciable segment of the public. This test had an advantage of relative objectivity, since it was possible, within limits, to determine whether an appreciable segment of the public would use the land after condemnation. But the rule did more than this: it established a hierarchy of values that is not expressly stated in the Constitution. If applied literally, the standard meant that, unless the service from the land was made available to a large part of the public, the public interest was served better by permitting a private landowner to furnish the service to those who wished it. Thus this test made the market allocation of resources the measure of highest public good. Only when government utilized the condemned property for many members of the public was a higher public interest recognized. The effect of this test, as Justice Douglas pointed out in the *Berman* case,[7] was to require the government to engage in a form of state socialism if it concluded that providing a particular service was in the public interest. It could not take property from owner *A*, who would not provide the service thought to be in the public interest, and dispose of it to citizen *B*, who was willing (or was induced by subsidy) to provide the service.

The constitutional doctrine limiting the condemnation power to the taking of property to be used by the public was dying long be-

---

[5] *Id.* at 556.

[6] 348 U.S. 26, 32 (1954).

[7] See *id.* at 33.

fore *Welch* and *Berman*. But these cases definitively established that use by the public is not essential to the power of condemnation. The major inroad on this "public use" limitation prior to *Welch* and *Berman* was the rule that government is permitted to take private property with compensation for the purpose of eliminating a use of the property thought to be harmful to the public. The early slum-clearance and urban-redevelopment cases in the State courts emphasized the elimination of a public evil as the public purpose served by the condemnation. It would seem that *Welch* and *Berman* also eliminate this alternative requirement.

Neither *Welch* nor *Berman* involved land taken for use by the public or for the purpose of the elimination of a public harm. In *Welch*, the TVA had decided that it was more efficient to condemn land not needed for any public use than it was to build a highway to private land denied access by the construction of a government reservoir. The TVA did propose, more or less as an afterthought, to convey this land to a park system, but this "public use" was not one that TVA had authority to promote. The case must be treated, therefore, as one in which the purpose of the condemnation was neither to eliminate a harmful use nor to provide property for public use. In *Berman*, the District of Columbia had decided that if the objector's land was joined with land cleared of slums and then sold to a private developer, who would develop it in accordance with an approved plan, a better-planned new use could be obtained than if only the land cleared of slums were involved. As in the *Welch* case, the land taken was part of a larger project that admittedly satisfied the current tests of condemnation. Both cases could have been rested on the proposition that, so long as the larger project met the public purpose test, the necessity for taking any one parcel is not a judicial question. In neither case did the Court proceed on this thesis. Both cases sustained the validity of a legislative judgment that a new use, public or private, of the objector's land, served the public interest better than the old uses, although the old uses were not in themselves harmful.

If use by the public or elimination of a public harm are no longer essential to permit expropriation of private property, then what guidelines remain for the judiciary to control the legislative judgment? As has been said, neither Black nor Douglas was willing to eliminate all judicial control by holding that as long as the private landowner receives just compensation, the government power may be utilized.

In the *Berman* case, Douglas purported to provide one affirmative guide: a legislative conclusion that the public interest will be served cannot be allowed to stand in the face of "specific constitutional limitations." However nice this may sound, the fact is that there are no "specific constitutional limitations." The Third Amendment, prohibiting quartering of troops without the consent of an owner, is about the only specific constitutional limitation on land use,[8] and even this would not prohibit condemnation of private property for the purpose of quartering troops.

It is possible that the "specific constitutional limitation" language would forbid government from granting condemnation power to a private group whose actions might, if carried on by the government, violate some constitutional provision. Thus, this language might mean that a delegation of condemnation power to a corporation whose purpose was to build racially segregated housing would be invalid. Another possible meaning is that the condemnation power cannot be used by government to acquire land for an admitted public purpose or use if the motive of the legislature in acquiring the land is suspect under some specific constitutional provision. Presumably a private owner's land could not be taken for the purpose of providing a government-operated church. But does this limitation mean that, in condemning land necessary for a "government town" near a large government installation, a landowner could object to the taking of his property because the "city plan" included provision for one or more churches on his land? Or does Douglas mean that government could not condemn private property for a new highway in order to avoid condemning a church? May the condemnation power be restricted because a community decides to locate all of its new public uses, such as courthouses, highways,

---

[8] It is possible that a particular condemnation could violate a treaty made under the treaty power. See consideration of this question in F.P.C. v. Tuscarora Indian Nation, 362 U.S. 99 (1960). State condemnation of federal property would violate the supremacy clause. But the federal government may condemn State property. See United States v. Carmack, 329 U.S. 230 (1946). The United States presumably could not, by use of the condemnation power, make a new State out of boundaries of an old State without its consent. Art. IV, § 3, cl. 1.

schools, and the like, on land occupied by Negro residents in order to remove them from the community boundaries? If the motive of the condemnor became subject to judicial review under Justice Douglas' test, then, while limiting judicial review of public purposes, he was reintroducing review of the "necessity" for taking, a matter not now subject to judicial review.[9] This possibility cannot be lightly dismissed because of *Gomillion v. Lightfoot.*[10] There is no "specific" constitutional provision prohibiting government from taking land on payment of compensation without disclosing its purpose. Thus, in order to reach Douglas' specific constitutional limitations, it would seem that the Court must retain enough of the older public-use or public-purpose test to compel disclosure of purpose.

Mr. Justice Black's language in *Welch*, to the effect that the legislative finding must be followed unless it "involve[s] an impossibility,"[11] may be of help in applying Douglas' test as to the motives of the condemnor. In a case where it was alleged that the purpose of condemning land for park purposes was really to prevent construction of integrated housing, the Illinois Supreme Court distinguished the *Lightfoot* case by stating that there an "inescapable illegal purpose" was involved, while in the case at hand, park use of the land was not beyond reason.[12] In other words, a declared purpose of promoting an admitted public interest is "well-nigh conclusive"[13] unless this purpose cannot possibly be the actual purpose of the condemnor.

The Equal Protection and Privileges and Immunities Clauses, even if these could be said to be "specific constitutional provisions," cannot easily be applied to condemnation.[14] Inherent in a transfer of private property is the fact that only that land is transferred. Consequently, whenever a private owner is compelled to sell his land to

---

[9] See cases cited in NICHOLS, EMINENT DOMAIN § 4.11 n. 82 (3d ed. Sackman & Van Brunt 1950).

[10] 364 U.S. 339 (1960). See Lucas, *Dragon in the Thicket: A Perusal of Gomillion v. Lightfoot*, [1961] SUPREME COURT REVIEW 194.

[11] 327 U.S. at 552.

[12] Deerfield Park District v. Progress Development Corp., 22 Ill. 2d 132, 140 (1961).

[13] 348 U.S. at 32.

[14] Discrimination in compensation goes to the question of "just compensation."

the government, the condemnor's decision is necessarily discriminatory. The only thing that distinguishes the person who must sell from the one who does not sell is the accident that the former owns land that the government wants and the latter does not. If this fact ever results in a denial of equal protection of the laws or invades the privileges of a citizen, it can only be because the purpose of the taking is wrongful, again the expression of judicial control of public purpose.

In *Berman v. Parker*, Douglas seems to offer another limitation on the condemnation power:[15] "[W]e deal, in other words, with what traditionally has been known as the *police power*." This would seem to mean that the condemnation power, in some circumstances at least, is not an independent power of government but is only a means of effectuating other government powers. If this means that wherever the legislature may regulate it may choose instead to take the property and pay compensation, then the statement only emphasizes the elimination of the limitations on condemnation deriving from such doctrines as public use or elimination of an evil. The statement cannot mean, however, that the condemnation power is no broader than the regulatory power, for the requirement of compensation may satisfy some of the constitutional objections to regulation.

If the power of eminent domain is, as Justice Douglas stated, a means of achieving a governmental objective labeled "police power," then a large percentage, if not all, of the cases involving the constitutionality of substantive provisions of regulatory statutes or orders really raised the question whether government could compel a person to act or use his property in a particular way without compensation.[16] The older tests for the power of expropriation and

---

15 348 U.S. at 32. (Emphasis added.)

16 In Thompson v. Consolidated Gas Co., 300 U.S. 55 (1937), the Texas Railroad Commission issued a regulatory order limiting production from petitioner's gas wells below its market requirements under existing contracts and below the capacity of its pipeline system. Petitioner claimed that the purpose of such an order was to compel petitioners and others owning their own pipeline and marketing facilities to purchase gas from well owners who had not provided themselves with such facilities. While it was weakly asserted that the purpose of the order was to prevent waste, the Commission elected to argue that it had constitutional power to regulate petitioners, even if the sole purpose was to furnish a market for those wells without pipeline facilities. Mr. Justice Brandeis, speaking for the Court, held the order uncon-

for the police power resulted in declarations of the absence of governmental power; the government could neither regulate nor obtain the desired end by taking property and paying compensation. These tests would also sustain the anomaly that government could, by regulation, destroy and even "take," in a realistic sense, a person's property without compensation, and yet it could not condemn the property and pay compensation if it desired to do so. Under the new tests, assuming that the power to regulate exists, whether there should be regulation without compensation or taking with compensation becomes a matter of legislative judgment. By freeing the legislature from an inability to pay compensation for a restriction on use of property even where the legislature thought it just to do so, these two landmark cases, *Welch* and *Berman*, enlarge legislative responsibility.

III. "Taking" without Compensation

The cases treated in this section are concerned with government action or non-action that results in financial loss to the objecting owner seeking compensation. Conventional legal analysis divides the cases into three distinct categories.

In one category fall the regulatory, police-power, or due-process and equal-protection cases, where the objector challenges, on constitutional grounds, legislative or administrative action that compels the private owner to act or prohibits his action at a financial sacrifice. *Nashville, C. & St. L. Ry. v. Walters,*[17] and *Goldblatt v. Town of Hempstead*[18] are illustrative. In the former, a railroad was

stitutional. He stated: "The use of the pipeline owner's wells and reserves is curtailed solely for the benefit of other private well owners. The pipeline owner, a private person, is, in effect, ordered to pay money to another private well owner for the purchase of gas which there is no wish to buy. . . . There is here no taking for the public benefit; nor is payment of compensation provided. . . . Our law reports present no more glaring instance of the taking of one man's property and giving it to another. . . . And this Court has many times warned that one person's property may not be taken for the benefit of another private person without a justifying public purpose, even though compensation be paid." *Id.* at 78, 79, 80. Given the state of the condemnation cases at that time, all Mr. Justice Brandeis had to do was to say that if the "taking" could not be accomplished by compensation a fortiori it could not be done without compensation.

[17] 294 U.S. 405 (1935). See Comment, *Cost Allocation and Substantive Due Process*, 27 U. Chi. L. Rev. 160 (1959).

[18] 369 U.S. 590 (1962).

ordered to separate, at its own expense, the grade of a railroad track from that of an interstate highway. In the latter, a sand company was ordered to stop quarrying sand and to fill in the quarry hole its operation had created. The basic contention of the claimants was that, however beneficial the results of the regulation might be, they could not be obtained without compensation.

The second category includes the cases labeled "consequential damage" or "taking" cases, where the constitutional claim is that government must pay the objector for damage caused to his property by governmental action or inaction in no way directed at him or his property as in the first category. Here *Reichelderfer v. Quinn*[19] and *Griggs v. Allegheny County*[20] are illustrative. In the former case, construction of a fire station in a public park allegedly damaged objector's land adjacent to the park. In *Griggs*, landing commercial jet airplanes at the Greater Pittsburgh Airport pursuant to a landing routine established by the United States Civil Aeronautics Administration was the alleged cause of damage to the objector's adjacent property.

The third conventional classification includes the cases involving the "justness" of the offered compensation. Here the constitutional claim is that the government, which has admittedly taken the objector's property, is not offering to pay for an item of damage or loss of value that the owner has suffered. The claim may result from the fact that the price obtainable in the market would not compensate him for his loss or from the fact that the government proposes to exclude from consideration some matter which the market price does consider. The major group of cases in this category has involved the price to be paid for fast lands near a stream that the government is admittedly taking for a project on the stream. In a large number of cases, for example, it was asserted that since the lands had a market value that recognized the lands' availability for water-power uses, taking the land for any use of the stream, including water power, requires the government to pay him for its water-power value. In this same category belong the cases where it is claimed that the government must pay an owner for his cost of removing himself and his other property from the property taken. Like the first category, and unlike the second, the government action is

19 287 U.S. 315 (1932).

20 369 U.S. 84 (1962).

aimed at the objector's property; but like the second, and unlike the first, the item of damage caused to plaintiff was in no way the desired objective of the government action.

These three categories of cases reveal a common trend in the thirty-year period studied. Older tests and guides have given way, and there is a tendency in the opinions to substitute a vague ethical standard for any objective standard.

A. POLICE POWER VERSUS EMINENT-DOMAIN POWER

That government may use the eminent-domain power to achieve almost any public purpose does not dispose of the question. Regulation as a means of achieving a governmental objective cannot necessarily be used wherever the eminent-domain power may be used. This subsection will deal with the cases in which the judiciary has been asked to tell a legislature that if it desires a particular end it may achieve it by paying compensation, but not by regulation.

Nashville Railway involved a Tennessee statute that required railroads to separate the grade of a railroad track and a state highway if "the elimination of any such grade crossing is necessary for the protection of persons traveling on any such highway or any such railroad."[21] The statute made an automatic allocation of the cost of the grade-crossing elimination, 50 per cent to the railroad and 50 per cent to the State highway system. It was conceded that previous cases had held that a State under its police power could impose the whole cost of elimination of grade crossings on railroads. The railroad urged that there were new circumstances that made these earlier cases inapplicable. These circumstances were: (1) the assumption by the federal government of the function of road building so that this road was not built for local traffic; (2) the change in the occasion for elimination of grade crossings from protection of local traffic to that of furthering the efficiency of rapid national highway travel in competition with the railroads; (3) the change in frequency and type of highway travel that changed the relative responsibility of railroad and highway users for grade-crossing accidents. The Supreme Court of Tennessee had refused to permit consideration of these factors as affecting the allocation of costs. In reversing the State court, Brandeis ruled that these factors

21 294 U.S. at 412.

must be considered. While it is true, Brandeis stated, that the police power embraces regulation designed to promote the public welfare as well as health and safety, this does not justify requiring a single person to bear the cost of advancing the public interest. The "imposition must bear some reasonable relation to the evils to be eradicated or the advantages to be secured."[22]

This principle was reaffirmed in *Atchison, T. & S. F. Ry. v. Public Utility Commission*,[23] where a 50 per cent assessment was upheld. Here the commission had considered all the evidence and found that the improvements were designed to meet local transportation needs and were made necessary by the growth of the communities involved. The railroad had contended that the assessment of cost could be made only on the basis of benefit, thus ignoring the "evils-to-be-eradicated" portion of the Brandeis principle.[24] Justice Minton, speaking for the Court, upheld the allocation, not on the basis of an advantage to be secured, but on the basis of the cause of the evil to be eradicated. "The presence of these tracks in the streets creates the burden of constructing grade separations in the interest of public safety and convenience. Having brought about the problem, the railroads are in no position to complain because their share of the cost of alleviating it is not based solely on the special benefits accruing to them from the improvements."[25] In the *Nashville* case, Minton said, the improvement was not required to meet local transportation needs or safety, but rather as part of a State highway system built primarily as part of a plan to qualify for federal aid.

Minton's thesis about responsibility resulting from the "creation" of the need for removing the "public harm" runs through several

---

[22] *Id.* at 429.

[23] 346 U.S. 346 (1953).

[24] See text *supra*, at note 22. State supreme courts sometimes miss the alternative in the quoted statement. In Georgia Railway & Electric Co. v. Decatur, 295 U.S. 165 (1935), the Supreme Court reversed a Georgia decision upholding a special assessment against a street railway for repaving a street on the basis of benefit conferred. As Sutherland, J., had anticipated, the case was back in the United States Supreme Court the following year, after Georgia said the assessment was not made on the basis of benefit conferred on the railroad but on the basis that its tracks contributed to the need for repaving. This time the Supreme Court upheld the Georgia court. Georgia Ry. & Electric Co. v. Decatur, 297 U.S. 620 (1936).

[25] 346 U.S. at 353.

other cases. In *Panhandle v. Highway Commission*,[26] decided at the same Term as the *Nashville Railway* case, it was held unconstitutional to impose on a gas transmission line the expense of relocating its pipeline on a private right of way to be crossed by a new highway. In a temporal sense the new highway created the need for eliminating the dangers from the gas transmission line. But in this sense the subsequently constructed highways created the need for the grade crossing in the railroad cases, too. In *Panhandle* the Court found no danger at all and distinguished the railroad case on this ground.[27]

The cases upholding the power to destroy property by regulation, in order to remove a harm "created" by the use destroyed or regulated, do not, of course, establish a hard rule that this relationship between regulated property and harm must exist before the government may act. But the standard, that regulation without compensation requires a causal relationship between the regulated activity and a harm, is a test with some element of objectivity. Doubt was cast on the scope of such a test by Mr. Justice Clark in *Goldblatt v. Town of Hempstead*[28] when he said: "There is no set formula to determine where regulation ends and taking begins." This would seem to be a refusal by the Court even to attempt a verbal formulation of a rule as to when compensation must be paid. The "elimination-of-evil" formula maintains some strength, nonetheless, in light of the dissents of Justices Black and Douglas in *Caltex*[29] and of Justice Harlan in *Eureka Mining*,[30] in which they appeal to this formula to demonstrate that regulation cannot be used simply to promote the public welfare. Indeed, the facts in *Hempstead* and other language of Clark's opinion support the requirement that the prohibition or regulation must compel an owner to eliminate a public evil created by him and cannot compel him to act only to promote the public interest by providing without cost something the public wants. It would seem, therefore, that Clark's "no-set-formula" language was really addressed to a second question. In his opinion he referred to *Pennsylvania Coal Co. v. Mahon*[31] as an illus-

26 294 U.S. 613 (1935). 27 *Id.* at 622. 28 369 U.S. 590, 594 (1962).

29 United States v. Caltex (Philippines), 344 U.S. 149, 156 (1952).

30 United States v. Central Eureka Mining Co., 357 U.S. 155, 179 (1958).

31 260 U.S. 393 (1922).

tration of a situation where the "onerousness" of the regulation may require compensation.[32] In other words, something more than "creation" of the harm is required. Without the causal relationship, regulation without compensation is, "in most cases," invalid; with the requisite causation the regulation may be invalid if the cost to the regulated party is "too onerous." On the question "how much is too much," courts have never been able to develop, even in common-law litigation involving nuisances, a standard more meaningful than balancing the public need against the private cost.

The *Griggs* case, involving damage caused by use of air space by jet airplanes as authorized by Congress, also supports the test developed by Brandeis in *Nashville.* Clearly the public interest was served by airplane approach to the airport over the objector's land. In a sense, the government was regulating the objector's use of his land just as much by allowing the noise and inconvenience to induce him to move as it would by compelling him to move or by zoning his land in the airport approaches so as to prohibit residential use.[33] But the objector was causing no harm, and the regulation, or lack of it, was not to eliminate an evil caused by the objector but rather to obtain a public advantage. In short, *Griggs* supports Brandeis' conclusion in *Nashville* that public benefit is not, in most cases, a sufficient reason in itself to destroy property use without compensation.

The qualification, "in most cases," is required by another concept. There may be an economic expectation recognized by society that the claimant is not "entitled" to assert against government action. This question has been litigated in each of the three categories mentioned at the beginning of this section. Sometimes the expectation, even though recognized in the market, is not entitled to protection against government action because the claimant is entitled to no protection against equivalent private action. Thus private utility companies seeking to enjoin competition by government-operated TVA facilities were met with the answer that there is no protection against competition.[34]

The *Gold Clause* cases[35] decided at the same Term as *Nashville*

---

[32] 369 U.S. at 594.

[33] See Miller v. Schoene, 276 U.S. 272 (1928).

[34] Alabama Power Co. v. Ickes, 302 U.S. 464 (1938); Duke Power Co. v. Greenwood, 302 U.S. 485 (1938); Tennessee Power Co. v. T.V.A., 306 U.S. 118 (1939).

[35] The two cases which raise the condemnation-power question are Norman v. B. & O. R.R. Co., 294 U.S. 240 (1935), and Perry v. United States, 294 U.S. 330 (1935).

are instructive here. Congress thought it necessary in promoting the public interest to prevent payments in gold on bonds calling for such performance. There was no assertion that these bond clauses "created" the economic problem dealt with by the legislation. The legislation was designed for the public benefit and not to eliminate any evil caused by the bonds held by the objecting creditors. In the case involving private debtors and private creditors, *Norman v. Baltimore & O. R.R.*, Chief Justice Hughes upheld the legislation against a claim, among others, that this involved a taking of private property without just compensation.[36] Throughout his opinion for the Court he emphasized the conclusion that these contracts concerned money, not a commodity, and "must be understood as having been made in reference to the possible exercise of the rightful authority of the Government" to regulate money.[37] In other words, a claim to a particular form of money was subject to an uncompensable risk that Congress would regulate the money to the detriment of the claimant.[38]

Two "regulatory" cases involving losses of property values during World War II are also relevant. In *United States v. Caltex*,[39] private oil-storage facilities in Manila were ordered destroyed by the retreating United States military command as part of a "scorched-earth" policy. In *United States v. Central Eureka Mining Co.*,[40] the War Production Board ordered cessation of gold mining in order, according to a finding of the Court of Claims, to allocate hard-rock miners to copper and other essential ore production. In both cases the Court, over strong dissents, held that the damage was not compensable under the Fifth Amendment. In both cases the opinion for the majority had trouble with the fact that the property in question, destroyed or regulated, was not injurious in the sense that it "created" public harm. In *Caltex*, the prior authorities, few in number, had said that, if in the field of battle private property were used by the military commander, compensation had to be paid, but if private property were destroyed in battle, the loss was to be borne by the owner. There were older authorities holding that in time of

---

36 294 U.S. at 330.

37 *Id.* at 305.

38 The Court thought this risk shifted when the United States was itself the debtor making the promise concerning gold payment of its own obligations, but it found no damage. Perry v. United States, 294 U.S. 330 (1935).

39 344 U.S. 149 (1952).

40 357 U.S. 155 (1958).

imminent peril, such as a great fire, private property in the face of the fire may be destroyed without compensation in order to stop the fire. Perhaps because history indicated that these cases were rare and, therefore, no guide for the future was needed, Chief Justice Vinson fell back on the unhelpful formula:[41] "No rigid rules can be laid down." Caltex had to bear the loss. Douglas and Black vigorously dissented on the ground that the Fifth Amendment required compensation:[42]

> The property was destroyed, not because it was in the nature of a public nuisance, but because its destruction was deemed necessary to help win the war. . . . Whenever the Government determines that one person's property—whatever it may be—is essential to the war effort and appropriates it for the common good, the public purse, rather than the individual, should bear the loss.

In the *Central Eureka Mining Co.* case the majority, which this time included Black and Douglas, also had trouble with the principle of the *Nashville* case as restated in the *Caltex* dissent. Justice Burton fell back on ancient and long-rejected meanings of "taking." The government did not occupy, use, or in any manner take physical possession of the gold mines; therefore, there was no taking governed by the Fifth Amendment:[43] "Traditionally, we have treated the issue as to whether a particular governmental restriction amounted to a constitutional taking as being a question properly turning upon the particular circumstances of each case." Burton redeemed himself somewhat by offering a "guiding principle":[44]

> In the context of war, we have been reluctant to find that degree of regulation which, without saying so, requires compensation to be paid for resulting loss of income. . . . The reasons are plain. War . . . makes demands which otherwise would be insufferable. But wartime economic restrictions, temporary in character, are insignificant when compared to the widespread uncompensated loss of life and freedom of action which war traditionally demands.

This time Harlan took up the cudgels for the public-harm test.[45] There was no finding that gold mining was injurious. All of the cases relied upon by the majority, *e.g.*, the OPA cases and the pro-

---

41 344 U.S. at 156.

42 *Ibid.*

43 357 U.S. at 168.

44 *Ibid.*

45 *Id.* at 182–83.

hibition order in World War I, involved either some fair compensation to the objector or an injurious activity. The only exception was *Caltex* and that occurred in a "theatre of war."

Cases from the "consequential-damage" and "meaning-of-market-value" categories also indicate how much the first step in analysis involves a judgment as to an appropriate allocation of risk of loss of an expectation. In *Reichelderfer v. Quinn*,[46] the District of Columbia proposed to erect a fire station on a portion of a park adjoining complainant's land, after he had paid a special assessment for the creation of the park. The landowner claimed that this would decrease the value of his land. Justice Stone, speaking for the Court, rejected the claim that the landowner had a compensable right. Enhancement of value does not create an interest. "The possibility that the United States might . . . rightfully exercise its power to change the use of the park lands, so far as it affected present value, was a proper subject for consideration," he said,[47] "in valuing the benefits" at the time of the assessment, and therefore the fact of change does not create a right to compensation.

The cases of greatest frequency in the past thirty years have involved allocation of risks from government action with reference to navigable streams. *United States v. Willow River Power Co.*[48] is illustrative. In that case, the United States raised the water level on the navigable St. Croix River so that the fall from the Willow River was reduced. Claimant, a riparian owner on the St. Croix, had a hydroelectric plant on the Willow, the efficiency of which was impaired by the backing-up of the water from the St. Croix. Compensation was denied. Justice Jackson, speaking for the Court, held that there had long been an overriding public interest with respect to navigable streams to which all riparian rights are inferior. The uncompensated damages sustained by a riparian owner on a public waterway are the same as those often suffered without compensation by owners of land abutting on public highways. In a general discourse on condemnation, Jackson emphasized the element of risk in Fifth-Amendment questions:[49]

> The Fifth Amendment, which requires just compensation where private property is taken for public use, undertakes to

46 287 U.S. 315 (1932).

47 *Id.* at 323.

48 324 U.S. 499 (1945).

49 *Id.* at 502.

> redistribute certain economic losses inflicted by public improvements so that they will fall upon the public rather than wholly upon those who happen to lie in the path of the project. It does not undertake, however, to socialize all losses. . . . It is clear, of course, that a head of water has value and that the Company has an economic interest. . . . But not all economic interests are "property rights"; only those economic advantages are "rights" which have the law back of them, and only when they are so recognized may courts compel others to forbear from interfering with them or to compensate for their invasion.

The results in these cases can be construed to be consistent with the *Nashville* principle that compensation must be paid for loss suffered to create a public benefit but need not be paid for loss suffered when government removes a public harm "created" by an owner or his property. The economic loss suffered by an objector must be compensated only if there has been a determination that the loss which the new government action has produced for the objector is one which he should not be expected to bear. But the courts have not stated a guiding principle to determine when an owner's expectation is protected against government action.[50] Nor can *Caltex* and *Central Eureka Mining*, where no compensation was payable for a loss resulting from government action to promote the war effort, be reconciled with *United States v. Causby*,[51] where landing patterns of government military aircraft on training missions were held to create a right to compensation for a nearby chicken farmer.

Justice Jackson's adoption of the Bentham principle, that property is only that economic advantage that has the sanction of law, is a description not a guide. If this principle were followed to its logical conclusion, government could redefine property rights as subordinate to all government claims and then destroy, take, or

---

50 Consider, in this connection, Mullen Benevolent Corp. v. United States, 290 U.S. 89 (1933), where a creditor (holder of municipal improvement bond) was denied compensation by Justice Roberts when the United States took all the land from which special taxes for bond payment could be levied, and Armstrong v. United States, 364 U.S. 40 (1960), where a creditor (holder of a mechanics lien) was held entitled to compensation by Justice Black when the United States, pursuant to its contract with the debtor-contractor, took title to the ships in construction from which the lien was to be paid.

51 328 U.S. 256 (1946).

damage without compensation because no "property rights" were taken. The converse proposition would seem more reasonable: compensate for the loss of any economic value recognized in the market place that results from government action to promote the public welfare. This would be the most objective test, since proof of the market is readily obtainable. The Illinois Supreme Court once utilized this test, even to the extent of ordering the condemnor to pay market value of an illegal bawdy house, since the market had discounted the chances of enforcing the law.[52]

The Court has many times noted that the question of "just" compensation involves largely an ethical judgment,[53] however much market value tends toward an objective standard devoid of such judgments in each individual case. The most that the Court has been able to develop as guiding principles are indications of some of the factors it considers relevant. The weight to be assigned to these factors in any given case has not yet been disclosed. The Justices follow the Holmesian tradition of stating that property expectations may be damaged "to a certain extent" but "if regulation goes too far it will be recognized as a taking."[54]

B. DAMAGES RESULTING FROM GOVERNMENT ACTIVITY

Unlike the cases in the preceding section, the instant group of cases was concerned with government action not generally directed toward complainant or his property: accidental loss from government action. Historically, the question whether compensation

---

52 Frieberg v. South Side Elevated R. Co., 221 Ill. 508 (1906).

53 "The law of eminent domain is fashioned out of the conflict between the people's interest in public projects and the principle of indemnity to the landowner." Douglas, J., in United States ex rel. T.V.A. v. Powelson, 319 U.S. 266, 280 (1943). "The Fifth Amendment . . . undertakes to redistribute certain economic losses inflicted by public improvements so that they will fall upon the public rather than wholly upon those who happen to lie in the path of the project." Jackson, J., in United States v. Willow River Power Co., 324 U.S. 499, 502 (1945). "The Fifth Amendment expresses a principle of fairness. . . ." Frankfurter, J., in United States v. Dickinson, 331 U.S. 745, 748 (1947). "The political ethics reflected in the Fifth Amendment reject confiscation as a measure of justice. But the Amendment does not contain any definite standards of fairness. . . ." Douglas, J., in United States v. Cors, 337 U.S. 325, 332 (1949). "The word 'just' in the Fifth Amendment evokes ideas of fairness. . . ." Black, J., in United States v. Commodities Trading Corp. 339 U.S. 121, 124 (1950).

54 Pennsylvania Coal Co. v. Mahon, 260 U.S. 393, at 415.

must be paid for this kind of loss was answered by determining whether there was a "taking," because of the Fifth Amendment's use of that term. Originally, unless there was a physical "taking," compensation was not payable. In 1872, in *Pumpelly v. Green Bay Co.*,[55] the Supreme Court concluded that "taking" included destruction, and since that date "taking" has had less of a physical connotation. This is partially due to the recognition that all property interests are intangible, consisting of rights, privileges, powers, and the like that the law gives a person with respect to an object. Although courts occasionally revert to the "taking" language—usually when compensation is not payable—the term today only describes the result: the claimant has or has not a compensable interest. The earlier cases on consequential damage were complicated by the fact that sovereign immunity from tort and other actions made it impossible to proceed on a nuisance, or other continuous-tort, theory. With few exceptions, the statutory removal of sovereign immunity has not converted these from eminent-domain cases into tort cases.[56]

United States v. Causby[57] and *Griggs v. Allegheny County*[58] illustrate the tendency toward fusion of "taking" and consequential damage. In *Causby*, suit was brought under the Tucker Act against the United States, lessee of the airport and operator of the military aircraft using the field. The planes made so much noise in landing at the field that commercial chicken farming on the adjacent land became impossible and the occupants themselves suffered great annoyance. Under the Tucker Act the United States had consented to be sued only on the grounds of an unconstitutional taking or breach of contract, express or implied. No action sounding in tort was authorized. The claimant proceeded on the theories that there was a taking of his land and that repeated trespasses of his air space —at altitudes ranging from eighteen to eighty-three feet—gave rise to an implied contractual obligation to pay for the use of the land. Recovery against the United States was allowed on the theory that it had taken an easement of flight across the claimant's land.

Mr. Justice Douglas, speaking for the Court, first dealt with the

---

[55] 13 Wall. 166, 177–78 (1872).

[56] See Dalehite v. United States, 346 U.S. 15 (1953), for consideration of the Federal Tort Claims Act in connection with a discretionary decision to "promote the public interest."

[57] 328 U.S. 256 (1946).

[58] 369 U.S. 84 (1962).

constitutional and Tucker Act requirement of a "taking." If land is rendered useless, he said, there is a taking. This is not a case of "incidental damage" from a legalized nuisance, for the line of flight was directly over claimant's land. Granted that there was a "taking," it was still necessary to determine its nature. In 1938 Congress declared that navigable air space belonged to the United States.[59] In *Causby*, the government claimed that by reason of the statute it was flying its airplanes through its own property. Douglas answered that the flights in question were not within the navigable air space that the act of 1938 had placed in the public domain. Only the space for horizontal flight was claimed in that act and not the angle of glide for landing. Douglas rejected the ancient common-law maxim about ownership to the sky and ruled that a surface owner owns as much air space as he can occupy or use in connection with the land. Flights over private land are not a taking, unless they are so low and so frequent as to be a direct and immediate interference with enjoyment.

This proposition sounded, as Black pointed out in dissent, more in nuisance than in traditional expropriation.[60] Moreover, Douglas' statement about the nature of the taking left open the question who the taker was. The United Sates claimed, under its aeronautics legislation, the right to direct and control proper approaches to airports; it was the lessee or operator of the airport; and it was the owner and operator of the aircraft. In which capacity had it "taken" claimant's land? Since the language of actual interference with claimant's possession and enjoyment sounded in nuisance, the actor or operator of the aircraft would appear to be the person liable.

The Civil Aeronautics Act was revised by Congress in 1958[61] so that the omission Douglas found in *Causby* was remedied. Congress redefined navigable air space in the public domain to include the air space needed to insure safety in take-off and landing of aircraft. Did this assertion of the right to use the air space for landing constitute a taking? Or is the idea of "taking" related more to the right

---

59 52 Stat. 973 (1938), now 49 U.S.C. § 1304 (1958).

60 The consequences of this decision to the aviation industry were considered in many law review comments. See, *e.g.*, 14 J. Air L. & Com. 112 (1947); 35 Calif. L. Rev. 110 (1947); 95 U. Pa. L. Rev. 224 (1946).

61 72 Stat. 731 (1958), 49 U.S.C. §§ 1301 *et seq.* (1958).

to exclude than the right to use? Under *Causby*, if the "taking" does not occur until actual interference with possession and enjoyment, then the assertion of a right to use the airspace does not constitute an assertion of a right to exclude the landowner from its use. The right to exclude or interfere with the landowner's use would not arise unless or until he used it.

An opportunity to answer some of these questions was presented in *Griggs*. Allegheny County, a municipal corporation of Pennsylvania, owned and operated the Greater Pittsburgh Airport. This airport was built under the National Airport Act[62] which provided that, if an airport were built according to approved specifications, a substantial federal grant-in-aid would help defray the cost. The pattern of flight to and from this airport would be controlled by federal regulations. In the approach zone to one runway, the CAA pattern of flight required airplanes to fly at very low altitudes over claimant's property, then used for residential purposes. The resulting noise, vibrations, and fear of injury forced claimant to move and he sought compensation for his loss. His alleged loss was not only a monetary evaluation of his suffering, but also the decreased value of his property resulting from the fact that a very substantial segment of those who might normally consider buying his property would react as he did to the low-flying aircraft.

The lack of clarity in the *Causby* case gave Griggs the choice of three defendants: the United States, which claimed the air space in the prescribed angle of flight; the operator of the airport; and the operators of the aircraft. He chose the airport operator. The Supreme Court of Pennsylvania, by a divided court, concluded that if there were a taking it was either by the United States or by the aircraft operators.[63] The United States Supreme Court reversed, again by a divided Court. The opinions and the form of the order do not indicate the basis for Supreme Court jurisdiction. Allegheny County asserted a right to do what it did because of federal authorization. To the extent that the Supreme Court of Pennsylvania held that the airport was immune from liability because of a federally created right, there was jurisdiction in the United States Supreme Court to determine the scope of that immunity.[64] It determined that

62 60 Stat. 170 (1946), as amended, 49 U.S.C. §§ 1101–19 (1946).

63 402 Pa. 411 (1961).

64 28 U.S.C. § 1257(3).

Allegheny County was not protected by any federal statute and went on to determine that Allegheny County was liable. On what theory was this second question within the province of the Supreme Court?[65] This was a federal question only on the basis that failure to compensate claimant constituted a violation of the Fourteenth Amendment. Presumably that part of the Fifth Amendment that requires "just compensation" has been read into the Fourteenth Amendment and controls the States. This aspect of the case should be compared with *Delaware River Commission v. Colburn*,[66] where a State court's rejection of a claim for interference with access and light by a public bridge approach was held not to present a federal question. The United States Supreme Court has seldom, if ever before this case, interfered with a State court's determination of what is a compensable taking rather than mere incidental damage.[67]

Unlike *Causby*, in *Griggs* the air space needed for approaches to an airfield was claimed under the 1958 act. Did the statute constitute a "taking"? Douglas answered in the negative. The airport's responsibility for the approaches was no different from its responsibility for the runways. Clearly, Allegheny County acquired the latter. But, as the dissent by Black pointed out, the county did not have to acquire even the runways if its permission to use was obtained from Congress. This would be true even if congressional appropriation were wrongful. In *Yearsley v. Ross Construction Co.*,[68] a suit was brought against a contractor building a dike in the Missouri River which allegedly "took" claimant's land by erosion. In an opinion by Chief Justice Hughes, the suit was dismissed on the ground that if the authority given the contractor was valid there was no liability on his part for executing congressional will. The proper remedy was to sue the United States in the Court of

---

65 "Our only power over state judgments is to correct them to the extent that they incorrectly adjudge federal rights." Herb v. Pitcairn, 324 U.S. 117, 125–26 (1945). See Weisberg, *Supreme Court Review of State Court Decisions Involving Multiple Questions*, 95 U. OF PA. L. REV. 764 (1947); Note, *Supreme Court Disposition of State Decisions Involving Non-federal Questions*, 49 YALE L. J. 1463 (1940).

66 310 U.S. 419 (1940).

67 See Cardozo, J., in Roberts v. New York City, 295 U.S. 264 (1935), to the effect that all the Fourteenth Amendment requires is a reasonable attempt at determining just compensation.

68 309 U.S. 18 (1940).

Claims. If Allegheny County claimed the right to use the air space over claimant's land pursuant to federal authority, it would seem that it should be as much protected as the contractor in the *Yearsley* case. Black, in dissent, adopted this position when he concluded that it was the United States that had appropriated respondent's air space.

Griggs, holding the airport liable, need not be interpreted as relieving the other two possible defendants from liability. Indeed, if, as *Causby* stated, a taking occurs by reason of the interference with possession and enjoyment, then the operator of the airplanes, and anyone under whose authority it acts is also liable. There need not be only one possible defendant. The question whether other persons, including the United States, may be liable would seem to remain open. But the airlines, even more than the airport, act pursuant to federal orders. Except for the weakening of the *Yearsley* case by *Griggs,* however, *Yearsley* might relieve the airlines of liability.

Whether the United States or Allegheny County be the proper defendant, did the claim become actionable when the right to use the air space was first asserted by the United States in 1958, or when the completed airport was first given permission to use it by the United States, or when the airport was first used? Apparently the statute of limitations had not run under any of these theories, so the point was not raised. Nuisance theory, basing the action on interference with enjoyment, would, of course, use none of these times to measure the bar. *United States v. Dickinson*[69] seems to allow the same flexibility for a taking. In *Dickinson,* a claimant who acquired his property interests after May, 1937 sought to recover from the United States the value of easements taken to flood his land permanently and damages for erosion to the part not otherwise taken. The United States asserted that the claim to compensation arose before claimant acquired the land. It claimed that the right arose when Congress authorized the dam in 1935, or when notice of the pool elevation was given to abutting landowners in 1936, or when the dam began to back up water before May, 1937. Justice Frankfurter said that the United States could have unilaterally fixed the time of taking by commencement of eminent-domain proceedings.

---

69 331 U.S. 745 (1947).

By its own decision the United States left it to physical events to determine damage, and this put upon the owner the onus of determining the correct date. Frankfurter then stated that, where no proceedings have been initiated by the United States,[70] "property is taken in the constitutional sense when inroads are made upon an owner's use of it to an extent that, as between private parties, a servitude has been acquired either by agreement or [by prescription]." It is believed that this is mistakenly phrased. For it would mean that the "taking" occurs only after the easement has arisen by prescription. If this were true there would be two statutes of limitation: one for the ripening of the use into a "taking" and one for the claim for damages for the taking under the Tucker Act. In private litigation there is no such rule and there should be none in condemnation cases. A better statement would be that the taking occurs when interference with the owner's use has occurred to such an extent that an easement by prescription will rise by lapse of time.

As indicated earlier, *Causby* found the "taking" to be interference with use and enjoyment, caused by noise, vibration, and fear of injury. Both *Causby* and *Griggs* involved situations where aircraft flew directly over claimant's land. Is this fact essential to a compensable taking? The interference by reason of noise, vibration, and fear of injury can occur to property adjacent to an airport that is not directly under the line of approach. While the Court found flying over claimant's land itself not to be a taking in *Causby*, Justice Douglas repeatedly referred to "flying over" and the acquisition of an easement of flight, as if acquisition of a property interest were essential to a taking. Long before *Causby*, however, it had been held that rendering land useless, or destruction of enjoyment, could constitute a taking. There is no justification in the precedents for a requirement that the condemnor actually go upon or over or under the objector's surface land. Yet "easement of flight" seems to imply a flight over objector's land. But a right to interfere with enjoyment of the claimant's property can be characterized as an easement, just as the right to interfere with a neighbor's use of his property has been called an easement of light and air.

This same problem occurred in the elevated-railway cases in the

[70] *Id.* at 748.

last century.[71] There it was noise and dirt from coal-fired steam locomotives that interfered with use and enjoyment of the objector's adjacent property. The State courts struggled with the requirement that there be a taking from the objector. But they concluded that the landowners were entitled to recover. The propensity of property law to pigeonhole everything into historic categories led to a characterization of this right as an easement of light, air, and view on the streets. But the basic question was whether the cost that the governmental activity imposed on others by reason of their propinquity should be borne by the public or by those injured. Once "taking" lost its meaning of physical possession, that factor became only one element contributing to a conclusion that the public should bear the cost. In other contexts the Court has not felt bound by a requirement that the government acquire a property interest from the claimant.[72] The question whether those adjacent to airports, but not in any flight path, should be compensated thus remains an open one as far as Supreme Court decisions are concerned. But the logic of *Causby* and its idea of fairness would seem to require compensation even where the planes do not fly directly over the objector's land.

Is the requirement of interference with actual possession and enjoyment a limitation on the compensation recoverable? In a typical condemnation case where only a portion of the claimant's land is taken, the formula for compensation is the difference between the value of the whole before condemnation and the value of that which remains after condemnation. Since the values are determined on the basis of the highest and best probable use of the land, this

---

[71] The final round of the litigation, on abandonment of the elevated, reached the Supreme Court in the *Roberts* case, *supra* note 67. For a discussion of the earlier New York cases, see Comment, *Valuation of Easements in Condemnation of Elevated Railroads,* 40 YALE L. J. 779 (1931); Comment, *"Property Right" and Its "Value," id.* at 1074; and Comment, *The Elevated Railway Condemnation Case—Another Analysis of the Property Interests Involved, id.* at 1309.

[72] *Cf.* Armstrong v. United States, 364 U.S. 40 (1960), where destruction of claimant's lien was held to be the "taking," not the acquisition of the lien rights; Cities Service Corp. v. McGrath, 342 U.S. 330 (1952), where the "taking" was the payment by the obligor to the Alien Property Custodian and to the holder of bearer bonds located outside of the United States. See also Douglas' dissent in *Caltex,* text *supra,* at note 42, where the taking was the destruction of claimant's oil storage facilities.

formula considers the effect, adverse or beneficial, that the public project will have on the possible uses of the land remaining. Suppose, at the time of construction of an airport, land beyond the ends of the runways is vacant. Construction of the airport will affect the market value of the vacant land as well as the market value of the built-upon land. The possible adverse effects on market value are two: If the highest and best use of the land that determines the market price the day before the airport is built is a use likely to be damaged by proximity to the airport or its runways, the value of the land will decline. If the new uses and consequent increased demand created by proximity of an airport are of a type damaged by overflight, the land in the approach area will increase in value less rapidly than other lands. In the first instance the owner will suffer an out-of-pocket loss, or at least loss of a highly likely expectation. In the second case there is no out-of-pocket loss but only the loss of equal advantage from the windfall arising from airport construction. Neither nuisance nor condemnation law has been concerned about inequality in treatment by windfall. Nuisance law and condemnation law have approached the problem differently, in dealing with loss arising from depreciation in value of expectations of development. Condemnation law normally dates the taking for purposes of measuring compensation as the date of the condemnation suit, or the date of first use by the condemnor. Thus the owner will recover on a market value uninfluenced by any adverse use by the condemnor. The nuisance approach, because interference with possession and enjoyment is the basis of the action, gives no recovery until interference with actual use and on that date measures the difference in value with and without the actor's adverse use. On this theory, if a sale occurs after knowledge of the potential adverse use but before it takes place, the buyer may receive a windfall where the potential use had reduced the purchase price of the land.

Finally, the effect of *Causby* and *Griggs* must be weighed in relation to the ability of the airport owner to do something about the adjacent land so as to reduce the public cost of the airport project. Since the *Welch* case,[73] if not before, the airport could acquire all the land in a foreseeable area of harm by voluntary or

---

[73] United States ex rel. T.V.A. v. Welch, 327 U.S. 546 (1946).

compulsory acquisition and then retain it or dispose of it in such a way that a purchaser and his successors take the risk of future harm. As discussion of *United States v. Miller*[74] will show, the time of taking, or of valuation, is not (within limits) continually specified so that a government could, by legislation, redefine the time of taking to the time of completion of the airport. This coupled with a short statute of limitations would put a substantial risk of airport damage on the underdeveloped land.

Do the holdings in *Causby* and *Griggs*, that interference with neighboring land use is a compensable taking, mean that the government cannot, without compensation, prevent the interference from arising, for example, by zoning? If the purpose of the zoning is to avoid paying the compensation that *Causby* and *Griggs* require, the *Nashville* case[75] would seem to make the zoning illegal without compensation. If it is asserted that structures and uses endanger the aircraft and its users so that the existing structures must be removed, as in the *Town of Hempstead* case, then the principle of the *Panhandle* case involving removal of an existing gas pipeline from the right of way of a new highway would apply, requiring compensation. For the problem under consideration here, the one thing that *Causby* and *Griggs* decide is that the expectation of enjoyment free from interference from landing aircraft, military or civil, is a protected expectation that can be destroyed only on payment of compensation.

C. JUST COMPENSATION

The terse constitutional requirement of "just compensation" has left to the courts the task of providing content for the phrase.[76] The common denominator of the cases in the present subsection is that the dispute is only as to the amount or the formula by which the amount of compensation is to be determined.

In spite of the fact that market value is a fact frequently found by the court rather than a jury, these cases exhibit a marked tendency by the Supreme Court to control the trier of fact as to the

---

[74] 17 U.S. 369 (1943), see text *infra*, at note 84 *et seq*.

[75] See text *supra*, at notes 21 *et seq*.

[76] For a general discussion of condemnation valuation, see ORGEL, VALUATION UNDER EMINENT DOMAIN (1953).

bases of awards.[77] The cases in this section reveal an inclination to keep, as far as possible, the older guide "market value" and to refine its definition by adding or subtracting items to be considered in arriving at a "just compensation."

The historic statement has been that "just compensation" is a judicial question that cannot constitutionally be controlled by legislature or executive. Unlike the recent cases involving "public purpose," the three cases growing out of World War II regulations of just compensation do not clearly tell us that the legislative judgment is "well-nigh conclusive," but neither do they say that it is not controlling. It should be noted that the question of legislative control of "just compensation" is a constitutional question exclusively as to the minimum amount payable. There is almost no question as to the power of the legislature to direct that more than "constitutional just compensation" be paid.[78]

United States v. Cors[79] gave the Court opportunity to consider legislative and administrative control of just compensation but it chose not to grasp it. The legislation in question there, a World War II amendment to the Merchant Marine Act,[80] provided that in determining just compensation "in no case shall the value of the property taken or used be deemed enhanced by the causes necessitating the taking or use." Several interpretations of this general language had been utilized. The Comptroller General had ruled that the statute meant that compensation paid must be the value of the requisitioned item on the date of the presidential declaration of emergency in 1939, if it were shown that higher values after that date were due to economic conditions caused by the emergency. Judges Hand, Parker, and Hutcheson, acting as an Advisory Board on Just Compensation, recommended that market value as of the time of taking be used as the base figure but that there be deducted

77 Compare the contrary result in Federal Employers' Liability Act cases, where the jury is usually the fact-finding agency.

78 Taxpayers in federal cases, at least, have no standing to assert that too much money was paid. See Massachusetts v. Mellon, 262 U.S. 447 (1923); Alabama Power Co. v. Ickes, 302 U.S. 464 (1938).

79 337 U.S. 325 (1949).

80 49 Stat. 2015, 2016 (1936), as amended by 53 Stat. 1255 (1939), 46 U.S.C. § 1242(*a*) (1940).

from this value sums attributable to three factors: (1) the government's need that caused the taking; (2) the previous taking of similar vessels by the government; and (3) the reasonable probability that the vessel being valued would be taken.

The Court unanimously avoided the question whether the legislative standard could control the judicial standard of just compensation. Justice Douglas, speaking for the majority, concluded that on the facts of the case the judicial and statutory standards were the same. In effect he adopted the standard of the Advisory Board. He asserted that it "is not fair that the government be required to pay the enhanced price which its demand alone has created."[81] Jackson, Burton, and Frankfurter, in a dissent by Justice Frankfurter, apparently disagreed with the conclusion of the Hand board as to the second factor: previous takings of similar vessels by the government. Frankfurter pointed out that enhancement of value of the particular item requisitioned because of previous government requisitions could not be due to government demand; rather it was due to private demand remaining unsatisfied because of earlier government requisitions of a portion of the supply. This would have occurred even if no further requisitions were contemplated by the government. He accepted the Court of Claims' position that it is not fair that the United States pay less than others would have to pay in the market. Although the case has some interesting discussions of the economics of market value, it gives no guide as to legislative power to reduce the price payable on requisition below that of the judicial standard.

In the other two cases where there was legislative control of prices, the question was whether OPA ceiling prices were the controlling measure of just compensation. Again there were available to the Court judicial standards that made it unnecessary to consider the conclusiveness of legislative definition of price. Judicial standards had previously included the rule that where there was no market available other tests had to be used. In a controlled market, as under OPA, there was no market price; obviously other standards had to be used. In *United States v. John J. Felin*,[82] involving requisition of pork products, no opinion commanded a majority of the Court. Justice Frankfurter, in an opinion in which Chief Jus-

[81] 337 U.S. at 333.

[82] 334 U.S. 624 (1948).

tice Vinson and Justice Burton concurred, rejected replacement cost, a standard used by the Court of Claims, and held that on refusal of respondent to accept the government's offer of ceiling prices, respondent had the burden to prove the damage it would suffer by not receiving more. The peculiar inability of the meat-packing industry to establish accurate cost accounting for each item meant that respondent could not sustain its burden unless the whole of its operations during the relevant period resulted in a loss. Respondent failed in this burden.

Justices Reed, Black, and Murphy also started with the inability to find a measure because of the absence of a market. They examined several substitutes for market price and found them all illusory. Absent any other standard, the constitutionally established ceiling prices were the only proper standard. This opinion indicated how far they would go in allowing constitutionally established legislative prices to control just compensation. They would hold that, if the government fixed prices with the "predominant" purpose of acquiring property affected by its order, ceiling prices could not be used. Justices Jackson and Douglas stated that just compensation cannot be the equivalent of a controlled price, and, absent a market, replacement cost should be used.

In *United States v. Commodities Trading Corp.*[83] the Court went much further in bowing to the legislative price of black pepper. Justice Black in writing for the Court pointed out that the word "just" in the Fifth Amendment was synonymous with "fairness" and "equity" in the congressional standards for OPA prices. Therefore, the ceiling price should be accepted unless the owner carried the burden of showing special circumstances and hardships as to the ceiling price.

The case that would sanction the greatest legislative and executive freedom in controlling the price is *United States v. Miller.*[84] It did not involve "just compensation," but rather the question when did the "taking" occur for purposes of measuring compensation. Partly as a survival of the earlier position that "taking" meant physical dominion, the prevailing rule invoked the day suit is commenced by the condemnor or possession or control taken, whichever is first, as the relevant time for measuring damages. Government action be-

83 339 U.S. 121 (1950).

84 317 U.S. 369 (1943).

fore either of those dates might affect the price of a particular parcel, favorably or adversely. *Miller* involved such earlier influence beneficial to the owner. In large irrigation and power projects taking many years to complete, it has been the practice of Congress to approve the project and then make annual appropriations toward its cost, with the work proceeding in accordance with the size of the appropriation. In the *Miller* case, Congress had approved, in August, 1937, the Shasta Dam plan that involved the relocation of a railroad. As a result of the dam project, a "boom town" grew on claimant's land that formerly had been low-grade agricultural land. Some of the land was subdivided for urban development. In December, 1938, the project officials began proceedings to condemn a portion of claimant's land for railroad relocation purposes. The claimant sought the value as of that date, which would, of course, include its urban or boom-town value, a value wholly attributable to the dam project. The Supreme Court, speaking through Justice Roberts, held that a date earlier than date of suit should be used. If the project from the beginning includes the taking of several tracts but only one is taken in the first instance, the owners of other tracts are not to be allowed an increased value due to the government activity. The questions, he said, were two: (1) Was the government committed to a project that included the present purposes? (2) Was the claimant's land probably within the scope of the project at the time of commitment? The Court accordingly held that value on the day of legislative commitment should be used.

Since the legislature and executive have substantial control over the events satisfying Roberts' two requirements, the legislature by this indirect method may succeed in controlling "just compensation." Slum clearance and redevelopment projects are large ventures taking many years. If the legislature were to provide that it would redevelop a designated large area but that in stage 1 only part would be taken and rebuilt, the *Miller* case would seem to permit the condemnor to exclude, in condemnation of the land needed for stage 2, any value increase after the day of commitment attributable to the success of stage 1. Absent legislative commitment to a taking of the whole area, however, the price payable for the second stage would have to include the increase in value.

The *Miller* principle is capable of judicial expansion and development. The dissenters in *Cors* indicated that they were willing to extend the *Miller* principle to exclude any speculative increase in price due to the possible condemnation of similar items. In *United States v. Virginia Electric & Power Co.*,[85] the majority of the Court held that, in allocating market value for agricultural uses between the owner of the fee and the owner of an easement of flowage for power purposes, the Court must exclude "any depreciation in value caused by the prospective taking," citing the *Miller* case. This is perhaps the most significant development of the *Miller* principle. It suggests that the Constitution requires this exclusion of depreciation. It is well known that many large-scale projects depreciate market value after "commitment," since buyers are frequently repelled by the thought of probable condemnation a few months or years after the announced commitment. But if the *Virginia Electric* case is read into the Fourteenth Amendment, the Illinois Supreme Court failed to award just compensation in a redevelopment case where the announcement of the project made the building unrentable and even caused destruction by vandalism before suit for condemnation was filed. The Illinois court rigidly followed the day-of-taking rule, so that the owner received substantially less than he would have received on the day of commitment.[86]

"Market value" has been the standard formula for determining just compensation almost from the beginning. "Value to the owner" and "value to the taker," the competing formulas, have long lost the battle.[87] It is said that it is "fair" that government should pay only value determined by general demand rather than a value computed on the basis of the unique and perhaps eccentric personal standards of the owner.

The assault on market value has not been a frontal assault. The market assesses expectations and values which, if openly stated as included in market price, would offend the sensibilities and moral standards of a large segment of the population. Newspaper scandals remind us how frequently, for example, the market assesses, in price determination, the chances of a regulatory law being enforced against the owner. Since market price is affected by so many considerations, the result is that both sides in eminent-domain proceed-

---

85 365 U.S. 624, 636 (1961).

86 Chicago Housing Authority v. Lamar, 21 Ill. 2d 362 (1961).

87 See discussion and criticism of these formulae in ORGEL, *op. cit. supra* note 76, at §§ 12–15.

ings try to separate from market value particular factors normally considered in the market and to obtain separate valuation of these items for purposes of enhancement or reduction of the total award.

One such factor is illustrated by the cases following World War II attempting to reopen a previously settled question whether the claimant is entitled to compensation for the cost of removal of personal property from the land taken and for the loss of good will or "business" value said to be destroyed by the condemnation. If one assumes a real market situation, it is clear that the "freely arrived at" decision of a "willing seller" to sell includes a decision on his part that the price, less whatever costs the sale involves, including the cost of removing his property from the premises, produce an amount of cash or net flow to his liking. A decision to sell shares of stock at market price, for example, means that the seller is willing to accept the gross price less costs of transfer, such as transfer taxes and brokerage fees. Thus the normal rule refusing to award the seller in condemnation extra compensation for cost of removal or loss of business is correct, given the basic assumption of a willing seller. The fact is, however, that there is almost never a willing seller in a condemnation suit; otherwise there would be no litigation. In fact it may be that these "costs of sale" have led him not to sell at market price. If the assumption is that the "average" man would sell at market, the conclusion that the "unreasonable" man shall not get more is easy to reach. But what of the situations where it is almost inconceivable that the average man would sell willingly? Four cases growing out of World War II presented this problem. In each of the four, the United States was taking a short-term use plus what was in effect an option to renew for the duration of the war. In *United States v. General Motors Corp.*,[88] condemnation of a one-year term and option to renew was sought from a lessee of a warehouse who had a twenty-year term. In this case Justice Roberts, while rejecting removal costs as an independent item of value, rephrased the market-value rule so as to allow its consideration. He said that the normal market-value rule would pay the rental value of a vacant building to be leased for a long term. Here he would construct a hypothetical market—the value which

[88] 323 U.S. 373 (1945).

a hypothetical long-term tenant in possession would exact when leasing to a temporary occupier requiring his removal.[89]

In the *Kimball Laundry* case,[90] involving temporary use of a laundry for a term with an option to renew, Justice Frankfurter attempted to explain why market value had been adopted as the formula. While an owner may have a "unique need for property or idiosyncratic attachment to it, . . . transferable value,"[91] he said, is thought to be a fair measure of public obligation because it has an external validity. Loss of "idiosyncratic values" on condemnation without compensation is like loss due to exercise of the police power; it is a "burden of common citizenship."[92] Extra compensation for loss of going-concern value is not given in cases where a fee is taken, because the owner can usually retain this value for use at alternative sites. But a seller of a temporary term cannot easily transfer the going-concern value to a new site, since he must remain ready to return to the original place of business. Therefore, in a temporary taking, government should pay for destruction of this value.

Justice Douglas dissented in the cases that deviated from the market-value rule, restricting himself to a reliance on precedent, to a phrase that appeared to reintroduce the long discarded rule of "value to the taker," and to chiding the majority for trying to state a guiding principle.

When Justice Frankfurter's "idiosyncratic attachment" to property is reduced to its meaning, he is simply telling us "some owners will not sell at market." This is true of all owners in condemnation suits. He is also telling us that in the temporary taking situations, the category of "some owners" becomes so large that it is hard to

---

89 There were two other removal-costs cases involving condemnation from a lessee: United States v. Petty Motor Co., 327 U.S. 372 (1946), where the one-year term condemned exhausted the lessee's remaining interest; United States v. Westinghouse Electric & Mfg. Co., 339 U.S. 261 (1950), where the original term taken did not exhaust lessee's unexpired term, but several renewals had exhausted the lessee's interest before litigation. In *Petty*, no removal costs were allowed since the entire interest of the lessee was taken. In *Westinghouse*, the Court held that it would wait until final termination of the condemned interest to determine whether the *Petty* rule or the *General Motors* rule should be applied.

90 Kimball Laundry Co. v. United States, 338 U.S. 1 (1949).

91 *Id.* at 5.

92 *Ibid.*

imagine a willing seller when less than all is taken. Since market price assumes that a large percentage of rational people would sell at such a price, market price becomes meaningless when most people will not sell. It is not fair to make one owner sell at a price where it is highly unlikely that any owner would sell at such a price. This seems to be the justification for the exceptions in the temporary taking cases.

The largest single group of cases studied involve the relationship of the federal government's paramount power over navigable waters to the compensation that government must pay in condemnation for use of lands adjacent to the stream. Since government controls the right to allocate the flowing stream, one central issue has been the question whether any special value can attach to fast lands adjacent to the stream by reason of their location. Thus lands adjacent to a stream may be usable if assembled in appropriate quantity for reservoir storage behind dams built for water power and other uses. No one can build the dam without the consent of the United States. If it withholds its consent and decides to build the dam itself, must it pay unique water-power value of the flowable lands?

Until the 1955 Term the Court controlled the market value of such lands by determining whether it was practically possible that someone could have assembled the land necessary to flow, or whether it was "too remote" that someone other than the government condemnor could undertake the project. Thus, in *Olson v. United States*[93] the Court refused to permit flowage rights on the Lake-of-the-Woods for a power project because, among other facts, the necessary land was owned in part by the Canadian government which, unlike the United States, had many years before indicated that only a public power project would be built in this area. The possibility that it would change its position was too remote for the market to consider. If the possibility of assembly existed because the owner of a parcel being condemned also had the power of eminent domain sufficient to assemble the lands, *United States ex rel. T.V.A. v. Powelson*[94] held, an unexercised and revocable power of condemnation was not compensable.

United States v. Twin City Power Co.[95] and *United States v.*

---

93 292 U.S. 246 (1934).

94 319 U.S. 266 (1943).

95 350 U.S. 222 (1956).

Virginia Electric Co.[96] finally dealt with situations where the claimant sought payment for value attributable to unique qualities for use as a power-dam site. The factual difference between the two cases was that, in *Twin City Power*, the claimant owned the fee simple, so that if power-site value was excluded, it admittedly was entitled to market value for the next highest and next best use. In *Virginia Electric*, however, the claimant owned only an easement to flow the servient lands for a power dam. In each case the United States was seeking to condemn the land necessary to build substantially the same power dam that the claimants at one time thought they could build. In both cases the private claimants had some reason to believe, during the time they were assembling land, that they might receive from the United States the necessary license to build. Unlike the Canadian situation in the *Olson* case involving the Lake-of-the-Woods, in the United States it seldom becomes clear that a private power project would not be permitted prior to congressional commitment to build the dam by appropriating money for it. Indeed, in the *Twin City Power* case, Congress on six different occasions had given permission for private construction of the dam in question. Even after establishment of the Federal Power Commission, it had granted licenses for construction of a private dam on the Savannah River. These licenses were allowed to lapse. After World War II an application for a license to build a private hydroelectric power project was denied on the ground that the United States had decided to build the dam itself.

In *Twin City Power*, the court of appeals held that the question whether the United States had to pay power-site value as just compensation depended on whether the river improvement by the United States was for navigation or for power purposes. Since it was found to be the latter, the court ruled that water-power value of the fast lands near the navigable river was to be included in market value. The Supreme Court, in a five-to-four decision, reversed. Both the majority and the minority rejected the suggested distinction. The United States has the power of condemnation and that is all the Court can ask about purpose in assessing just compensation. The minority stood squarely on the principle of the *Olson* case: in the light of fifty years of private activity concerning

[96] 365 U.S. 624 (1961).

this dam, power-site value was far from speculative. It would be considered in a voluntary sale and the United States should be in no more favorable position than private persons in the market place. The majority, speaking through Justice Douglas, saw a very simple situation: the fast lands had no unique value except in connection with the flow of the stream; therefore, to grant the claimant value for this connection is to grant him compensation for the flow of the stream which already belonged to the United States. "If the owner of the fast lands can demand water-power value as part of his compensation, he gets the value of a right that the Government in the exercise of its dominant servitude can grant or withhold as it chooses. The right has value or is an empty one, dependent solely on the Government. What the Government can grant or withhold and exploit for its own benefit has a value that is peculiar to it and that no other user enjoys."[97]

Justice Douglas' argument concerning the power of government to grant or withhold a license for development is too simple to serve as a guiding principle. When analyzed in connection with earlier decisions it can have meaning only if there is something unique about public power. It is true, as the *Olson* case held, that an announced policy concerning something the government owns may prevent a reasonable expectation of being able to acquire the object owned by government. Thus, once Yellowstone National Park was established in a manner indicating that it was inconceivable that the United States would sell any of its park lands, private lands could not thereafter acquire any additional value attributable to the fact that assembly of the private parcel with a portion of Yellowstone Park would make for a higher and better use than that possible on the private parcel considered alone. The possibility of assembly of the requisite parcel would be "too remote," as the *Olson* case recognizes, to be considered in the market place. On condemnation of the adjacent lands any value attributable to association with the Yellowstone lands would be excluded. This was not the case, however, in either *Twin City Power* or *Virginia Electric*, for the United States had no clearly announced or long-established policy that only public power projects would be built on the rivers. Almost every year some private power licenses are granted by the FPC, and

[97] 350 U.S. at 228.

important public political debates are concerned with the advisability of public or private power projects on other locations.

It is also true that, if prior to the establishment of Yellowstone National Park the market had already given adjacent private lands an added value, because of the possibility that under existing government policies it would sell some of that land, an announcement by the United States of the establishment of Yellowstone Park would destroy, in the market place, the added value attached to the neighboring private lands. Such a destruction, resulting from a change of government policy, is, as the *Reichelderfer* case[98] indicated, noncompensable. If thereafter, and in a manner unconnected with the announcement, the United States were to condemn the private lands for an addition to the park, the market value payable would not include the previously destroyed associative value. This is the reverse of the dicta of Justice Roberts in the *Miller* case, that a second and independent condemnation project must pay to the private owners any value which the market considered the first condemnation added to the land involved in the second. But this was not the case in *Twin City Power* and *Virginia Electric*, where, for reasons independent of the forthcoming condemnation, the United States had made no announcement concerning the right which it held.

Up to the point of the announced public use, there was nothing unique about United States control of development on navigable streams. The economic impact of a government's decision granting a power license differs in no way from the impact of an announced decision concerning use or disposition of some non-power land that it owns in fee simple. The problem in the two power cases was not unique to power. Wherever government controls something that adds associative value to privately owned property, it is within government's economic power to destroy this associative value in connection with the condemnation of the private land for some public purpose. Even if no associative value is involved, it is within government power to reduce or destroy value of land about to be condemned by use of its regulatory or condemnation power, just before the condemnation of the particular parcel in question. The question is whether government can make the action previously

---

[98] Reichelderfer v. Quinn, 287 U.S. 315 (1932).

mentioned non-compensable as part of the condemnation of the land in question.

In *Reichelderfer*, the property adjacent to Rock Creek Park "enjoyed" some added value by reason of the government creation of the park. This enjoyment was no less contributed by government decision than would power value be contributed to fast lands by a government decision to permit private development of a power site. Unless there is something unique about power, therefore, the fact that the private owner enjoys something that a government decision could grant or withhold is no reason not to include in "just" compensation the value of this enjoyment that a government decision contributes. This is the dicta in *Miller*.

It is also clear that the fact that government could have made a power announcement like that which the Canadian government made in *Olson*, or could have built a fire station on the park lands adjacent to claimant's property as in *Reichelderfer*, or could have regulated the private lands so as to eliminate the possibility of enhancement due to a particular use, is not a reason to eliminate from just compensation this aspect of value that government could have destroyed without compensation. Mr. Justice Douglas himself made this point in *United States ex rel. T.V.A. v. Powelson*:[99] "The United States no more than a state can be excused from paying just compensation measured by the value of the property at the time of the taking merely because it could destroy that value by appropriate legislation or regulation." Since this case was also a water-power case, it is fair to conclude that the quoted language of Justice Douglas is as applicable to water power as it is to a zoning regulation.

Twin City Power and *Virginia Electric* are not "could have" situations; they are situations where government action was taken that destroyed expectations. The denial of the license to build a private power dam or the commencement of a condemnation suit to acquire flowage rights served notice on the market that only the government could build that which gave the lands associative value. In most situations the rule that market value is determined as of the moment before the condemnation suit is commenced is sufficient to secure for the owner the value that the condemnation destroys,

---

[99] 319 U.S. at 284.

be it value added by earlier government or private action or by the probable prospect of government or private action. Thus, in *Reichelderfer*, if the government had condemned claimant's land for the fire station instead of using the park land as it did, the market value of claimant's land would be determined without regard to the adverse impact that a fire station would have on residential land.

Unless there is something unique about public power, the question reduces itself to this: Can government make decisions to regulate or to use its own property as part of the project for which the private land is wanted, so that when it is time to condemn the private land the value of the private land is now affected by these decisions? Prior cases have considered this question. In *Felin*, Justices Reed, Black, and Murphy, in a concurring opinion concluding that OPA prices should be used, said that a different situation would be presented if the government established ceiling prices with the predominant purpose of acquiring property affected by its order, thus implying at least that government does not have unlimited power to issue a regulatory order for the purpose of affecting market price in condemnation. In the same case, Justices Jackson and Douglas were unwilling even to consider the OPA ceiling as controlling because of the possible use of the order for condemnation purposes. Thus, while there appears to be no holding that an order cannot be issued for the purpose of affecting price, there is strong indication, where public power is not involved, that a government decision cannot be used to affect "just compensation" if that is the purpose of its promulgation.

It was held in *United States v. Miller* that decisions made after the government is "committed" to a project cannot be used to affect the market value of land being taken, at least to increase the value of the adjacent land. That case, too, involved a water-power and irrigation project. *Miller* left open the question whether the principle was applicable in reverse: exclusion from valuation of reductions caused by the government decision. The issue was not considered in *Twin City Power*, but *Virginia Electric* held the *Miller* principle applicable to water-power value in both aspects: "The value of the easement must be neither enhanced nor diminished by the special need which the Government had for it. . . . The court must exclude any depreciation in value caused by the prospective taking once the government 'was committed' to the project."[100]

Thus, Mr. Justice Douglas' opinion in *Twin City Power* cannot, consistently with other case law, be based simply on the power of the condemnor to grant or withhold that which gives the private lands associative power value. Unless this other authority is rejected, *Twin City Power* has to rest on a proposition that flowing water is a national resource that belongs to the sovereign for allocation, so that no expectation of profit from this resource can attach—for purposes of just compensation—to adjacent private lands. Nothing warrants giving this kind of government property such unique status in condemnation law.

Because of the divided ownership of the private property there involved, *Virginia Electric* gave the Court opportunity to throw new light on *Twin City Power*. In *Virginia Electric*, the power company owned the right to flow certain lands for power purposes, a recognized easement of flowage. The owner of the servient estate in fee had sold its rights to the United States for $1.00. In the suit to condemn *Virginia Electric's* flowage rights, the United States asserted that they had no value because of *Twin City Power* and because all possibility of private development had ceased when the United States undertook the project and denied the license application of Virginia Electric. The majority of the Court, including Justice Douglas, concluded that the flowage easements had value apart from their power value, for the easement, a right to flow the lands for power purposes, was also a right to destroy other uses. This "right" to destroy other uses was valuable or not depending on the probability of private power development. If it was highly unlikely that power development by a private person would occur, then the right to destroy the next highest use (agricultural use) had almost no value and the agricultural use value belonged to the fee owner, which the United States had purchased for $1.00. If on the other hand, private power development was highly likely, the fee owner had almost no value, and the agricultural use value was attached to the right to destroy it.

In 1956, *Virginia Electric* had been remanded by the Supreme Court for reconsideration in light of the *Twin City Power* deci-

100 365 U.S. at 636.

sion.[101] The holding of *Twin City Power*, that power value could not be considered in arriving at just compensation, was in effect the "law of the case," so that no major reconsideration of *Twin City Power* was possible. Nevertheless, by refining the property right being valued, so that the right to destroy, not the right to enjoy power uses, was being valued, the stated basis of Justice Douglas' position in *Twin City Power* was substantially weakened. If, as *Virginia Electric* holds, it is the right to destroy other uses that is the basis for condemnation, what justification is there for limiting the value of this right of destruction to the value of the right to destroy non-power uses? Douglas' opinion in *Twin City Power* held that since the government controlled the right to enjoy power uses, that could not be included. But government doesn't control the right to prevent or destroy power uses except after condemnation.

A further holding of *Virginia Electric* is a retreat from *Twin City Power*. The government decision to deny a license to develop in order to develop itself cannot, under the *Miller* doctrine, be used to depreciate the value of the right to destroy; the denial of the license for the purpose of condemning the land cannot be used to affect condemnation value. Thus, the only thing left of *Twin City Power* is its unexpressed conclusion that a great natural resource, such as water power, must belong to the sovereign until expressly allocated. That conclusion remains as a possible basis for *Twin City Power* but its expressed reasons are no longer tenable.

IV. Conclusion

When a problem that the Constitution itself states in ethical terms, "just compensation," must be answered by courts with few, if any, guides, it is not surprising that there are floundering and differences among judges and among generations of judges. That the problem is difficult of rational statement is no reason not to try. At the same time the failure of the courts offers a reason why the legislature should try its hand at stating what is just compensation. *Berman v. Parker*[102] has eliminated any reason that a legislature might have to try to regulate without compensation, other than a desire to save taxpayers' money or a belief that it is fair to destroy an economic expectation without compensation, particularly if the property own-

---

101 350 U.S. 956 (1956).

102 348 U.S. 26 (1954).

er "created" the evil that the regulation is designed to remove. It once was possible, under existing constitutional doctrine, that the legislature could only act without paying compensation because its objective could not meet the public-use test. This is no longer true. The legislature, like the courts, can now ask: What is fair? Perhaps Congress is ready to assume this responsibility. The Committee on Public Works of the House of Representatives has created a Subcommittee on Real Property Acquisition to consider the question of "adequacy of payments to persons affected by public improvements."[103] It may be that this Committee can succeed in providing appropriate structure where the Court has failed. That it has failed would seem to be clear from the evidence set out here.

---

103 Congressman Clifford Davis is chairman of the Subcommittee and Mr. Henry H. Krevor is chief counsel.

HERBERT L. PACKER

MENS REA AND THE SUPREME COURT

"The existence of a *mens rea*," the late Chief Justice Vinson once opined, "is the rule of, rather than the exception to, the principles of Anglo-American criminal jurisprudence."[1] Mr. Justice Brennan later quoted the remark with evident approval, but went on to add a qualification: "Still, it is doubtless competent for the States to create strict criminal liabilities by defining criminal offenses without any element of scienter. . . ."[2] Then, he qualified the qualification: "[But] there is precedent in this Court that this power is not without limitations."[3] To paraphrase: *Mens rea* is an important requirement, but it is not a constitutional requirement, except sometimes.

One purpose of this paper is to examine how far the Supreme Court has gone in deciding when *mens rea* is a constitutional requirement and why. The thesis advanced here is that the Court has accomplished little not contained in the paraphrase attempted above. There are difficulties, but the Court's failure to make the effort is a mark of inadequate performance in an increasingly important area of its adjudication. It will also be suggested that the shortcomings on the constitutional level, both in result and rationale, have been

Herbert L. Packer is Professor of Law, Stanford University.

1 Dennis v. United States, 341 U.S. 494, 500 (1951).

2 Smith v. California, 361 U.S. 147, 150 (1959).

3 *Ibid.*

compounded by the Court's failure to develop an adequate method of interpretation of criminal statutes that do not explicitly provide for *mens rea.*

It may be ventured that a good deal of the trouble results from the disorderly state of traditional criminal law with respect to the mental element in the definition of offenses, a highly complex cluster of problems for which the tag of *mens rea* stands as a convenient but elliptical symbol. Blackstone talks about a "vicious will."[4] American statutes are often framed in terms of a "union of act and intent."[5] It is only recently that careful analysts have given us more nearly precise concepts to work with.[6]

Attempts to provide a compendious definition of *mens rea* do not get far beyond a gloss on the translation from the Latin: the guilty mind. In general, two closely related but distinguishable notions are involved in the idea of *mens rea.* One is that conduct is criminal only if the actor is aware of the facts making it so. For example, it may be criminal under certain circumstances to possess narcotics. The question arises, does the actor know that the substance that he possesses is a narcotic? If he claims that he does not, will he be allowed to introduce evidence to that effect? If he may not, we have what is commonly described as an offense of strict liability, *i.e.*, one dispensing with *mens rea.*[7] The other and rather more difficult notion includes what is sometimes referred to as awareness of wrongdoing. For example, does the possessor of narcotics know there is a legal norm that renders his possession criminal?[8] It is hornbook law that the first of these two notions is usually a limitation on criminality, that the second is usually not.[9] Or, to put it in the disarmingly simple way that has confused generations of law students: ignorance or mistake of fact excuses; ignorance or mistake

---

[4] 4 BL. COMM. *21.

[5] *E.g.*, CALIF. PENAL CODE § 20: "In every crime or public offense there must exist a union, or joint operation of act and intent, or criminal negligence."

[6] See note 123 *infra* and accompanying text.

[7] See People v. Winston, 46 Cal. 2d 151 (1956), holding that knowledge of the narcotic character of the thing possessed is an essential element of the offense of possession of marijuana.

[8] For an example of the confusion of the two concepts, see People v. Gory, 28 Cal. 2d 450, 555 (1946), explained, or possibly explained away, in *Winston*, note 7 *supra.*

[9] *Cf.* PERKINS, CRIMINAL LAW 806, 807, 825 (1957) (hereinafter PERKINS).

of law does not excuse.[10] As we shall see, however, analysis of the first notion reveals, in addition to the classic "exceptions," many unsuspected instances in which ignorance or mistake of fact does not excuse; while analysis of the second reveals that there are times when ignorance or mistake of law does excuse and further suggests that there are other times when it perhaps should.

The role of *mens rea* in the criminal law has been the subject of much discussion. The consensus can be summarily stated: to punish conduct without reference to the actor's state of mind is both inefficacious and unjust. It is inefficacious because conduct unaccompanied by an awareness of the factors making it criminal does not mark the actor as one who needs to be subjected to punishment in order to deter him or others from behaving similarly in the future, nor does it single him out as a socially dangerous individual who needs to be incapacitated or reformed. It is unjust because the actor is subjected to the stigma of a criminal conviction without being morally blameworthy. Consequently, on either a preventive or a retributive theory of criminal punishment, the criminal sanction is inappropriate in the absence of *mens rea*.[11]

It may be asked why so disarmingly simple and persuasive a position has not commanded the deference from courts that it has received from legal scholars. Dr. Johnson's answer, "Ignorance, madam," can hardly be taken as a complete one. A less offensive explanation may be that the conventional *mens rea* notion, that the actor must be consciously aware of the factors making his conduct criminal, places so heavy a burden on law enforcement that it is bound to be resisted. If there is no concept between *mens rea* in the conventional sense and strict liability, then the agencies of enforcement will choose strict liability when the pressure to do so exists, as it notably does in the case of offenses that are handled on an assembly-line basis. But there is a "half-way house":[12] criminal

---

10 The maxim *ignorantia legis neminem excusat* and its counter-maxim *ignorantia facti excusat* afford the convenient symbols *ignorantia legis* and *ignorantia facti* for shorthand reference to these concepts.

11 A concise statement of this position, together with citation of representative authorities, may be found in A.L.I., MODEL PENAL CODE, Tent. Draft No. 4, Comments § 2.05 (1956).

12 WILLIAMS, CRIMINAL LAW: THE GENERAL PART 271 (1953) (hereinafter WILLIAMS).

liability predicated upon negligence. There are many situations in which criminal liability is so based, but they have not been adequately generalized.[13] In the analysis that follows, I shall argue that the idea of criminal responsibility based upon the actor's failure to act as carefully as he should affords an important and largely unutilized means for avoiding the tyranny of strict liability in the criminal law. Although negligence as a mode of culpability should be viewed as an exceptional resort, it can do service. Whether it does violence to the premises upon which the principle of *mens rea* rests, as some have argued, is a point that I shall leave to subsequent discussion.[14]

This problem becomes the concern of the Supreme Court when it is presented in cases testing the constitutionality of State criminal statutes that have been construed to dispense with *mens rea* and in cases raising the constitutionality or the construction of federal criminal statutes. The contemporary resurgence of interest in the substantive criminal law makes it apparent that questions about the constitutional status of *mens rea* will be pressed on the Court with increasing frequency and insistence. That the Court has not so far been able to deal adequately with these questions emerges from an historical review of the Court's treatment of the *mens rea* problem[15] and a close examination of *Lambert v. California*,[16] where the Court held that a municipal ordinance was unconstitutional as applied to one who was unaware of its requirements. That pitfalls lie ahead is suggested by analysis of the problems likely to emerge in various contexts as the confrontation becomes more acute.[17]

I. Mens Rea in the Supreme Court: A Brief History

The history of the problem in the Supreme Court is an unedifying example of how constitutional doctrine comes to be fashioned. There are two lines of decision that bear on the issue, one of them apparently establishing that *mens rea* has no constitutional significance, or very little, and the other suggesting that in some situations, at least, it has considerable significance. The odd

---

13 See A.L.I., *op. cit. supra* n. 11, at 126–27.

14 See text *infra* at notes 133–37.

15 See text at notes 18 *et seq. infra*.

16 355 U.S. 225 (1957), discussed in the text at notes 72 *et seq. infra*.

17 See text at notes 117 *et seq. infra*.

thing about these two lines of decision is that each has developed almost without acknowledgement of the other's existence. Viewed in perspective, these decisions suggest that contemporary criticism of the Court's lack of craftsmanship[18] is, if intended to contrast with the assumed glories of a bygone day, somewhat unhistorical.

The first case to raise the issue squarely, *Shevlin-Carpenter Co. v. Minnesota*,[19] is an example of constitutional adjudication at its worst. Shevlin-Carpenter, a Minnesota corporation engaged in the lumbering business, complained of a statutory penalty assessed by the State of Minnesota for cutting timber on State lands without a permit to do so. The company's defense in the State courts had been that it was not a willful trespasser but merely a casual and involuntary one, since it had been misled by official action into believing in good faith that it had a valid permit. In the State supreme court this defense had secured a reduction in the penalty from treble to double damages, in accordance with the statutory discrimination between willful and casual trespassers.[20] The statute also, however, made violation a felony, punishable by a year's imprisonment and a substantial fine. This criminal provision had been interpreted by the Minnesota Supreme Court as applicable to willful and casual violators alike.[21] Shevlin-Carpenter was not prosecuted under the criminal provisions; it was merely subjected to the statutory penalty of damages. As a kind of last-ditch argument in the United States Supreme Court, however, the company urged that the Minnesota statute was unconstitutional because its criminal provision eliminated the "question of intent," and, consequently, it contended, violated the Due Process Clause of the Fourteenth Amendment.[22] Of course, this question was not properly before the Supreme Court. All that the Court had to decide was whether the Fourteenth Amendment forbade the State to exact a statutory penalty of double damages from a casual trespasser. It was easily able to hold that the

---

18 See, *e.g.*, Hart, *The Time Chart of the Justices*, 73 HARV. L. REV. 84 (1959); Bickel & Wellington, *Legislative Purpose and the Judicial Process*, 71 HARV. L. REV. 1 (1957).

19 218 U.S. 57 (1910).

20 State v. Shevlin-Carpenter Co., 102 Minn. 470 (1907).

21 State v. Shevlin-Carpenter Co., 99 Minn. 158 (1906).

22 Brief of Plaintiffs in Error, p. 65.

Constitution contained no such proscription. In addition, it readily held the criminal provision separable.[23] It is not immediately apparent why the Court did not stop there. It went on to deal with the contention that the criminal provision, which was not before it, was unconstitutional.

The Court's job was made easy by the form in which the company cast its argument. The company began by postulating a universal rule of intent in criminal cases, but conceded that this rule might have exceptions "where so-called criminal negligence supplied the place of criminal intent,[24] or where, in a few instances, the public welfare has made it necessary to declare a crime, irrespective of the actor's intent."[25] No cases were cited, nor did the company suggest any basis for differentiating such cases from the one presented. The Court had no trouble in disposing of the contention by asserting that the concession vitiated the alleged principle. The Court cited no authority for the proposition that criminal punishment could be visited upon persons unaware of the circumstances making their conduct criminal. Its failure to cite cases is perhaps explained by the fact that the Court spoke against a background of State and federal decisions, many of them the work of strong judges, affirming criminal convictions under statutes that had been construed to dispense with any *mens rea* requirement.[26] It is fair to say, however, that none of those cases explicitly involved a sentence of imprisonment, nor did any of them deal with the issue in terms of a possible constitutional limitation on the use of the criminal sanction. Rather, the focus was upon the evil—sale of adulterated food products, commerce in intoxicating liquor, etc.—and the power of the legislature to deal with the evil, resting in general upon an expansive view of the "police power," without any examination of the method adopted. Then, too, the Court may have

---

[23] 218 U.S. at 65–67.

[24] Had the Court been so inclined, this contention might have afforded the basis for a significant expansion of the *mens rea* concept. See text at notes 133–37 *infra*.

[25] Brief of Plaintiffs in Error, p. 66.

[26] *E.g.*, Commonwealth v. Smith, 166 Mass. 370 (1896) (*per* Holmes, J.); People v. Roby, 52 Mich. 577 (1884) (*per* Cooley, C. J.); United States v. Leathers, 6 Sawyer 17 (D.C. Nev. 1879). For an account of the rise of strict liability in England and the United States, see J. HALL, GENERAL PRINCIPLES OF CRIMINAL LAW ch. 10 (2d ed. 1960) (hereinafter HALL).

felt that a matter not directly germane to the case before it required no elaborate treatment. Whatever the reason, the statements on the point in *Shevlin-Carpenter* are very weak dicta indeed.

If *Shevlin-Carpenter* was somewhat casual in its approach to the problem, the next and key decision in the sequence, *United States v. Balint*,[27] must be regarded as egregiously so. Once again, the circumstances of the case forced presentation of the issue in an abstract and unsatisfying way. The occasion was the construction of an indictment under the Harrison Narcotics Act. The indictment charged the defendants with the sale of narcotics without the requisite order form supplied by the Commissioner of Internal Revenue. The defendants demurred to the indictment on the ground that it failed to charge that they had sold the narcotics knowing them to be such. The statute did not in terms make knowledge an element of the offense. The district court sustained the demurrer and the Government, which appears to have framed the indictment as it did for the purpose of raising this very question, took the case directly to the Supreme Court under the Criminal Appeals Act.[28] The Government's brief relied upon the numerous State cases in which criminal convictions had been upheld (usually without discussion of constitutionality) even though the statutes were construed to dispense with *mens rea*.[29] There was no appearance for the defendants in the Supreme Court. So it came about that this all-important case was presented on an abstract issue and decided on the basis of an *ex parte* presentation.

Unfortunately, the unanimous opinion of the Court, written by Mr. Chief Justice Taft, did not remedy the deficiency in the presentation. The constitutional point, only fleetingly referred to in the Government's brief, was quickly dismissed by the Court. The basis for this action was only a reference to *Shevlin-Carpenter*, followed by the assertion that:[30] "Many instances of this [dispensation with

---

[27] 258 U.S. 250 (1922). See also the related decision in United States v. Behrman, 258 U.S. 280 (1922), decided the same day, note 33 *infra*.

[28] 18 U.S.C. § 3731; see ROBERTSON & KIRKHAM, JURISDICTION OF THE SUPREME COURT OF THE UNITED STATES §§ 175–91 (Wolfson & Kurland ed. 1951); Friedenthal, *Government Appeals in Federal Criminal Cases,* 12 STAN. L. REV. 71 (1959); Kurland, *The* Mersky *Case and the Criminal Appeals Act: A Suggestion for Amendment of the Statute,* 28 U. CHI. L. REV. 419 (1961).

[29] Brief on Behalf of the United States, pp. 5–11.

[30] 258 U.S. at 251.

mens rea] are to be found in regulatory measures in the exercise of what is called the police power where the emphasis of the statute is evidently upon achievement of some social betterment rather than the punishment of the crimes as in cases of mala in se." The opinion did not pause to defend this peculiar dichotomy, nor even to suggest criteria for applying it. The question, then, the Chief Justice continued, was not one of constitutionality at all but simply of ascertaining the intention of Congress.

By a similarly obscure process of divination, the Chief Justice concluded that the omission of any reference to knowledge in the statute indicated an intention on the part of Congress to force persons dealing in narcotic drugs to do so at their peril. "Doubtless considerations as to the opportunity of the seller to find out the facts and the difficulty of proof of knowledge contributed to this conclusion."[31] Here again, the intermediate concept of negligence might have been pressed into service, although it is not easy to conceive of situations in which a prosecution for selling narcotics would be impeded by requiring the prosecution to show that the defendant actually knew the nature of the commodity in which he trafficked. But the Court showed no concern about the imposition of severe criminal sanctions without proof of blameworthiness. There was not a whisper in the opinion about the maximum penalty under the Act: five years' imprisonment, as it then stood. Nor was anything said about the trivial nature of the offenses dealt with in the State cases cited by the Court, although the distinction had not escaped the attention of State court judges.[32]

---

[31] *Id.* at 254. The suggestion may be that persons charged with selling narcotics, as Balint and his co-defendant were, invariably know the nature of the commodity in which they are dealing. That was the view of one federal court, which distinguished *Balint* in reversing a conviction for purchasing narcotics. Nigro v. United States, 4 F. 2d 781 (8th Cir. 1925). The Government did not seek review of *Nigro* in the Supreme Court. The distinction is hardly persuasive. In any event, it is difficult to see why the improbability that the defense will succeed should militate against permitting it to be advanced.

[32] "But in sustaining the power to fine, we are not to be understood as sustaining to a like length the power to imprison. . . . The statute is not void as a whole though some of its penalties may be excessive." People v. Sheffield Farms-Slawson-Decker Co., 225 N.Y. 25, 32–33 (1918) (strict liability aspect of Child Labor Law) (per Cardozo, J.). *Cf.* Tenement House Department v. McDevitt, 215 N.Y. 160 (1915). For a more recent attempt to draw the same distinction, see Commonwealth v. Koczwara, 397 Pa. 575 (1959).

Upon this flimsy basis, dictum became holding, and the doctrine passed into our constitutional law that severe criminal punishment may be inflicted at the legislature's will, regardless of whether the defendant had any opportunity to conform his conduct to the requirements of law. And the more far-reaching doctrine that legislative silence is to be construed as a direction to dispense with *mens rea* took a firm hold.[33] One wonders whether the result would have been the same if a high officer of the Shevlin-Carpenter Company

---

[33] *Balint* itself did not enunciate a general presumption against *mens rea*. In the *Behrman* case, decided the same day, the Court may have done so. "If the offense be a statutory one, and intent or knowledge is not made an element of it, the indictment need not charge such knowledge or intent." 258 U.S. at 288. As the Court later recognized, this language "if read literally, would work far-reaching changes in the composition of all federal crimes." Morissette v. United States, 342 U.S. 246, 259 (1952); see text at notes 44 *et seq. infra*.

The *Behrman* decision illustrates the shaky basis of the *Balint* doctrine. The question in *Behrman* was whether an indictment under the Harrison Act adequately negatived the statutory exception for dispensation by a physician "in the course of his professional practice only" by alleging that the defendant gave a known addict a large quantity of narcotics to be taken in divided doses over a period of days, without in terms alleging that this was not "in the course of his professional practice only." Relying on *Balint*, the Court sustained the indictment, thereby holding irrelevant a doctor defendant's good-faith belief that what he was doing comported with professional medical standards.

This decision evoked the dissent of Justice Holmes, joined by Justices McReynolds and Brandeis. The dissent pointed out the trap which the Government had laid and into which the Court had fallen: "The indictment for the very purpose of raising the issue that divides the Court alleges in terms that the drugs were intended by the defendant to be used by King in divided doses over a period of several days. The defendant was a licensed physician and his part in the sale was the giving of prescriptions for the drugs. In view of the allegation that I have quoted and the absence of any charge to the contrary it must be assumed that he gave them in the regular course of his practice and in good faith. Whatever ground for scepticism we may find in the facts we are bound to accept the position knowingly and deliberately taken by the pleader and evidently accepted by the Court below.

"It seems to me impossible to construe the statute as tacitly making such acts, however foolish, crimes, by saying that what is in form a prescription and is given honestly in the course of a doctor's practice, and therefore, so far as the words of the statute go, is allowed in terms, is not within the words, is not a prescription and is not given in the course of practice, if the Court deems the doctor's faith in his patient manifestly unwarranted. *It seems to me wrong to construe the statute as creating a crime in this way without a word of warning*." 258 U.S. at 289–90. (Emphasis added.)

Why is it wrong so to construe the statute? If a *mens rea* requirement is not to be implied in *Balint*, why should it be in *Behrman?* The dissenters' position is an appealing one; but it is inconsistent with *Balint*.

had been convicted and sentenced to a year's imprisonment under the criminal provision of the Minnesota statute, or if Balint had come before the Supreme Court after conviction and sentence of five years' imprisonment, rather than in the posture of one protesting the omission of a word from an indictment.

When the question of *mens rea* next arose directly, it was intertwined with and possibly obscured by an issue of statutory interpretation relating to the imposition of vicarious liability. The narrow issue in *United States v. Dotterweich*[34] was whether the president of a company that shipped misbranded or adulterated products in interstate commerce was a "person" who had done so under the Food, Drug, and Cosmetic Act,[35] notwithstanding that he had nothing to do with the shipment. The facts of the case are instructive.[36] Buffalo Pharmacal Company, a drug wholesaler, purchased drugs from manufacturers, repackaged them under its own label, and shipped them on order to physicians. Dotterweich and the company were prosecuted for two interstate shipments alleged to be adulterated or misbranded. The first consisted of a cascara compound that conformed to specifications but whose label included reference to an ingredient that had, a short time before, been dropped from the National Formulary. One infers that the old labels were still being used. The other shipment was of digitalis tablets that were of less than the potency proclaimed by their label. The company did not manufacture these tablets but merely repackaged them under its own label. So far as appears, there was no way short of conducting a chemical analysis of the tablets for their seller to know that they were not what their label declared them to be. The jury found Dotterweich guilty but for "some unexplainable reason"[37] disagreed as to the company's guilt. Dotterweich was sentenced to pay a fine and to "probation for 60 days."[38] The court of appeals reversed, on the ground that the statute should not be

---

[34] 320 U.S. 277 (1943).

[35] 52 Stat. 1040 (1938), 21 U.S.C. § 301 (1940).

[36] The description that follows is taken from the opinion in the court of appeals, United States v. Buffalo Pharmacal Co., 131 F. 2d 500 (2d Cir. 1942). The opinion in the Supreme Court does not detail the facts.

[37] The phrase is Judge Swan's, writing for the court of appeals. 131 F. 2d at 501.

[38] *Ibid.* Under the statute he could have been sentenced to a year's imprisonment. 21 U.S.C. § 333(a) (1959).

read as applying to an individual agent of the principal (here the company), since only the principal was in a position to exculpate itself by obtaining a guaranty of non-adulteration from its supplier. Since there appeared to be no statutory basis for distinguishing between a high corporate agent, like Dotterweich, who might have obtained such a guaranty, and a shipping clerk or other menial employee who might be instrumental in causing the forbidden shipment and who would not be covered by the guaranty, a divided court of appeals concluded that Dotterweich's conviction could not stand.

It will be noticed that the answer to the question whether this was indeed a "forbidden shipment" was dealt with rather cursorily. The court of appeals held merely that "intention to violate the statute" was not an element of the offense.[39] The shipments in question were illegal under the statute, and that was that. Whether Dotterweich (or anyone else) had failed to take reasonable precautions was not put to the jury. Once again, negligence as a possible mode of culpability was overlooked.

The court of appeals opinion had at least the merit of keeping separate two questions that it would only confound analysis to blur: (1) whether whoever was responsible for the shipment could be held criminally liable, notwithstanding the absence of culpability on his part: the issue of "strict liability"; and (2) whether Dotterweich could be held criminally liable, notwithstanding his own lack of connection with the shipment: the issue of "vicarious liability."[40]

---

[39] 131 F. 2d at 502.

[40] The distinction is well drawn in Sayre, *Criminal Responsibility for the Acts of Another*, 43 HARV. L. REV. 689, 721–22 (1930): "In view of the close parallelism between the problem of *mens rea* and the problem of vicarious criminal responsibility, it is not surprising that some courts have fallen into the error of basing upon the *mens rea* requirement the inapplicability of the doctrine of *respondeat superior* to all serious crimes. In the case of crimes requiring *mens rea*, it is argued, it is impossible to convict one for the unauthorized crime of his servant or agent of which he had no knowledge, since his lack of knowledge necessarily disproves *mens rea* on his part. But this is specious reasoning. If one's criminal liability may be based upon the physical activity of his servant, why may it not equally be based upon the accompanying mental activity of his servant? A close parallel is to be found in the problem of the criminal liability of corporations. For centuries it was held that because a corporation possessed no soul or mind, it could not be convicted of any crime requiring *mens rea*. Today we realize that the liability of corporations may be based upon another's state of mind quite as easily as upon

It is obvious that the second issue is dependent on the first; if no one committed a crime, there was no crime for which Dotterweich could have been held vicariously liable. The underlying issue was whether the statute imposed strict liability.

The opinion for the Court, by Mr. Justice Frankfurter, did not make the essential distinction between the issues of strict and vicarious liability. It is not an unfair paraphrase to say that the Court held that since the liability was strict it was also vicarious.[41] But the premise that the Act dispensed with *mens rea* and imposed strict liability was assumed rather than examined:[42]

> The prosecution to which Dotterweich was subjected is based on a now familiar type of legislation whereby penalties serve as effective means of regulation. Such legislation dispenses with the conventional requirement for criminal conduct—awareness of some wrongdoing. In the interest of the larger good it puts the burden of acting at hazard upon a person

---

another's physical act; and we freely convict corporations for crimes requiring not only *mens rea,* but specific intent as well. It will not do, therefore, to argue that because a crime does not require *mens rea,* one should be convicted for his servant's unauthorized commission of it, or *vice versa.* The dispensing with the usual requirement of *mens rea* and the imposition of criminal liability for the unauthorized acts of one's servant are parallel but disconnected results flowing from a common cause."

[41] *Cf.* WILLIAMS 285–86 (1953): "The same statute may, of course, create both strict and vicarious responsibility. In that event, since the responsibility is strict, there will be no need to prove *mens rea* on the part of anyone; and since the responsibility is vicarious, there will be no need to prove an *actus reus* on the part of the accused master. It may be hoped that such a tyrannous combination will be found to be rare."

[42] 320 U.S. at 280–81. The passage quoted by the Court is from United States v. Johnson, 221 U.S. 488, 497–98 (1911) (*per* Holmes, J.), holding that intentionally misleading statements as to curative effects on the label of a patent medicine which did not, however, import any statement as to the identity of the compound did not constitute misbranding under the 1906 Act. The quoted passage reads in full as follows: ". . . it should be noticed that although the indictment alleges a wilful fraud, the shipment is punished by the statute if the article is misbranded, and that the article may be misbranded without any conscious fraud at all. It was natural enough to throw this risk on shippers with regard to the identity of their wares, but a very different and unlikely step to make them answerable for mistaken praise."

As Professor Henry Hart has observed: "Morality and rationality alike, it is submitted, could hardly be more completely inverted." *The Aims of the Criminal Law,* 23 LAW & CONTEMP. PROB. 401, 432–33 n. 71 (1958). Beyond that, it should be noted that the snippet of this passage quoted by Mr. Justice Frankfurter's opinion is very cursory dictum. The question of strict liability was not involved in *Johnson.*

> otherwise innocent but standing in responsible relation to a public danger. *United States* v. *Balint*, 258 U.S. 250. And so it is clear that shipments like those now in issue are "punished by the statute if the article is misbranded [or adulterated], and that the article may be misbranded [or adulterated] without any conscious fraud at all. It was natural enough to throw this risk on shippers with regard to the identity of their wares. . . ."

It is well to note that this offhand passage is precisely all that the opinion had to say on the *mens rea* issue, despite the fact that this was the first time that the Supreme Court had before it the construction of the mental element in this important federal criminal statute. *Balint* had done its work thoroughly. It is also well to note the primitive and rigid view of *mens rea* that the quoted passage reflects. "Conscious fraud" and "awareness of some wrongdoing" are impossibly high standards, the opinion seems to say, and that leaves only strict liability. Did the company or its responsible agents behave recklessly or negligently with respect to the possibility that these shipments were not up to standard? Perhaps it was inexcusably careless not to have destroyed the old cascara labels and prepared new ones. Perhaps not. But could not the lower courts have been told that this question should be submitted to the jury? The case posed an obvious opportunity for framing a more discriminating set of standards for the mental element, but the opportunity was foregone. Instead, unquestioning reliance on *Balint* strengthened that doctrine's hold. The four dissenters[43] confined themselves to a discussion of the vicarious liability point, leaving unexposed the weaknesses of the majority's opinion with respect to the *mens rea* problem.

It fell to a judge intimately familiar with the corruption of the criminal process in a totalitarian society to raise the first note of skepticism about the dogma thus established. In *Morissette v. United States*,[44] Mr. Justice Jackson wrote for the Court in reversing a conviction for knowing conversion of government property. The defendant had taken used bomb casings that he had found

---

[43] The dissent was written by Mr. Justice Murphy and concurred in by Justices Roberts, Reed, and Rutledge. In this as in other decisions dealing with the substantive criminal law the division within the Court was such as to confound simplistic practitioners of the "box-score" technique.

[44] 342 U.S. 246 (1942).

upon a government reservation. He asserted the defense that he had regarded them as abandoned. The trial court refused to allow Morissette the benefit of this defense. The trial judge's view was based on his belief that the failure of Congress to express explicitly a mental element meant that, under the *Balint* rule, no such mental element was required.

Mr. Justice Jackson's opinion recognized the difficulty in which this unthinking adherence to *Balint* placed the federal courts in their construction of federal criminal statutes. Unless Congress had expressly defined the mental element in the offense, it could not be implied, notwithstanding the strength of common-law tradition with respect to *mens rea.*[45] But recognizing the problem was not the same as solving it. The distinction for which Jackson reached, while perhaps adequate for the case at hand, did not come to grips with the underlying problem. What he said, in short, was that *mens rea* was presumptively to be implied in the statutory redefinition of offenses taken over from the common law. From this category, Mr. Justice Jackson distinguished cases like *Balint*, which dealt with "public welfare offenses." What is a public welfare offense? Mr. Chief Justice Taft had referred to "prosecutions under statutes the purpose of which would be obstructed" by a *mens rea* requirement.[46] It did not escape Mr. Justice Jackson's attention that the "purpose" of any criminal statute, if it be to secure convictions, is "obstructed" by allowing a *mens rea* defense.[47] The line between common-law crimes and public welfare offenses could hardly be drawn on that basis. But, lacking a basis for drawing the line, Jackson drew it nonetheless. "The conclusion reached in the *Balint* and *Behrman* cases has our approval and adherence for the circumstances to which it was there applied."[48] One is left to ponder what those circumstances are supposed to be. Mr. Justice Jackson may have wanted to say that it is proper to construe a statute as dispensing with *mens rea* when the penalty for its violation is slight and when conviction under it does not involve the stigma usually associated with the criminal sanction. But he did not say so and, indeed, hardly could have said so in view of the "circumstances" of *Balint*,

---

[45] *Id.* at 263.

[46] 258 U.S. at 252.

[47] 342 U.S. at 259.

[48] *Id.* at 260.

involving as they did a felony punishable then by five years' imprisonment and now, under some circumstances, by even more severe penalties.[49] Whether a satisfactory line can be drawn between "public welfare offenses" and more serious crimes is a question to which we will recur; but clearly it is impossible to draw such a line and leave the *Balint* case standing.

Perhaps the most revealing feature of the *Morissette* opinion is its highly labored quality. The decadence of substantive criminal law is never more starkly revealed than in the fact that a unanimous Supreme Court found it necessary to buttress by an opinion running to thirty pages the conclusion that claim of right is a defense to a charge of theft.[50] *Morissette* may represent a turning point of sorts in judicial attitude toward *mens rea.* If it does, we must recognize how far we had come down the road to obliterating any general principles in the substantive criminal law.

Morissette dealt only with an issue of statutory construction.[51] There was no hint in the opinion of any constitutional objection to the imposition of criminal penalties in the absence of the actor's awareness (or blameworthy unawareness) of facts making his conduct criminal. On the federal level, *Balint* remained unimpaired as constitutional doctrine, although severely if indeterminately restricted as a guide to statutory construction. *Morissette* appears to have had a fairly salutary effect on the construction of federal criminal statutes.[52] It said nothing, of course, about what should be done with State criminal cases in which a statute comes to the Supreme Court authoritatively construed as dispensing with *mens rea.* That problem lay ahead.

---

49 See 26 U.S.C. § 7237 (1958).

50 *Cf.* the treatment of "Mr. Justice Jackson's spread-eagle dissertation," in Hart, *supra* note 42, at 431, n. 70.

51 It also rejected the trial court's reliance on a "presumption" of intent, citing Tot v. United States, 319 U.S. 463 (1943), for the proposition that "[e]ven congressional power to facilitate convictions by substituting presumptions for proof is not without limit." 342 U.S. at 275. It remains an intriguing question why Congress may not resort to an admittedly irrational presumption to supply proof of an element even though it has power to eliminate the element itself. See Brosman, *The Statutory Presumption,* 5 TUL. L. REV. 17 (1930); Scott, *Constitutional Limitations on Substantive Criminal Law,* 29 ROCKY MT. L. REV. 275, 289–92 (1957).

52 But see note 151 *infra.*

As of the time *Morissette* was decided, the Court appears, if this line of cases alone is considered, to have eliminated *mens rea* as a constitutional issue. But these cases do not tell the whole story. In another group of decisions the Court has relied on *mens rea* to save some statutes and on its absence to strike down others, without once recognizing that its actions cast any doubt on either the limits or the intrinsic validity of the constitutional proposition asserted in *Balint*.

There has always been a strong undercurrent of dictum about the importance of *mens rea*.[53] But there are two groups of decisions in which the principle has assumed controlling importance. The first group includes decisions in which the principle of *mens rea* was called into play to save the constitutionality of criminal statutes that otherwise were thought to be void for vagueness.[54] The bellwether case, *Screws v. United States*,[55] upheld the constitutionality of a criminal conviction under the provision of the Civil Rights Act making it a crime for one acting under color of State law to deprive any person "of any rights, privileges, or immunities secured or protected by the Constitution or laws of the United States" on account of alienage, color, or race.[56] The statute was attacked because of the vagueness of its substantive reach. The plurality opinion rejected this attack on the ground that the statutory requirement that the defendant had acted "willfully," interpreted to mean with a specific intent to deprive the victim of some constitutional right, supplied the "ascertainable standard of guilt" that would otherwise be lacking.[57] In the conventional formulation of the

---

[53] See, *e.g.*, Felton v. United States, 96 U.S. 699, 703 (1878); Baender v. Barnett, 255 U.S. 224 (1921). It is interesting to note that the same Court that unanimously decided *Balint*, had, only a year earlier in *Baender*, unanimously upheld the federal counterfeiting statute against the claim that it penalized "innocent" possession of coinage dies by rejecting that construction in the following terms: "The statute is not intended to include and make criminal a possession which is not conscious and willing. While its words are general, they are to be taken in a reasonable sense and not in one which works manifest injustice *or infringes constitutional safeguards*." 255 U.S. at 225–26. (Emphasis added.)

[54] Screws v. United States, 325 U.S. 91 (1945); Hygrade Provision Co. v. Sherman, 266 U.S. 497 (1925); Omaechevarria v. Idaho, 246 U.S. 343 (1918).

[55] 325 U.S. 91.

[56] The provision now appears at 18 U.S.C. § 242 (1958).

[57] 325 U.S. at 103.

vagueness doctrine, adequate notice was thereby given the defendant as to what conduct was made unlawful by the statute.

The dissenting opinion pointed out that importing a *mens rea* requirement into the definition of the offense did nothing to make the definition more precise.[58] Accepting the "decent advance notice" rationale for the vagueness requirement, the dissenters asked how it could help to be told that you must not do something "willfully" if you are not told what that something is.[59] Their question seems unanswerable. *Screws* and the decisions on which it purports to rely, however, raised some interesting questions about the relationship between the vagueness doctrine and the notion of *mens rea.*

If the function of the vagueness doctrine is, as is so often said in the cases, to give the defendant fair warning that his conduct is criminal, then one is led to suppose that some constitutional importance attaches to giving people such warning or at least making such warning available to them. If a man does an act under circumstances that make the act criminal, but he is unaware of those circumstances, surely he has not had fair warning that his conduct is criminal. If "fair warning" is a constitutional requisite in terms of the language of a criminal statute, why is it not also a constitutional requisite so far as the defendant's state of mind with respect to his activities is concerned? Or, even more to the point, if he is unaware that his conduct is labeled as criminal by a statute, is he not in much the same position as one who is convicted under a statute which is too vague to give "fair warning"? In both cases, the defendant is by hypothesis unblameworthy in that he has acted without advertence or negligent inadvertence to the possibility that his conduct might be criminal. If warning to the prospective defendant is really the thrust of the vagueness doctrine, then it seems inescapable that disturbing questions are raised, not only about so-called strict-liability offenses in the criminal law, but about the whole range of

---

[58] *Id.* at 138, 149–57. The opinion bears the comparatively unusual notation of joint authorship: "Mr. Justice Roberts, Mr. Justice Frankfurter and Mr. Justice Jackson, dissenting." Intrinsic evidence suggests that Mr. Justice Frankfurter's pen was largely responsible for this opinion.

[59] *Id.* at 154.

criminal liabilities that are upheld despite the defendant's plea of ignorance of the law.[60]

Without stopping to examine in detail the rationale of the vagueness doctrine, it may suffice to observe that its principal thrust, despite the language that the courts habitually resort to, may not be so much to give any literalistic "warning" to the individual but rather to confine the discretionary power of prosecutors and judges within decent limits, particularly in areas where a failure to do so is thought to press heavily on constitutionally sensitive areas of human activity.[61] On that view of the doctrine's function, which I think is the more realistic one, the asserted relationship between vagueness and *mens rea* disappears. Once it is postulated that a statute is unconstitutionally vague if and only if it confers upon prosecutors and judges intolerably large discretion to impose a judgment of criminality, then the defendant's state of mind as to the facts or his awareness of illegality is immaterial. If the statute expresses its scope with sufficient clarity, then there is no *mens rea* analogue to the vagueness doctrine. For example, a prohibition of some very specific activity such as spitting on the sidewalk is not rendered unconstitutional because the actor is unaware that spitting on the sidewalk is illegal. The problem is simply whether the prohibition is expressed with sufficient clarity so that a prosecutor knows what conduct to prosecute and a judge knows what range of circumstances will support a conviction. What the defendant knows is immaterial. Nevertheless, even if it be conceded that the "fair notice" rationale of the vagueness doctrine is highly fictional, the frequency with which that rationale is reiterated suggests that it has some independent, although perhaps irrational, validity. To the extent that it does, the existence of the doctrine may afford some basis for a broad frontal attack on the elimination of *mens rea* in both the *ignorantia facti* and *ignorantia legis* situations. More likely, when the thrust of that attack is noted, the Court may be impelled to articulate with a little more precision than it has so far

---

[60] For a decision invalidating as unconstitutionally vague a criminal statute that dispensed with *mens rea,* see State v. Prince, 52 N.M. 15 (1948); Note, 24 IND. L. J. 89 (1948).

[61] This view is taken in a discerning treatment of the vagueness doctrine. See Note, *The Void-For-Vagueness Doctrine in the Supreme Court,* 109 U. Pa. L. Rev. 67, 81 (1960).

done just what considerations govern the application of the vagueness doctrine.

The other group of decisions in which the presence or absence of a *mens rea* requirement has been deemed controlling on the issue of a statute's constitutionality have all involved in one way or another the problems of freedom of speech and of association. The Court has repeatedly relied on *mens rea* to limit the applicability of State and federal criminal (and, on occasion, non-criminal) sanctions to conduct which is thought to require constitutional protection. In the loyalty-oath cases, the result has often turned on whether the enactment in question was construed to cover membership in "subversive" organizations *simpliciter* or only membership with knowledge of the organizations' suspect character.[62] In *Watkins v. United States*,[63] the fulcrum of the Court's discursive examination of congressional investigative power appears to be that the particular contempt conviction under scrutiny was bad because the defendant had not been made aware of the pertinency of the particular question asked to the legitimate purpose of the inquiry. In the Smith Act cases,[64] the Court made much of the protective nature of the requirement that the defendants must have had a specific intent to overthrow the government as speedily as circumstances would permit.

None of the opinions variously upholding and striking down enactments thought to impinge on First Amendment rights evinces the slightest awareness that their reliance on *mens rea* as a constitutional test might conceivably have ramifications outside that area.[65]

---

[62] *Compare* Wieman v. Updegraff, 344 U.S. 183 (1952), *with* Garner v. Board of Public Works, 341 U.S. 716 (1951); Gerende v. Board of Supervisors, 314 U.S. 56 (1951). See also Adler v. Board of Education, 342 U.S. 485, 494 (1952).

[63] 354 U.S. 178 (1957). See the gloss placed on the Court's opinion in the concurring opinion of Mr. Justice Frankfurter, *id.* at 216–17.

[64] Dennis v. United States, 341 U.S. 494 (1951); Yates v. United States, 354 U.S. 298. *Mens rea* was also heavily relied upon in the decision at the 1960 Term that upheld the "membership" clause of the Smith Act. Scales v. United States, 367 U.S. 203 (1961).

[65] The *Balint* doctrine is referred to in the plurality opinion in *Screws*, 325 U.S. at 103, but only as predicate for the argument that by the addition of the word "wilfully" to Section 20 in 1909, Congress meant to limit the sweep of the statute. "Prior to that time it may be that Congress intended that he who deprived a person of any right protected by the Constitution should be liable without more. That was

It was not until the Court's eyes were opened to the generality of the *mens rea* problem in *Lambert v. California*[66] that its opinions in the speech cases began to perceive, if not to deal with, these ramifications.[67] Recent evidence may tend to suggest that the awakening was as fleeting as it was incomplete.[68]

The implication of the *mens rea* point in these cases has not been fully articulated but it appears to rest on the premise that requiring a man to act at his peril is likely to inhibit his engaging in the activity in question. Where that activity is constitutionally protected, the argument then runs, the imposition of strict liability is an unreasonable restraint on his freedom to act. Speech is such an area of activity. Consequently, inhibitions on speech must at the very least be imposed only on persons who are adequately aware of what they are doing and of its relation to relevant legal norms.

Whatever may be thought of this argument as a justification for the results reached in the cases where it has been applied, it suggests that notions about *mens rea* cut a little deeper than the Court has been willing to recognize in other contexts. It may be conceded that "there is an important difference in the scope of the power of a State to regulate what feeds the belly and what feeds the brain."[69] But if strict liability is overly strong medicine in the one case, that does not prove it is just right in the other. One might even suggest that what is too harsh to be tolerable for the imposition of non-penal sanctions on constitutionally favored activity ought to be deemed too harsh for the imposition of the severer forms of penal sanctions on any activity at all. Constitutional limits may be appropriate not only when the question is one of the power to regulate a given activity but also when it is one of the nature of the sanction em-

---

the pattern of criminal legislation which has been sustained without any charge or proof of scienter [citing *Shevlin-Carpenter* and *Balint*]." To which one might reply, in language used by the dissenters in a cognate context: "It is true also of a statute that it cannot lift itself up by its bootstraps." *Id.* at 154.

[66] 355 U.S. 225, see text at notes 72 *et seq. infra.*

[67] See the remarks of Mr. Justice Brennan in *Smith v. California,* quoted in the text at note 2 *supra.*

[68] The opinion of the Court in the *Scales* case, *supra* note 64, despite its heavy reliance on *mens rea,* made no reference either to *Lambert* or to the *Balint* doctrine.

[69] Mr. Justice Frankfurter, concurring, in Smith v. California, 361 U.S. 147 at 162.

ployed. As Professor Hart has put it, there are "unmistakable indications that the Constitution means something definite and something serious when it speaks of 'crime.' "[70] It would be anomalous if that "something" turned out to concern only the procedures by which criminal sanctions are brought to bear and not what conduct they are brought to bear upon. The First Amendment decisions suggest that some constitutional doctrines about the substantive limits of criminal law may soon be born.[71]

This rapid review of the strands of decision about *mens rea* has hardly produced a more helpful set of generalizations about its constitutional role than was ventured at the outset. Perhaps a more sympathetic scrutiny of what the Supreme Court has done would produce a clearer picture. A less sympathetic scrutiny might, on the other hand, produce this gloss: The Supreme Court regards *mens rea* as constitutionally unimportant except when it serves as a convenient peg on which to hang a result that it thinks desirable but is unwilling or unable to defend on other grounds. Judgment on that gloss should be reserved, probably indefinitely, but at least pending an examination of *Lambert v. California.*

II. An Examination of Lambert v. California

Not the least of the paradoxes that surround the *Lambert* case,[72] the first invalidation by the Supreme Court on *mens rea* grounds of legislation unrelated to the First Amendment, is that it involved not the conventional issue of strict liability that was the subject of the *Balint-Dotterweich-Morissette* line of cases, but rather the more difficult problem posed by the defense of ignorance that the particular conduct involved had been declared to be criminal. Under a Los Angeles municipal ordinance[73] of an increasingly familiar type, a person who has been convicted of any offense that would be a felony in California, or of certain misdemeanors, wheth-

---

70 Hart, *supra* note 42, at 431. He goes on to remark that the Court "has hardly got to first base in working out what that something is." *Ibid.*

71 For a possible premature delivery, see Robinson v. California, 370 U.S. 660 (1962), discussed in note 144 *infra.*

72 Lambert v. California, 355 U.S. 225 (1957).

73 Los Angeles Municipal Code §§ 52.38–52.39. See Note, 130 U. Pa. L. Rev. 60 (1954).

er committed within or without California, at any time subsequent to January 1, 1921, must not remain in the city of Los Angeles for more than five days without registering with the Chief of Police. Failure to register was made a misdemeanor, punishable by fine or imprisonment, and each day's violation was made a separate offense.[74] Miss Lambert, a person who fell within the statutory category by reason of having been convicted of forgery in California, was charged with a violation of the ordinance. At her trial, she offered to testify that she did not know that she had a duty to register, but the trial court excluded the testimony[75] and the jury convicted. The facts of the case appeared to raise disturbing questions about the use of the registration ordinance to harass suspected criminals and to circumvent the limitations on the police power to arrest. Indeed, the principal burden of Miss Lambert's initial complaint was that her arrest was illegal. On appeal to the Appellate Department of the Superior Court for Los Angeles County, the highest State court in which the appeal could be heard, her conviction was affirmed, on the ground that wrongful intent was not an element of the crime created by the ordinance and that it was no defense that appellant did not know the registration requirement.[76] Without elaboration, the court declared that there was no merit to the argument that the ordinance was unconstitutional.[77]

The case apparently gave the Supreme Court some difficulty. It was argued at the 1956 Term. Re-argument was ordered and the Court invited the Attorney General of California to file a brief and participate in the re-argument.[78] Three weeks later another order was entered inviting a member of the Court's Bar to appear as *amicus curiae* for the appellant.[79] Perusal of the briefs submitted on both sides before the original argument suggests that the Court had even less help than usual from counsel. Other weaknesses aside, neither appellant nor appellee had cited any of the *mens rea* cases previously decided by the Court. Although it was apparently the

---

[74] Los Angeles Municipal Code §§ 11.00(m), 52.43.

[75] Record, p. 17.

[76] *Id.* at 30.

[77] *Ibid.*

[78] 353 U.S. 979 (1957).

[79] Inquiry of the Clerk's Office elicited no recollection of another instance in which the Court had invited an *amicus* to participate on behalf of a private party already represented by counsel.

weakness of the City's brief that in the first instance brought the call for reinforcement, Miss Lambert ended the gainer. The Attorney General's brief was minimally competent, but the brief filed by *amicus curiae* for the appellant was one of those rare performances that must gladden the hearts of the Justices. It appears to be the only instance in which counsel has given the Court a basis for considering the constitutional dimensions of the *mens rea* problem. As a consequence of its high quality, this brief appears to have dominated consideration of the case. Echoes of it can be found throughout the Court's opinion.

The *amicus* brief relied on two points. The first point was the *mens rea* argument, which I shall examine in detail. The second was that the registration ordinance was an "unwarranted invasion of the right of privacy, right to liberty, and privileges and immunities of a citizen of the United States in that it penalizes a morally innocent and passive status and is not reasonably restricted to the evil with which it purports to deal."[80] In other words, a substantive due process argument was directed against the "reasonableness" of the ordinance, with all the difficulties that attend such a position in the climate of constitutional adjudication that has prevailed since the judicial crisis of the mid-1930's.[81] This portion of the argument was marked by an impressive marshalling of criminological data tending to show that it was unreasonable for an ordinance purporting to deal with the evil of "professionalism in crime"[82] to cast as wide a net as the Los Angeles ordinance did. At the argument of the case, the Court apparently exhibited at least as much interest in the question of the ordinance's reasonableness as it did in the *mens rea* issue.[83] When the opinion emerged, however, this second issue had entirely dropped out. There is not the slightest reference in either the majority or the dissenting opinion to the very impressive

---

[80] Brief of Amicus Curiae for Appellant, p. 21.

[81] *Cf.* Mr. Justice White's recent reference to "the present Court's allergy to substantive due process." Robinson v. California, 370 U.S. 660, 689 (1962). See McCloskey, *Economic Due Process and the Supreme Court: An Exhumation and Reburial,* [1962] SUPREME COURT REVIEW 34, *supra.*

[82] Brief, *supra* note 80, at 35. Counsel for the city had been incautious enough so to describe the ordinance's purpose. Appellee's Brief, p. 3.

[83] This conclusion is based on an account of the argument in a memorandum prepared after the argument by the *amicus curiae*, Warren M. Christopher, Esq.

argument that *amicus curiae* urged against the reasonableness of the ordinance apart from the *mens rea* point. It may be surmised that the Court found it easier to dispose of the case on the *mens rea* issue.

The *mens rea* argument for appellant seized on the obvious infirmity of the ordinance, its applicability to wholly neutral, indeed passive, conduct. The point was made that Miss Lambert neither knew nor had any reason to know of the existence of the ordinance making her condition of residence in Los Angeles criminal. Much emphasis was placed on the inaccessibility of municipal ordinances and on the lack of any attempt by the city of Los Angeles to bring the registration requirement to the attention of convicted persons. As the brief pointed out: ". . . the effect of appellant's lack of knowledge of her duty to register is seriously aggravated by the fact that neither her status nor her conduct provided any 'built-in' notice that she was committing a crime punishable by imprisonment."[84] On these facts, *amicus curiae* submitted, "wrongful intent" could not constitutionally be eliminated as an element of the offense.

The brief made it clear at the outset that the term "wrongful intent" meant, in this instance, "an intention not to comply with the ordinance despite knowledge of its requirements."[85] *Amicus* obliquely recognized that the term is only rarely used in that sense, and attempted to bridge the gap by the suggestion that knowledge of the ordinance fulfils the same function in a crime of this type as is fulfilled by the more conventional requirement of factual awareness characteristic of crimes that "are harmful to others or objectively immoral."[86] The distinction thus made unfortunately escaped the Court's attention, as did other subtleties in the *amicus* brief.

The burden of the *amicus* argument with respect to wrongful intent was as follows: "When (1) an ordinance makes unlawful a morally innocent and passive status, (2) the accused neither knew nor should have known that her status had been made unlawful by the ordinance, and (3) the crime created is punishable by imprisonment . . . , due process requires that a wrongful intent be proved."[87] The *amicus* brief then faced with considerable aplomb the problem of dealing with the line of cases previously described. It took

---

84 Brief *supra* note 80, at 11–12.

85 *Id.* at 13 n.

86 *Ibid.*

87 *Id.* at 13.

Morissette as the key case, even though that case had not involved a constitutional issue, and viewed its analysis as weighing heavily against the constitutionality of a statute dispensing with *mens rea* in any except a "limited class of offenses."[88] The brief then went on to deal with *Shevlin-Carpenter*, *Balint*, and *Dotterweich* in terms that suggested the presence in those cases of factors making dispensation with *mens rea* constitutional, primarily that the circumstances were such as to place the defendants on notice that their conduct might be in violation of the law, so that their asserted lack of awareness of the material facts must have been at least culpably negligent. Whether *mens rea* in the sense of knowledge of the circumstances making conduct criminal can be thus easily equated with *mens rea* in the sense of awareness of illegality was a point that the brief did not stop to deal with and that did not seem to trouble the Court when it came to decide the case. This portion of the brief concluded with reference to Sayre's classic article on public welfare offenses[89] and concluded that the offense here involved did not fall into any of the categories in which *mens rea* has been dispensed with. There was an interesting suggestion that the ordinance was in fact used for selective harassment of convicted persons, although *amicus* conceded that the record in the instant case did not support that conclusion. Nonetheless, the suggestion was advanced that the importation of a *mens rea* requirement would reduce the possibilities of unfair harassment.[90]

The Court divided sharply, five members voting for reversal and four for affirmance. The opinions were brief and unilluminating. The majority opinion by Mr. Justice Douglas made no attempt to examine the argument that *Morissette* had substantially qualified the scope of the constitutional doctrine laid down in *Balint*. Indeed *Morissette* was not mentioned, although it was *amicus curiae's* primary reliance.[91] The opinion opened with a rejection of the generalization that *mens rea* is necessary to constitute a crime. "There is wide latitude in the lawmakers to declare an offense and to exclude

88 Quoting *Morissette,* 342 U.S. at 258, 260.

89 Sayre, *Public Welfare Offenses,* 33 COLUM. L. REV. 55 (1933).

90 Brief *supra* note 80, at 20.

91 It may be of interest that Mr. Justice Douglas alone had concurred not in the opinion but only in the result in *Morissette.* 342 U.S. at 276.

elements of knowledge and diligence from its definition."[92] Mr. Justice Douglas did not tell us how wide is wide, or indeed, what calipers are to be used in measuring the width. Having in effect laid down a general rule, he proceeded to qualify it for purposes of the case at hand: "But we deal here with conduct that is wholly passive—mere failure to register. It is unlike the commission of acts or the failure to act under circumstances that should alert the doer to the consequences of his deed."[93] At this point, a purpose signal identifies and disposes of the *Balint* doctrine.[94] And that is precisely all that the majority opinion has to say on that subject. It is a little hard to know what distinction Mr. Justice Douglas was drawing. He appeared to recognize that it was not merely a distinction between doing and not doing. There are, his formulation recognized, circumstances of omission under which the actor ought to be aware that he has a duty to act. But if that is true, why is it not equally true that one may commit acts "under circumstances that [do not] alert the doer to the consequences of his deed." If it is, in truth, the variant circumstances that either should or should not alert the potential wrongdoer to the nature of his act rather than the distinction between active and passive conduct that is properly involved, it is hard to see how Mr. Justice Douglas was able to refrain from dealing with the case in terms responsive to the relevance of the *Balint* line of cases. As it is, all that we got was some talk about "notice," citing puzzlingly inapplicable cases.[95] The opinion was further confused by the uncertainty whether "actual knowledge" of a duty to register is required or only "the probability of such knowledge." "Probable knowledge" as a standard for any given case seems in conflict with the normal standard of proof in criminal cases. Perhaps the Court meant to suggest a negligence standard: whether in the generality of

---

[92] 355 U.S. at 228.

[93] *Ibid.*

[94] "*Cf.* Shevlin-Carpenter Co. v. Minnesota, 218 U.S. 57; United States v. Balint, 258 U.S. 250; United States v. Dotterweich, 320 U.S. 277, 284." *Ibid.*

[95] Mullane v. Central Hanover Trust Co., 339 U.S. 306 (1950); Covey v. Town of Somers, 351 U.S. 141 (1956); Walker v. Hutchinson City, 352 U.S. 112 (1956). These cases all dealt with the inadequacy of notice by publication as a predicate for civil proceedings affecting property interests. The point made in all of them was that under the circumstances some more direct form of notice *in the pending suit* could have been given the persons whose property interests were affected by the proposed action. Miss Lambert, like any criminal defendant, had received that kind of notice.

cases a felon would reasonably be expected to know of the registration requirement. There might be considerable merit in such an approach, but the elliptical reference in the opinion hardly seems an adequate basis for extrapolation.

Given the flabbiness of the majority opinion, one wonders what purpose other than the purely rhetorical was served by the ringing quotation that capped it:[96] "A law which punished conduct which would not be blameworthy in the average member of the community would be too severe for that community to bear." The sentiment does the Court credit, but the opinion provides no very solid basis for assertion of that view in subsequent cases.

Mr. Justice Frankfurter, speaking for himself and for Justices Harlan and Whittaker,[97] dissented in an opinion that matched the majority's both in brevity and in obscurity. It started by blurring the distinction between *ignorantia facti* and *ignorantia legis*, seemingly treating *Balint* as if it stood for nothing more than the familiar proposition that ignorance of the law does not excuse.[98] Then came a polite nod in the direction of *mens rea* as an interpretative presumption, which appears to suggest that there may be circumstances under which the maxim *ignorantia legis* will not be applied.[99] Neither citation nor example was given. Having intimated that there might be a pea under some shell, never mind which one, the opinion then accused the Court of having looked under the wrong shell:[100]

> But what the Court here does is to draw a constitutional line between a State's requirement of doing and not doing. What

---

96 355 U.S. at 229. The quotation is from HOLMES, THE COMMON LAW 50 (1881).

97 Mr. Justice Burton noted his dissent "because he believes that, as applied to this appellant, the ordinance does not violate her constitutional rights." 355 U.S. at 230. This statement may perhaps be explained by a footnote in Mr. Justice Frankfurter's dissent: "This case does not involve a person who, convicted of a crime in another jurisdiction, must decide whether he had been convicted of a crime that 'would have been punishable as a felony' had it been committed in California. Appellant committed forgery in California, and was convicted under California law. Furthermore, she was convicted in Los Angeles itself, and there she resided for over seven years before the arrest leading to the present proceedings." *Id.* at 231.

98 *Id.* at 230.

99 "Considerations of hardship often lead courts, naturally enough, to attribute to a statute the requirement of a certain mental element—some consciousness of wrongdoing and knowledge of the law's command—as a matter of statutory construction." *Id.* at 231.

100 *Ibid.*

> is this but a return to Year Book distinctions between feasance and nonfeasance—a distinction that may have significance in the evolution of common-law notions of liability, but is inadmissible as a line between constitutionality and unconstitutionality.

It should be observed that the distinction that the Court drew, although weak enough, was not quite so simple-minded as the distinction that the dissent accused it of drawing. The Court had not spoken of omissions in general but of "the failure to act under circumstances that should [not] alert the doer to the consequences of his deed."[101] As already pointed out, this distinction is not an adequate one, since it leaves out of account the fact that acts as well as omissions may be engaged in under such circumstances. But one is entitled to ask whether a dissenting opinion adequately discharges its function when, having conceded that there may be a problem, it attacks an untenable solution without stopping to inquire whether some other solution might be tenable.

Then Mr. Justice Frankfurter produced a sentence that was doubtless intended to brand the intellectual irresponsibility of the majority opinion:[102] "If the generalization that underlies, and alone can justify, this decision were to be given its relevant scope, a whole volume of the United States Reports would be required to document in detail the legislation in this country that would fall or be impaired." To which one can only reply: "What generalization?" Having rejected the feasance-nonfeasance distinction, Mr. Justice Frankfurter can hardly mean that. What generalization, then, "alone can justify" the majority opinion? Ignorance of the law is always an excuse? Some less sweeping generalization? What is the least sweeping generalization that will justify the position taken in the majority opinion? How much legislation will be invalidated or brought into question by the application of such a generalization? These are questions that would have to be answered in an attempt to construct a rational doctrine of *mens rea* in constitutional terms. Since the dissenters were not prepared to go into these questions and thereby to vindicate the role of a dissenting opinion, they might have done better merely to note the fact of their disagreement.

In view of the unresolved complexities of the *Lambert* opinion,

---

101 *Id.* at 228.

102 *Id.* at 232.

it might well be thought that the Court took the wrong fork in the road in its search for the "easy" ground of disposition. The unnecessary breadth of the Los Angeles ordinance, viewed in the light of rational legislative purpose, might have afforded a sounder basis for decision if the Court was as unprepared as it seems to have been to get below the surface of the *mens rea* issue. It may also be suggested that the case was not a meet one for adjudication of the *mens rea* issue because of the unsettled background of California law.[103] Ironically, the ordinance was eventually held invalid in its entirety by the Supreme Court of California, not because of the *mens rea* deficiency, but because it was deemed to conflict with State legislation on the same subject.[104]

Perhaps too little time has gone by since the decision in *Lambert* for an assessment of its generative force to be possible. The indications presently available are not encouraging. In two cases[105] involving the validity of a federal statute[106] making it a crime for one convicted of a narcotics offense to leave the country without registering as a narcotics offender, the lower federal courts have rejected constitutional attacks based on *Lambert* in terms that give some weight to Mr. Justice Frankfurter's prediction that the case will turn out to be "a derelict on the waters of the law."[107] One ground of distinction, asserted in apparent seriousness, is that *Lambert* was concerned with omissions, while leaving the country with-

103 At the time *Lambert* was pending in the Supreme Court, the highest court of California had just handed down a series of decisions the cumulative effect of which was to strengthen the role of *mens rea* as an interpretative presumption. See note 150 *infra*. *Lambert* could have been remanded for consideration in the light of those decisions. *Cf.* Brief *supra* note 80, at p. 20 n.

104 Abbott v. City of Los Angeles, 53 Cal. 2d 674 (1960). In so holding, the court refused to deal with the question whether the Appellate Department had correctly construed the ordinance in *Lambert* as not including knowledge of a duty to register. *Id.* at 680–81. See also Lambert v. Municipal Court, 53 Cal. 2d 690 (1960), terminating, on the authority of *Abbott,* the City's attempt to retry Miss Lambert following the Supreme Court's decision.

105 Reyes v. United States, 258 F. 2d 774 (9th Cir. 1958); United States v. Juzwiak, 258 F. 2d 844 (2d Cir. 1958), *cert. den.* 359 U.S. 939 (Douglas, J., dissenting). *See also* Burks v. United States, 287 F. 2d 117, 125 (9th Cir. 1961) (failure to register and pay wagering tax).

106 18 U.S.C. § 1407 (1958).

107 355 U.S. at 232.

out registering is an affirmative act.[108] Another distinction offered is that *Lambert* left *Balint* untouched, and the federal statute is one falling within the category of public welfare offenses, because it deals with narcotics.[109] The contemptuous tone of the *Lambert* dissent may be partially responsible for the way in which the decision has been brushed aside, but the failure of the controlling opinion to provide a reasoned basis for its novel result is probably the main cause.[110]

The Court has not itself paid much attention to *Lambert.* In *Smith v. California,*[111] a Los Angeles ordinance subjecting a bookseller to criminal penalties for possession of obscene books was held unconstitutional because the bookseller's lack of awareness of the nature of the books had been held no defense by the State courts. *Lambert* got only a passing nod,[112] primary reliance being placed on *Wieman v. Updegraff*[113] and the notion that *mens rea* is important in free speech cases. At the 1960 Term, the membership clause of the Smith Act was upheld,[114] largely on the basis of the very strong *mens rea* construction placed on it, without even perfunctory recognition that something more than the protection of speech and association may be involved in the idea of *mens rea.*[115] And

---

108 "Here there was no mere nonfeasance . . . there was misfeasance. They crossed the border (ordinarily lawful) in an unlawful manner (without registering)." Reyes v. United States, 258 F. 2d at 784. *Cf.* the similar distinction attempted in *Juzwiak,* 258 F. 2d at 847. *But see* the separate opinion of Chief Judge Clark rejecting the distinction. *Id.* at 847.

109 258 F. 2d at 845, 847.

110 "Whether or not Mr. Justice Frankfurter is correct in his estimate of Lambert . . . does not here concern us. We hold the holding of the majority in Lambert inapplicable, both on its facts and its reasoning, to the statute involved in the instant cases." 258 F. 2d at 785.

111 361 U.S. 147 (1959). Readers of this Review are doubtless familiar with the penetrating discussion of the *Smith* case in Kalven, *The Metaphysics of the Law of Obscenity,* [1960] Supreme Court Review 1, 35–40.

112 It was cited in support of the Court's observation, quoted in the text at note 3 *supra,* that the legislative power to dispense with *mens rea* is not absolute, even in cases outside the "protected" area.

113 Note 62 *supra,* and accompanying text.

114 Scales v. United States, 367 U.S. 203 (1961).

115 Justices Frankfurter and Harlan, who dissented in *Lambert,* wrote separate concurrences in *Smith* placing their disapproval of the obscenity ordinance on dif-

Robinson v. California,[116] invalidating a California narcotics statute on closely related grounds, made no mention at all of *Lambert*.

If this first foray in the direction of a general doctrine of *mens rea* in constitutional law has been, as it seems, abortive, it does not follow that the problem has been settled. It may be relevant, therefore, to consider some of the issues that sooner or later will have to be faced.

III. The Future of Mens Rea

The difficulties in evolving an adequate theory of *mens rea* as a constitutional requisite rest in large part, although not entirely, upon the inadequate framework within which problems of the mental element in criminal offenses have traditionally been analyzed. Somehow the generative powers of the common law dried up in the criminal area, perhaps because of the premature rigidity forced upon the criminal law by the codification movement of the nineteenth century, perhaps also because the proliferation of criminal enactments tended to emphasize the disparity of rules at the expense of the unity of principles. Whatever the explanation, neither courts nor legislatures have exhibited any notable capacity for dealing with the extraordinarily difficult problems of the mental element. Unfortunately, their deficiencies have not been adequately exposed by legal scholarship, at least, not until quite recently. One searches the treatises in vain for any articulation of underlying principles or for the construction of any analytical framework that would serve either to explain or to criticize the development of the law. The reasons for this failure of scholarship are probably complex and, in any event, are not our present concern, although they would, properly explored, provide an important if dispiriting chapter in the history of Anglo-American legal scholarship.[117]

It is only in comparatively recent times that this analytic gap has begun to be filled, especially by the work of Glanville Wil-

---

ferent grounds. Mr. Justice Brennan, who was with the majority in *Lambert*, wrote for the Court in *Smith*. Mr. Justice Harlan delivered the majority opinion in *Scales*.

116 Robinson v. California, 370 U.S. 660, see note 144 *infra*.

117 For an excellent analysis of the deficiencies in criminal law scholarship, see Allen, *Book Review*, 27 U. Chi. L. Rev. 406 (1960).

liams[118] in England and of Jerome Hall[119] in this country. By far the most precise and useful set of constructs, however, has come out of the current work of the American Law Institute in its formulation of a Model Penal Code. The provisions of that Code with respect to the mental element in offenses and the accompanying comments of the Reporter constitute by far the best treatment we now have of the subject.[120] One of the basic contributions of this analytic framework is its recognition of the complexity of the concept of "criminal conduct" and of the concomitant necessity for distinguishing among the various components of such conduct, with respect not only to the conduct itself but to the mental elements accompanying it.[121]

It can be shown that criminal conduct involves, in varying proportions with respect to the various offenses, the conduct itself, *i.e.*, an act or omission, the accompanying circumstances, and the result. The important basic insight of the Code's framers is that the requisite mental element for a criminal offense must, in the interest of clear analysis, be faced separately with respect to each material element of the offense.[122] Thus, in a case of homicide, which involves bringing about a certain result, it is not enough to inquire whether the homicidal act was "intentional." It must also be asked whether the actor intended to bring about the homicidal result. The point has the simplicity of the obvious, yet inattention to it has been perhaps the major source of analytical difficulty in substantive criminal law. The paradoxical consequence of this insight is that when the traditional corpus of the criminal law is analyzed with it in mind, it becomes apparent that the allegedly pervasive principle of *mens rea* is not pervasive at all. To the contrary, the hard core of the criminal law is seen to be riddled with exceptions to the principle, if it be asserted in any meaningful sense. What might be called the unconscious abandonment of *mens rea* is a major embarrassment to any attempt to construct a constitutional doctrine of *mens rea*.

This difficulty is somewhat mitigated, however, by the other

118 See WILLIAMS, CRIMINAL LAW: THE GENERAL PART (1953).

119 See HALL, GENERAL PRINCIPLES OF CRIMINAL LAW, first published in 1947 and extensively revised in a second edition published in 1960.

120 A.L.I., *op. cit. supra* note 11, at §2.02.

121 *Id.* at 123.

122 *Ibid.*

major contribution of modern analysis: the differentiation of various modes of culpability. The mental elements in criminal offenses have traditionally been dealt with in terms of "intent," elaborated by such unilluminating qualifications as "specific intent," "general intent," "presumed intent," and the like. The framers of the Model Penal Code have swept away these categories and in their place articulated four modes of culpability: purpose, knowledge, recklessness, and negligence.[123] The first three of these represent a re-

---

123 The rationale of these categories is provided in the *Comments* to § 2.02, at 124–26: "2. . . .

"The purpose of articulating these distinctions in detail is, of course, to promote the clarity of definitions of specific crimes and to dispel the obscurity with which the culpability requirement is often treated when such concepts as 'general criminal intent,' '*mens rea*,' 'presumed intent,' 'malice,' 'wilfullness,' 'scienter' and the like must be employed. What Justice Jackson called 'the variety, disparity and confusion' of judicial definitions of 'the requisite but elusive mental element' in crime (*Morissette v. United States,* 342 U.S. 246, 252 [1952]) should, in so far as possible, be rationalized by the Code. . . .

"3. In defining the kinds of culpability, a narrow distinction is drawn between acting purposely and knowingly, one of the elements of ambiguity in legal usage of 'intent.' Knowledge that the requisite external circumstances exist is a common element in both conceptions. But action is not purposive with respect to the nature or the result of the actor's conduct unless it was his conscious object to perform an action of that nature or to cause such a result. The distinction is no doubt inconsequential for most purposes of liability; acting knowingly is ordinarily sufficient. But there are areas where the discrimination is required and is made under existing law, using the awkward concept of 'specific intent.' . . .

"The distinction also has utility in differentiating among grades of an offense for purposes of sentence, *e.g.* in the case of homicide.

"A broader discrimination is perceived between acting either purposely or knowingly and acting recklessly. As we use the term, recklessness involves conscious risk creation. It resembles acting knowingly in that a state of awareness is involved but the awareness is of risk, that is of probability rather than certainty; the matter is contingent from the actor's point of view. Whether the risk relates to the nature of the actor's conduct or to the existence of the requisite attendant circumstances or to the result that may ensue is immaterial: the concept is the same. The draft requires, however, that the risk thus consciously disregarded by the actor be 'substantial' and 'unjustifiable'; even substantial risks may be created without recklessness when the actor seeks to serve a proper purpose, as when a surgeon performs an operation which he knows is very likely to be fatal but reasonably thinks the patient has no other, safer chance. Accordingly, to aid the ultimate determination, the draft points expressly to the factors to be weighed in judgment: the nature and degree of the risk disregarded by the actor, the nature and purpose of his conduct and the circumstances known to him in acting. . . .

"The fourth kind of culpability is negligence. It is distinguished from acting purposely, knowingly or recklessly in that it does not involve a state of awareness. It is the case where the actor creates inadvertently a risk of which he ought to be

fined elaboration of the traditional *mens rea* notion: conscious awareness of the facts. They suggest that the idea of *mens rea* is at once more complex and more flexible than traditional analysis has made it out to be. The fourth mode, negligence, represents an extension of *mens rea* and arguably a departure from it.[124] When applied to the various material elements of an offense these modes of culpability afford a series of choices that obviates the false dichotomy of "intent" and "strict liability."

However appealing the prospect for using these refined constructs as a basis for proposing a constitutional theory of *mens rea*, it has to be recognized, as previously suggested, that existing criminal law has deviated substantially from the path. There are four categories that must be considered in determining how responsive the traditional common law has been to the notion of *mens rea*. These may be characterized as:

1. Basic offenses dispensing in whole or in part with *mens rea*.
2. Negligence as a mode of culpability.
3. The barrier of *ignorantia legis*.
4. Public welfare offenses.

A. BASIC OFFENSES

The usual examples are those that arise in the field of sexual offenses, notably "statutory rape" and bigamy. These are universally regarded, in their traditional manifestations, as examples of strict liability in the criminal law. They serve as a predicate for the assertion that might otherwise seem surprising, that there is no adequate operational distinction between offenses that dispense entirely with *mens rea* and offenses that dispense with *mens rea* only partially, or with respect to one material element of the offense. Indeed, there is no such thing as a "strict liability" offense except in terms of a partial rather than a complete discarding of *mens rea*, since there is always some element of any offense with respect to which a mental

---

aware, considering its nature and degree, the nature and the purpose of his conduct and the care that would be exercised by a reasonable person in his situation. Again, however, it is quite impossible to avoid tautological articulation of the final question. The tribunal must evaluate the actor's failure of perception and determine whether, under all the circumstances, it was serious enough to be condemned. . . ."

124 See note 134 *infra* and accompanying text.

element is attached. In both the statutory rape and bigamy situations, it is the exclusion of *mens rea* with respect to the "circumstance" element of the offense that results in the imposition of strict liability: in the case of statutory rape, the circumstance that the girl is under the age of consent; in the case of bigamy, the circumstance that one or both of the parties is not legally free to remarry. Although there is an encouraging trend of contrary decisions in the bigamy field,[125] it probably remains the majority rule in this country that a good faith belief that one is legally free to remarry is not a defense to a charge of bigamy.[126] Indeed, this view apparently has constitutional sanction.[127] In the area of statutory rape, the strength of the traditional strict liability view has not been appreciably diminished.[128]

These examples are familiar ones. It might perhaps be thought that they represent rather unusual exceptions to a generally pervasive principle of applicability of *mens rea*. Actually, the contrary is true. Two conspicuous examples arise in the area of homicide. Both the felony-murder and the misdemeanor-manslaughter rules, insofar as they have independent force and are not simply instances of the more general operation of homicide doctrines, reflect the imposition of strict liability as to the homicidal result. Thus, the felony-murder rule has independent operation only in those aberrational cases where the defendant, although adverting to his felonious conduct and possibly to some other ulterior risk of harm, does not

---

125 See, *e.g.*, Long v. State, 5 Ter. 262 (Del. 1949); People v. Vogel, 46 Cal. 2d 798 (1956).

126 PERKINS 835–40.

127 Williams v. North Carolina, 325 U.S. 226, 238: "The legitimate finding of the North Carolina Supreme Court that the petitioners were not in truth domiciled in Nevada was not a contingency against which the petitioners were protected by anything in the Constitution of the United States. . . . The objection that punishment of a person for an act as a crime when ignorant of the facts making it so, involves a denial of due process of law has more than once been overruled. In vindicating its public policy and particularly one so important as that bearing upon the integrity of family life, a State in punishing particular acts may provide that 'he who shall do them shall do them at his peril and will not be heard to plead in defense good faith or ignorance.' *United States v. Balint*, 258 U.S. 250, 252. . . . Mistaken notions about one's legal rights are not sufficient to bar prosecution for crime."

128 PERKINS 127.

advert to the risk of death and is not negligent in failing to do so. The same is true with respect to the misdemeanor-manslaughter doctrine. If a robber is automatically to be held for the death of an accomplice who is shot by their intended victim,[129] or if one commits a battery that leads to the unforeseen and reasonably unforeseeable result of the victim's death,[130] liability for the homicide rests upon the absence of *mens rea* as to the result.

The standard rejoinder to the argument that strict liability is being imposed in such a situation is that habitually given in the sex-offense cases. It comes down to the assertion that since the underlying conduct is "wrongful" the actor must take all the consequences of that conduct whether or not he foresaw or desired them.[131] But it begs the question to assert that one who has intercourse with an underaged girl, even though he is ignorant of her age, is to be held for statutory rape because his underlying conduct is "wrongful." The question is whether he should be held for an offense to whose elements he did not advert as well as for an offense to whose elements he did advert. The fact that various limitations have been worked out to prevent some of the most absurd consequences of rigid adherence to this "at peril"[132] notion serves only to underline that the notion involves the imposition of strict liability in the only sense in which that term has meaning.

The point is significant as one illustration of how frequent is the absence of *mens rea* in our received criminal law, a point that surely has some relevance to the question whether *mens rea* is so fundamental a conception, so essential to "ordered liberty," that it must be protected by force of the Due Process Clause.

---

129 *E.g.*, People v. Harrison, 176 Cal. App. 2d 330 (1959). Compare the line of Pennsylvania decisions culminating in Commonwealth v. Redline, 391 Pa. 486 (1958). The character of the felony-murder rule as a rejection of *mens rea* is well analyzed in Morris, *The Felon's Responsibility for the Lethal Acts of Others*, 105 U. Pa. L. Rev. 50 (1956).

130 *E.g.*, State v. Frazier, 339 Mo. 966 (1936).

131 "This seems to be at variance with the familiar 'reasonable mistake of fact' doctrine, but it is a recognized exception due to the fact that what was done would have been unlawful and highly immoral even under the facts as the offender supposed them to be." Perkins 127.

132 See the discussion of limitations on the felony-murder rule in A.L.I. Model Penal Code, Tent. Draft. No. 9, 37 (1959).

B. NEGLIGENCE

If a man purposely or recklessly brings about a forbidden harm, we have no hesitation in saying that he had the requisite *mens rea* with respect to his conduct. But if he negligently brings about the forbidden harm, a different problem is presented. Negligence is not readily transformable into a state of mind. It is, by hypothesis, the absence of a state of mind. Negligence is, in short, an extension rather than an example of the idea of *mens rea* in the traditional sense.[133]

There are those who argue that negligence as a mode of culpability has no place in the criminal law, because the threat of punishment for causing harms inadvertently must be either inefficacious or unjust or both.[134] Whatever the merits of this philosophic position, it is plain that negligence has a very strong foothold in the criminal law. It finds its most explicit formulation in the statutes

---

[133] This is the view taken by most of the leading writers on the subject, including Glanville Williams, Jerome Hall, and the framers of the Model Penal Code. One writer, concerned to demonstrate the prevalence of *mens rea* at common law, has argued that negligence is "*mens rea* . . . of an omissive nature." Mueller, *On Common Law Mens Rea*, 42 MINN. L. REV. 1043, 1063–64 (1958). It is presumably less important to settle that issue, conceived semantically or even historically, than it is to determine whether the ideas that give vitality to the concept of *mens rea* are consistent with the use of negligence as a mode of culpability. See text at notes 134–37 *infra*.

[134] WILLIAMS, 98–100; HALL, 135–41. *But see* A.L.I., *op. cit. supra* note 11, at 126–27: "Of the four kinds of culpability defined, there is, of course, least to be said for treating negligence as a sufficient basis for imposing criminal liability. Since the actor is inadvertent by hypothesis, it has been argued that the threat of punishment for negligence must pass him by, because he does not realize that it is addressed to him. [Quoting WILLIAMS.] So too it has been urged that education or corrective treatment not punishment is the proper social method for dealing with persons with inadequate awareness, since what is implied is not a moral defect. [Citing HALL.] We think, however, that this is to over-simplify the issue. Knowledge that conviction and sentence, not to speak of punishment, may follow conduct that inadvertently creates improper risk supplies men with an additional motive to take care before acting, to use their faculties and draw on their experience in gauging the potentialities of contemplated conduct. To some extent, at least, this motive may promote awareness and thus be effective as a measure of control. Certainly legislators act on this assumption in a host of situations and it seems to us dogmatic to assert that they are wholly wrong. Accordingly, we think that negligence, as here defined, cannot be wholly rejected as a ground of culpability which may suffice for purposes of penal law, though we agree that it should not be generally deemed sufficient in the definition of specific crimes, and that it often will be right to differentiate such conduct for the purposes of sentence. . . ."

penalizing negligent homicide in the driving of an automobile. But its hold on the criminal law is far more pervasive than that. Negligence suffices as a mode of culpability whenever the question asked with respect to the actor's perception is not whether he knew but whether he should have known. In the field of homicide, the difference between negligent inadvertence to the risk of death and conscious advertence to that risk is, very roughly speaking, the dividing line between manslaughter and murder. But beyond that, murder itself is sometimes treated as an offense that may be committed negligently, either by applying an external standard to the actor's perception of the risk[135] or by applying an external standard to his perception of the basis for some excuse, such as self-defense.[136] To the extent that we subject persons to liability for murder on the basis of an external standard of care, we are treating negligent conduct as being sufficient to establish liability. To the extent that negligence suffices as a mode of culpability in the criminal law, the force of the generalization with respect to *mens rea* in the traditional sense is considerably diminished. Beyond that, it has been suggested that negligence has closer affinities with strict liability than it has with those modes of culpability that reflect subjective awareness on the part of the actor.[137] There are important and, for me, decisive differences between a legislative determination that certain conduct is unacceptable, made in advance of such conduct, and a jury's determination after the fact that a particular instance of such conduct fell below a previously established community standard. Nonetheless, negligence and strict liability share reliance on an external standard that ignores the actual state of mind of the offender.

To these objections it may be replied that a finding of negligence does import blameworthiness, that it does require a jury to say with respect to the case before it that the actor deviated unjustifiably from generally accepted standards of conduct, and that it may serve the corrective function of promoting future awareness. So viewed, it seems plausible for the criminal law to employ an occa-

---

135 See Collings, *Negligent Murder*, 49 CALIF. L. REV. 254 (1961).

136 See, *e.g.*, People v. Manzo, 9 Cal. 2d 594 (1937).

137 See Wasserstrom, *Strict Liability in the Criminal Law*, 12 STAN. L. REV. 731, 741–45 (1960).

sion, although not as a matter of course, a negligence standard without being charged with having abandoned the substance of *mens rea.* To put it another way, it seems to me proper to view negligence as an extension of rather than a departure from the values symbolized by the *mens rea* concept.

C. IGNORANTIA LEGIS

The principle that ignorance of the law is no excuse is deeply imbedded in our criminal law.[138] If the criminal law faithfully reflected prevalent community standards of minimally acceptable conduct, there would be no difficulty in reconciling the principle *ignorantia legis* with the requirements of *mens rea.* The proliferation of minor sumptuary and regulatory offenses, however, many of them penalizing conduct under circumstances where the fact of illegality can scarcely be known to a first offender, creates a sharp problem.[139] This in effect was the problem of the *Lambert* case, although it is a far more general one than is suggested by the language of the majority opinion. Sometimes a legislature specifies that awareness of the law's requirement is a necessary ingredient of guilt.[140] More often it does not. Courts rarely remedy the deficiency by fashioning a doctrine that bridges the gulf between innocent and guilty conduct in contravention of an esoteric legal proscription.[141]

It has been suggested by the framers of the Model Penal Code that a limited defense should be available to persons accused of crime if they can show a good faith belief that their conduct does not legally constitute an offense, owing to lack of publication or reasonable availability of the enactment.[142] It is not entirely clear how broad this defense is meant to be. I read it as establishing a

---

[138] See PERKINS 807 *et seq.*, for a brief account of the conventional view.

[139] The range of problems is exhaustively treated in HALL, ch. 11. For a stimulating discussion of the *ignorantia legis* dilemma, see Hart, *supra* note 42, at 417–22.

[140] *E.g.*, 18 U.S.C. § 835 (1958), subjecting to criminal penalties "[w]hoever knowingly violates" regulations of the Interstate Commerce Commission respecting the safe transportation of explosives and other dangerous articles. See Boyce Motor Lines v. United States, 342 U.S. 337 (1952).

[141] Perhaps the leading exception is the "corrupt motive" doctrine in the law of conspiracy, see People v. Powell, 63 N.Y. 88 (1875), which probably represents a judicial attempt to create a special *mens rea* requirement for that offense.

[142] A.L.I., *op. cit. supra* note 11, at § 2.04(3), and Comments, at 138–39.

negligence standard for the defense of ignorance or mistake of law. As so read, the proposal goes a long way toward resolving the *ignorantia legis* paradox. If an actor is by hypothesis unblameworthy in failing to know that his conduct violates a legal norm (a condition that will ordinarily obtain only if either he or the enactment is a stranger to prevailing standards in the relevant community), then criminal punishment is objectionable for precisely the same reasons as obtain in respect to strict liability. Adjustments in the burden of proof can meet whatever substance there may be in the argument that allowing a defense of *ignorantia legis* would subvert the practical enforcement of the law.

Of course, all of this lies in the future. It is plain that present law does not go so far. To the extent that it does not, the *ignorantia legis* paradox remains inconsistent with the asserted universality of *mens rea*. *Lambert* could have contributed to a resolution of the paradox but did not.

D. PUBLIC WELFARE OFFENSES

Ever since Sayre gave the phrase currency,[143] this category of offenses has been treated by commentators as the main "exception" to the principle of *mens rea* and by courts as a convenient pigeonhole for any crime construed to dispense with *mens rea*. Perhaps the principal significance of the public welfare offenses lies in their open flouting of *mens rea*, as opposed to the rather more covert erosions that have gone on in the main body of the criminal law. Despite the enormous body of decisional law that affirms dispensing with the mental element in violations of food and drug regulations, liquor regulations, traffic rules, and the like, there is a conspicuous lack of authority explicitly considering and avowing the propriety of distinctively "criminal" sanctions as applied to minor infractions. On the contrary, these offenses have been treated as something different from traditional criminal law, as a kind of hybrid category to which the odium and hence the safeguards of the criminal process do not attach. The primary departure from this generalization is *Balint* and its progeny in federal criminal law. However limited in application the departure from *mens rea* may be in this category of offenses, it cannot be doubted that its recog-

143 Sayre, *supra* note 89.

nition as an operational concept has been a powerful brake on the development of a general theory of *mens rea* in the criminal law.

E. SUMMARY

The departures from *mens rea* are a good deal more widespread than they are usually thought to be. It is a noteworthy feature of these departures that for the most part they are judicially created. Legislatures are open to severe criticism for their undiscriminating resort to the criminal sanction. But they have rarely given a clear direction to the judiciary to impose the stigma of a criminal conviction on persons who are unaware of the factual circumstances that make their conduct potentially criminal or upon persons who are, without fault on their part, unaware of the existence of a legislative norm affecting their conduct. The onus for the erosion of *mens rea* rests on the courts in their wooden interpretation of criminal statutes. It remains to inquire whether we are entitled to look to courts or to legislatures, or to both, for an adequate elaboration of *mens rea* in the criminal law. And, to return to the starting point of this inquiry, what role in this process of elaboration should be expected of the Supreme Court, especially in the exercise of its unique powers to invalidate both State and federal legislation deemed incompatible with the Constitution?

IV. Conclusion

The concept of *mens rea* poses formidable difficulties of articulation and equally formidable inconveniences in application. Small wonder, then, that it has been subjected to such vicissitudes. But however great the difficulties, the effort needs to be made, because what underlies the concept is the insight that there is something distinctive about the criminal sanction and that its distinctive character must be recognized, not only in the procedures by which it is invoked and applied, but also in the substance of what is invoked and applied.[144] Few today cavil at strict liability in tort. *Ives*

---

[144] Robinson v. California, 370 U.S. 660 (1962), invalidated a California statute making it a crime to be addicted to the use of narcotics. The decision raises far more questions than it answers. If its premise, that the legislature may not make it a "crime" to be "sick" is to be taken literally, the demise of the criminal law may be at hand. If, as seems more probable, the Court simply struck down an awkward phrase in a statute while leaving the substance of the statutory scheme intact, the

v. South Buffalo Railway[145] is dead and gone. But the transfer of money from one pocket to another is one thing, and the judgment of community condemnation expressed in a criminal conviction is quite another. So long as that sanction is resorted to, moral blameworthiness should be the indispensable condition precedent to its application.[146] Whether it is a sufficient condition is a question that needs more thought,[147] but that it is a necessary condition cannot be seriously doubted.

The recognition of its prime importance is a conspicuous feature of the re-examination of the substantive criminal law that is coming to assume major proportions. No doubt, well-considered legislative formulations will do much to rescue *mens rea* from its desuetude.[148]

---

decision may not be of much moment. Whatever its rationale, the constitutional peg on which the result is hung, the ban against cruel and unusual punishments, hardly seems apposite and is probably to be explained, as Mr. Justice White explained it, as reflecting the Court's "allergy to substantive due process." *Id.* at 689.

When all this is said, however, *Robinson* remains an intriguing instance of the Court's increased concern about the substance of the criminal law. It may turn out to be, in the words of Mr. Justice Frankfurter's anathema upon *Lambert*, "a derelict on the waters of the law." Perhaps so. But a body of water that is liberally strewn with navigational hazards is not the same calm, untroubled sea that it was in the good old days of *Balint* and *Dotterweich*.

145 201 N.Y. 271 (1911) (invalidating an early workmen's compensation statute on the ground that strict liability contravenes due process). *Cf.* New York Central R. Co. v. White, 243 U.S. 188 (1917).

146 See A.L.I., *op. cit. supra* note 11, at § 2.05 and Comments, p. 140: "This section makes a frontal attack on absolute or strict liability in penal law, whenever the offense carries a possibility of sentence of imprisonment....

"... The liabilities involved are indefensible in principle, unless reduced to terms that insulate conviction from the type of moral condemnation that is and ought to be implicit when a sentence of imprisonment may be imposed. In the absence of minimal culpability, the law has neither a deterrent nor corrective nor an incapacitative function to perform.

"It has been argued, and the argument undoubtedly will be repeated, that absolute liability is necessary for enforcement in a number of the areas where it obtains. But if practical enforcement can not undertake to litigate the culpability of alleged deviation from legal requirements, we do not see how the enforcers rightly can demand the use of penal sanctions for the purpose. Crime does and should mean condemnation and no court should have to pass that judgment unless it can declare that the defendant's act was wrong. This is too fundamental to be compromised...."

147 *Cf.* the debate occasioned by Lord Devlin's Maccabean Lecture, The Enforcement of Morals (1959).

148 See, *e.g.*, Ill. Crim. Code art. 4 (1961).

But the legislative process is glacially slow. Beyond that, it does not free courts from the obligation to think about the law's development in terms of its ultimate purposes. There is encouraging evidence that this kind of constructive thought is under way in State courts, where closer attention is being paid to the centrality of *mens rea* than was formerly the case. This development has its most spectacular manifestation in decisions invalidating legislation construed to dispense with *mens rea*.[149] But a more important, more constructive line of decision has made substantial inroads on the dogma that legislatures mean to dispense with *mens rea* by failing explicitly to provide for it.[150]

The Supreme Court made a major contribution to establishing an interpretative presumption that *mens rea* is the rule rather than the exception by its decision in *Morissette*. The contribution would have been more substantial if a misplaced deference to *stare decisis* had not impeded fresh consideration of the *Balint* doctrine in its interpretative aspect.[151] That shortcoming was compounded in *Lambert*. The basic trouble with *Balint* is that it focuses on the nature of the activity being regulated rather than on the nature of the sanction being used to effect that regulation. The basic trouble with *Lambert* is that it left *Balint* standing. Until the anomaly there-

---

[149] See, *e.g.*, People v. Estreich, 75 N.Y.S. 2d 267 (1947); State v. Prince, 52 N.M. 15 (1948); State v. Williams, 94 Ohio App. 249 (1952); People v. Nangapareet, 210 N.Y.S. 2d 446 (1960).

[150] A group of California cases decided within a short time of each other is illustrative. People v. Winston, 46 Cal. 2d 151 (1956) (narcotics); People v. Vogel, 46 Cal. 2d 798 (1956) (bigamy); People v. Stuart, 47 Cal. 2d 167 (1956) (manslaughter).

[151] See, *e.g.*, the restrictive interpretation placed on *Morissette* by Chief Judge Magruder, concurring, in St. Johnsbury Trucking Co. v. United States, 220 F. 2d 393, 397, 398 (1st Cir. 1955). Other lower court decisions restricting *Morissette* include Razete v. United States, 199 F. 2d 44 (6th Cir. 1952); United States v. Hart Motor Express, 160 F. Supp. 886 (D. Minn. 1958).

On the other hand, a number of post-*Morissette* decisions have demonstrated its affirmative impact by reversing criminal convictions for erroneous dispensation with *mens rea*. See, *e.g.*, Rent v. United States, 209 F. 2d 893 (5th Cir. 1954); Smith v. United States, 230 F. 2d 935 (6th Cir. 1956); United States v. Nedley, 255 F. 2d 350 (3rd Cir. 1958); Levine v. United States, 261 F. 2d 747 (D.C. Cir. 1958); Mullen v. United States, 263 F. 2d 275 (D.C. Cir. 1958). See also Gordon v. United States, 203 F. 2d 248 (10th Cir. 1953), *rev'd per curiam on confession of error*, 347 U.S. 909 (1954).

by created is recognized and corrected, the federal courts will not have available a rational and understandable set of criteria for applying the interpretative presumption that a judgment of criminality requires a showing of blameworthiness.

Perhaps one day the Supreme Court will recognize that it is precisely wrong to adhere to the conclusion reached in *Balint* "for the circumstances to which it was there applied." That recognition will have to be accompanied by some standard for deciding when *mens rea* ought to be read into criminal statutes, unless by then the millennium has arrived when legislatures take it upon themselves to think through the use of the criminal sanction and to make their rationales articulate. If the *Balint* doctrine has any basis in reason at all, it resides in the perception that the criminal sanction is used for a very wide range of social purposes and that not everything the legislature chooses to treat as "criminal" needs to be dealt with on the same basis. If we avoid the error of supposing that the criminal sanction is differentiated according to the nature of the conduct proscribed—the fallacy of the "public welfare offense"—we need also to avoid the error of supposing that everything the legislature treats as "criminal" should require proof of *mens rea.* The fact is that the processes of criminal justice are used, or misused, for purposes that have no odor of criminality except that which resides in the use of the word itself. Traffic offenses are perhaps the most extreme example. It makes trivial the concept of criminality to apply it to such minor infractions of the laws.

The relevant distinctions may perhaps be found in the consequences of a "criminal conviction." While we have few clues about the indirect consequences of a judgment formally denominated "criminal" with respect to relatively minor infractions, the direct consequence is easily assessable. The combination of stigma and loss of liberty involved in a conditional or absolute sentence of imprisonment sets that sanction apart from anything else the law imposes. Here at the very least the line should be drawn. No one should be sentenced to imprisonment or its equivalent without being afforded the opportunity to litigate the issue of *mens rea* or, to use the term adopted by the framers of the Model Penal Code, culpability.[152] No criminal statute should be construed as depriving such a defendant of that opportunity in the absence of the plainest kind of indication that the legislature meant to do so. In the field of federal criminal law, it seems likely that an adequately formulated interpretative presumption should solve the problem. *Morissette* should be generalized and the view taken that no criminal statute should be construed to dispense with blameworthiness (whether through traditional *mens rea* or through its extension to include negligence) merely because it does not contain language explicitly imposing that requirement. Rather *mens rea* or its equivalent should be required unless a legislative purpose to dispense with it plainly appears. By taking that step, the Supreme Court can make a major contribution without committing itself to any sharp departures from existing law.

On the State level, the problem is a more difficult one. State criminal convictions come to the Supreme Court with questions of State law, including the construction of statutes, already determined. How authoritatively they have been determined is another matter, particularly when the highest State court in which an appeal could have been heard is not the highest State court. The Court is not without methods of getting State courts to take another look at their own statutes.[153] It may even be that the Supreme Court can teach the State courts to swim without getting into the water itself.

Yet the constitutional question remains. Faced with the hard case that inescapably poses the issue, is there any basis for a constitutional doctrine of *mens rea?* Given the erosion of *mens rea* in traditional criminal law it takes some temerity to assert that due process now requires a constitutional doctrine of *mens rea* to be fashioned. But the suggestion that it does is less temerarious than it would be if these questions had been given due consideration by the courts. As we have seen, they have not. And the Supreme Court itself bears

---

152 That is the line drawn by the framers of the Model Penal Code. See A.L.I., *op. cit. supra* note 11, at § 2.05 and accompanying Comments; note 146 *supra*. *Cf.* the construction of the term "infamous crime," U.S. CONST. AMEND. V, in United States v. Moreland, 258 U.S. 433 (1922).

153 See, *e.g.*, Musser v. Utah, 333 U.S. 95 (1948); State v. Musser, 118 Utah 537 (1950).

prime responsibility for having sanctioned the erosion of *mens rea* in what can be restrainedly described as an intellectually unsatisfying way. Strict liability in the criminal law is irrational, in the substantive due process sense of that word.[154] *Mens rea* as extended to include negligence as a mode of culpability ought to find its way into constitutional doctrine.

[154] *But see* Robinson v. California, 370 U.S. 660 (1962), note 144 *supra*. It may be aesthetically offensive to some when the Court uses the Eighth Amendment to strike down a statute it considers irrational. Still, we should be free enough of the shibboleths of the 1930's to be encouraged by the Supreme Court's willingness to inquire into the rationality of criminal statutes.

DALLIN H. OAKS

THE "ORIGINAL" WRIT OF HABEAS CORPUS IN THE SUPREME COURT

A significant proportion of the United States Supreme Court's business in recent years has been concerned with motions for leave to file a petition for the "original" writ of habeas corpus.[1] Some 2,000 such motions have been filed with the Court during the past three decades,[2] an astonishing total in the light of the fact that relief has been denied in every instance. Indeed, it seems that not since 1925

Dallin H. Oaks is Associate Dean of the Law School and Associate Professor of Law, The University of Chicago.

[1] The "Great Writ," the writ of habeas corpus ad subjiciendum, is among the most precious safeguards of personal liberty. See, *e.g.*, Smith v. Bennett, 365 U.S. 708, 712–14 (1961). This article is concerned with issues raised when the petitioner seeks to obtain that writ directly from the United States Supreme Court. For excellent studies of problems incident to issuance of that writ by the federal district courts, consult Reitz, *Federal Habeas Corpus: Postconviction Remedy for State Prisoners*, 108 U. PA. L. REV. 461 (1960); Reitz, *Federal Habeas Corpus: Impact of an Abortive State Proceeding*, 74 HARV. L. REV. 1315 (1961).

Although the papers submitted to the Court are seldom so styled, the practice for some years has been to docket them as "motions for leave to file a petition for the writ of habeas corpus." In the interest of brevity this article will forgo use of the formal title and use the terms "motion" and "petition" interchangeably, unless the context otherwise indicates.

[2] These figures are taken from the table in the Appendix *infra*, at pp. 209–11.

has anyone succeeded in obtaining discharge directly from the Supreme Court.[3] The continued popularity of this motion with the untutored petitioners (counsel rarely appear on the motions)[4] would seem to stem from the popular reverence for the "Great Writ," from the public image of the Supreme Court as the surest guardian of liberty, and from a misconception of the role that the Court is competent to play. As a result the Court is faced with a problem of no mean proportions. There is evidence that many uninformed petitioners have pursued this unobtainable remedy to the exclusion or prejudice of more feasible alternatives. Furthermore, the burden imposed on the Court in disposing of such petitions is significant[5] and, perhaps, unnecessary. In recent Terms the Court has made some effort to mitigate the prejudice sometimes suffered by such petitioners and, in doing so, has significantly altered the pattern of its disposition of such petitions, without in any way decreasing their quantity. In light of the hardship imposed on the petitioners as well as the Court, an examination of the controlling principles seems appropriate.

I. Constitutional Limitations—Original and Appellate Jurisdiction

A. SOME BASIC PRINCIPLES OF FEDERAL JURISDICTION

There are a few basic postulates of federal jurisdiction that underlie consideration of the Court's power to issue the Great Writ.

First. Federal courts have no "inherent" or "common-law" jurisdiction to issue the writ of habeas corpus. Unless the case is one falling within the range of judicial power granted in Article III, § 2 of the Constitution,[6] the Supreme Court is powerless to award the writ. Thus, when it was argued in *Ex parte Bollman*[7] that the Su-

---

[3] Ex parte Grossman, 267 U.S. 87 (1925).

[4] Only 39 of the 2,000 motions disposed of since 1929 bore the names of counsel. See the table in the Appendix *infra.*

[5] Harlan, *Manning the Dikes,* 13 Record 541, 548 (1958).

[6] The constitutional powers relating to cases arising under the Constitution and laws of the United States are sufficient to provide jurisdiction for most habeas corpus cases. Although less frequently invoked, other sources of Article III power, such as the diversity jurisdiction and the jurisdiction incident to suits by a State against citizens of another State, text *infra,* at note 23, may also be feasible.

[7] 4 Cranch 75, 79–82 (1807).

preme Court, like the superior courts of record in England, was invested by the common law with jurisdiction to issue the writ, Chief Justice Marshall rejected the argument: "[F]or the meaning of the term *habeas corpus*, resort may unquestionably be had to the common law; but the power to award the writ by any of the courts of the United States, must be given by written law."[8] Although the Article III powers and the applicable statutes on habeas corpus are so comprehensive that this jurisdictional limitation is not often tested, there is sufficient authority to demonstrate the continued vitality of the principle.[9]

Second. The so-called "original writ of habeas corpus"[10] is not "original" in the sense that it issues in the exercise of the Court's original jurisdiction. With a few exceptions to be considered later, the Supreme Court can only issue the writ under its appellate jurisdiction.[11] Any legislation purporting to enlarge the Supreme Court's original jurisdiction to issue a writ of habeas corpus beyond those cases specified in Article III, § 2 would, of course, be unconstitutional.[12]

Third. The Supreme Court's appellate jurisdiction is limited to that which Congress has expressly conferred.[13] The Court has no implied constitutional or common-law supervisory powers over the decisions of inferior courts.[14]

The provision in Article II, § 9 of the Constitution that the right

---

8 *Id.* at 93–94.

9 United States v. Hudson, 7 Cranch 32 (1812); In re Burrus, 136 U.S. 586 (1890); Carbo v. United States, 364 U.S. 611, 614 (1961). *But see* Eisentrager v. Forrestal, 174 F. 2d 961 (D.C. Cir. 1949), *rev'd on other grounds sub nom.* Johnson v. Eisentrager, 339 U.S. 763 (1950). Justices Black, Douglas, and Burton, dissenting, approved the court of appeals' reasoning.

10 See, *e.g.*, Mooney v. Holohan, 294 U.S. 103, 109 (1935); Vinson, *Work of the Federal Courts*, 69 S.Ct. v, vii (1949).

11 U.S. Const. Art. III, § 2, cl. 2.

12 Marbury v. Madison, 1 Cranch 137 (1803); Ex parte Bollman, 4 Cranch 75 (1807).

13 Durousseau v. United States, 6 Cranch 307, 317–18 (1810); United States v. More, 3 Cranch 159, 173 (1805); 2 Story, Constitution of the United States § 1773 (3d ed. 1858).

It has been suggested that if Congress had not defined the limits of the Court's appellate jurisdiction, it would have possessed all of the jurisdiction it could exercise under the Constitution. Durousseau v. United States, *supra*, at 313.

14 Clark v. Bazadone, 1 Cranch 212 (1803).

to habeas corpus shall not be suspended has been urged in opposition to some of the above principles. Thus, critics of a limited federal jurisdiction cite it as evidence that the federal courts were meant to have a general common-law jurisdiction.[15] Limited to a claim of common-law jurisdiction in habeas corpus, the argument has more force, for the clause does stand as evidence that the Framers contemplated the existence of the privilege whose suspension they forbade. Alternatively, one might concede that the federal courts are limited to the powers conferred by Article III but use the clause to argue that insofar as the Article III powers relate to habeas corpus they are self-executing. On this approach, Congress has no more power to withhold the privilege than it has to suspend it, at least where Congress has established courts constitutionally capable of exercising the power.[16] For obvious reasons there appear to be no direct holdings on this question, although a dictum by Marshall suggests that had Congress not acted the great privilege would never have come into existence.[17] Whether Congress could withdraw the habeas corpus jurisdiction altogether, after it was once granted, is a question not yet resolved by judicial authority.[18]

B. ORIGINAL JURISDICTION

In *Marbury v. Madison*,[19] the Court held that its original jurisdiction was limited to the cases specified in Article III, §2, cl. 2 of the Constitution: "Cases affecting Ambassadors, other public Ministers and Consuls, and those in which a State shall be a Party. . . ." Research has disclosed only one instance where the first half of this clause has been invoked in support of an application to the Supreme Court for habeas corpus.[20] In that case the petition was summarily

---

15 *E.g.*, 1 CROSSKEY, POLITICS AND THE CONSTITUTION 625 (1953); Eisentrager v. Forrestal, *supra* note 9.

16 See Eisentrager v. Forrestal, *supra* note 9.

17 Ex parte Bollman, 4 Cranch 75, 95 (1807).

18 See HART & WECHSLER, FEDERAL COURTS AND THE FEDERAL SYSTEM 335–39 (1953) (hereafter HART & WECHSLER).

19 1 Cranch 137 (1803).

20 Ex parte Fiala, 319 U.S. 733 (1943). In this case, as in other cases where the information set forth does not appear in the orders of the Court, the facts have been

denied "for the want of original jurisdiction," apparently in reliance upon the Solicitor General's representation that the petitioner was no longer performing the duties of vice-consul and was not accredited with the State Department as a consular officer.

The remaining ground of original jurisdiction for habeas corpus, cases "in which a State shall be a party," has lain fallow. Only last Term, however, the Court took occasion to remind the bar that this facet of its original jurisdiction was a viable instrument for resolving conflicting claims to personal property.[21] It seems possible that the Court would be equally willing, in an appropriate case, to exercise this jurisdiction in protection of personal liberty.

There is theoretical justification for making a State a party to an original habeas corpus proceeding. The historical characterization of the writ as a means by which the sovereign inquired into the cause of detention of any of its subjects[22] suggests aligning the State as party plaintiff,[23] a nominal position it in fact occupies under the habeas corpus practice of many of our States.[24] This theory was utilized in *Ex parte Virginia*,[25] which appears to be the only habeas corpus case that sought to invoke the Court's original jurisdiction on the basis of a State being a party. This was an attempt by a State to secure the release of one of its judges who was detained in the

---

obtained by an examination of the original papers on file in the Office of the Clerk, United States Supreme Court.

If this infrequently asserted clause, see HART & WECHSLER 260–61, has served as the basis for other petitions for habeas corpus, the attempts are veiled by the inscrutability of the Court's memorandum orders. Such cases have arisen in other courts. *E.g.*, Emmett v. Lomakin, 84 N.Y.S. 2d 562 (S.Ct. N.Y. Co. 1948); Ex parte Cabrera, 4 Fed. Case 964 (No. 2278) (C.C. Pa. 1805).

21 Western Union Tel. Co. v. Pennsylvania, 368 U.S. 71, 77 (1961). (Rival States claiming funds subject to escheat "can invoke our original jurisdiction." Neither party had ventured this suggestion.)

22 See Crowley's Case, [1818] 2 Swan. Ch. 1, 50; 3 BL. COMM. *131; HALE, HISTORY OF THE COMMON LAW 193 (4th ed. 1779); 1 CHITTY, CRIMINAL LAW 97 (1819); Re Barry, reported in 136 U.S. 597 (C.C. S.D. N.Y. 1844).

23 The possibility of considering the State a defendant may be precluded by the Eleventh Amendment or by the doctrine of sovereign immunity, bolstered by the practice of naming the individual custodian as defendant.

24 See, *e.g.*, Pennsylvania ex rel. Herman v. Claudy, 350 U.S. 116 (1956); United States v. Hamilton, 3 Dall. 17 (1795) (Supreme Court's first habeas corpus case).

25 100 U.S. 339 (1880). See also the discussion of Mahon v. Justice, 127 U.S. 700 (1888), *infra* note 30.

State by a federal marshal under a bench warrant issued on an indictment in federal court. Rejecting this basis of original jurisdiction, the Court simply declared that "it is not readily perceived how the fact that a State applies for the writ to be directed to one of her own citizens can make a case for our original jurisdiction."[26] This passage implies that the Court was without original jurisdiction because the defendant was a citizen of the plaintiff State,[27] not because the State could not invoke the original jurisdiction as a party plaintiff in a habeas corpus case.[28]

If a case were to arise on a petition by a State[29] on the relation of one of its citizens who was incarcerated by another State,[30] the Court would probably disclaim jurisdiction on the ground that the State was only a formal party. There is no original jurisdiction "where it appears that the suit brought in the name of the State is in reality for the benefit of particular individuals."[31] If the prisoner

---

26 100 U.S. at 341.

27 *Cf.* Texas v. I. C. C., 258 U.S. 158, 164 (1922). Since both *Texas v. I. C. C.* and *Ex parte Virginia* were cases arising under the Constitution or laws of the United States, and since the Supreme Court has original jurisdiction of cases "in which a State shall be a Party," Art. III, § 2, cl. 2, the jurisdictional defect is not readily apparent. The rulings apparently rely on the language of clause 1, which confers judicial power in controversies "between a State and Citizens of another State." It has been suggested in explanation of *Texas v. I. C. C.* that the original jurisdiction authorized in clause 2 extends only to those cases which clause 1 describes in terms of parties rather than subject matter. HART & WECHSLER 226; see California v. Southern Pacific Co., 157 U.S. 229, 257–58 (1895).

28 It is well settled that one person can apply for habeas corpus on behalf of another in whom he has some interest. CHURCH, WRIT OF HABEAS CORPUS §89 (1893).

29 For purposes of the original jurisdiction, a suit by a governor on behalf of his State is equivalent to a suit by the State. Kentucky v. Dennison, 24 How. 66, 97–98 (1861).

30 *Cf.* Mahon v. Justice, 127 U.S. 700 (1888), where the governor of West Virginia, on behalf of his State, sought a writ of habeas corpus in a lower federal court for the release of a West Virginia resident who had been abducted from that State and was incarcerated by respondent, a Kentucky jailer. The writ was denied upon the Court's holding that there was no statutory warrant for use of the writ inasmuch as no constitutional or statutory right was violated. In dissent, Justices Bradley and Harlan argued (without contradiction in the majority opinion) that the State was a proper party to apply for the writ and that "perhaps the writ might have been sued out of this court, as the controversy had come to be a controversy between the States. . . ." *Id.* at 717. And see Kentucky v. Dennison, 24 How. 66 (1861).

31 Georgia v. Pennsylvania R. Co., 324 U.S. 439, 446 (1945); Massachusetts v. Missouri, 308 U.S. 1, 17 (1939); Oklahoma v. Cook, 304 U.S. 387, 394 (1938).

were an officer of the plaintiff State, as in *Ex parte Virginia*, the State interest might be sufficient to sustain the original jurisdiction. There might also be justification for aligning the State as a party plaintiff if it were appearing as *parens patriae* in an original proceeding concerning the custody of a child.[32]

C. APPELLATE JURISDICTION

In contrast to the tenuous and unproved nature of the Supreme Court's original jurisdiction in habeas corpus, its authority to issue the writ as an exercise of appellate jurisdiction is well recognized.[33] It is the requirement that the jurisdiction be "appellate" that is the major feature distinguishing the habeas corpus authority of the Supreme Court from that of other federal courts. The requirement of "appellate jurisdiction"[34] embodies the major limitation on the habeas corpus powers of the Supreme Court.

1. *Review of decisions of Article III courts.* The first judicial definition of "appellate jurisdiction" as it pertained to petitions for

---

[32] Where a guardian is entitled by State law to bring an action in his own name "he is the real party in interest" and his citizenship, not that of his ward, is determinative for purposes of the diversity jurisdiction. Mecom v. Fitzsimmons Co., 284 U.S. 183 (1931); *cf.* Mexican Central Ry. v. Eckman, 187 U.S. 429, 433–34 (1903).

Domestic-relations cases, including habeas corpus cases, have ordinarily been excluded from the federal courts for inability to satisfy statutory jurisdiction. *E.g.*, Matters v. Ryan, 249 U.S. 375, 378 (1919); Horn v. Mitchell, 243 U.S. 247, 249 (1917); see HART & WECHSLER 1016–18; Dobie, *Habeas Corpus in the Federal Courts*, 13 VA. L. REV. 433, 450–51 (1927). Since the Court's original jurisdiction is not subject to such statutory limitations, the plaintiff State might have to show only sufficient interest to be aligned as a party plaintiff in a suit against a citizen of another State to come within the Court's original jurisdiction. On the other hand, it has been suggested that where a habeas corpus case involves the question of the custody of a child, "with reference to which the court sits parens patriae," the proceeding is simply an inquisition by the sovereign and does not constitute a case or controversy within the meaning of the Constitution. King v. McLean Asylum, 64 Fed. 331, 334–35 (1st Cir. 1894); Re Barry, reported in 136 U.S. 597 (C.C. S.D. N.Y. 1844).

[33] Research has disclosed eighteen instances where prisoners have been discharged by this means. See *infra* notes 99, 111, 124, 195–97.

[34] "It is the essential criterion of appellate jurisdiction, that it revises and corrects the proceedings in a cause already instituted, and does not create that cause." Marbury v. Madison, 1 Cranch 137, 175 (1803). No. 81 of the Federalist Papers called appellate jurisdiction "nothing more than the power of one tribunal to review the proceedings of another. . . ."

habeas corpus was stated in *Ex parte Bollman*.[35] Bollman and his copetitioner Swartwout, associates of Aaron Burr, were seized in New Orleans because of their connection with Burr's infamous New Orleans expedition. During the period of their confinement on the voyage from New Orleans, they became the objects of great public excitement, deliberately aroused by the Administration. They arrived in Washington on Thursday evening, January 22, 1807, and without the benefit of warrant were immediately confined in the Marine barracks. On the following day, at the very moment when counsel was petitioning the circuit court for a writ of habeas corpus, the Administration closed the doors of the Senate and by unanimous vote rushed through a bill to suspend the writ of habeas corpus in cases of treason and related offenses. The measure was secretly conveyed to the House when it reconvened on the following Monday, but that body promptly made the shameful attempt public and rejected the bill by a vote of 113 to 19.

In the meantime, the circuit court had issued a writ of habeas corpus, returnable on Monday, but the Marine commandant failed to make return and a writ of attachment for contempt was refused because the three days that the common law allowed the respondent had not yet passed. On Tuesday, January 27, on the motion of the Government, a divided circuit court made a finding of probable cause and issued a bench warrant charging Bollman and Swartwout with treason, thus bringing them under civil jurisdiction. The circuit court's hearings on January 29 and 30, to determine whether there was sufficient evidence to hold defendants for trial, were such an attraction that the Senate could scarcely form a quorum, and the House actually adjourned.[36] At the conclusion of these hearings a divided court ordered defendants committed on the charge, the two Jefferson appointees again comprising the majority.

---

[35] 4 Cranch 75 (1807). The best source of information on the various proceedings and preliminaries in this case are the Jan. 26, 28, 30, and Feb. 2, 4, 6, 9, 11, 13, and 18, 1807, issues of the *National Intelligencer*, a Washington newspaper. The statement in the text is drawn principally from the day-to-day accounts in that paper, which published verbatim reports of the arguments and opinions in the circuit as well as the Supreme Court. Abbreviated accounts appear in 3 BEVERIDGE, JOHN MARSHALL 343–48 (1919); 1 WARREN, SUPREME COURT IN UNITED STATES HISTORY 303–06 (1926); SCHACHNER, AARON BURR 364–73, 387–94 (1961). The congressional proceedings appear in 9 ANNALS OF CONG. 39–42, 402–25 (1807).

[36] 3 BEVERIDGE, *op. cit. supra* note 35, at 345–46.

The following Monday, February 2, petitioners' counsel orally moved the Supreme Court for writs of habeas corpus for Bollman, Swartwout, and Alexander, a New Orleans lawyer who was thereafter discharged by a district judge for lack of evidence. Although the Court had issued a writ of habeas corpus on two prior occasions with little discussion,[37] Justices Chase and Johnson orally voiced doubts about the Court's constitutional or statutory authority to issue the writ. The Chief Justice thereupon announced that the whole subject would be taken up "*de novo*, without reference to precedents."[38]

The doubting Justices had identified two jurisdictional obstacles that petitioners had to clear. First, there were legitimate doubts that section 14 of the Judiciary Act authorized the Court to issue the writ.[39] Second, the recent opinion in *Marbury v. Madison*,[40] which struck down as unconstitutional that portion of the act that authorized the Court to issue the writ of mandamus, suggested grave doubts about the constitutionality of the similar habeas corpus authorization. It is remarkable that, in the face of these doubts and despite two days of argument in favor of jurisdiction, the Attorney General declined to argue the point on behalf of the United States. Two days later the Chief Justice, in what is undoubtedly the most important habeas corpus opinion ever issued by the Supreme Court, opened the way for a consideration of the evidence by sustaining the Court's jurisdiction. Bollman and Swartwout were actually brought into Court in response to the writ, and, after an additional period of argument covering portions of five succeeding days (the Attorney General now taking a vigorous part), they were discharged upon the Court's ruling that the evidence of treason was insufficient to justify their continued detention.

The major significance of *Ex parte Bollman* for present purposes lies in the reasons Marshall gave for holding that the issuance of the writ was an exercise of appellate jurisdiction:[41]

---

37 United States v. Hamilton, 3 Dall. 17 (1795); Ex parte Burford, 3 Cranch 448 (1806).

38 4 Cranch at 75, n. (*a*).

39 See text *infra*, at note 87, where this question is explored further.

40 1 Cranch 137 (1803).

41 4 Cranch at 101.

> It is the revision of a decision of an inferior court, by which a citizen has been committed to gaol. . . .
>
> The decision that the individual shall be imprisoned must always precede the application for a writ of *habeas corpus*, and this writ must always be for the purpose of revising that decision, and, therefore, appellate in its nature.

Thus was established the major premise upon which almost all Supreme Court habeas corpus jurisdiction was thereafter to be based.

The Court's second effort to delineate the extent of its constitutional appellate jurisdiction in habeas corpus came in *Ex parte Watkins*.[42] While Watkins was serving a three-month sentence for embezzling government funds, the Attorney General sued out a writ of *capias ad satisfaciendum* against him, returnable to the May Term of the circuit court.[43] No return was made to the writ. On May 14, 1830, petitioner completed service of his sentence, but the marshal kept him in jail, apparently on the understanding that he had been ordered into commitment in connection with the *capias*. Still confined in January, 1833, Watkins petitioned the Supreme Court for a writ of habeas corpus, contending that the applicable Maryland law did not authorize detention under a *capias* beyond the return date shown on the writ. In reply, Attorney General Taney suggested petitioner's dilemma. On the merits Watkins was not entitled to release unless he was being detained for a period in excess of that authorized by the *capias*. Consequently he was complaining of detention without process, not detention under process, and therefore his case was not one over which the Supreme Court had appellate jurisdiction. The only possible grounds for relief on the merits established a want of jurisdiction in the Court. The majority opinion purported to avoid this dilemma by phrasing a broader definition of appellate jurisdiction. Since the award of the *capias* was a judicial act of the circuit court, Story reasoned, the Court would clearly be exercising appellate jurisdiction if it should hold that the *capias* justified the confinement and remand the prisoner:[44]

---

42 7 Pet. 568 (1833).

43 The writ commanded the marshal to "take Watkins, and him safely keep, so that he have his body before the circuit court, on the first Monday of May then next, to satisfy unto the United States the fine, costs and charges." 7 Pet. at 570.

44 7 Pet. at 572–73. (Emphasis added.)

> But the jurisdiction of the court can never depend upon its decision upon the merits of a case brought before it; but upon its right to hear and decide it at all. . . . In all these cases the issuing of the writ was treated as an exercise of appellate jurisdiction; and it could make no difference in the right of the court to entertain jurisdiction, whether the proceedings of the court below were annulled or confirmed. Considering then, as we do, that we are but *revising the effect of the process awarded by the circuit court*, under which the prisoner is detained, we cannot say, that it is the exercise of an original jurisdiction.

The writ was issued, and after argument on its return a divided court ordered Watkins discharged.

The next doctrinal development in this area came in *Ex parte Yerger*,[45] which simply supplied a corollary to the *Watkins* principle that the Court has constitutional jurisdiction if its writ would revise the effect of process issued by a lower federal court. In each of the successful habeas corpus petitions up to this point the petitioner's confinement had been under a warrant and order of a federal court. Yerger, however, was a civilian held without judicial warrant for trial by military commission. A writ of habeas corpus had been denied by a United States circuit court prior to his petition to the Supreme Court. In opposition to that petition the Attorney General argued that the issuance of the writ would be an exercise of original jurisdicion inasmuch as petitioner was not held under the order of a circuit court. The Court disagreed:[46]

> It is unimportant in what custody the prisoner may be, if it is a custody to which he has been remanded by the order of an inferior court of the United States. . . . We are obliged to hold, therefore, that in all cases where a Circuit Court of the United States has, in the exercise of its original jurisdiction, caused a prisoner to be brought before it, and has, after inquiring into the cause of detention, remanded him to the custody from which he was taken, this court, in the exercise of its appellate jurisdiction, may, by the writ of *habeas corpus*, aided by the writ of *certiorari*, revise the decision of the Circuit Court, and if it be found unwarranted by law, relieve the prisoner from the unlawful restraint to which he has been remanded.

---

[45] 8 Wall. 85 (1869).

[46] *Id.* at 102–03.

The Supreme Court's last major discussion of the question of its constitutional appellate habeas corpus jurisdiction was in 1879 in *Ex parte Siebold*.[47] There, petitioners convicted in a United States district court sought habeas corpus from the Supreme Court on the ground that the statute under which they had been indicted was unconstitutional. Before denying relief on the merits, Justice Bradley's opinion sustained the Court's jurisdiction and held that the ground asserted by petitioner could be reviewed by petition for habeas corpus. On the subject of jurisdiction Bradley explained that, although the Court had no appellate jurisdiction to review the judgment by writ of error, the *Bollman* and *Yerger* decisions showed that its review of the circuit court's act in issuing the warrants of commitment was appellate in character. The opinion then continued:[48]

> That this court is authorized to exercise appellate jurisdiction by *habeas corpus* directly is a position sustained by abundant authority. It has general power to issue the writ, subject to the constitutional limitations of its jurisdiction, which are, that it can only exercise original jurisdiction in cases affecting ambassadors, public ministers and consuls, and cases in which a State is a party; but has *appellate jurisdiction in all other cases of Federal cognizance, "with such exceptions and under such regulations as Congress shall make."* Having this general power to issue the writ, the court may issue it in the exercise of original jurisdiction where it has original jurisdiction; and may issue it in the exercise of appellate jurisdiction where it has such jurisdiction, *which is in all cases not prohibited by law except those in which it has original jurisdiction only*. *Ex parte Bollman and Swartwout, supra; Ex parte Watkins*, 3 Pet. 202; 7 id. 568; *Ex parte Wells*, 18 How. 307, 328; *Abelman* v. *Booth*, 21 id. 506; *Ex parte Yerger*, 8 Wall. 85.

If the emphasized portions of this paragraph mean that the Court has appellate jurisdiction over all cases over which it does not have original jurisdiction,[49] they cannot be sustained upon reason and are directly contrary to earlier authorities.[50]

---

[47] 100 U.S. 371 (1880).

[48] *Id.* at 374–75. (Emphasis added.)

[49] *Cf.* 2 Crosskey, *op. cit. supra* note 15, at 1041, which suggests the converse: that the Court has original jurisdiction over all cases Congress excepts from its appellate jurisdiction.

[50] *E.g.*, Marbury v. Madison, 1 Cranch 137 (1803); Ex parte Barry, 2 How. 65 (1844).

Bollman, *Watkins*, and *Yerger* conclusively establish the Court's appellate jurisdiction under the Constitution to issue a writ of habeas corpus wherever the petitioner's confinement was initiated by or has subsequently been judicially reviewed by an inferior United States court. Where a federal judge ordered the confinement from his chambers, one early case held that appellate jurisdiction was wanting,[51] but subsequent opinions have criticized the holding and declared, by way of dicta, that the "appellate jurisdiction by habeas corpus extends to all cases of commitment by the judicial authority of the United States. . . ."[52]

History records at least one instance where parties seriously considered invoking the Court's appellate jurisdiction by first securing denial of habeas corpus from a single Justice,[53] but the attempt was not made and there appear to be no decisions on the question.[54] If the habeas corpus jurisdiction which the single Justice has enjoyed since the first Judiciary Act[55] is appellate, then its erroneous exercise or refusal would of course confer no authority on the Court to grant relief. If it is original, then there would seem to be no reason why a denial of habeas corpus by a single Justice could not be just as effective a basis for the Court's appellate jurisdiction as a similar denial by a district judge.[56]

---

51 In the matter of Metzger, 5 How. 176 (1847).

52 Ex parte Virginia, 100 U.S. 339, 342 (1879); Ex parte Yerger, 8 Wall. 85, 99 (1869). In addition, the *Metzger* opinion can be read as a limitation on statutory rather than constitutional power. Fong Yue Ting v. United States, 149 U.S. 698, 714 (1893). *Cf.* Carper v. Fitzgerald, 121 U.S. 87 (1887) (no statutory appellate jurisdiction to review order of circuit judge in habeas corpus case).

53 See the discussion of Ex parte Quirin, *infra* note 75.

54 In at least two cases the Court has attempted to characterize the habeas corpus jurisdiction exercised by a single Justice. In both cases the jurisdiction of the Court itself was soundly premised on review of an act of a lower federal court, and the only jurisdictional question was whether the Court could give relief when the petition was presented first to a single Justice who issued the writ or a rule to show cause and then "transferred" the cause by making it returnable before the whole Court. In the first, a majority denied the efficacy of the transfer on the premise that the asserted jurisdiction over the case must be original, since a single Justice could not exercise appellate jurisdiction. In re Kaine, 14 How. 103, 116, 131 (1852). Twenty-seven years later the Court upheld such a transfer, reasoning that the power exercised by a single Justice in granting or denying habeas corpus relief was appellate in character. Ex parte Clarke, 100 U.S. 399, 403 (1880).

55 See the statute quoted in text *infra*, at note 87.

56 Supreme Court review of decisions of a circuit court presided over by a Justice was a familiar occurrence in earlier days. The fact that a Justice, in denying habeas

2. *Review of decisions of non-Article III courts.* Familiar instances of Supreme Court review of State courts, of territorial courts, and of special tribunals like the Court of Claims teach that the Court has constitutional appellate jurisdiction to review an exercise of judicial power other than that conferred by Article III. In each of these examples the Supreme Court is of course reviewing the action of a "court." But a petition for a writ of habeas corpus may seek release from confinement not initiated or reviewed by judicial authority. Familiar examples include armed-forces restraint over a selective-service inductee, confinement of an alien under an Immigration and Naturalization Service order arresting him for deportation or excluding him from admission into the United States, confinement by order of the Senate or Congress for contempt of either of those bodies, and confinement by order of a court-martial.[57] Except for the court-martial cases discussed hereafter,[58] there is practically no direct authority on the question whether the Supreme Court has constitutional appellate jurisdiction to effect release from such confinements by its own writ of habeas corpus.

The Court's reasoning in other cases sheds some light on the problem.[59] According to these authorities, the Supreme Court will

---

corpus, acted individually and not in the capacity of a court would seem to make no difference for this purpose. But *cf.* In the matter of Metzger, *supra* note 51.

[57] Eagles v. Samuels, 329 U.S. 304 (1946) (inductee); 8 U.S.C. §§ 1103, 1105(*a*) (9), 1105*a*(*b*), 1503(*c*); 8 C.F.R. § 242.2(*a*); United States v. Ju Toy, 198 U.S. 253 (1905) (deportation and exclusion); Jurney v. McCracken, 294 U.S. 125 (1935) (contempt); Burns v. Wilson, 346 U.S. 137 (1953) (court-martial). See 3 Davis, Administrative Law § 24.08 (1958); Comment, *Federal Habeas Corpus Review of "Final" Administrative Decisions,* 56 Colum. L. Rev. 551 (1956).

[58] See text *infra,* at notes 63 *et seq.*

[59] "[T]he essential criterion of appellate jurisdiction [is] that it revises and corrects the proceedings in a cause already instituted, and does not create that cause." Marbury v. Madison, 1 Cranch 137, 175 (1803). Appellate jurisdiction, according to other opinions, implies a review of "an exercise of judicial power," In re Sanborn, 148 U.S. 222, 224 (1893); Williams v. United States, 289 U.S. 553, 566 (1933); Old Colony Trust Co. v. Commissioner, 279 U.S. 716, 723 (1929), or acts rendered in a "judicial capacity," Pope v. United States, 323 U.S. 1, 13 (1944), a "judicial judgment," Postum Cereal Co. v. California Fig Nut Co., 272 U.S. 693, 698–700 (1927), a "judicial act," Pope v. United States, *supra;* United States v. Coe, 155 U.S. 76, 86 (1894), a "judicial procedure," Tutun v. United States, 270 U.S. 568, 577 (1926), or a "judicial determination," The Alicia, 7 Wall. 571, 573 (1869); Gordon

have constitutional appellate jurisdiction by habeas corpus to review any confinement initiated or reviewed by a "court of justice" or by "judicial" authority. This in turn requires a definition of "judicial" authority, a matter that has frequently bemused the Court.[60] The Court has usually reasoned that the question whether the initiating or reviewing body was a "court" or whether its authority was "judicial" depends upon whether its proceedings followed the customary forms of law or equity, "instituted and conducted throughout according to the regular course of judicial procedure."[61] This formulation would seem to preclude the Supreme Court from issu-

---

v. United States, 2 Wall. 561, Taney's opinion reported at 117 U.S. 697, 702 (1865). The Court does not review legislative, Prentis v. Atlantic Coastline Co., 211 U.S. 210 (1908); Keller v. Potomac Electric Co., 261 U.S. 428 (1923); *cf.* Olney v. Arnold, 3 Dall. 308 (1796), or administrative, Postum Cereal Co. v. California Fig Nut Co., *supra;* Federal Radio Comm. v. General Electric Co., 281 U.S. 464 (1930); *cf.* Upshur County v. Rich, 135 U.S. 467, 477 (1890), actions. "[I]t is not sufficient that there has been a decision by some officer or department of the United States, it must be by one clothed with judicial authority, and acting in a judicial capacity." 2 Story, *op. cit. supra note* 13, at § 1761.

60 It will be recognized that the question here is not the currently confused issue whether a certain tribunal is an Article I or an Article III "court." See Glidden Co. v. Zdanok, 370 U.S. 530 (1962); Comment, *The Distinction between Legislative and Constitutional Courts and Its Effects on Judicial Assignment*, 62 Colum. L. Rev. 133 (1962). Appellate jurisdiction may lie to review the action of either type of tribunal. *E.g.*, United States v. Coe, 155 U.S. 76 (1894); O'Donoghue v. United States, 289 U.S. 516, 535–38 (1933). See Robertson & Kirkham, Jurisdiction of the Supreme Court §§ 228, 259, 264 (Wolfson & Kurland ed. 1951).

61 See Gordon v. United States; Marbury v. Madison; In re Sanborn; Prentis v. Atlantic Coastline Co.; Postum Cereal Co. v. California Fig Nut Co.; Upshur County v. Rich; The Alicia; all *supra* note 59.

Most to the point here is the statement by Mr. Justice Brandeis for a unanimous Court in Tutun v. United States, 270 U.S. 568, 576, 577 (1926): "Whether a proceeding which results in a grant is a judicial one, does not depend upon the nature of the thing granted, but upon the *nature of the proceeding* which Congress has provided. . . . Whenever the law provides a *remedy enforceable in the courts according to the regular course of legal procedure,* and that remedy is pursued, there arises a case within the meaning of the Constitution. . . . The [citizenship] *proceeding is instituted and is conducted throughout according to the regular course of judicial procedure.*" (Emphasis added.)

To the same effect are the general definitions of "case" as that word is used in the constitutional grant of judicial power. See Muskrat v. United States, 219 U.S. 346, 356 (1911); In re Pacific Ry. Comm'n, 32 Fed. 241, 255 (C.C. N.D. Cal. 1887); Old Colony Trust Co. v. Commissioner, 279 U.S. 716, 723 (1929); Smith v. Adams, 130 U.S. 167, 173–74 (1889); Cohens v. Virginia, 6 Wheat. 264, 405 (1821); see generally, Robertson & Kirkham, *op. cit. supra* note 60, at § 260.

ing its writ of habeas corpus for any of the types of confinements suggested above, unless they had first been reviewed by some intervening judicial authority. As will be seen, the instances where the Supreme Court has been requested to review confinements not initiated or reviewed by lesser judicial authorities are consistent with this hypothesis, but such cases are not numerous.

It is clear at one extreme that the Court has no appellate jurisdiction to issue the writ where the confinement is by a private party, as in a petition growing out of a controversy over the custody of a child.[62] Almost all of the remaining cases in this area involve confinement by military authorities.[63]

The leading case is *Ex parte Vallandigham*,[64] where the Court held that the Constitution gave it no appellate jurisdiction to review by certiorari proceedings of a military commission which had tried petitioner and sentenced him to confinement for the duration of the war for expressing southern sympathies. After referring to the judicial powers conferred on a territorial judge in an earlier case, the Court's opinion continued:[65]

> Nor can it be said that the authority to be exercised by a military commission is judicial in that sense. It involves discretion to examine, to decide and sentence, but there is no original

---

62 Ex parte Barry, 2 How. 65 (1844). Not only is appellate jurisdiction lacking, but such cases may not come within the judicial power of the United States. In re Burrus, 136 U.S. 586 (1890); HART & WECHSLER, 1016–18, 1238; authorities cited *supra* note 32. If a lower federal court has acted without jurisdiction in such a case, the Supreme Court of course has appellate jurisdiction to correct the error. In re Burrus, *supra*.

63 In Ex parte Mirzan, 119 U.S. 584 (1887), the Court expressly left open the question of its jurisdiction to issue the writ to one confined by the now-defunct consular courts. In Ex parte Hung Hang, 108 U.S. 552 (1883), the Court held itself to be without appellate jurisdiction to issue a writ of habeas corpus for an alien detained under a warrant of arrest issued by the police judge of the city and county of San Francisco. The Court's brief opinion does not explain its assertion that the petition does not seek "review of the judicial decision of some inferior officer or court." *Id.* at 553.

64 1 Wall. 243 (1864).

65 *Id.* at 253. A district judge had refused habeas corpus relief before petitioner came to the Supreme Court. Ex parte Vallandigham, 28 Fed. Cas. 374 (No. 16816) (C.C. S.D. Ohio 1863). Five years later, in Ex parte Yerger, *supra* note 45, a similar circumstance was used to sustain the Court's jurisdiction to issue the writ of habeas corpus.

> jurisdiction in the Supreme Court to issue a writ of *habeas corpus ad subjiciendum* to review or reverse its proceedings, or the writ of certiorari to revise the proceedings of a military commission.

Although the reasoning in *Vallandigham* was just as applicable to habeas corpus as to certiorari, and although its holding and its dictum as to habeas corpus should have been important landmarks in an area where precedents are few, over eighty years elapsed before the Court cited the case as applicable to habeas corpus.[66] In the meantime, the Court was notably indecisive on the question of its appellate jurisdiction over military bodies. In ruling on an 1881 petition for the original writ by a soldier convicted by a general court-martial, the Court identified the question at the outset as "whether this court has jurisdiction to issue such a writ as is asked, inasmuch as it has no power to review the judgments of courts-martial."[67] "Upon this question," Chief Justice Waite declared, "there is not entire unanimity of opinion among the members of the court, and we purposely withhold any decision at this time in respect to it." The Court was unanimous in denying relief on the merits.[68]

In the wake of World War II the Supreme Court was showered with petitions by individuals convicted by or held for trial before United States or international military courts, commissions, or tribunals. In large part the petitioners were Germans, but a few Japanese and some United States citizens were also involved. So far as appears in the published descriptions of these cases,[69] none of the petitioners had first sought relief in a lower federal court, except Quirin and Yamashita, whose cases are discussed below. Presumably, those few petitioners who were well enough advised to have considered the question thought that the statute which authorizes district courts and circuit judges to grant writs of habeas corpus "within their respective jurisdictions"[70] would preclude relief from

---

66 See text *infra,* at note 76.

67 Ex parte Mason, 105 U.S. 696, 697 (1882).

68 *But cf.* Wales v. Whitney, 114 U.S. 564, 570 (1885) (semble).

69 See Fairman, *Some New Problems of the Constitution Following the Flag,* 1 Stanf. L. Rev. 587, 589–603 (1949); Hart & Wechsler 284–87.

70 Now 28 U.S.C. § 2241(*a*). See Ahrens v. Clark, 335 U.S. 188 (1948). The general problem is discussed in Fairman, *supra* note 69, at 631–43; Wolfson, *Americans Abroad and Habeas Corpus,* 9 Fed. B.J. 142 (1948); 10 Fed. B.J. 69 (1948).

overseas confinement. Subsequently, this rule was relaxed in the District of Columbia, at least as to United States citizens held by United States authorities,[71] but the modification came too late to offer an alternative forum for any of the original group of petitioners. The feasibility of applying to an individual Justice occurred to at least one counsel who acted on behalf of certain of these petitioners, but this imaginative lawyer did not present such a petition because he was advised in advance that the ruling would not be favorable.[72]

Only two of the so-called war-crimes cases were heard on the merits before the Supreme Court, *Ex parte Quirin*,[73] and *In re Yamashita*.[74] Neither of these cases posed the problem of direct Supreme Court habeas corpus review of a military tribunal; in each case a lower court had already denied habeas corpus.[75] But Chief

---

[71] Eisentrager v. Forrestal, *supra* note 9; Cozart v. Wilson, 236 F. 2d 732 (D.C. Cir. 1956). *Cf.* United States v. Dulles, 222 F. 2d 390 (D.C. Cir. 1954). The territorial limitation issue as it pertains to habeas corpus writs other than *ad subjiciendum*, the "Great Writ," is discussed in Carbo v. United States, 364 U.S. 611 (1960).

[72] See Wolfson, *supra* note 70, 10 Fed. B.J. at 72–73. This may have been the same event discussed *infra* note 75.

[73] 317 U.S. 1 (1942).

[74] 327 U.S. 1 (1946).

[75] In *Quirin*, seven Nazi saboteurs were seeking relief from their trial and conviction by a military commission appointed by the President. Their counsel and the assistants to the attorney general considered obtaining relief from the Circuit Justice (Black, J.) as a predicate for Supreme Court habeas corpus relief, but, because of doubts about the efficacy of this method, they decided to proceed first in the district court instead. Mason, Harlan Fiske Stone 657 (1956). The district court denied habeas corpus on July 28, 1942. The following day the Supreme Court convened and counsel asked leave to file a petition for habeas corpus and a petition for certiorari to review the order of the district court. Argument was held July 29 and 30, while counsel perfected an appeal from the district court to the court of appeals and sought certiorari to the court of appeals before judgment. The final steps were accomplished on July 31, only a few minutes before the Court met to announce its decision. Cushman, *The Nazi Saboteur Case*, 28 Corn. L. Q. 54, 57–58 (1942). In a brief per curiam opinion, certiorari before judgment was granted, the district court order denying habeas corpus relief was affirmed on the merits, and leave to file petitions for habeas corpus was denied. 317 U.S. 18 (1942). A full opinion was filed on Oct. 29, 1942. 317 U.S. 1 (1942).

In *Yamashita*, a Japanese general being tried by a military tribunal in the Philippines petitioned for writs of prohibition and habeas corpus. On being informed that the Supreme Court of the Philippines had denied similar relief and that a petition for a writ of certiorari to that decision was on its way, the Supreme Court stayed all further proceedings. 326 U.S. 693. After hearing argument on the motion and

Justice Stone's prevailing opinion in *Yamashita* contained this significant dictum:[76]

> In the present cases it must be recognized throughout that the military tribunals which Congress has sanctioned by the Articles of War are not courts whose rulings and judgments are made subject to review by this Court. See *Ex parte Vallandigham*, 1 Wall. 243; *In re Vidal*, 179 U.S. 126; cf. *Ex parte Quirin, supra*, 39.

As was true with the dictum in *Vallandigham*, this observation seems to have been overlooked in subsequent cases.

In about 125 other cases (where the petitioners had not gone first to a lower court) relief was denied without argument in all but one case, but the Court was not as decisive as one might have expected. Chief Justice Vinson and Justices Reed, Frankfurter, and Burton consistently voted to deny these motions. In the first case, *Ex parte Betz*,[77] decided almost a year after *Yamashita*, these four were joined by Mr. Justice Douglas in an order denying leave to file "for want of original jurisdiction." Justices Black and Rutledge would have denied without prejudice to a petition to the appropriate district court, and Justice Murphy was for argument on the jurisdictional question. As in all of these cases, with the exception noted below, Justice Jackson took no part. The next two groups of cases[78] were simply "denied," but with Justices Black, Douglas (in the first but not the second), Murphy, and Rutledge of the opinion that the petition should be set down for hearing on the jurisdictional question. Then followed the only "war-crimes" petition in which the Court was unanimous in denying relief: "Petition denied."[79]

The remaining cases followed a pattern. The Chief Justice and Justices Reed, Frankfurter, and Burton were "of the opinion that there is want of jurisdiction," citing Article III, § 2, cl. 2, *Ex parte*

---

petition, the Court vacated the stay, 327 U.S. 757, denied the writ of certiorari, and denied leave to file the petitions for habeas corpus or prohibition, with an opinion holding that petitioner was not entitled to relief on the merits.

76 327 U.S. at 8.

77 329 U.S. 672 (1946).

78 Milch v. United States, 332 U.S. 789 (1947); Brandt v. United States, 333 U.S. 836 (1948).

79 In re Eichel, 333 U.S. 865 (1948).

Betz, and some of the other early cases.[80] Justices Black, Douglas, Murphy, and Rutledge adhered to their view that argument should be had on the jurisdictional question.

In the German cases considered up to this point, Justice Jackson had taken no part, "for reasons which are obvious."[81] On December 6, 1948, he joined Justices Black, Douglas, Murphy, and Rutledge to bring about a hearing in *Hirota v. MacArthur*,[82] a petition by former Premier Hirota and other Japanese convicted by the International Military Tribunal of the Far East. The matter was argued ten days later, and on December 20, 1948, the Court denied leave to file the petitions in a brief per curiam opinion stating that because the tribunal which sentenced the petitioners was not a tribunal of the United States, the courts of the United States had no power to review, affirm, set aside, or annul its judgments and sentences. Mr. Justice Douglas wrote a concurring opinion; Justice Murphy dissented without opinion; Justice Rutledge reserved decision (he died before announcing a vote), and Justice Jackson took no part in the final decision.

After *Hirota v. MacArthur*, the Court continued throughout its 1948 Term to dispose of the German cases by its four-to-four split, although now Justices Black, Douglas, Murphy, and Rutledge desired argument "in order to settle what remedy, if any, the petitioners have."[83] Before the Court convened for its 1949 Term, Justices Clark and Minton had replaced Justices Murphy and Rutledge. The final petition of this series was denied without opinion, with Justices Black and Douglas voting to "deny without prejudice to making applications in a District Court."[84]

In retrospect it seems unfortunate that the Supreme Court did not appoint counsel and hear argument on the jurisdictional issue in

---

[80] Everett v. Truman, 334 U.S. 824 (1948); In re Krautwurst, 334 U.S. 826 (1948); In re Ehlen, 334 U.S. 836 (1948); In re Gronwald, 334 U.S. 857 (1948); In re Strattman, 335 U.S. 805 (1948); In re Vetter, 335 U.S. 841 (1948); In re Eckstein, 335 U.S. 851 (1948); In re Heim, 335 U.S. 856 (1948).

[81] Hirota v. MacArthur, 335 U.S. 876, 877 (1948) (memorandum of Jackson, J.).

[82] 338 U.S. 197 (1948).

[83] In re Dammann, 336 U.S. 922, 923 (1949); In re Muhlbauer, 336 U.S. 964 (1949); In re Steimle, 337 U.S. 913 (1949); In re Felsch, 337 U.S. 953 (1949).

[84] In re Hans, 339 U.S. 976 (1950).

the earliest cases so that the unavailability of the writ from the Supreme Court could have been established, thus channeling the energies of subsequent litigation into the development of a more feasible alternative. Instead, as time wore on, the accumulation of indecisive denials only served to cloud the jurisdictional issue until it was possible for more than one able commentator who wrote about these cases to overlook, or at least fail to mention, that entirely apart from the merits of these cases the Supreme Court simply had no power to review them by the "original" writ of habeas corpus.[85] The Court's decision to place its disclaimer of jurisdiction in *Hirota v. MacArthur* on a ground common to all United States courts, rather than on its own want of appellate jurisdiction, may have been warranted, in view of the short-range instructive effect of that decision for all federal courts. Unfortunately, however, it served further to disguise the fact that relief was specifically outside the range of Supreme Court power.[86]

II. Statutory Authority—the Nature of the Writ of Habeas Corpus

Section 14 of the Judiciary Act of 1789 contained the following provision:[87]

> That all the before-mentioned courts of the United States, shall have power to issue writs of *scire facias*, *habeas corpus*, and all other writs not specially provided for by statute, which may be necessary for the exercise of their respective jurisdic-

---

85 See Fairman, *supra* note 69, at 602–03, 621, 632. Not even the more exhaustive comments on the noteworthy war-crimes cases mentioned the question of the Supreme Court's appellate jurisdiction to review these questions by its own writ of habeas corpus. *E.g.*, 56 Harv. L. Rev. 631 (1943) (*Quirin*); 41 Mich. L. Rev. 481, 483–84 (1942) (*Quirin*); 44 Mich. L. Rev. 855 (1946) (*Yamashita*); see also Robertson & Kirkham, *op. cit. supra* note 60, at § 255 n. 2. Cushman, *supra* note 75, at 55, 57–58, on the other hand, recognized the jurisdictional problem and observed that the court in *Quirin* was without constitutional jurisdiction to review the action of the military commission directly.

86 See, *e.g.*, 47 Mich. L. Rev. 835, 837 (1949). Mr. Justice Douglas' concurring opinion in Hirota v. MacArthur, 338 U.S. 197, 200 (1948), filed six months after the Court's per curiam opinion was issued, seems to assume that the Supreme Court has constitutional appellate jurisdiction by habeas corpus in any case within the potential jurisdiction of a lower federal court. See Hart & Wechsler 286. The assumption is obviously in error.

87 1 Stat. 73, 81–82 (1789).

> tions, and agreeable to the principles and usages of law. And that either of the justices of the supreme court, as well as judges of the district courts, shall have power to grant writs of *habeas corpus* for the purpose of an inquiry into the cause of commitment.—Provided, That writs of *habeas corpus* shall in no case extend to prisoners in gaol unless where they are in custody, under or by colour of the authority of the United States, or are committed for trial before some court of the same, or are necessary to be brought into court to testify.

The major question of construction under this statute, the ancestor of the habeas corpus[88] and "all-writs"[89] sections of the present Judicial Code, was whether it gave the Supreme Court jurisdiction to issue the writ of habeas corpus *ad subjiciendum*, the "Great Writ." The problem stemmed from the fact that the second sentence of section 14 (which specifically authorized a use of the writ to inquire into the cause of commitment) conferred no authority on the Supreme Court (or any other court), whereas the first sentence had a qualifying clause that seemed to limit the authority of a *court* to issue the writ to circumstances where it was "necessary for the exercise of their respective jurisdictions."

The idea of using the writ of habeas corpus in aid of a court's jurisdiction was not a novel one. In its earliest forms the writ of

---

88 28 U.S.C. § 2241:

"(*a*) Writs of habeas corpus may be granted by the Supreme Court, any justice thereof, the district courts and any circuit judge within their respective jurisdictions. . . .

"(*c*) The writ of habeas corpus shall not extend to a prisoner unless—

(1) He is in custody under or by color of the authority of the United States or is committed for trial before some court thereof; or

(2) He is in custody for an act done or omitted in pursuance of an Act of Congress, or an order, process, judgment or decree of a court or judge of the United States; or

(3) He is in custody in violation of the Constitution or laws or treaties of the United States; or

(4) He, being a citizen of a foreign state and domiciled therein is in custody for an act done or omitted under any alleged right, title, authority, privilege, protection, or exemption claimed under the commission, order or sanction of any foreign state, or under color thereof, the validity and effect of which depend upon the law of nations; or

(5) It is necessary to bring him into court to testify or for trial."

89 28 U.S.C. § 1651(a): "The Supreme Court and all courts established by Act of Congress may issue all writs necessary or appropriate in aid of their respective jurisdictions and agreeable to the usages and principles of law."

habeas corpus was simply an auxiliary device to assure the presence of a party before the court.[90] It was not until the late sixteenth and early seventeenth centuries that the Great Writ was definitely established as a substantive remedy and independent means for inquiring into the cause of detention.[91] But the auxiliary usages of the writ remained, and at the time the first Judiciary Act was passed there were several developed forms of the writ that simply served to bring a person before the court in aid of pending litigation.[92]

Against this history one could argue that the authority of a court under the first sentence of section 14 was limited to writs in aid of cases otherwise within a court's statutory jurisdiction, and that the Great Writ could only be issued under the second sentence, which bestowed its authority on judges but not on courts. The argument was never made. The question was raised by Justice Johnson in *Ex parte Bollman*,[93] but the issue was decided in favor of jurisdiction without the benefit of argument to the contrary.

Marshall stated three reasons why Congress had authorized the Court to issue the Great Writ in circumstances other than those "in aid of" jurisdiction in a case already pending: (1) A construction that would deny the power to the Supreme Court would deny it to every other federal court, and Congress could not have intended to

---

[90] For discussions of the early history of the writ, see Jenks, *The Story of Habeas Corpus*, 18 L. Q. REV. 64, 65–71 (1902), reprinted in 2 SELECTED ESSAYS IN ANGLO-AMERICAN LEGAL HISTORY 531 (1908); WALKER, CONSTITUTIONAL AND LEGAL DEVELOPMENT OF HABEAS CORPUS AS THE WRIT OF LIBERTY (1960); Cohen, *Habeas Corpus Cum Causa*, 18 CAN. BAR. REV. 10 (1940); 9 HOLDSWORTH, HISTORY OF ENGLISH LAW 108–12 (1926).

[91] Jenks, *supra* note 90, at 73–75; 9 HOLDSWORTH, *op. cit. supra* note 90, at 111. More recently scholars have pointed to evidence indicating that the writ of habeas corpus cum causa may have been used for the purpose of inquiring into the cause of detention as early as the fourteenth century, although they concede that the *ad subjiciendum* form of the writ did not appear until the 1500's. WALKER, *op. cit. supra* note 90 at 13, 29–32; Cohen, *supra* note 90 at 19, 25.

[92] *Ad respondendum* (to remove a prisoner confined by process of an inferior court to charge him with an action in the court above); *ad satisfaciendum* (to remove a prisoner to charge him with execution in the court above); *ad faciendum et recipiendum* (to remove a cause and a prisoner from an inferior court to the courts in Westminster); *ad prosequendum, testificandum*, or *deliberandum* (to remove a prisoner in order to prosecute or testify in an action or to be tried in the proper jurisdiction). Ex parte Bollman, 4 Cranch 75, 97–98 (1807); 3 BL. COMM. *129–*31; 3 COMYNS, DIGEST 453–62 (1785).

[93] 4 Cranch at 75 n. (*a*).

confer the power on Justices and judges and to deny it to the courts on which they sat. (2) The first sentence in section 14 must refer to the Great Writ, since most (although not all) of the other forms of the writ were inapplicable in our system of federal courts. (3) Since the 33d section of the Judiciary Act included the Supreme Court among those who could admit to bail in a capital case, it presupposed that the power to award the writ of habeas corpus (the appropriate process for bringing up a prisoner to be bailed) was granted by the 14th section. According to Marshall, the function of the second sentence was simply to insure a remedy when the courts were not in session, which, although Marshall did not say so, was one of the principal purposes served by the Habeas Corpus Act of 1679.[94]

None of the Chief Justice's reasons compelled the conclusion reached;[95] as a matter of technical construction Justice Johnson's dissent had the better of the argument. Yet the desirability of the Supreme Court's having an independent habeas corpus power in reserve was quite evident in the circumstances under which Bollman and Swartwout had filed their pleas for relief. The stress of the political cannonade under which the Supreme Court's power to issue the Great Writ was created served to emphasize, despite technical doubts, the timeliness of its appearance and the desirability of its existence. Subsequent adherence to the decision by the courts and the acquiescence of Congress have long since removed the matter from the area of any legitimate controversy, although from time to time the Supreme Court has fallen into the error of attributing its

[94] 31 Car. II, ch. 2 (1679). Prior to this famous act it was thought that the writ was unavailable during vacation except, perhaps, in the Court of Chancery. Crowley's Case, [1818] 2 Swan. Ch. 1; 9 HOLDSWORTH, *op. cit. supra* note 90, at 115–16; WALKER, *op. cit. supra* note 90, at 81–85.

[95] It was possible, for example, to construe the limiting clause ("which may be necessary for the exercise of their respective jurisdictions") to permit issuance of the Great Writ by district and circuit courts, which could exercise an original jurisdiction, and to preclude issuance by the Supreme Court, which could not. The argument that Congress would not have conferred the habeas corpus power on Justices while denying it to the Court was refuted in 1833 when Congress did just that in enlarging the circumstances under which the writ could issue. 4 Stat. 634–35 (1833). See *infra* note 113.

habeas corpus jurisdiction to the authority of the "all-writs" section.[96]

The holding that section 14 of the Judiciary Act empowered the Supreme Court to exercise its appellate jurisdiction by issuing a writ of habeas corpus produced anomalous results in later years, due largely to the confusion resulting from the use of the word "jurisdiction" to indicate both the limits of constitutional appellate powers and the extent to which Congress had authorized the exercise of those powers. Thus, in the first half of the nineteenth century the Court held: (1) that it had no "jurisdiction" to issue the writ where there had been no lower-court decision to review;[97] (2) that it had no "jurisdiction" to issue the writ where the petitioner was held under the judgment of a lower federal court;[98] but (3) that it did have "jurisdiction" where the petitioner had been committed to await trial.[99] These decisions were of course consistent with one another, but the Court's failure to distinguish between the constitutional jurisdiction that was wanting in the first case and the statutory jurisdiction that was the basis for decision in the other two fostered some misunderstanding. So, too, did the rule that the Court had appellate jurisdiction in habeas corpus over an interlocutory order of a lower federal court in a criminal case, but no jurisdiction over the final judgment. This apparent anomaly can be explained best by reference to the history of appellate review.

Among the several means by which one English court reviewed

---

96 Ex parte Abernathy, 320 U.S. 219, 220 (1943); see Ex parte Burrus, 136 U.S. 586, 590 (1890). The predecessor of the present "all-writs" section, 28 U.S.C. § 1651, was held to authorize the courts of appeals to issue writs of habeas corpus in aid of their appellate jurisdiction. Whitney v. Dick, 202 U.S. 132, 136 (1906); Adams v. McCann, 317 U.S. 269 (1942); Price v. Johnson, 334 U.S. 266 (1948). A more recent case has suggested, perhaps unwittingly, that the power to issue writs of habeas corpus was removed from the "all-writs" section in 1875 and incorporated in the sections expressly referring to habeas corpus. Carbo v. United States, 364 U.S. 611, 615–16 (1961). If so, courts of appeals no longer have authority to issue the writs, for they are not so empowered in the habeas corpus section. 28 U.S.C. § 2241, *supra* note 88.

97 Ex parte Barry, 2 How. 65 (1844).

98 Ex parte Watkins, 3 Pet. 193, 202–03, 207 (1830); Ex parte Kearney, 7 Wheat. 38 (1822).

99 Ex parte Bollman, 4 Cranch 75 (1807); Ex parte Burford, 3 Cranch 448 (1806); United States v. Hamilton, 3 Dall. 17 (1795).

the decisions of another were the statutory remedy of appeal and the common-law writs of error and certiorari. The remedy of appeal was ordinarily confined to causes in the chancery, admiralty, and ecclesiastical courts and did not pertain to the criminal jurisdiction until the procedural reforms of the late nineteenth century.[100] The writ of error, by far the most common device, was the appropriate method of review of a final judgment of a court of record upon indictment in a criminal case.[101] The writ of certiorari, in general, did not issue in any circumstances where a writ of error was appropriate. So far as can be determined, the writ of habeas corpus was not considered as a means by which one court reviewed the action of another. If a petitioner was held under the judgment of a court of competent jurisdiction upon indictment in a criminal case, the writ of habeas corpus would not issue.[102] Thus, it could be said that habeas corpus, like certiorari, was not available in any circumstance in which a writ of error would have been appropriate.[103]

By the first Judiciary Act, the Supreme Court was empowered to exercise its appellate jurisdiction by writ of error in civil cases,[104] but there was no provision for a writ of error in criminal cases.[105] The Court received no jurisdiction by appeal.[106] The writ of certiorari was only authorized under the "all-writs" provision, *i.e.*,

---

[100] United States v. Coe, 155 U.S. 76, 83 (1894); 2 STORY, *op. cit. supra* note 13, at § 1762; 1 STEPHEN, HISTORY OF THE CRIMINAL LAW OF ENGLAND ch. 10 (1883).

[101] 3 BL. COMM. *406–*07; 1 STEPHEN, *op. cit. supra* note 100; Gordon, *Challenging Convictions by Habeas Corpus and Certiorari*, 2 CRIM. L. Q. 296, 298–300 (1959).

[102] Ex parte Corke, [1954] 2 All E. R. 440; Ex parte Lees, [1858] E. B. & E. 828, 836; 1 HOLDSWORTH, *op. cit. supra* note 90, at 227; 4 BACON, ABRIDGEMENT 563 (1852 ed.). The Habeas Corpus Act, 31 Car. II., ch. 2 (1679), makes exceptions for persons "detained upon legal process, order or warrant, out of some court that hath jurisdiction in criminal matters. . . ." See 1 CHITTY, *op. cit. supra* note 22, at 100–01.

[103] Gordon, *supra* note 101, at 297–305. Gordon suggests that this followed from the statute of 4 Hen. IV, ch. 23 (1403), which provided that "after judgment given in the courts, the parties and their heirs shall be thereof in peace until the judgment be done by attaint or by error, if there be error."

[104] 1 Stat. 73, 84 (1789).

[105] United States v. More, 3 Cranch 159 (1805).

[106] Section 21 of the first Judiciary Act authorized an appeal from the district court to the circuit court in admiralty causes, 1 Stat. 73, 83–84 (1789), but the Supreme Court could review these matters only by writ of error. Wiscart v. D'Auchy, 3 Dall. 321, 328 (1796). Jurisdiction by appeal in admiralty and equity was added in 1802. 2 Stat. 244 (1803).

only when necessary in the exercise of a jurisdiction otherwise acquired.[107] Consequently, the first Judiciary Act gave the Supreme Court no appellate jurisdiction in criminal matters, unless that jurisdiction could be found in the section 14 provision empowering the Court to issue the writ of habeas corpus.[108]

The construction of section 14 adopted in *Ex parte Bollman* thus gave the Supreme Court some measure of supervisory control over the lesser federal courts in criminal matters. Since Congress had chosen to confer this authority through the medium of the common-law writ of habeas corpus, however, the limits of this control were coextensive with the Court's definition of the usage and functions of that writ. Accordingly, each decision that expanded the scope of review by habeas corpus would effect a corresponding expansion in the statutory appellate jurisdiction of the Court.

In *Bollman,* Marshall declared "that for the meaning of the term *habeas corpus,* resort may unquestionably be had to the common law; . . ."[109] Under this definition the Court had no statutory appellate jurisdiction to review a final judgment of a court of competent jurisdiction in a criminal case.[110] Consequently, the Court could only issue the writ of habeas corpus when the petitioner was held under a judicial order that was not the final judgment of a court of general criminal jurisdiction, a circumstance sufficiently rare that only four petitioners seem to have been discharged by means of the writ in the first eighty years of the Court's existence.[111]

The history of the expansion of the scope of inquiry under the writ of habeas corpus is an account often told.[112] Except for two relatively insignificant additions, the circumstances in which the statutes authorized issuance of the writ remained unchanged until

---

[107] 1 Stat. 73, 81–82 (1789), quoted in text *supra,* at note 87.

[108] *Ibid.*

[109] 4 Cranch at 93, 94; McNally v. Hill, 293 U.S. 131, 136 (1934). *But cf.* Price v. Johnston, 334 U.S. 266, 282 (1948).

[110] Note 102 *supra.*

[111] Ex parte Watkins, 7 Pet. 568 (1833), and cases cited *supra* note 99.

[112] Dobie, *supra* note 32; Note, *The Writ of Habeas Corpus in the Federal Courts,* 35 Colum. L. Rev. 404 (1953); Note, *The Freedom Writ—The Expanding Use of Federal Habeas Corpus,* 61 Harv. L. Rev. 657 (1948); Hart, *The Supreme Court, 1958 Term—Foreword,* 73 Harv. L. Rev. 84, 103–06 (1959).

1867.[113] In that year Congress authorized the writ for any case where a person was restrained of his liberty in violation of the constitution or laws of the United States, and empowered the courts to look beyond the written return to the writ to determine the facts by hearing testimony.[114]

In the meantime, the Court had begun, without the aid of legislation, to expand the strict common-law scope of habeas corpus. The constitutional limitation of "appellate jurisdiction" played an important part in this expansion of the scope of habeas corpus, for it presented the Court with the alternatives of having its habeas corpus jurisdiction confined to an occasional review of interlocutory judicial orders, on the one hand, or of wresting some additional area from the common-law province of the writ of error, on the other. More importantly, the constitutional rule was so effective in focusing attention on the requirement that there be a lower-court decision that the Court sometimes omitted to inquire whether such a decision was one which, by the common law, could be reviewed by habeas corpus or only by writ of error.[115] For example, it became firmly established by 1840 that a writ of error was an appropriate means to review lower-court habeas corpus decisions,[116] although statutory requirements such as jurisdictional amount usually rendered that remedy ineffective.[117] Without mentioning the suitability of a writ of error in the circumstances, however, the Supreme Court commenced, in opinions rendered in 1852, 1855, and 1868, to review such decisions through the medium of its own writ of habeas corpus.[118] In one,[119] and perhaps in all three, cases the

---

113 The various statutes relating to habeas corpus are discussed in Carbo v. United States, 364 U.S. 611 (1961); see also HART & WECHSLER 1236–37.

114 14 Stat. 385 (1867).

115 *E.g.*, Ex parte Yerger, 8 Wall. 85 (1869); Ex parte Wells, 18 How. 307 (1856); Ex parte Watkins, 7 Pet. 568 (1833). *But see* Ex parte Siebold, 100 U.S. 371, 374–75 (1880).

116 Holmes v. Jennison, 14 Pet. 540, 597 (1840); Lee v. Lee, 8 Pet. 44 (1834); Tinsley v. Anderson, 171 U.S. 101, 105–06 (1898); Yates v. People, 6 Johns. (N.Y.) 337 (1810).

117 Kurtz v. Moffitt, 115 U.S. 487 (1885); Barry v. Mercein, 5 How. 103 (1847); Holmes v. Jennison, 14 Pet. 540 (1840).

118 In re Kaine, 14 How. 103 (1852); Ex parte Wells, 18 How. 307 (1856); Ex parte Yerger, 8 Wall. 85 (1869).

119 Ex parte Yerger, 8 Wall. 85 (1869).

Court derived its constitutional jurisdiction solely from the lower court's habeas corpus decision, since the confinement reviewed by the lower court was not by judicial authority. Despite that fact, the Court appears to have taken these lower-court cases (that were within the common-law province of its writ of error, though perhaps excluded by statutory-amount requirements) and reviewed them, not to test whether the lower court acted without jurisdiction, but rather to determine whether it committed error.[120]

The culmination of the habeas corpus infringement on the province of the writ of error, if such it was, came with *Ex parte Lange*[121] in 1874. There, for the first time, the Court used the writ of habeas corpus to relieve from the effect of a judgment of a court of concededly competent jurisdiction, establishing that there were errors so egregious that their commission would deprive a court of its "jurisdiction" or authority to punish and render its judgment subject to collateral attack by habeas corpus.

The decision in *Ex parte Lange*, and the 1867 legislation that first made the federal writ generally available to State prisoners,[122] stimulated an expansion of federal jurisdiction with limits even yet to be defined. These innovations brought the Supreme Court under great pressure to utilize habeas corpus in criminal cases because it was the only available means of appellate review.[123] In the eighteen years following *Ex parte Lange*, the Court utilized its habeas corpus powers to give relief in at least ten of the scores of criminal or contempt cases in which relief was sought.[124]

Two legislative developments stemmed the tide.[125] In 1885 Congress provided an appeal to the Supreme Court from the decisions

---

120 Ex parte Wells, 18 How. 307 (1856). The Court did not consider the merits in *Yerger*.

121 18 Wall. 163 (1874).

122 See Ex parte Dorr, 3 How. 103 (1845).

123 See Ex parte Parks, 26 Wall. 18 (1876); Ex parte Siebold, 100 U.S. 371 (1880).

124 Ex parte Rowland, 104 U.S. 604 (1882); Ex parte Wilson, 114 U.S. 417 (1885); Ex parte Fisk, 113 U.S. 713 (1885); Ex parte Bain, 121 U.S. 1 (1887); In re Sawyer, 124 U.S. 200 (1888); Medley, Petitioner, 134 U.S. 160 (1890); Savage, Petitioner, 134 U.S. 176 (1890); In re Mills, 135 U.S. 263 (1890); In re Burrus, 136 U.S. 586 (1890); In re Mayfield, 141 U.S. 107 (1891).

125 See Hart & Wechsler 1244.

of lower federal courts on habeas corpus petitions,[126] and in 1891 Congress made the writ of error generally available to review criminal judgments in the federal courts.[127] As the Supreme Court soon observed, these direct avenues of appellate review of criminal convictions left very little occasion for the exercise of the "original" writ.[128] Thereafter the Court's opinions became preoccupied with the questions of discretion that determine the rare circumstances under which the Court would exercise its powers.

III. The Contemporaneous Development of the Common-Law Writ of Certiorari

At common law the writ of certiorari was used by an appellate court to supply defects in the record and to remove an indictment or presentment before trial in order to pass upon its validity or to assure trial in the higher tribunal.[129] It was often used in conjunction with habeas corpus.[130] The two were complimentary. Certiorari removed the record, but not the prisoner; habeas corpus removed the prisoner, but not the record.[131]

Although quantitatively less significant, certiorari also had an-

---

126 23 Stat. 437 (1885). Prior to this time the Court could issue a writ of error to review the habeas corpus decisions of certain territorial courts. Rev. Stats. § 1909 (1875). It could also review a circuit court decision under the certification procedure. See, *e.g.*, Ex parte Milligan, 4 Wall. 2 (1866). In 1867 the Court was first authorized to review habeas corpus decisions by appeal. 14 Stat. 385, 386 (1867); Ex parte McCardle, 6 Wall. 318 (1867). But the right was abolished the following year. 15 Stat. 44 (1868); Ex parte McCardle, 7 Wall. 506 (1868).

127 The writ of error was made available in capital cases by 25 Stat. 655, 656 (1889), and extended by § 5 of the Evarts Act, 26 Stat. 826, 827 (1891), to "infamous crimes," a term comprehending all offenses punishable by penitentiary confinement. In re Claasen, 140 U.S. 200 (1891).

128 See, *e.g.*, Ex parte Mirzan, 119 U.S. 584 (1887); Ex parte Terry, 128 U.S. 289 (1888).

129 4 Bl. Comm. *320–*21; 1 Chitty, *op. cit. supra* note 22, at ch. 9; Hartranft v. Mullowny, 247 U.S. 295, 299–300 (1918).

130 Professor Jenks concluded that during the fifteenth and sixteenth centuries, before the Great Writ evolved from the writ of habeas corpus cum causa, the latter was used only to enforce the more important writ of certiorari. Jenks, *supra* note 90, at 69–72, 533–41. Other writers agree that habeas corpus cum causa was used in aid of certiorari in this period, but suggest that it also had other and independent usages. Walker, *op. cit. supra* note 90, at 21–22; Cohen, *supra* note 90, at 14–19, 25.

131 2 Hale, Pleas of the Crown 210 (Am. ed. 1847).

other usage at common law: to review the judgments of inferior courts. Here its principal function was to review interlocutory orders and decisions in which Quarter Sessions were exercising appellate jurisdiction over summary orders and convictions of lesser courts. This was consistent with the principle that certiorari could not be used in any circumstance in which a writ of error was appropriate.[132]

The "common law writ of certiorari"[133] was never issued as freely in federal courts as it had been in England, because the only source of authority to issue this writ was the narrowly confined language in section 14 of the first Judiciary Act.[134] The principal usage of the writ of certiorari in the nineteenth century became that of supplementing the record in cases already within the jurisdiction of the appellate court.[135] In this connection, it was frequently used in conjunction with the writ of habeas corpus, in order to bring before the Court portions of the lower-court record necessary to a decision of the habeas corpus petition.[136] Although one

---

[132] See Gordon, *supra* note 101; Goddard, *The Prerogative Writs*, 32 N.Z.L.J. 199 (1956); STEPHEN, CRIMINAL LAW 278 (1834); 2 HALE, *op. cit. supra* note 131, at 215.

[133] Supreme Court Rule 31-2 refers to this writ as the "common law writ of certiorari," apparently to distinguish it from the statutory writ.

[134] Ex parte Vallandigham, 1 Wall. 243 (1864); American Construction Co. v. Jacksonville Ry., 148 U.S. 372, 380 (1893).

Ex parte Bollman had extricated the writ of habeas corpus from the narrowing effect of the "which" clause in § 14, but no such feat could be performed for certiorari, since the general language that served as authority for its issuance was clearly subject to the limiting clause. See text *supra*, at note 87. It was thought that the common-law writ of certiorari could not be employed as an independent means of reviewing the judgments of inferior courts, even in cases not within the appellate jurisdiction by writ of error or appeal. United States v. Young, 94 U.S. 258, 259–60 (1877); American Constr. Co. v. Jacksonville Ry., 148 U.S. 372, 380 (1893); *cf.* Ex parte Lange, 18 Wall. 163, 166 (1874). The appellate courts of the District of Columbia, which enjoyed special common-law powers, Hartranft v. Mullowny, 247 U.S. 295, 299 (1918), did employ the writ of certiorari to review the actions of the lower courts, but only to determine whether those courts had acted without jurisdiction. Harris v. Barber, 129 U.S. 366 (1889).

[135] Barton v. Petit & Bayard, 7 Cranch 288 (1813) (auxiliary to writ of error); United States v. Young, 94 U.S. 258 (1877) (auxiliary to appeal); United States v. Adams, 9 Wall. 661 (1870) (auxiliary to writ of error). See CURTIS, JURISDICTION OF THE COURTS OF THE UNITED STATES 90–91 (1880). The Supreme Court abolished this usage of the writ by rule in 1954. Supreme Court Rule 32.

[136] Ex parte Burford, 3 Cranch 448 (1806); Ex parte Bollman, 4 Cranch 75 (1807); Ex parte Lange, 18 Wall. 163 (1874). In numerous other cases the writ was re-

dictum supported use of the writs together to perform the function of a writ of error,[137] the Court ordinarily intoned the familiar formula that habeas corpus could not be used as a substitute for a writ of error, and the Court never undertook to develop the potentialities inherent in the combination of these two writs. Nor, in light of the statute, was certiorari used by superior United States courts to bring up for trial cases currently pending in lower courts.[138]

Another obstacle existed to the use of that writ as a means of effecting appellate review. It was the rule, purporting to come from the common law, that certiorari could only be used to review judgments where the lower tribunal had acted without jurisdiction, and not to correct mere error.[139] Although this idea gained real force in this country, it was never the rule at common law.[140]

The development that led to the abolition of these two limitations on the use of certiorari dates from Congress' creation of the statutory writ of certiorari as a means of discretionary Supreme Court review.[141] There is, of course, a significant difference in the source of the Court's authority to issue the statutory and the common-law writ, and in the prescribed conditions under which each can be issued.[142] It is likely, however, that the frequent usage of

---

quested but not issued, either because the record was attached to the petition and apparently came in by agreement, Ex parte Jackson, 96 U.S. 727 (1877); Ex parte Hudgings, 249 U.S. 378 (1919), or because the petitioner failed to demonstrate merit in his habeas corpus petition, *e.g.*, In re Kaine, 14 How. 103 (1852); Ex parte Moran, 203 U.S. 96 (1906).

137 Wales v. Whitney, 114 U.S. 564, 571 (1885).

138 Ex parte Royall, 112 U.S. 181 (1884); American Constr. Co. v. Jacksonville Ry., 148 U.S. 372, 380 (1892); Fowler v. Lindsey, 3 Dall. 411 (1799). The federal courts performed this function when they exercised their statutory prerogative to remove suits or prosecutions from State courts for trial in the federal system. See Hart & Wechsler 1147–50. The writ of certiorari was the authorized means of enforcing this removal in cases not involving a personal arrest; otherwise the courts used a writ of habeas corpus cum causa. Rev. Stats. § 643 (1875); see Ex parte Crouch, 112 U.S. 178, 180 (1884).

139 Harris v. Barber, 129 U.S. 366, 371–72 (1889); Degge v. Hitchcock, 35 App. D.C. 218, 226, aff'd, 229 U.S. 162, 170 (1913); cases cited *infra* notes 146 and 148. State cases are cited in Ferris, Extraordinary Remedies §§ 157–58 (1926).

140 See text *infra*, at note 159.

141 Circuit Court of Appeals (Evarts) Act, 26 Stat. 826 (1891).

142 The statutory writ is presently issued under 28 U.S.C. §§ 1254, 1257, and is limited by the requirement of timeliness. 28 U.S.C. § 2101. Federal cases must have

statutory certiorari as a means of reviewing for error encouraged abandonment of the limitations that prevented the same use being made of the common-law writ.

In re Chetwood[143] was the first case to use certiorari other than as an auxiliary writ. There, the Court held, in annulling a judgment of contempt brought before it by means of the common-law writ, that "whenever the circumstances imperatively demand that form of interposition the writ may be allowed, as at common law, to correct excesses of jurisdiction *and in furtherance of justice*."[144]

In the two decades following *Chetwood*, two cases, *Whitney v. Dick* and *McClellan v. Carland*,[145] utilized the common-law writ as an independent means of reviewing courts of appeals' judgments not otherwise reviewable, without bothering to discuss the authority to the contrary. But in *United States v. Dickinson*,[146] falling chronologically between these two, the Court unanimously reaffirmed the holdings that the writ was "an auxiliary process only, to supply imperfections in the record of a case already before it; and not, like a writ of error, to review the judgment of an inferior court."[147] The old rule against using the writ to reverse for error also came in for its share of confusion. In *Whitney* and *McClellan* the Court obviously reversed the judgments for error, but without mentioning the authority to the contrary. In *Dickinson*, on the other hand, and subsequently in *United States v. Beatty*,[148] the Court unanimously reaffirmed the principle that the proper use of the writ was for "preventing excesses of jurisdiction . . . and that certiorari cannot be independently used to supply the place of a writ of error for the mere correction of error."

The 1925 revisions of the Judicial Code enlarged the scope of the statutory writ of certiorari and commensurately reduced the

---

been "in" a court of appeals. In State cases the judgment must be "final" and rendered by the highest State court. The common-law writ is issued under the "all-writs" section, 28 U.S.C. § 1651, and is only limited (within the bounds of constitutional appellate jurisdiction and the construction of this general statute) by the common-law usages of the writ.

143 165 U.S. 443 (1897).

144 *Id.* at 462. (Emphasis added.)

145 Whitney v. Dick, 202 U.S. 132, 135 (1906); McClellan v. Carland, 217 U.S. 268, 277–79 (1910).

146 213 U.S. 92 (1909).

147 *Id.* at 102.

148 232 U.S. 463, 467–68 (1914).

practical importance of these expansions of the scope of the common-law writ.[149] But the inroads made on the old law remained to serve as the basis for later expansion.

The modern significance of the common-law writ of certiorari has been that of reviewing interlocutory rulings and of reviewing courts of appeals' decisions in cases that for one reason or another were not "in" a court of appeals so as to be reviewable by the statutory writ.[150] The writ has been employed in reviewing courts of appeals' denials of leave to appeal in forma pauperis[151] and refusals to issue certificates of probable cause prerequisite to appeals from a final order in a habeas corpus proceeding challenging State detention.[152] It is in these two areas that the most recent expansion in the scope of the common-law writ has taken place.

The culmination of this development came in *Holiday v. Johnston*,[153] and *House v. Mayo*.[154] Holiday was a federal prisoner whose habeas corpus petition had been denied by a federal district court, which also denied him leave to appeal in forma pauperis. After the court of appeals also denied leave to appeal, the Supreme Court granted his petition for certiorari and reversed the judgment

---

149 See ROBERTSON & KIRKHAM, *op. cit. supra* note 60, at § 309.

150 *Ibid.* See In re 620 Church St. Corp., 299 U.S. 24, 26 (1936). The Court held that the court of appeals did not abuse its discretion in declining to allow an appeal.

151 Holiday v. Johnston, 313 U.S. 342 (1941); Wells v. United States, 318 U.S. 257 (1943); Steffler v. United States, 319 U.S. 38 (1943). More recently, the Supreme Court has been reviewing numerous in forma pauperis denials by means of the statutory writ of certiorari, without discussing these earlier cases. See Coppedge v. United States, 369 U.S. 438 (1962), and cases cited. This may be justified by the fact that the statute governing appeals when the earlier cases were decided spoke of an appeal being "allowed," see Wells v. United States, *supra,* at 260–61; Nye v. United States, 313 U.S. 33, 43–44 (1941), whereas under the present law the jurisdiction of the court of appeals attaches upon the filing of the notice of appeal, with or without in forma pauperis approval.

152 In House v. Mayo, 324 U.S. 42, 44 (1945), the Court declared that it could not issue a statutory writ of certiorari where a certificate of probable cause had been denied since "the case was never 'in' the court of appeals, for want of a certificate of probable cause." See 28 U.S.C. § 2253. Unlike the case with the analogous problem of in forma pauperis permission discussed *supra* note 151, there have been no statutory changes since 1948 to justify change of this rule. In Burwell v. Teets, 350 U.S. 521, 808 (1956), however, the Court did not specify whether it was using the statutory or common-law writ in reversing a court of appeals judgment that refused to consider on its merits an application for a certificate of probable cause.

153 313 U.S. 342 (1941).

154 324 U.S. 42 (1945).

of the district court for error in failing to give petitioner a hearing. The Court achieved this novel result by disposing of the certiorari question in a two-line footnote, which stated only that the common-law writ was being issued and cited *In re 620 Church Street Corp.* as authority.[155] The *Church Street* case, however, had not used the writ to reach the merits, but only to consider whether the court of appeals had abused its discretion in declining to allow the appeal.

House involved a State prisoner who had been denied federal habeas corpus and the necessary certificate of probable cause for appeal by the district court and had been denied leave to appeal in forma pauperis by the court of appeals. He petitioned the Supreme Court for certiorari but also requested the Court to issue a writ of habeas corpus. Acting on the authority of *Holiday* and *620 Church Street*, and without additional discussion of the point, the Court held that it could review the case by the common-law writ of certiorari, asserting that the scope of review extended not only to whether the court of appeals should have allowed the appeal, but "also to the questions on the merits sought to be raised by the appeal."[156] The judgment of the district court was reversed on the merits; the accompanying petition for habeas corpus was denied.

With *House v. Mayo*, the Supreme Court completed the abolition of two historic limitations on the common-law writ of certiorari: that the statutory authorization of writs "in aid of their respective jurisdictions" required that the case be one over which the Court then had jurisdiction[157] and that certiorari could not be used to review non-jurisdictional errors.[158] It is of interest that the aboli-

---

155 313 U.S. at 348, n. 2; see *supra* note 150.

156 324 U.S. at 44–45.

157 *But cf.* Price v. Johnston, 334 U.S. 266, 279 (1948). It is noteworthy that two years earlier the Supreme Court had approved a similar usage of the writs of prohibition and mandamus. Ex parte Peru, 318 U.S. 578 (1943). Mandamus had gone through a similar development. *Compare* In re Glasser, 198 U.S. 171 (1905), and In re Massachusetts, 197 U.S. 482 (1905), *with* Ex parte United States, 287 U.S. 241 (1932); Ex parte Peru, 318 U.S. 578 (1943); and Roche v. Evaporated Milk Ass'n, 319 U.S. 21, 25 (1943). See, generally, Wolfson, *Extraordinary Writs in the Supreme Court since Ex parte Peru,* 51 COLUM. L. REV. 977 (1951).

158 A subsequent decision indicates that the rule may be different where property rights are at issue. In De Beers Consol. Mines v. United States, 325 U.S. 212, 217 (1945), the Court stated that the common-law writ of certiorari "can, of course,

tion of the second proposition, summary as it was, actually corrected a long-standing error about the proper scope of the common-law writ of certiorari. In *Rex v. Northumberland Compensation Appeal Tribunal*,[159] the opinions of Lord Chief Justice Goddard and Lord Denning surveyed the ancient law and "restored certiorari to its rightful position" with the conclusion that it was properly used to correct errors of law appearing on the record even though they did not go to the jurisdiction of the court.[160]

As for habeas corpus, the leviathan proportions of the companion writ of certiorari, as utilized in *Holiday* and *House*, have largely overshadowed the occasions for its exercise. Out of constitutional necessity the Court cannot award either writ unless its action would be reviewing a decision of some judicial body.[161] But if the case meets that requirement for purposes of habeas corpus, the Court also has power to review and, if necessary, reverse the judgment by the less limited process of common-law certiorari.[162] The Court has made clear, however, that as a matter of discretion its power to use the common-law writ will seldom be exercised.[163] In this context, the writ of habeas corpus would only be necessary to effect an immediate release. If so, the writ of habeas corpus in the Supreme Court may have moved from its nineteenth-century role, as the foundation of jurisdiction in aid of which certiorari might issue,

---

not be availed of to correct a mere error in the exercise of conceded judicial power. But when a court has no judicial power to do what it purports to do—when its action is not mere error but usurpation of power—the situation falls precisely within the allowable use of sec. 262."

159 [1951] 1 K.B. 711, [1952] 1 K.B. 338, 346 (C.A.).

160 "Until about 100 years ago, certiorari was regularly used to correct errors of law on the face of the record. It is only within the last century that it has fallen into disuse, and that is only because there has, until recently, been little occasion for its exercise." [1952] 1 K.B. at 348 (Denning, L.J.).

161 In respect to certiorari, see United States v. Perrin, 131 U.S. 55 (1889); Jewell v. Knight, 123 U.S. 426 (1887); White v. Turk, 12 Pet. 238 (1838); Robertson & Kirkham, *op. cit. supra* note 60, at § 164, all discussing the constitutional limitations on bringing cases to the Supreme Court by certified questions before decision below.

162 Certiorari is less limited because it is direct rather than collateral review and is thus free from the controversies about what errors are "jurisdictional." In addition, habeas corpus is, of course, limited to those circumstances where the petitioner is actually under confinement. Ex parte Royall, 112 U.S. 181 (1884).

163 Ex parte Fahey, 332 U.S. 258 (1947), and cases cited *supra* notes 157–58.

back to the function of the sixteenth-century *corpus cum causa*, a mere auxiliary available to enforce the process of certiorari.

IV. Some Procedural and Discretionary Considerations

A. PROCEDURE

At common law habeas corpus was a writ of right: it issued immediately upon showing of some ground for its issuance.[164] The issues were argued when the prisoner was brought before the court on the "return," and he was either "remanded" to custody or discharged.[165] About 1805 the English courts began to resolve habeas corpus cases by the issuance of a rule to show cause why the writ should not issue (rule nisi).[166] This was done as a matter of administrative convenience to obviate the necessity for producing the prisoner where this was difficult or unnecessary.

The procedure upon application for the writ in the Supreme Court has been less consistent. In the earliest cases the writ seems to have issued as of right, with the argument occurring on its return.[167] The rule to show cause soon made its appearance, however, and with it the alternative of making a "motion for the writ of habeas corpus." In one case Marshall suggested use of the rule because the Court ought not to issue the writ until its jurisdiction to do so had been made apparent,[168] but most of the cases contain no discussion of why one procedure was used rather than another.[169] Most of the cases decided in the half-century following 1807 were considered upon motion[170] or upon the return to the rule to show cause.[171]

In 1867 Congress passed a comprehensive act governing pro-

---

164 Goddard, *supra* note 132 at 214; Dicey, Law of the Constitution 211 (6th ed. 1902). It was not a writ "of course," which a court was bound to grant without any showing. *Ibid.*

165 Goddard, *supra* note 132, at 214.

166 *Id.* at 214–15; Cox v. Hakes, [1890] 15 App. Cas. 506, 509.

167 Ex parte Burford, 3 Cranch 448 (1806); Ex parte Bollman, 4 Cranch 75 (1807).

168 Ex parte Milburn, 9 Pet. 704, 704(a) (1835).

169 In Ex parte Watkins, 3 Pet. 193 (1830), the parties argued over whether the case should be submitted on the rule or by motion. Marshall directed the parties to reach agreement on the matter and issued a rule when they failed to do so.

170 *E.g.*, Ex parte Kearney, 7 Wheat. 38 (1822); Ex parte Wells, 18 How. 307 (1856).

171 *E.g.*, Ex parte Watkins, 7 Pet. 568 (1833); Ex parte Milburn, 9 Pet. 704 (1835).

cedure upon habeas corpus petitions,[172] which provided for the writ to issue "forthwith" on application, unless it appeared on its face to require denial.[173] Thereafter, the writ was issued as of right in a number of cases, although it appears that the parties sometimes agreed that the petitioner need not be brought into court in response thereto.[174] Despite the mandatory language of the statute, however, the practice of hearing these cases on rule to show cause[175] or on motion (now a motion for leave to file a petition for the writ of habeas corpus)[176] continued. In one early case the use of the rule was justified as a matter of "convenience in the administration of justice,"[177] but not until 1941 did the Court explicitly measure this practice against the statute and indorse its validity.[178] The routine use of the rule was given statutory sanction in the 1948 Judicial Code.[179] In 1954, the Supreme Court amended its Rules to provide that habeas corpus petitions directed to the Court should be preceded by an *ex parte* motion for leave to file such a petition.[180]

B. EXHAUSTION

One of the earliest discretionary rules in respect to habeas corpus stated that the Court would not issue the writ for a State prisoner in advance of his trial in the State court.[181] Later, the Court enlarged

---

172 14 Stat. 385 (1867).

173 The language was rephrased in 1875. Rev. Stats. 755 (1875), 28 U.S.C. § 455 (1940).

174 Ex parte Lange, 18 Wall. 163 (1874); Ex parte Clarke, 100 U.S. 399 (1879); Ex parte Curtis, 106 U.S. 371 (1882); Medley, Petitioner, 134 U.S. 160 (1890); Savage, Petitioner, 134 U.S. 176 (1890).

175 *E.g.*, Ex parte Rowland, 104 U.S. 604 (1882); In re Lane, 135 U.S. 443 (1890); Ex parte Spencer, 228 U.S. 652 (1913); Ex parte Grossman, 267 U.S. 87 (1925).

176 *E.g.*, Ex parte Fonda, 117 U.S. 516 (1885); Ex parte Mirzan, 119 U.S. 584 (1887); Ex parte Hudgings, 249 U.S. 378 (1919).

177 Ex parte Yarborough, 110 U.S. 651, 653 (1884). And see Ex parte Jackson, 96 U.S. 727 (1878), where the Court remarked that the rule was being issued by consent.

178 Walker v. Johnston, 312 U.S. 275, 283–84 (1941).

179 28 U.S.C. § 2242.

180 Supreme Court Rules 32-1, 31-5. We are told by Lord Chief Justice Goddard that most habeas corpus matters in the High Court are presently submitted by application for leave or by notice of motion. Goddard, *supra* note 132, at 215.

181 Ex parte Royall, 117 U.S. 254 (1886).

this rule by stating that it applied to petitions after final decision in the State court as well as those before, and that the writ would not issue where the petitioner had opportunity to make his contentions by direct appeal.[182] In time this same rule evolved into the requirement that the petitioner must have exhausted all of his State remedies before applying for federal habeas corpus,[183] a requirement embodied in the Judicial Code in 1948 and re-emphasized in the Court's own rules.[184]

The Court enunciated a similar policy for federal prisoners. One early case indorsed the "judicious and salutary" rule of non-interference with proceedings pending in the federal courts in advance of their final determination.[185] A later decision added that the interests of orderly administration required that the writ not issue where the error could be corrected by writ of error to the court of appeals.[186]

C. RELIEF AVAILABLE FROM LOWER COURT

Another of the Court's standards was phrased this way in an early leading case:[187] "[T]his court will not issue such a writ . . . in cases where it may as well be done in the proper Circuit Court, if there are no special circumstances in the case making direct action or intervention by this court necessary or expedient." This rule, or its equivalent, often appears in opinions denying habeas corpus.[188]

---

182 Ex parte Spencer, 228 U.S. 652 (1913).

183 *E.g.*, Ex parte Hawk, 321 U.S. 114 (1944); Mooney v. Holohan, 294 U.S. 103 (1935).

184 28 U.S.C. § 2254; Supreme Court Rule 31-5.

185 In re Chapman, 156 U.S. 211, 217 (1895).

186 In re Lincoln, 202 U.S. 178 (1906).

187 Ex parte Mirzan, 119 U.S. 584, 586 (1887).

188 *E.g.*, Ex parte Tracy, 249 U.S. 551 (1919); Ex parte Abernathy, 320 U.S. 219 (1943); Ex parte Hawk, 321 U.S. 114 (1944).

Courts of appeals have followed a similar rule. United States ex rel. Bernstein v. Hill, 71 F. 2d 159 (3d Cir. 1934) (dictum); Whitaker v. Johnston, 85 F. 2d 199 (9th Cir. 1936); Brosius v. Botkin, 110 F. 2d 49 (D.C. Cir. 1940); Sweetney v. Johnston, 121 F. 2d 445 (9th Cir. 1941), cert. den. 314 U.S. 607 (1941); In re Gersing, 145 F. 2d 481 (D.C. Cir. 1944); Wright v. Johnston, 74 F. Supp. 25 (9th Cir. 1947). But see Ex parte Haumesch, 82 F. 2d 558 (9th Cir. 1936). The 1948 Code incorporates this principle. 28 U.S.C. § 2242.

The Court also evolved a corollary rule that the petitioner need not apply to the lower federal courts where it would clearly be fruitless to do so.[189]

The mandatory language of the Judicial Code and of the Court's rule[190] suggest that, if the petition fails to allege that an application for relief has been made to a lower court or fails to give reasons for not doing so, this is a sufficient ground for the appellate court to deny relief. Nevertheless, the Court's oft-voiced conviction that a "petition for *habeas corpus* ought not to be scrutinized with technical nicety"[191] suggests that a petitioner with an otherwise meritorious claim would not fail to secure relief simply because he did not conform to this requirement.[192]

D. INABILITY TO TRY FACTUAL ISSUES

A third major consideration in the denial of habeas corpus does not seem to have been explicitly stated by the Court. With the expanding scope of habeas corpus, more and more applications for relief turn on factual issues. The traditional means of resolving factual questions in the Supreme Court is by reference to a commissioner, but the Court has held that the statutes preclude this in the case of habeas corpus petitions.[193] Accordingly, where a petition raises factual issues, unless the Court chooses to exercise the new

---

189 Ex parte Terry, 128 U.S. 289 (1888); In re Sawyer, 124 U.S. 200 (1888); Mooney v. Holohan, 294 U.S. 103 (1935). This factor figured in each of the post-1891 cases where habeas corpus relief was granted. See text *infra,* following note 197.

190 22 U.S.C. § 2242; Supreme Court Rule 31-5. Ex parte Hawk, 321 U.S. 114, 117–18 (1944), decided before the relevant statute was passed, phrased the rule in a way that seems to render an appeal before seeking relief in the Supreme Court unnecessary, although the reasons behind the rule would seem to require it. Mr. Justice Douglas has cited a petitioner's failure to appeal a habeas corpus denial as one reason for refusing, as a circuit Justice, to grant habeas corpus relief. Norris v. Swope, 72 S. Ct. 1020 (1952) (Douglas, J.).

191 *E.g.,* Holiday v. Johnston, 313 U.S. 342, 350 (1941).

192 *Accord:* Stidham v. Swope, 83 F. Supp. 370 (9th Cir. 1949). The petitioner was ultimately discharged in this case. Stidham v. Swope, 96 F. Supp. 773 (N.D. Calif. 1951).

193 Holiday v. Johnston, 313 U.S. 342 (1941), held that by stating in Rev. Stat. § 761, that the "court, or justice, or judge shall proceed in a summary way to determine the facts of the case," Congress had precluded a district court from having the facts heard by a commissioner. This statutory requirement originated in the 1867 Act. 14 Stat. 385, 386 (1867). 28 U.S.C. § 2243 is to the same effect.

statutory power of transfer,[194] the Court has no alternative other than to deny it. Thus, the "original" writ is suitable only where the petitioner's claim for discharge presents only a legal question.

It is significant that each of the three instances since 1891 when the Supreme Court has used its writ of habeas corpus to give relief from confinement, *Matter of Heff*,[195] *Ex parte Hudgings*,[196] and *Ex parte Grossman*,[197] involved undisputed facts, and the petitioner's right to discharge turned solely on a sharply drawn legal question of real moment. In fact, the legal questions were of such substance that the Court and counsel were almost entirely diverted from the initial question of the propriety of their resolution by the "original" writ. None of the opinions contains any discussion of the jurisdictional issues, and only the *Hudgings* case even so much as cites a statute, rule, or decision concerning Supreme Court power to issue the writ. The cases have one common feature, however. In each there was a possible barrier to effective or immediate appellate relief, although in retrospect even that seems to have been misunderstood or misapplied.

Heff, who had been convicted of selling liquor to an emancipated Indian, came directly to the Supreme Court because the court of appeals in another case had already decided adversely to his contention that the prohibitory act was unconstitutional, surely an insufficient reason by today's standards. Hudgings and Grossman had been committed for contempt. Hudgings' counsel cited one case to the effect that a judgment of contempt was not reviewable by writ of error or appeal;[198] the Court's opinion simply asserted without explanation that the case was one of exceptional character allowing the applicant to bypass other available sources of judicial power. In Grossman's case there was not a word about the suitability of habeas corpus relief in either party's brief or in the Government briefs. The Court's opinion is equally silent. In view of the availability of common-law certiorari to review contempt commit-

---

194 See text *infra*, at notes 200–03.

195 197 U.S. 488 (1905).

196 249 U.S. 378 (1919).

197 267 U.S. 87 (1925).

198 Ex parte Fisk, 113 U.S. 713 (1885), cited in Preliminary Brief of Petitioner, p. 40, Ex parte Hudgings, 249 U.S. 378 (1919).

ments,[199] the suitability of original habeas corpus in both *Hudgings* and *Grossman* seems questionable.

E. TRANSFERS

In 1948 Congress gave the Court an alternative to denial of petitions involving factual issues by providing that the Supreme Court or any of its Justices or any circuit judge "may decline to entertain an application for a writ of habeas corpus and may transfer the application for hearing and determination to the district court having jurisdiction to entertain it."[200]

Despite the large number of applications being received in this period, the Supreme Court reported no transfers under the statute until the closing months of the 1961 Term. Then it issued two transfer orders of surprisingly diverse form. In *Chaapel v. Cochran*,[201] the Court's order simply transferred the motion "for hearing and determination" to the appropriate United States district court in Florida. In *Hayes v. Maryland*,[202] decided about a month later, the Court denied the motion, granted certiorari upon the motion papers (a practice discussed hereafter), and then ordered the case transferred to the United States District Court for the District of Maryland. The diverse procedures probably derive from the fact that the *Hayes* petition would have been timely as a petition for certiorari whereas *Chaapel* would not.[203] Whatever the procedures employed, however, the fact that the Supreme Court has now begun to transfer cases under the statute is a significant development in the administration of this aspect of its business.

---

199 In re Chetwood, 165 U.S. 443 (1897), discussed in text *supra*, at note 143.

200 28 U.S.C. § 2241 (*b*). See Stidham v. Swope, 83 F. Supp. 370 (9th Cir. 1949); Knetzer v. Schultz, 344 U.S. 908 (1952) (dissent suggests transfer). Query whether the Supreme Court could, under 28 U.S.C. § 2241(*b*) or otherwise, transfer a case over which it had no constitutional appellate jurisdiction? *Cf.* Western Union Telegraph Co. v. Pennsylvania, 368 U.S. 71, 77 (1961), hinting that the Court might transfer original actions between the States to district courts.

201 369 U.S. 869 (1962).

202 370 U.S. 931 (1962).

203 See text *infra*, at note 236. Since 28 U.S.C. § 2241(*b*) relates only to habeas corpus cases there is room for doubt whether it authorizes a transfer where, as in *Hayes*, the Court has already denied the habeas corpus petition when it grants certiorari and orders the case transferred.

V. Disposition of Motions since 1929

The wave of post-conviction petitions that has swamped the lower federal courts since the landmark constitutional decisions in the 1930's is familiar knowledge. The Court has docketed its share of this increase, but, since not one of the 2,000 petitioners who have come to the Court during the last three decades has been ordered discharged, any study of the Court's administration of the habeas corpus device in this period necessarily resolves into an inquiry into the manner in which relief was denied. The table in the appendix, which classifies all of these cases, summarizes the results of that inquiry.

A. In General

The Court rarely furnishes any reasons for its denial of habeas corpus. It seldom writes an opinion or even adds a word of elaboration to its order. As the table discloses, 1,686 of the petitions denied in this period, over 84 per cent, were disposed of by a bare notation in the orders that the motion was denied. It seems likely that some of these were cases over which the Court lacked constitutional appellate jurisdiction or cases in which the Court lacked statutory authority because the errors alleged did not come within the current concept of what was correctible by habeas corpus. Others must have been denied because the petitioner had failed to exhaust his State remedies or failed to apply first to lower federal courts. Many of the remainder were probably denied because they involved factual questions that the Court had no practical means to resolve.

Fortunately, the Court has occasionally contributed an opinion or a few words of elaboration to its habeas corpus orders. An examination of these cases yields the impression that the Court's deviations from its normal brevity have been motivated by a desire to instruct the petitioner on his rights and remedies, to encourage the granting of relief by the State or lower federal courts, or to condemn judicial or executive practices deemed improper. In short, many of these orders read like open letters to a particular prisoner, judge, or warden.

If there is justification for this deviation from the normal judicial function, it stems from the fact that almost all of the petitioners in these cases are striving for relief without the benefit of counsel.[204] But, if the absence of counsel in these cases is one reason for the occasional amplifications in the language of orders denying relief, it is also a circumstance that weighs against the Court's saying too much. The questions of constitutional and statutory law and the intricacies of procedure tangled in these *pro se* petitions are raw materials that the Court normally should not attempt to process without the aid of counsel.

B. RULE TO SHOW CAUSE

Six times during the administration of Chief Justice Hughes and twice during the tenure of Chief Justice Stone, the Court issued a rule to show cause why a motion for leave to file a petition for habeas corpus should not be granted.[205] In five of these the rules were subsequently discharged and the motions for leave to file were denied, apparently because the return to the rule satisfied the Court. One became moot. In none of these six cases was an opinion filed.

In the two remaining cases the rules were discharged by full opinions. The disparity is intriguing. The length and coverage of these opinions bespeak a purpose other than to render the petitioner some gratuitous legal aid or to enlighten the authorities who would next deal with petitioners' claims. Nor is the primary purpose of the opinions that of explaining why the rule is being discharged, although that is mentioned. Rather, these seem to be instances

---

[204] Only 39 of the 2,000 petitions disposed of in this period, less than 2 per cent, bore the name of counsel. See the last column of the table in the appendix. The petitioners who did have counsel were frequently those whose case had become a cause célèbre: Mooney, Hauptman, Quirin, Yamashita, Hirota, Touhy, Chessman.

[205] Mooney v. Holohan, 293 U.S. 529 (1934) (rule issued): 294 U.S. 103 (1935) (rule discharged with opinion); Ex parte House, 303 U.S. 626 (1938) (rule discharged, no reasons given; issuance of rule apparently not reported); Ex parte Holchak, 305 U.S. 561 (1938) (rule issued); 306 U.S. 616 (1939) (rule discharged after argument, no reasons given); Ex parte Becker, 311 U.S. 618 (1940) (rule issued); 312 U.S. 650 (1941) (rule discharged, no reasons given); Ex parte Offill, 311 U.S. 622 (1940) (rule discharged, no reasons given; issuance of rule apparently not reported); Ex parte Cleio Hull, 312 U.S. 546 (1941) (rule discharged with opinion; issuance of rule apparently not reported); Ex parte Weil, 317 U.S. 597 (1942) (rule discharged and motion denied as moot, petitioner no longer being in respondent's custody; issuance of rule apparently not reported); Ex parte Wells, 321 U.S. 748 (1944) (rule discharged, no reasons given; issuance of rule apparently not reported).

where the Court has seized an opportunity to issue a corrective and prospective declaration of policy. In *Mooney v. Holohan,*[206] the per curiam opinion explained that leave to file was denied because the petitioner had not made use of the corrective judicial process available in the State courts, but the Court nevertheless used this occasion to promulgate what immediately became a leading due-process doctrine: a conviction obtained by knowing use of perjured testimony was violative of due process. It is noteworthy that Mooney was represented by counsel, so the substantive questions that the Court expounded had passed through the adversary process.

In *Ex parte Hull*[207] a unanimous opinion by Mr. Justice Murphy discharged the rule for failure to allege sufficient grounds for relief, but nevertheless declared the invalidity of a Michigan warden's regulation that had the effect of suppressing papers that prisoners sought to file in the courts. This end is obviously laudable, but the wisdom of disposing of substantive questions that are not necessary to the present or future disposition of the case and which have not been subjected to argument is, of course, questionable.

An equally interesting question is why the Court issued rules in some few of these cases and not in others and, in particular, why no rules have been reported since 1944. The answer may lie in the immediate effect of issuing the rule, which is to provoke a response from the committing authority, a response that may be sorely needed in cases where the petitioner is seldom represented by counsel and the only information available to the Court is the petitioner's account. There is some evidence that the Court is now using more informal procedures for obtaining additional information about certain petitions on its docket. These procedures may now be serving the purpose formerly served by issuance of the rule to show cause. Of a sample of about thirty habeas corpus files docketed during Chief Justice Warren's tenure, three were found to contain responses by the committing authority assertedly submitted at the request or direction of the Court.[208]

---

206 294 U.S. 103 (1935).

207 312 U.S. 546 (1941).

208 Parker v. United States, 364 U.S. 808 (1960); Ramirez v. United States, 362 U.S. 986 (1960); Rose v. Bell, 355 U.S. 805 (1957). The Court's order list contains no statement that a response was requested, but it does note in each of these instances the participation of the attorney for the custodian. Since the Court's rules expressly provide that habeas corpus proceedings "will be ex parte, unless the court requires

C. MOTION DENIED WITHOUT PREJUDICE

Another practice employed by Hughes, and continued by his immediate successor, was that of denying the motion "without prejudice to an application to the United States District Court" or other words of like import.[209] Under Hughes most of these orders gave no reason for the special form of words (which the table shows was employed in only 11 of the 200 motions denied in his tenure). Since the Supreme Court had already declared that its denial of leave to file a petition for habeas corpus was without prejudice to the petitioner's application to other and appropriate sources of judicial power,[210] the employment of this form on some orders and not on others raises some question. A similar phenomenon in the Court's denial of petitions for certiorari is discussed in Professor Reitz's exhaustive articles on habeas corpus in the United States district courts. He suggested that when the Court attaches this form to a denial of certiorari it probably indicates that there is a substantial impediment to the Court's review of an apparently meritorious claim,[211] and that the words are inserted in the order to encourage the lower federal courts to make an independent inquiry into the case.[212] Professor Hart has suggested that the form is "only a bit of gratuitous legal aid to prisoners combined with extracurricular communications of Delphic encouragement to federal district judges."[213] These observations probably explain some of the "without prejudice" habeas corpus denials also, but in the case of habeas

---

the respondent to show cause why leave to file the petition for a writ of habeas corpus should not be granted," Supreme Court Rule 31-5, it seems probable that most of the other cases where counsel has appeared for respondent (from 5 to 10 per cent in recent years) are instances where the Court has directed such participation. This would indicate a fairly frequent use of this device.

A related informal procedure, less suitable for habeas corpus petitions, was employed by Chief Justice Hughes, who is said often to have directed the Clerk to procure a proper record from the court below in in forma pauperis petitions for certiorari. McElwain, *The Business of the Supeme Court as Conducted by Chief Justice Hughes*, 63 HARV. L. REV. 5, 22 (1949).

209 Cases cited *infra*, at notes 214–24.

210 Ex parte Tracy, 249 U.S. 551, 552 (1919).

211 Reitz, *supra* note 1, 74 HARV. L. REV. at 1359.

212 Reitz, *supra* note 1, 108 U. PA. L. REV. at 507, 511.

213 Hart, *supra* note 112, at 114, n. 88.

corpus there is evidence from which more definite conclusions may be drawn. In approximately two-thirds of the denials of petitions for original habeas corpus "without prejudice," the Court made the reasons for the denial explicit, and from those reasons one may glean some significant impressions about what the words mean even when unaccompanied by reasons.

The practice of stating reasons along with a denial "without prejudice" began with Hughes but was practiced with greater frequency by Stone. The most frequent occasion for denying habeas corpus "without prejudice" during this period was for failure to exhaust State remedies. Some of the earliest denials referred to "appropriate application to the proper Court of the State of Michigan"[214] and to "appropriate application for review of the judgment of the Supreme Court of California on writ of certiorari or appeal."[215]

Under Stone, who was plagued with the brunt of the "exhaustion" tangle, some of the Court's "without prejudice" orders began to be a little more direct with their legal aid. One case stated that the motion was denied without prejudice because petitioner had failed to exhaust his State remedies by applying for a writ of error coram nobis, citing a pertinent Indiana decision for petitioner's enlightenment.[216] Later, two other petitioners from the same State had their motions denied "without prejudice" because, the Court said, they had not yet obtained from the Indiana Supreme Court an order finally disposing of their appeals from denials of coram nobis.[217] Michigan and Nebraska petitioners[218] drew the "without prejudice" form because they had not yet exhausted their State remedies by applying to the State supreme courts for habeas corpus. Pertinent statutes and cases were cited for the Nebraska petitioner, and, when he returned to the Court six months later, he again drew a gentle "without prejudice" order, that redirected his attention to the remedy that the Nebraska Supreme Court had suggested in his

214 Ex parte Van Dyke, 296 U.S. 541 (1935).

215 Ex parte Lee, 303 U.S. 624 (1938).

216 Ex parte Botwinski, 314 U.S. 586 (1942).

217 Ex parte Davis, 318 U.S. 412 (1943); Ex parte Wood, 318 U.S. 745 (1943).

218 Ex parte Ross, 319 U.S. 729 (1943); Ex parte Williams, 317 U.S. 604 (1943).

case.[219] Finally, one other petition was denied without prejudice "on the ground that it does not appear that all the matters alleged in the petition have been previously presented to the state courts of Indiana."[220]

These denials for failure to exhaust State remedies were decided in the 1941 and 1942 Terms. In the 1943 Term the Court issued, under the style of *Ex parte Abernathy*,[221] a short opinion denying seventeen motions. The opinion, which clearly seems designed to discourage applications for the original writ of habeas corpus, cautioned that the Court does not exercise its discretionary jurisdiction (save in exceptional circumstances) where an adequate remedy may be had in a lower federal court or where the petitioner has not exhausted his remedies in the State courts. "Refusal of the writ, without more," the Court concluded, "is not an adjudication on the merits and is to be taken as without prejudice to an application to any other court for the relief sought."[222] Stone seems never again to have employed the "without-prejudice" form in an original habeas corpus case, except in one case in the 1944 Term that steered the petitioner back into exhausting his remedies by coram nobis and habeas corpus and re-emphasized the considerations set forth in the *Abernathy* opinion.[223]

The "without-prejudice" form was employed twice by Chief Justice Vinson, and then apparently died as a means of denying original habeas corpus relief.[224] The strong statement in *Ex parte Abernathy* that all denials are without prejudice and the 1954 incorporation of this declaration in the Supreme Court rules[225] probably deprived the device of any further utility.

---

219 Ex parte Williams, 319 U.S. 730 (1943), citing "*Williams* v. *Olson,* 8 N.W. 2d 830."

220 Ex parte McConnell, 319 U.S. 731, 732 (1943).

221 320 U.S. 219 (1943).

222 *Id.* at 220.

223 Ex parte Hawk, 321 U.S. 114 (1944).

224 Francis v. Resweber, 331 U.S. 786 (1947); see PRETTYMAN, DEATH AND THE SUPREME COURT 126–27 (1961); In re Bush, 336 U.S. 971 (1949); Hirota v. MacArthur, 338 U.S. 197, 201–02, n. 3 (1948) (Douglas, J., concurring).

225 Supreme Court Rule 31-5.

D. CONSIDERATION AND DENIAL OF PAPERS AS PETITIONS FOR CERTIORARI

Throughout the first four Terms under Chief Justice Warren there were practically no deviations from the form denials of leave to file. Then, midway through the 1957 Term, the Court issued the following order in *Cheeks v. Maryland*:[226] "Motion for leave to file petition for writ of habeas corpus denied. Treating the papers submitted as a petition for writ of certiorari, certiorari is denied."

This form had been introduced and briefly used by Chief Justice Stone[227] following the decision in *Ex parte Hawk*[228] which held that before State prisoners could qualify for federal habeas corpus they must ordinarily exhaust all of the available State remedies, including certiorari to the United States Supreme Court. In view of this sequence and of the specific facts in the initial cases,[229] there can be little doubt that the purpose of the gratuitous certiorari denial in Chief Justice Stone's Court was to assure that these petitioners would not be barred from district court relief for failure to exhaust their State remedies by petitioning for certiorari. But, if that is the case, it is surprising that this form abruptly disappeared

---

226 355 U.S. 929 (1958).

227 Ex parte Welch, 322 U.S. 708 (1944); Ex parte Hanley, 322 U.S. 708 (1944); Ex parte King, 322 U.S. 716 (1944); Ex parte Hall, 322 U.S. 717 (1944); Ex parte Dreksler, 323 U.S. 672 (1944); Ex parte Caulo, 323 U.S. 669 (1944); Ex parte Lee, 323 U.S. 669 (1944).

228 321 U.S. 114, 116–17 (1944).

229 Shortly after the *Hawk* opinion was issued portions of it were incorporated in a mimeographed letter that an Illinois federal district judge apparently used to inform State prisoners why he was denying them habeas corpus relief. One of these prisoners then filed a petition for habeas corpus in the Supreme Court, making this plea for relief from the exhaustion requirement: "Not seeing how he has grounds for a writ of certiorari when no grounds have been furnished by the Illinois Supreme Court's action [the court issued no opinion], Petitioner asks this honorable Court to accept jurisdiction in this case and grant his plea for Habeas Corpus or order that he be granted a hearing in the Federal Court at Chicago, Illinois." Petition for Habeas Corpus, Ex parte Welch, 322 U.S. 708 (1944). The Court responded by denying habeas corpus relief and by adding that the petition was treated as a petition for certiorari and denied. In the succeeding few months similar orders were issued in response to six other Illinois habeas corpus petitions, all of which, like the *Welch* case, were filed within the time when they would have been timely as a petition for certiorari. Cases cited *supra* note 227.

after October 9, 1944.[230] Stone's death in 1946 furnishes one possible explanation for the disappearance of this form. His successor was far less inclined to add anything to the two-word order with which these motions are ordinarily denied.

Although the practice of denying certiorari upon habeas corpus papers was of short duration, the reasons for its use survived its discontinuance. After a brief period of indecision on the necessity for obtaining a denial of certiorari to exhaust State remedies,[231] the requirement was reaffirmed in *Darr v. Burford*.[232] In no instance did this unpopular rule operate more unfairly than with respect to the uncounseled prisoners who actually came to the Supreme Court directly after a denial of relief in a State court but who mistakenly styled their papers as a petition for habeas corpus, an understandable mistake, particularly where the petitioner was seeking habeas corpus relief in the State court.[233] Following the Supreme Court's denial of habeas corpus these petitioners must presumably institute new State proceedings, ascend the appellate ladder, and, on again arriving at the Supreme Court, take care to style their papers as a petition for certiorari so that the order list will carry the magic words without which the lower federal courts may refuse them access. It seems certain that the practice that the Warren Court renewed in 1957 in *Cheeks v. Maryland* and has used in a large proportion of cases since that time is a procedural reform designed to alleviate this hardship.

Its use is not without problems, however. There is no statutory warrant for treating an unambiguous request for a writ of habeas corpus as a petition for certiorari, although there is a suggestive

[230] There are cases thereafter where a single order denies both certiorari and habeas corpus relief, but at least some of these cases are situations where the petitioner has actually requested both writs. *E.g.*, Grand v. Mayo, 332 U.S. 766 (1944); Foxall v. Ragan, 323 U.S. 748 (1944).

[231] Wade v. Mayo, 334 U.S. 672 (1948). [232] 339 U.S. 200 (1950).

[233] A case in point is Kirby v. Maryland, 261 F. 2d 345 (4th Cir. 1958). There a prisoner who had been denied habeas corpus relief in the State courts made the mistake of petitioning the Supreme Court for habeas corpus instead of certiorari (although the papers would not have been timely as a petition for certiorari). 357 U.S. 901 (1958). Thereafter, federal habeas corpus relief was denied on the merits and because, on an examination of this history, "it is clear that by failing to apply for writ of certiorari from the decision of the Court of Appeals of Maryland he has failed to exhaust his State remedies." Kirby v. Maryland, *supra*, at 346.

analogy in a provision of the Judicial Code relating to improvident appeals.[234] Probably few would object to the practice on this ground, however, so long as its purpose is merely to supply the procedural formality of a denial of certiorari. A more interesting question is why the Court denies certiorari in only a part of these cases: 20 per cent in the last four Terms. Consistent with the exhaustion rationale, it is not surprising that the Court does not seem to deny certiorari for federal petitioners,[235] but there are many State prisoners for whom the Court does not deny certiorari either, and at least one of these was subsequently denied district court habeas corpus relief for this reason.[236]

An examination of the original papers in a large number of these cases suggests that certiorari is only denied in those cases where the petition reveals: (1) that the petitioner had been denied relief by a State court; and (2) that his habeas corpus papers were filed in the Supreme Court within ninety days after the State court action so that they would have been timely as a petition for the statutory writ of certiorari. The first prerequisite is hardly subject to argument, but the second is questionable. Ordinarily, if a petition for certiorari is out of time, the Court simply denies the petition and rarely notes that it failed for jurisdictional (timeliness) grounds.[237] So far as a district court could observe, the State remedies would then have been exhausted. Therefore, if the purpose of denying certiorari in response to a request for habeas corpus is to put the uncounseled petitioner in the position he would have been if he had not misstyled his papers, the device should be employed without regard to the timeliness of filing.

If the practice of denying certiorari on habeas corpus petitions was simply designed to aid uncounseled petitioners in exhausting their State remedies, the practice soon outgrew its purpose. In

---

234 See 28 U.S.C. § 2103, which provides that where an appeal is improvidently taken "the papers whereon the appeal was taken shall be regarded and acted on as a petition for writ of certiorari. . . ."

235 *But cf.* Broadus-Bey v. Clemmer, 361 U.S. 804 (1959), where the petition of a prisoner held in the District of Columbia reformatory was treated and denied as certiorari.

236 Kirby v. Maryland, *supra* note 233.

237 *But see* Foxall v. Ragen, 323 U.S. 748 (1944).

Reynolds v. Cochran[238] and *Carnley v. Cochran*,[239] habeas corpus petitions submitted just two and three years after the certiorari practice was reinstituted, the Court issued the following order: "Motion for leave to file petition for writ of habeas corpus denied. Treating the papers submitted as a petition for writ of certiorari, certiorari to the Supreme Court of Florida granted." After argument the judgments of the Florida Supreme Court denying these petitioners relief on their claims of a constitutional right to counsel were reversed.[240]

In both of the foregoing cases the habeas corpus petitions were "timely" and the certiorari granted by the Supreme Court was apparently the statutory writ. In the third and most recent case, however, the Court was rather clearly granting the common-law writ, because the case was not "in" the court of appeals for purposes of satisfying the statutory certiorari requirement.[241] In *Matter of Shuttlesworth*,[242] the petitioner was a Negro clergyman convicted in an Alabama court of a misdemeanor for his actions in connection with a bus terminal sit-in. A federal district court denied habeas corpus and a court of appeals judge denied the certificate of probable cause necessary for appeal. Thereafter, Shuttlesworth, in completely unambiguous papers drawn and filed by the attorney who had represented him in the lower courts, prayed that the Supreme Court issue a writ of habeas corpus. The Court treated these papers (which did not mention certiorari) as a petition for certiorari, granted certiorari, and proceeded without argument to vacate the court of appeals order and remand the case to the district court with instructions. This is probably as far as the Court has ever gone in giving legal aid to a habeas corpus petitioner, and it is ironic that this special effort was exerted in behalf of a petitioner who was represented by counsel.

Now that the Court has demonstrated its willingness to grant the common-law writ of certiorari to aid a petitioner whose counsel has requested a writ of habeas corpus, it should be at least equally willing to use its common-law writ to supply the denial of certiorari

---

238 363 U.S. 801 (1961).

239 366 U.S. 958 (1961).

240 Reynolds v. Cochran, 365 U.S. 525 (1961); Carnley v. Cochran, 369 U.S. 506 (1962).

241 See *supra* note 152.

242 369 U.S. 35 (1962).

necessary for the out-of-time petitioner to exhaust his State remedies. It would be consistent for the Court routinely to deny certiorari on all petitions that request a writ of habeas corpus from the Supreme Court within a reasonable time after denial of relief by a State court.

On the other hand, perhaps the Court should abolish the practice and deny certiorari in none of them. Now that the Court has established that it can grant certiorari on any habeas corpus petition, it would seem that a State prisoner whom the Supreme Court has denied a writ of habeas corpus following a reviewable State court decision should be held to have exhausted his State remedies.

The most that can be said for the Supreme Court's "denial as certiorari" policy is that it is a partial solution for a vexing problem. The real malady is the rule that makes a denial of certiorari part of the required exhaustion of State remedies, and it is to this problem that the Court should direct its attention. It is gratifying that the Court has already begun. In a per curiam opinion filed during the 1961 Term, denying certiorari in *Mattox v. Sacks*,[243] the Court expressly held that *Darr v. Burford* did not require an application for certiorari where petitioner "is without a State remedy to challenge his conviction upon the Federal constitutional grounds asserted"—in other words, when the State court judgment rests on an adequate State ground.[244] This innovation seems to portend the eventual demise of *Darr v. Burford*.[245] At the very least its acceptance by the district courts will significantly reduce the circumstances under which the "denial as certiorari" would be necessary or desirable. With this relaxation of the exhaustion requirement

243 369 U.S. 656 (1962).

244 This decision at least arguably overrules Daniels v. Allen, 344 U.S. 343, 482 (1953). Compare Reitz, *supra* note 1, 74 HARV. L. REV. at 1363 *et seq.*, *with* Hart, *supra* note 112, at 117 *et seq.*, and *with* Brennan, *Federal Habeas Corpus and State Prisoners: An Exercise in Federalism*, 7 UTAH L. REV. 423 (1961).

245 The Court seemingly paid no attention to the exhaustion requirement in *Chaapel v. Cochran*, 369 U.S. 869 (1962), discussed in text *supra*, at note 201. Although the petitioner had not obtained a denial of certiorari to the State appellate court judgments affirming his convictions or denying him habeas corpus relief, the Supreme Court's order seems to imply that the exhaustion requirement was not to be an obstacle, since the habeas corpus petition was transferred to the federal district court "for hearing and determination."

added to the reasons suggested earlier, it seems that the function of the mutation has ceased and that it should disappear.

VI. Conclusion

For over seventy years the "original" writ of habeas corpus has been an anachronism in the United States Supreme Court. Significant expansions in the nature and scope of review by the writ of certiorari and the Court's present willingness to treat as a petition for certiorari (statutory or common law) even the most unambiguously styled habeas corpus petition have completely eliminated the function that the writ once served as a means of appellate review. Yet uncounseled petitioners, seemingly oblivious of the fact that relief is invariably denied and certainly unaware that this mistaken choice of relief may actually prejudice their cases, continue to burden the Court with eighty to one hundred habeas corpus petitions each year. The Court can and should take steps to relieve itself and its petitioners of this hardship.

During the 1943 Term, Chief Justice Stone tried to discourage habeas corpus petitions by issuing an opinion emphasizing that the Court would only exercise this jurisdiction in exceptional circumstances.[246] The appendix shows that the quantity of petitions did not appreciably decrease. Either the opinion did not come to the attention of subsequent petitioners or they chose, out of misunderstanding, optimism, or desperation, to conclude that it did not apply to them. Any solution will have to reckon with all these possibilities.

A desirable reduction might be achieved if the Court routinely transferred all petitions for original habeas corpus relief.[247] The fear that the Court might overlook a meritorious claim by this procedure should be diminished by an appraisal of the figures in the appendix. The proper provision for the occasional meritorious claim or for the case where exhaustion rules may continue to require a denial

---

[246] Ex parte Abernathy, 320 U.S. 219 (1943), discussed in text *supra,* at note 221.

[247] See Chaapel v. Cochran, 369 U.S. 869 (1963), discussed in text *supra,* at note 201. Except in circumstances like the war-crimes cases, where it is not apparent what district court "[has] jurisdiction to entertain it," 28 U.S.C. § 2241(*b*), it would seem that the burden of disposing of such papers could be borne by the Clerk's office, perhaps without even entering the cases on the docket or order list. The fact that the transfer statute in terms authorizes the Court to decline to "entertain" applications supports this procedure.

of certiorari is to create procedures by which the papers can be resubmitted as a petition for certiorari. If the Court were to continue examining all petitions, denying or granting certiorari on the meritorious ones[248] and transferring the balance, it would perpetuate an unnecessary burden and do nothing to discourage further habeas corpus petitions. It would be better to transfer all habeas corpus petitions without regard to merit, but to do so in a manner that would inform the petitioner of his proper remedy and permit him to reapply for a writ of certiorari in an appropriate case. This might be accomplished on transferring the first group of cases by issuing a rule or an opinion explaining the impropriety of the habeas corpus remedy in the Supreme Court and suggesting instead the appropriateness of a petition for certiorari where there was a lower-court decision to review. If copies of this opinion or rule were thereafter mailed by the Clerk's Office to every petitioner who submitted a request for habeas corpus, the petitioner could then submit a petition for certiorari in an appropriate case.[249] In time the explanatory reply and the invariable transfer of habeas corpus petitions would convey to the prison grapevine the desirability of petitioning for certiorari and the futility of seeking an "original" writ of habeas corpus in the United States Supreme Court.

---

[248] *E.g.*, Reynolds v. Cochran, 363 U.S. 801 (1960), and Carnley v. Cochran, 366 U.S. 958 (1961), discussed in text *supra*, at notes 238–39.

[249] The timeliness problem could be solved through subsequent use of the common-law writ of certiorari, Matter of Shuttlesworth, 369 U.S. 35 (1962), discussed *supra*, at note 242, or perhaps by providing in the rule or opinion that the transfer is without prejudice to reconsideration of the papers as a petition for certiorari. *Cf.* United States v. Ohio Power Co., 353 U.S. 98 (1957).

APPENDIX

United States Supreme Court—Disposition of Motions for Leave To File a Petition for a Writ of Habeas Corpus* 1929–61 Terms

Term and Volumes of U.S. Reports	Total Motions Denied (None Was Granted)	Denied without Opinion	Denied with Opinion or with Order Containing More than Word "Denied": Majority Simply Denied but Dissent Written[a]	Denied "without Prejudice": No Reasons Given[b]	Denied "without Prejudice": Some Reasons Given[c]	Papers Also Treated and Denied as Certiorari[d]	Denied for Want of Jurisdiction[e]	Denied after Rule Issued and Discharged[f]	Other Denials	Petitions Where Counsel Appeared
	Chief Justice Hughes									
1929 (280–81)	1	1								
1930 (282–83)	3	3								
1931 (284–86)	0									
1932 (287–89)	5	3		2						1
1933 (290–92)	13	13								1
1934 (293–95)	17	14		2				1		1
1935 (296–98)	20	18		1	1					3
1936 (299–301)	17	17								
1937 (302–04)	31	28		1	1			1		
1938 (305–07)	30	28		1				1		1
1939 (308–11)	35	35								
1940 (311–13)	45	40		1	1			3		
Total	217	200	0	8	3	0	0	6	0	7

APPENDIX—*Continued*

Term and Volumes of U.S. Reports	Total Motions Denied (None Was Granted)	Denied without Opinion	Denied with Opinion or with Order Containing More than Word "Denied": Majority Simply Denied but Dissent Written[a]	Denied "without Prejudice": No Reasons Given[b]	Denied "without Prejudice": Some Reasons Given[c]	Papers Also Treated and Denied as Certiorari[d]	Denied for Want of Jurisdiction[e]	Denied after Rule Issued and Discharged[f]	Other Denials	Petitions Where Counsel Appeared
					Chief Justice Stone					
1941 (314–16).....	53	50	...	2	1	...	...	...	...	1
1942 (317–19).....	81	60	...	6	8	...	...	1	6[g]	6
1943 (320–22).....	96	74	...	...	17	4	...	1	...	1
1944 (323–25).....	84	81	...	...	...	3	...	...	...	...
1945 (326–28).....	54	51	...	...	...	...	...	...	3[h]	3
Total.........	368	316	0	8	26	7	0	2	9	11
					Chief Justice Vinson					
1946 (329–31).....	75	67	...	...	1	...	7	...	...	...
1947 (332–34).....	178	73	15	...	...	...	89	...	1[i]	1
1948 (335–38).....	114	89	...	...	1	...	24	...	...	6
1949 (338–39).....	60	57	3	...	...	...	...	...	...	1
1950 (340–41).....	70	70	...	...	...	...	...	...	...	2
1951 (342–43).....	56	56	...	...	...	...	...	...	...	...
1952 (344–45).....	66	65	1	...	...	...	...	...	...	3
Total.........	619	477	19	0	2	0	120	0	1	13

	Chief Justice Warren									
1953 (346–47).....	59	58	1	....	....	....	....	....	....	1
1954 (348–49).....	82	82	....	....	....	....	....	....	....	1
1955 (350–51).....	85	85	....	....	....	....	....	....	....	....
1956 (352–54).....	102	102	....	....	....	....	....	....	....	1
1957 (355–57).....	94	85	....	....	....	9	....	....	....	1
1958 (358–60).....	101	78	....	....	....	23	....	....	....	....
1959 (361–63).....	105	74	....	....	....	30	....	....	1[j]	3
1960 (364–67).....	85	69	....	....	....	15	....	....	1[j]	....
1961 (368–70).....	83	60	1	....	....	19	....	....	3[k]	1
Total.........	796	693	2	0	0	96	0	0	5	8
Grand total...	2,000	1,686	21	16	31	103	120	8	15	39

* Neither the Administrative Office of the United States Courts nor the Clerk's Office of the Supreme Court compiles data on the number and disposition of "original" habeas corpus petitions. Letter of E. P. Cullinan, Chief Deputy Clerk, Supreme Court of the United States, Dec. 9, 1961.

The data in this table were compiled by paging through the memorandum orders of the Court. Only those papers docketed as specified above were included, but it seems probable that this does not exhaust all of the requests for habeas corpus relief. During many of these Terms, the Court docketed and denied from five to as many as twenty-five "Applications." It seems probable from their style that many of these sought habeas corpus relief, and an examination of the original papers in some has shown this to be the fact. E.g., case cited *supra* note 20. The basis for differentiating between these cases and those docketed as habeas corpus cases is not apparent.

The 1929 Term, the first Term under Chief Justice Hughes, was selected as the starting point, and the table is subdivided according to the presidency of the four Chief Justices. This was done because the various Chief Justices seem to have shouldered the principal burden in the consideration of these petitions and markedly influenced the form of the orders by which they were denied. Hughes and Stone examined all habeas corpus petitions themselves. 2 Pusey, Charles Evans Hughes 727–28 (1951); Mason, *op. cit. supra* note 75, at 639, 788. Chief Justice Warren has also assumed the principal responsibility for these petitions, according to the practice described by Mr. Justice Harlan. Harlan, *supra* note 5, at 555; see also Prettyman, *supra* note 224, at 305. Finally, per curiam orders have normally been prepared under the direction of the Chief Justice; see McElwain, *The Business of the Supreme Court as Conducted by Chief Justice Hughes*, 63 Harv. L. Rev. 5, 15 (1949).

[a] Cases cited *supra*, at notes 78 and 84; Knetzer v. Schultz, 344 U.S. 908 (1952); Ex Parte Sztwiertnia, 346 U.S. 930 (1954); Bandy v. United States, 369 U.S. 815 (1962).

[b] *E.g.*, Ex Parte Miles, 287 U.S. 567 (1932); Ex Parte Current, 314 U.S. 578 (1941). In all of these cases the order provides, in substance, that the motion for leave to file a petition for a writ of habeas corpus is denied without prejudice to an application to the United States District Court or judge.

[c] Cases cited *supra*, at notes 214–24.

[d] Cases cited *supra*, at notes 226–27.

[e] Cases cited *supra*, at notes 77–80 and 82–84. Fairman, *supra* note 69, at 597, states that the petition in Everett v. Truman, 334 U.S. 824 (1948), was on behalf of 74 individuals, and it is so treated for numerical purposes in this table.

[f] Cases cited *supra*, at note 205.

[g] Case cited *supra*, at note 73.

[h] Case cited *supra*, at note 74; Homma v. Patterson, 327 U.S. 759 (1946); Brown v. Mayo, 327 U.S. 768 (1946) (moot).

[i] Hawkins v. Clemmer, 332 U.S. 812 (1947) (motion for leave to file granted, petition denied, and application for stay of execution denied).

[j] Cases cited *supra*, at notes 238–39.

[k] Cases cited *supra*, at notes 201–02 and 242.

WILLIAM M. BEANEY

THE CONSTITUTIONAL RIGHT TO PRIVACY IN THE SUPREME COURT

Decisions of the Supreme Court involving the right to privacy or containing extensive references to that right have been part of the staple fare of constitutional litigation for many decades. Only last Term, in *Lanza v. New York*,[1] the Court was split asunder on the question of the existence of such a constitutional right, although it did not—nor did it have to—resolve the question. Even the casual reader soon realizes, however, that the phrase "right to privacy" is used to describe a variety of interests, that it is urged upon the courts in a wide range of circumstances, and that judges use it in different senses and for varying purposes.[2]

William M. Beaney is Professor of Politics, Princeton University.

Author's acknowledgment: This paper was completed during the term of the author's appointment as Ford Research Professor, Princeton University, 1962–63.

1 370 U.S. 139 (1962).

2 To take examples from a single Term: There was extensive use of the concept in a conventional, though significant, search-and-seizure case. Mapp v. Ohio, 367 U.S. 643 (1961). It was invoked in dissent against a State law making punishable the use of contraceptives. Poe v. Ullman, 367 U.S. 497, 509, 522 (1961). Privacy was involved in a decision repudiating electronic eavesdropping. Silverman v. United States, 365 U.S. 505 (1961). Finally, it was resorted to, in vain, by the dissenters, in Wilson v. Schnettler, 365 U.S. 381, 388 (1961), where they sought to preclude

This paper seeks to determine whether it is meaningful to speak of a constitutonally protected right to privacy and, if it is, to describe the meaning and scope of that right as used by the Justices. In this undertaking a number of limitations have been imposed. No effort has been made to elaborate the law of arrests or of search and seizure, which have been the subject of detailed analysis by highly competent authorities.[3] These topics, however, provide a major share of the litigated cases involving official intrusion on personal privacy, so that a good deal of what follows necessarily involves a discussion of Fourth and Fifth Amendment rights, with occasional references to the Fourteenth, as they affect the right to privacy. If this necessitates the threshing of old straw, my excuse is that the objective of this brief paper cannot be accomplished in any other way. A second limitation is that I have not yet gathered the empirical data necessary to decide many of the crucial questions posed by the analysis that follows. For example, judgment as to whether health inspectors should be permitted to inspect houses, with a consequent invasion of privacy, without first obtaining a warrant depends on some knowledge of the complexities of public health administration in modern urban areas and the extent to which the duty of procuring a warrant would obstruct effective health enforcement.[4] Obviously, courts must commonly decide cases presenting such questions, armed with nothing more than the limited data offered by the trial record. One feels that the Court's judgment in *Frank v. Maryland*,[5] for example, that the claim of privacy is overbalanced by another social interest, in this instance public health as protected by warrantless inspection, may rest on very little substantial evidence.[6] A final limitation is that a number of problems have been set forth toward the conclusion of the paper without any

testimony of a federal agent at a State trial on the ground that he had engaged in an unlawful search.

3 4 WHARTON, CRIMINAL LAW AND PROCEDURE chs. 62, 63 (rev. ed. Anderson 1957); 8 WIGMORE, EVIDENCE §§ 2180–86 (rev. ed. McNaughton 1961).

4 I hope to investigate at least some of these problems as part of a larger study of the right to privacy on which I am presently engaged.

5 359 U.S. 360 (1959).

6 See Comment, *State Health Inspections and "Unreasonable Search": The* Frank *Exclusion of Civil Searches*, 44 MINN. L. REV. 513 (1960), and data presented there on Minneapolis–St. Paul experiences with health inspections.

sustained effort to provide solutions. Perhaps time and further thought will yield stronger insights.

Since the right to privacy is not specifically mentioned at any place in the Constitution, where does one look in that document to find safeguards for the right? Or perhaps the earlier question is: Why should one assume that the right to privacy is protected by fundamental law? The fact that the right has received increasing recognition in tort law in the last seventy years,[7] a development stimulated by the deservedly famous essay by Brandeis and Warren,[8] hardly disposes of the problem because of the different interests involved when the question of the public-law right arises. The answer in a few words must be that our Constitution and our system of constitutional government reflect a decision that government is limited in the powers and in the methods it may use. Powers are withheld from government or, alternatively stated, freedoms or liberties of the citizen are set forth in order to guarantee that the individual, his personality, and those things stamped with his personality shall be free from official interference, except where a rational basis for intrusion exists. "Liberty against government," a phrase used by Professor Corwin, expresses this idea forcefully.[9] In this sense virtually all enumerated rights in the Constitution can be described as contributing to the right to privacy, if by the term is meant the integrity and freedom of the individual person and personality. It was more than mere literary license, then, that Mr. Justice Douglas indulged when he included freedom of religion, academic freedom, freedom to travel, the right to resist improper questioning by legislative investigating committees, and a number of other rights, among the rights to privacy or the rights to be let alone.[10] Nonetheless, his broadly inclusive scheme seems better suited to literary than to legal analysis. Apart from requiring a coverage of virtually all of the recognized constitutional rights, such a category involves the use of a new concept in situations where adequate, if imperfect, categories under which analysis can proceed already exist. It seems, for example, more natural to treat

---

[7] PROSSER, TORTS ch. 20 (2d ed. 1955); Prosser, *Privacy*, 48 CALIF. L. REV. 383 (1960).

[8] Brandeis & Warren, *The Right to Privacy*, 4 HARV. L. REV. 193 (1890).

[9] LIBERTY AGAINST GOVERNMENT (1948).

[10] RIGHT OF THE PEOPLE ch. 2 (1958).

academic freedom as a special case of freedom of speech and press, which are other forms of the more general category of freedom of expression, than to conceive academic freedom as part of the right to privacy on the ground that the claimant asks government to "let him alone." If the right to privacy is viewed as a broad, major category, then any attempt to give it meaning and use it with precision will require that each of its subcategories be identified. What is attempted here is more modest. It is a brief survey to see if the right to privacy as considered by the Court is simply a protected area defined by one or more specific constitutional guaranties, or if it represents an extension of one or more enumerated rights, or if it possesses a status virtually independent of any specified right or rights. Finally, it will be asked whether there is any real purpose in utilizing the concept and, if not, whether it should be discarded?

I. Early Fourth Amendment Cases

The nearest to an explicit recognition of a right to privacy in the Constitution is contained in the Fourth Amendment: "The right of the people to be secure in their persons, houses, papers, and effects, against unreasonable searches and seizures, shall not be violated, and no warrants shall issue, but upon probable cause, supported by oath or affirmation, and particularly describing the place to be searched, and the persons or things to be seized."

As numerous writers have pointed out, the Fourth Amendment represented a reaction against the use of writs of assistance and general warrants by the Crown in the period before the Revolution, a feeling that was also reflected in State constitutions adopted in the period following independence.[11] The early Supreme Court decisions expressed a generous attitude toward the purpose and meaning of the Fourth Amendment especially when it was joined to the Fifth. In *Boyd v. United States*,[12] the Court invalidated a law requiring the defendant to produce private books, invoices, and

---

[11] Lasson, History and Development of the Fourth Amendment to the United States Constitution (1937); Dickerson, Writs of Assistance as a Cause of the Revolution (1939); Reynard, *Freedom from Unreasonable Search and Seizure—A Second Class Constitutional Right?*, 25 Ind. L. J. 259 (1950); Barrett, *Personal Rights, Property Rights, and the Fourth Amendment*, [1960] Supreme Court Review 46.

[12] 116 U.S. 616 (1886).

papers on demand or have the allegations of the Government treated as admitted. In a technical sense there certainly was no search or seizure, as the concurring opinion of Mr. Justice Miller clearly explained, but the Court thought that the principles laid down in *Entick v. Carrington*[13] required a non-technical view of the scope of the Fourth and Fifth Amendments. Referring to this celebrated English decision, where Lord Camden allowed a recovery in a private suit against officers of the Crown who had conducted a search for papers without warrants, Mr. Justice Bradley wrote:[14] "The principles laid down in this opinion affect the very essence of constitutional liberty and security. They reach farther than the concrete form of the case then before the court, with its adventitious circumstances; they apply to all invasions on the part of the government and its employés of the sanctity of a man's home and the privacies of life." And in language that has been cited many times, Bradley tried to underline the nature of the offense committed: "It is not the breaking of his doors, and the rummaging of his drawers, that constitutes the essence of the offense; but it is the invasion of his indefeasible right of personal security, personal liberty and private property, where that right has never been forfeited by his conviction of some public offense. . . ."[15] In an even earlier decision, *Ex parte Jackson*,[16] the Court, in holding valid a statute prohibiting the use of the mails to carry on a lottery or fraudulent scheme, suggested in a dictum that a sealed letter entrusted to the postal system could be opened only in response to a warrant.

The essence of these early decisions is that the Fourth Amendment guaranties applied to government action that was not a search or seizure in the traditional sense; that it was the intrusion on privacy, whether of the home, the person, or his effects, that was prohibited by the amendment, especially when supported by the Fifth Amendment's privilege against self-incrimination. The dual barrier against government action was made particularly effective in 1914 when the Court announced that federal courts would no longer follow the common-law principle[17] that evidence was admissible regardless of the method used to obtain it. In *Weeks v. United*

---

[13] 19 Howell's St. Tr. 1029 (C.P. 1765).

[14] 116 U.S. at 630.

[15] *Ibid.*

[16] 96 U.S. 727 (1878).

[17] See Adams v. New York, 192 U.S. 585 (1904).

States[18] the Court adopted the rule that papers illegally seized by federal officials could not be received in evidence in federal trials. It rested its conclusion on the importance of exclusion as a means of protecting the Fourth Amendment rights. The government officers in this case had broken into Weeks's home without warrant and seized various papers.

In other conventional seizure cases arising before the prohibition era, the Court demonstrated a tendency to view the provision against unreasonable searches and seizures broadly in order to effectuate the central purpose of the amendment, except for two special categories. One exception was the power of officials to inspect a ship and its cargo without a warrant. An early statute granted that power because of the difficulty, if not impossibility, of procuring a warrant where the object of the search was movable.[19] This suggested that a search of an automobile would be fitted into the same exception, as it was in *Carroll v. United States*,[20] one of the important prohibition-era cases. The other exception, also of ancient origin, permitted officers to search a suspect at the time of arrest, and as an incident of arrest to seize unlawful objects found on his person or which were in plain view and under the control of the arrestee.[21] One of the many prohibition-era cases involved a seizure of a ledger and other business documents not described in the search warrant after defendant was arrested at his speak-easy. In *Marron v. United States*,[22] the Court upheld the seizure as an incident to a lawful arrest. Much was made of the fact that a speak-easy was a "common nuisance" under the National Prohibition Act and that the "authority of officers to search and seize the things by which the nuisance was being maintained, extended to all parts of the premises used for the unlawful purpose."[23]

The broader significance of these "exceptions" should not be

---

18 232 U.S. 383 (1914).

19 1 Stat. 29, 43 (1789). See Appendix to Mr. Justice Frankfurter's dissenting opinion in Davis v. United States, 328 U.S. 582, 616 (1946). The same justification exists for arrests for which warrants are not normally required.

20 267 U.S. 132 (1925).

21 See cases cited in Harris v. United States, 331 U.S. 145, 150–51, nn. 11, 12, 13 (1947); 4 WHARTON, *op. cit. supra* note 2, at § 1538.

22 275 U.S. 192 (1927).

23 *Id.* at 199.

overlooked. Their perseverance meant that the duty to obtain a warrant to justify a search and seizure was not an absolute. And since a warrant was not necessary to make an arrest at common law, a search incident to arrest could take place frequently. Nevertheless, the early decisions of the Court seemed to establish a presumption in favor of requiring a search warrant, and the Fourth and Fifth Amendments had been interpreted to give substantial protection to one's home and possessions.

II. Olmstead—the Great Retreat

One may doubt whether the large-scale resort to the Fourth Amendment by defendants in liquor-prohibition cases provided a desirable environment for the development of legal doctrine. Foes of the "noble experiment," including some judges, could and did use search-and-seizure rules in technical ways to defeat law enforcement efforts. Other judges, disturbed by the growth of crime and the spirit of lawlessness engendered by prohibition, hesitated to invoke a broad doctrine of personal privacy in favor of those engaged in large-scale, well-organized criminal activities. As Pringle has told us, among those who believed in strict enforcement, in spite of some early misgivings, was Chief Justice Taft:[24] "It sometimes seemed as though there were no lengths to which the Chief Justice would not go, and along which he would not attempt to lead the court, in his determination to uphold prohibition enforcement."

Perhaps the high point of Taft's crusade was reached in the celebrated *Olmstead* case.[25] Given the Chief Justice's attitude toward prohibition and his usual ability to muster support from the conservatives, the facts in *Olmstead* were hardly favorable to a decision enlarging the area of personal security. Olmstead was involved in a $200,000-a-month bootlegging ring which ran illegal liquor from British Columbia into Seattle and environs. For several months federal agents, who had tapped the defendant's telephone line, overheard conversations between various members of the organization and finally gathered sufficient evidence to support the indictment and conviction of the twenty-one members of the group. Efforts at the trial to exclude the evidence obtained by the wire taps were in

---

[24] 2 Pringle, Life and Times of William Howard Taft 989 (1939).

[25] Olmstead v. United States, 277 U.S. 438 (1928).

vain. The majority of the court of appeals agreed with the trial judge, who had refused to view wire tapping as a search or seizure, and held that violation of the Washington statute prohibiting wire tapping was of no concern to the jury. "The protection of [the Fourth and Fifth] amendments, however, has never been extended to the exclusion of evidence obtained by listening to the conversation of persons at any place or under any circumstances."[26] This was quite true, though there was no evidence that a case presenting this issue had arisen previously. "The purpose of the amendments," Judge Gilbert of the court of appeals observed, "is to prevent the invasion of homes and offices and the seizure of incriminating evidence found therein. Whatever may be said of the tapping of telephone wires as an unethical intrusion upon the privacy of persons who are suspected of crime, it is not an act which comes within the letter of the prohibition of constitutional provisions."[27] In support of his conclusion, he asserted that evidence obtained by seeing through, or listening at, doors or windows has always been held admissible and that evidence obtained by wire tapping was not distinguishable. The judge's authority for his conclusion was not impressive. He cited a State case in which evidence of conversations overheard by means of a detectaphone was held competent,[28] and other State and a few federal cases in which the manner of obtaining evidence was held not to affect admissibility. In effect, the majority looked upon the Fourth Amendment as a guaranty against a particular method of invading privacy or personal security—as a ban on physical intrusion of the house and seizure of material objects—rather than a protection of the right to privacy itself.

The dissenting opinion of Judge Rudkin was based on a wholly different view of the purpose of the Amendments and the scope of the right protected by them.[29] While the protection of the Fourth and Fifth Amendments "has been invoked more often and more successfully during the past 10 years then [sic] during the entire previous history of the republic," he thought it a "matter of common knowledge that there is a growing tendency to encroach upon and ignore constitutional rights."[30] But, in his opinion, the Supreme

[26] Olmstead v. United States, 19 F. 2d 842, 847 (9th Cir. 1927).

[27] *Ibid.*

[28] State v. Hester, 137 S.C. 145 (1926).

[29] 19 F. 2d at 848.

[30] *Id.* at 849.

Court had set its face against this tendency. "That court has consistently and persistently declared that the amendments in question must be liberally construed in favor of the citizen and his liberty, and that stealthy encroachments will not be tolerated."[31] He differed sharply with the majority of his brethren as to the object of the Amendments. "Nor are the guaranties contained in these amendments limited to houses and papers. Their chief aim and purpose was not the protection of property, but the protection of the individual in his liberty and in the privacies of life."[32] To Judge Rudkin the appropriate analogy to talking over the telephone was the use of the mails:[33] "[I]t is the contents of the letter, not the mere paper, that is thus protected. What is the distinction between a message sent by letter and a message sent by telegraph or by telephone? True, the one is visible, the other invisible; the one is tangible, the other intangible; the one is sealed, and the other unsealed; but these are distinctions without a difference."

The issues were thus sharply defined when presented to the Supreme Court, which first denied the petition for certiorari and then agreed to hear the case. As would be expected, counsel for petitioners stressed the broader concept of privacy while the Government concentrated on the limited nature of the search-and-seizure provision. The purpose of tapping, argued petitioners,

> was to secure evidence by which to convict them [the defendants] of crime. And this purpose alone condemns the whole proceeding if accompanied by violation of their fundamental right of privacy. That it is this fundamental right of privacy which it was the purpose of the Fourth Amendment to protect, rather than any mere right of property, is evident not only from the language of the amendment itself, but is attested by the ... [language of] the *Boyd* case ...[34]

which was then quoted as showing the broad objective of the Fourth and Fifth Amendments. *Ex parte Jackson* and other leading decisions, it was argued, "uniformly hold that the Fourth and Fifth Amendments were designed primarily to protect *personal rights*, one of the most valuable of which is the *right of privacy*."[35] In an effort to show that the use of the telephone deserved protection,

---

[31] *Ibid.*

[32] *Ibid.*

[33] *Id.* at 850.

[34] Brief of Petitioners Green *et al.*, p. 10.

[35] *Id.* at 14.

petitioners observed:[36] "If a private telephone line to a man's home or office is not one of the privacies of life, then it is difficult for the human mind to conceive what would be included in that phrase." In a similar vein, counsel for another group of petitioners asked, "What constitutes 'an invasion of the privacies of life' . . . ?" The answer was clear:[37] "It would indeed be difficult to attempt to enumerate all of those things coming within the phrase 'the privacies of life,' but it would be equally difficult to suggest any more sacred or any greater *privacy of life* under present conditions than that of using a private telephone line for transmitting private and confidential communications to one's family and business associates."

The Government's position was also clear. Even if there could be a search and seizure of a verbal communication (which was thought impossible), nothing in the Constitution prohibited such an action by the authorities.[38] Tapping of a telephone was analogous to eavesdropping by an officer, an action that always had been upheld.[39] In its brief on the merits, the Government minimized the significance of certain "sweeping statements" in the *Boyd* case "which have ever since been the favorite resort of all litigants who have sought to extend the scope of the Fourth Amendment."[40] The proper construction of the Fourth Amendment was a literal one, counsel argued:[41]

> In every case in which a violation of the Fourth Amendment was found to have occurred the decision without exception dealt with a case in which the object of the search and seizure condemned was literally described by the language of the Amendment; that is, "persons, houses, papers, and effects," "effects" used in the sense of tangible personal property.

Finally, the Government brief paraded horrors. Law officers would be prevented from putting an eye to a keyhole, joining a conspiratorial band, eavesdropping, or using detectaphones, if wire tapping was deemed within the Fourth Amendment guaranty.[42] A well-written *amicus curiae* brief by the telephone companies stressed the

---

36 *Id.* at 15.

37 Brief of Petitioners McInnis *et al.*, p. 9.

38 Brief for United States in Opposition, p. 15.

39 *Id.* at 15–16.

40 Brief for the United States, p. 21.

41 *Id.* at 33.

42 *Id.* at 38–39.

necessity for privacy of telephone conversations and pointed out that it was not only the privacy of a suspect that was infringed by a wire tap but that of every person to whom he might talk once the tap was made.[43]

Unfortunately for the purposes of analysis, the *Olmstead* case involved more than the issue whether the Fourth Amendment had been transgressed by the wire tapping activities of federal agents. The State of Washington, where the tapping had taken place, had made wire tapping a misdemeanor. The question of admissibility of evidence obtained in violation of this State law by federal officers had been raised and disposed of below, adversely to the petitioners. When the Supreme Court agreed to review the decision of the court of appeals, it limited the review to the Fourth Amendment question.[44] To the intense irritation of Taft, however, the law-violation issue, which he assumed had been shunted aside by the Court's order granting certiorari, was treated by three of the Justices.[45] This action, which undoubtedly served to strengthen the over-all position of the dissenters, deprived the decision of the clarity and force that undivided attention to the Fourth Amendment issue could have provided.

The opinions reveal considerable diversity. The Chief Justice, speaking for a majority that included Van Devanter, McReynolds, Sutherland, and Sanford, refused to treat wire tapping as an unreasonable search and seizure. It was not a "search and seizure" in any sense, said Taft, because the search referred to in the Fourth Amendment must "be of material things—the person, the house, his papers or his effects."[46] In this case there was no trespass, no entry of a house. "The evidence was secured by the use of the sense of hearing and that only. . . . [T]he wiretapping here disclosed did not

---

[43] Brief in Support of Petitioners' Contention, pp. 4, 9.

[44] 276 U.S. 609 (1928).

[45] The strength of the Chief Justice's feelings is revealed in a letter to his colleague, Justice Sanford. "I agree that there was a specific limitation on the certiorari and that Brandeis in writing his first opinion violated the limitation, but as Holmes bases his dissent not on the unconstitutional feature but on the crime, as he called it, we cannot throw those two men out." WHT to ETS, May 31, 1928, The Papers of William Howard Taft, the Library of Congress (hereafter Taft Papers). I am indebted to my colleague, Walter F. Murphy, for making available this and other references to the *Olmstead* case in the Taft Papers.

[46] 277 U.S. at 464.

amount to a search or seizure within the meaning of the Fourth Amendment."[47] He gave short shrift to the second issue, whether evidence obtained by wire tapping was not admissible either because obtained by unethical means or in violation of State law. He pointed out that the Court had agreed not to consider the question but that some members had breached their agreement. But he invoked the well-established common-law rule that admissibility of evidence is not affected by the illegality of the means by which it was obtained and asserted that precedent was lacking for a refusal to admit evidence because obtained by unethical means. Taft suggested that there was power in Congress to protect the secrecy of telephone messages by making inadmissible evidence obtained by wire tap.[48] The majority thus viewed the Fourth Amendment guaranty against searches and seizure in its narrowest terms. Taft relied on his own opinion in *Carroll v. United States*:[49] "The Fourth Amendment is to be construed in the light of what was deemed an unreasonable search and seizure when it was adopted, and in a manner which will conserve public interests as well as the interests and rights of individual citizens." The Chief Justice agreed with the statements of Justice Bradley in the *Boyd* case[50] and Justice Clark in the *Gouled* case[51] that the Fifth Amendment and Fourth Amendment "were to be liberally construed to effect the purpose of the framers of the Constitution in the interest of liberty." "But," he added, "that can not justify enlargement of the language employed beyond the possible practical meaning of houses, persons, papers, and effects, or so to apply the words search and seizure as to forbid hearing or sight."[52]

Of the dissenting opinions, that of Holmes[53] is of little significance for the purpose of this paper. Initially inclined to go along with the majority, he eventually agreed with one of the points set forth by Brandeis, that evidence obtained by lawbreaking activities of

---

47 *Id.* at 464, 466.

48 *Id.* at 465–66.

49 267 U.S. 132, 149 (1925).

50 Boyd v. United States, 116 U.S. 616 (1886).

51 Gouled v. United States, 255 U.S. 298 (1921).

52 277 U.S. at 465.

53 *Id.* at 469.

federal officers was inadmissible.[54] It is not clear whether Holmes's famous phrase "dirty business" refers specifically to wire tapping or to any form of illegal official action designed to help convict criminals. At the outset Holmes made clear his unwillingness to say that the terms of the Fourth and Fifth Amendments prohibited this action.

Butler's dissent announced that because of the limitation in the certiorari order he would concentrate on the Fourth Amendment issue. He refused to read search and seizure in the literal manner adopted by the majority; he thought that wire tapping was a search and seizure. "During their transmission the exclusive use of the wire belongs to the persons served by it. Wire tapping involves interference with the wire while being used. Tapping the wires and listening in by the officers literally constituted a search for evidence."[55] He remonstrated against the literal approach used by the Chief Justice:[56] "The direct operation or literal meaning of the words used does not measure the purpose or scope of [the Constitution's] provisions. Under the principles established and applied by this Court, the Fourth Amendment safeguards against all evils that are like and equivalent to those embraced within the ordinary meaning of its words."

Justice Stone's one-paragraph dissenting opinion expressed agreement with those of Holmes, Butler, and Brandeis. His sole contribution was a sentence in defense of the action of Holmes and Brandeis in going beyond the limits of the certiorari order.[57]

Brandeis' celebrated opinion in *Olmstead* rested on two principal arguments.[58] The violation of State law by a federal officer required that the government not be allowed to use the fruits of the crime in a federal court: "Decency, security and liberty alike demand that government officials shall be subjected to the same rules of conduct

---

[54] The Chief Justice in a letter to his brother, Horace, blamed Brandeis for Holmes's change of heart. "The truth is that Holmes voted the other way till Brandeis got after him and induced him to change on the ground that a state law of Washington forbade wiretapping." In the same letter he referred to Holmes's opinion as "the nastiest" of the dissenting opinions. WHT to HT, June 12, 1928, Taft Papers.

[55] 277 U.S. at 487.

[56] *Ibid.*

[57] *Id.* at 488.

[58] *Id.* at 471.

that are commands to the citizens."[59] Of greater significance for our purpose was his analysis of the constitutional claims based on the Fourth and Fifth Amendments. At the outset, Brandeis set the tone for the argument that was to follow. Marshall's reminder, "that it is a constitution we are expounding," prefaced a statement showing how federal powers had been extended to meet unforeseen situations. The statement of general limitations had not prevented meeting new conditions.[60] "Clauses guaranteeing to the individual protection against specific abuses of power, must have a similar capacity of adaptation to a changing world. . . . [A] principle to be vital must be capable of wider application than the mischief which gave it birth."[61] This led naturally to a discussion of the form that invasions of privacy had assumed in an earlier period: physical entry of the home, seizure of papers, and torture of the suspected individual. "Subtler and more far-reaching means of invading privacy have become available to the Government. Discovery and invention have made it possible for the Government, by means far more effective than stretching upon the rack, to obtain disclosure in court of what is whispered in the closet."[62] Scientific advances in the future threatened even greater invasions of individual security. He recalled, in most favorable terms, the broad spirit reflected in *Boyd* and its reference in turn to the generous language of *Entick v. Carrington*. Previous decisions of the Court had not, in Brandeis' view, placed an unduly literal construction upon the Fourth Amendment. He would go even further. "They [the framers of the Constitution] recognized the significance of man's spiritual nature, of his feelings and of his intellect. They knew that only a part of the pain, pleasure and satisfactions of life are to be found in material things. They sought to protect Americans in their beliefs, their thoughts, their emotions and their sensations."[63] Because of these objectives, the framers "conferred, as against the Government, the right to be let alone—the most comprehensive of rights and the right most valued by civilized men."[64] For Brandeis, the Fourth Amend-

---

[59] *Id.* at 485.

[60] Citing Euclid v. Ambler Realty, 272 U.S. 365 (1926), and Buck v. Bell, 274 U.S. 200 (1927).

[61] 277 U.S. at 472–73.

[62] *Id.* at 473.

[63] *Id.* at 478.

[64] *Ibid.*

ment, with the support of the Fifth, provided full protection of the right to privacy. "[E]very unjustifiable intrusion by the Government upon the privacy of the individual, whatever the means employed, must be deemed a violation of the Fourth Amendment. And the use, as evidence in a criminal proceeding, of facts ascertained by such intrusion must be deemed a violation of the Fifth."[65]

Brandeis thought it immaterial that no trespass to property had occurred. The contention that the wire tapping should be viewed tolerantly because used in aid of law enforcement was brushed aside. "Experience should teach us to be most on our guard to protect liberty when the Government's purposes are beneficent. . . . The greatest dangers to liberty lurk in the insidious encroachment by men of zeal, well-meaning but without understanding."[66]

In summary, it is clear that only two Justices, Brandeis and Stone, advocated an expansive interpretation of the Fourth Amendment in order to safeguard a broadly defined right to privacy. Justice Butler's position was that wire tapping was a modern variant of the classic search and seizure. And, while his failure to concur in the dissents of Holmes and Brandeis is explainable by his refusal to agree that the issue of violation of State law was properly before the Court, the modesty in conception of his opinion on the constitutional question suggests that he was not prepared to accept the broadly defined right propounded by Brandeis. Butler would have found the Fourth Amendment inapplicable to an invasion of privacy lacking any characteristic of a search and seizure. Perhaps the demand for entry by a health inspector would fall in this category. Conceivably the use of a detectaphone might lie outside Butler's zone of protected individual security, since he emphasized that the wire and its contents belonged to the subscribers. Brandeis, in contrast, gave the interest to be protected—the right to privacy or the right "to be let alone"—a comprehensive, if imprecise, meaning. The individual was to be secured against "every unjustifiable intrusion" by the government. Brandeis thus conceded that the right to privacy was not an absolute, a position hardly surprising since the Fourth Amendment itself justifies an intrusion by one armed with a proper search warrant.

The decision of the Court in *Olmstead* was the object of imme-

---

[65] *Id.* at 478–79.

[66] *Id.* at 479.

diate criticism. To the chagrin of the Chief Justice, many of the law-review comments were hostile.[67] By September, he had sufficiently recovered his equanimity so that he could write to Justice Sutherland:[68]

> I was a good deal disturbed at first by the very severe criticism of the opinion in the wiretapping case, but I thought the opinion was entirely logical and rested on authority. . . . I thought the language of Judge Holmes and Judge Brandeis was unjustified, and it was that kind of language that drew the condemnation of people who were opposed to prohibition, no matter what the law is, but [he added more cheerfully], I hope that ultimately it will be seen that we in the majority were right.

The *Olmstead* decision represents one of the decisive moments in the history of liberty in the United States. The theory of Brandeis, rejected by all but one of his brethren, would have made the Fourth Amendment a guaranty of a broad right to privacy. Had the Brandeis analysis prevailed, all government intrusions on a person's privacy at home, in his papers and effects, and on his free movement would have had to be justified, with the government forced to bear the burden of showing why a particular form of interference was reasonable. Privacy, though not an absolute, would have a high place in the hierarchy of protected values. It was the position of Taft and the majority, however, and their opposition to any enlarged theory of the Fourth Amendment that was to prevail in the decades ahead. It is perhaps reading too much into the opinion to say that by this time the Court had begun to regard the Fourth Amendment primarily as a safeguard for the criminal element. But any

---

67 Some of the criticism was directed to the court of appeals decision. See 28 COLUM. L. REV. 669 (1928); 41 HARV. L. REV. 258 (1927); 18 GA. L. REV. 120 (1930). For examples of adverse comment on the Supreme Court decision, see 15 VA. L. REV. 62 (1928); 77 U. PA. L. REV. 139 (1928). For a favorable reaction, see 27 MICH. L. REV. 78, 927 (1928). Two letters, written four days apart, to his brother Horace express the Chief Justice's reaction. In one, he commented "His [Brandeis'] claques in the law school contingent will sound his praise and point the finger of scorn at us, but if they think we are going to be frightened in our effort to stand by the law and give the public a chance to punish criminals, they are mistaken." WHT to HT, June 8, 1928, Taft Papers. In a second letter he stressed the value of the telephone to criminals. The dissenters in *Olmstead* were described as "idealist gentlemen [who] urge a conclusion which facilitates crime." WHT to HT, June 12, 1928, Taft Papers.

68 WHT to GS, Sept. 14, 1928, Taft Papers.

large-scale resort to its protection would inevitably give rise to that feeling. In its origins the Amendment was directed toward the safeguarding of political offenders and "good citizens" who might be suspected of such "innocent" offenses as evading customs regulations.[69] The object was to limit the possibilities of arbitrary, overzealous governmental action. But it should be remembered that the common-law rule allowed the admission at trial of evidence illegally seized, while permitting the offended person an action against the officer. The adoption of the exclusionary rule in 1914 had introduced a new and serious complication in the interpretation and application of the Fourth Amendment, because the price of securing the rights protected by the Amendment was the escape of many guilty defendants in federal trials. That fact undoubtedly affected the views of Taft and other Justices who found it difficult to accept the large-scale use of the Fourth Amendment by organized criminal enterprises during the prohibition era and thereafter. The larger the view of Fourth Amendment rights, the wider the road to safety for criminals. The majority in *Olmstead* and other restrictive Fourth Amendment decisions was obviously influenced by the desire to give suitable expression to the social interest in convicting criminals.[70]

III. Unconventional Eavesdropping after Olmstead

Olmstead made it clear that congressional action could provide for the privacy of the telephone. Taft suggested that it was to Congress rather than the courts that those affected by wire tapping must look for relief. Brandeis referred to the statutes banning wire tapping in various jurisdictions and to a relevant provision of the 1927 Radio Act providing that "no person not being authorized by the sender shall intercept any message and divulge or publish the

---

69 See references cited in note 11 *supra.*

70 Mr. Justice Frankfurter, who asserts that privacy has a high though not an absolute value, has opposed this form of balancing of interests and has insisted that the balance was struck in favor of protecting criminals and innocent alike at the time the Fourth Amendment was adopted. His dissenting opinions in Harris v. United States, 331 U.S. 145, 155 (1947), and Rabinowitz v. United States, 339 U.S. 56, 68 (1950), state this position. He has consistently supported claimants in Fourth Amendment cases. See Jacobs, Justice Frankfurter and Civil Liberties 153–60 (1961). *But see* Section V, *infra.*

contents, substance, purport, effect, or meaning of such intercepted message to any person"[71] to show a public policy against official wire tapping.

The Radio Act provision on intercepted messages was included and expanded in the Federal Communications Act of 1934, adopted primarily to achieve an extensive reorganization of government agencies regulating communications.[72] Beginning in 1937 in the first *Nardone* case,[73] the Supreme Court found in this provision a barrier to the admission of wire-tap evidence in federal courts, whether secured by federal or State officers[74] and regardless of whether the intercepted messages were intrastate or interstate.[75] Nor can evidence resulting from leads produced by wire tapping be used.[76] Federal officers may not testify in State trials where their evidence is derived from wire tapping.[77] This reading of the statutory provision was accomplished without the benefit of supporting legislative history. Congress had failed to enact bills introduced after *Olmstead* that would have made wire tapping a crime. The debates on the Federal Communications Act contain nothing on the crucial Section 605.[78] The Court, however, seemed almost eager to find a congressional policy forbidding wire tapping. Ironically, in the period following the *Nardone* decisions, the Court was criticized for its generous interpretation of the statute, as it had been criticized following *Olmstead* for its narrow reading of the Fourth Amendment

---

[71] 44 Stat. 1162, 1172 (1927), cited 277 U.S. at 479, n. 13 at 481.

[72] 48 Stat. 1103 (1934), 47 U.S.C. § 605 (1958).

[73] Nardone v. United States, 302 U.S. 379 (1937).

[74] Benanti v. United States, 355 U.S. 96 (1957).

[75] Weiss v. United States, 308 U.S. 321 (1939).

[76] Nardone v. United States, 308 U.S. 338 (1939).

[77] *Cf.* Rea v. United States, 350 U.S. 214 (1956). For a picture of the extensiveness of wire tapping in our society, see DASH, SCHWARTZ, & KNOWLTON, THE EAVESDROPPERS (1959); *Wiretapping, Eavesdropping, and the Bill of Rights, Hearings Before the Subcommittee on Constitutional Rights of the Senate Committee on the Judiciary*, 85th Cong., 2d Sess. pts. 1-4 (1958) and pt. 5 (1959); *Wiretapping and Eavesdropping Legislation*, 87th Cong., 1st Sess. (1961).

[78] See Westin, *The Wire-Tapping Problem: An Analysis and a Legislative Proposal*, 52 COLUM. L. REV. 165, 172-77 (1952).

right.[79] But the Court's generosity in applying Section 605 has been limited.

In 1942 the Supreme Court, perhaps affected by the criticism of the *Nardone* decisions, held in *Goldstein v. United States*[80] that the protection of Section 605 could not be invoked by one not a party to the intercepted telephone conversation. This meant that the flat prohibition in Section 605, which the Court had previously viewed as expressing congressional hostility to all wire tapping, was transformed into a remedy available to a limited class of persons whose privacy had been infringed. The new rule would, of course, encourage tapping by law-enforcement officials, who might derive valuable evidence from intercepted calls during which the speakers gave information implicating others. This analysis was contrary to a clearly expressed public policy, argued Justice Murphy, whose dissent in *Goldstein* was joined by Frankfurter and Stone.[81] Congress had laid a flat prohibition on interception and divulgence to protect "society at large against the evils of wire-tapping and kindred unauthorized intrusions into private intercourse conducted by means of the modern media of communication. . . ."[82] A more recent case has made further inroads on the protection furnished by Section 605.[83] One may listen to a telephone conversation on an extension with the consent of the subscriber without running afoul of the statutory prohibition against "interception and divulgence."

In spite of these limitations on the effect of Section 605, it is fair to say that the Court has gone a considerable distance toward filling in the huge gap in the protection of privacy created by the *Olmstead* decision. Congress could, of course, destroy the limitations on wire tapping created by the Court under Section 605. But none of the many bills seeking such a result has yet been enacted.

If the Court's treatment of Section 605 cases has, on the whole, been favorable to individuals whose phone calls have been intercepted, it has shown little disposition to apply the Fourth Amendment to protect citizens against other forms of electronic eavesdropping. Taft's rationalization in *Olmstead*, that the "reasonable view is that one who installs in his house a telephone instrument with con-

---

79 *Id.* at 175, n. 55.

80 316 U.S. 114 (1942).

81 *Id.* at 122.

82 *Id.* at 125.

83 Rathbun v. United States, 355 U.S. 107 (1957).

necting wires intends to project his voice to those quite outside, and that the wires beyond his house and messages while passing over them are not within the protection of the Fourth Amendment,"[84] suggested to the petitioners in *Goldman v. United States*[85] that the Court should be asked to overrule *Olmstead* or, at least, to distinguish it. In *Goldman*, two federal agents, seeking evidence against a lawyer and his associates suspected of fraudulent conduct in violation of the Bankruptcy Act, entered the suspected lawyer's office with the assistance of the building superintendent and placed a listening device in a small aperture in the room. When the device failed to work properly, the agents entered an adjacent office and placed a detectaphone on the wall that enabled the agents to overhear conversations in the office and over the telephone, including the lawyer's calls to clients and other persons not under suspicion. Petitioners also urged that the overheard telephone calls were intercepted and divulged in violation of Section 605. But the counterarguments prevailed with the Court. Speaking through Justice Roberts, a majority of five said they were unwilling to overrule *Olmstead*. "That case was the subject of prolonged consideration by this court. The views of the court, and of the dissenting justices, were expressed clearly and at length. . . . Nothing now can be profitably added to what was there said. It suffices to say that we adhere to the opinion there expressed."[86] The factual distinctions were "too nice for practical application of the Constitutional guarantee. . . ."[87] And Section 605 simply did not apply to overhearing one end of a telephone conversation.

In a short paragraph Chief Justice Stone and Justice Frankfurter expressed their complete agreement with the dissenting opinions in *Olmstead*, which they would apply to the facts in *Goldman*.[88] Justice Murphy chose to write a dissenting opinion in which he argued that a broad construction of the Fourth Amendment was necessary to protect the right to privacy, "as dear as any to free men." He pleaded that to prevent the Amendment from becoming obsolete "we must give mind not merely to the exact words of the Amendment, but also to its historic purposes, its high political character,

84 277 U.S. at 466.

85 316 U.S. 129 (1942).

86 *Id.* at 135–36.

87 *Id.* at 135.

88 *Id.* at 136.

and its modern social and legal implications."[89] An interesting and important feature of Murphy's opinion was the suggestion that, even on his construction, the Fourth Amendment did not necessarily rule out all uses of detectaphones by the police to obtain evidence. Safeguards might be devised, he thought, that would make their use "reasonable."[90]

It has been suggested that the decision in *Goldman* was attributable in part to the fact that it was rendered in time of war, when it might have been feared that a rule excluding evidence obtained by electronic eavesdropping would handicap the government's counterintelligence activities.[91] But there were again only four dissenting votes in *On Lee v. United States*[92] in 1952. There admission of evidence gained through a transmitting device secreted on an agent who engaged a suspect in conversation was held not to violate the Fourth Amendment. In addition to Justice Frankfurter, who had wanted to reverse *Olmstead* at the time *Goldman* was decided, the dissenters were Justice Burton, who thought spoken words could be the subject of search and seizure, and Justice Douglas, who had changed his mind and now expressed regret for his vote with the majority in *Goldman*. By way of penance, the latter quoted extensively from the Brandeis dissent in *Olmstead* and expressed his support for a generous view of the Fourth Amendment right to privacy, the right to be let alone. As he phrased it:[93] "The nature of the instrument that science or engineering develops is not important. The controlling, the decisive factor is the invasion of privacy against the command of the Fourth and Fifth Amendments." A fourth dissenter, Justice Black, whose general support for individual rights has been less evident in Fourth Amendment cases than elsewhere, would have found the government's behavior in *On Lee* improper by invoking the supervisory power of the Court over the administration of criminal justice in the federal judicial system.[94]

A more recent case involving an unconventional form of search and seizure, *Silverman v. United States*,[95] saw the Court in unani-

89 *Id.* at 137, 138.

90 *Id.* at 140, n. 7.

91 Westin, *supra* note 78, at 180.

92 343 U.S. 747 (1952).

93 *Id.* at 765.

94 *Id.* at 758.

95 365 U.S. 505 (1961).

mous agreement that the particular form of electronic eavesdropping violated the Fourth Amendment. The reason for the holding, however, gives little cheer to those who would oppose all forms of electronic surveillance. In *Silverman*, the Washington, D.C., police used a spike microphone, a slim, nail-like object that was driven into the wall between the suspect's house and an adjacent row house. The lower court decisions had turned on the question whether driving the spike into the wall constituted a trespass. The district court[96] and the court of appeals[97] said that no trespass had occurred or, if it had, that it was so trivial that it should not call constitutional safeguards into play. There was a strong dissent by Judge Washington.[98] The Supreme Court based its judgment on the trespass committed by driving the spike into the common wall until it struck a heating conduit, which had the effect of permitting the police to overhear all that was said throughout the house for a nine-day period. Mr. Justice Stewart, speaking for all of the Court save Justice Douglas, refused the invitation of counsel to re-examine the rationale of *Olmstead*, *Goldman*, and *On Lee*, and chose the simple, if mechanical, route of trespass. This actual invasion of the home by way of the spike microphone served to distinguish this case from *Goldman*. Douglas, concurring, thought that the Court, in concentrating on the elements of trespass, had missed the essential wrong which was the invasion of privacy, whether accomplished by trespass, as in the present case, or without trespass, as in *Goldman*. He concluded that "the invasion of privacy is as great in one case as in the other."[99]

The decision in the *Silverman* case, it should be noted, is perfectly consistent with *Olmstead;* because of the trespass there was an invasion of property that was missing in the earlier case. But the distinction itself suggests the irrationality of making a trespass, no matter how slight, decisive. The lower court's resolution of the issue whether a trespass had occurred turned on a matter of a few inches in the penetration of the common wall. Stewart, sensing the quixotic nature of such a rationale, preferred to stress the fact that a heating conduit was contacted by the spike microphone, thus in effect making the officers' action which enabled them to hear all

---

[96] 166 F. Supp. 838 (D.D.C. 1958).

[97] 275 F. 2d 173 (D.C. Cir. 1960).

[98] See text at notes 144 *et seq., infra.*

[99] 365 U.S. at 512–13.

that was said a trespass throughout the whole house. But is it not the intention of all electronic eavesdropping to make an "auditory trespass"?

The most recent statement of the Court's views on electronic eavesdropping occurred in *Lanza v. New York*.[100] Since the opinion of the Court represents the views of only three, or perhaps four, Justices[101] and the discussion of the constitutional issue was not essential to a disposition of the case, the comments dealing with search and seizure cannot be given much weight. The defendant Lanza had been granted immunity by a New York legislative committee investigating State parole practices but had refused to answer a series of questions relating to his recent release on parole. He was found guilty of a misdemeanor under State law for his refusal. Most of the questions to which answers were sought were based on information obtained by an electronic interception of a conversation between the defendant and his brother that took place in a visiting room at a jail where the latter was confined. Two of the questions asked by the committee were not based on the intercepted conversation and since the refusal to answer these was sufficient to support the conviction, all of the Justices of the Supreme Court agreed that an independent State ground existed for affirming the State court action. The interesting feature of the case, however, was Stewart's treatment of the constitutional issue and his not surprising conclusion that "a jail shares none of the attributes of privacy of a home, an automobile, an office, or a hotel room."[102] He then argued that even if the search-and-seizure guaranty applied to the jail room, there was no precedent for upsetting a conviction in the present case. A puzzling aspect of Stewart's treatment of this point, however, was his failure to refer to *Goldman v. United States* which would seem to be crucial here. For, if evidence obtained by electronic eavesdroping on conversations of suspects does

---

[100] 370 U.S. 139 (1962).

[101] Mr. Justice Harlan concurred on his understanding that nothing "in the Court's opinion [suggested] either that the Fourteenth Amendment 'incorporates' the provisions of the Fourth, or that the 'liberty' assured by the Fourteenth Amendment is, with respect to 'privacy,' necessarily coextensive with the protection afforded by the Fourth." *Id.* at 147.

[102] *Id.* at 143.

not violate the Fourth Amendment, it is hard to believe that a convicted person in jail should have a higher claim to constitutional protection.

IV. Conventional Searches and Seizures

We have seen that the Supreme Court has been reluctant to include unconventional forms of eavesdropping in the ban of the Fourth Amendment. On the other hand it has been relatively generous in its interpretation of the statutory ban on wire tapping. The conclusion must be that, in the Court's view, the interest in privacy has been outweighed by the interest in effective law enforcement through electronic eavesdropping. In the conventional type of search-and-seizure cases, the Court has been confronted with a wide variety of difficult fact situations and has been unable to reach agreement on clear rules or principles capable of ready application.[103]

It is clear that at common law the sanctity of an individual's home received greater protection than the privacy of his person.[104] To search one's house required a warrant issued by a judicial officer. To arrest a person suspected of crime, it was sufficient if the officer had reasonable grounds for believing that a felony had been committed and that the arrestee was the person responsible.[105] This, of

---

[103] For excellent discussions of the problems see Comment, *Search and Seizure in the Supreme Court: Shadows on the Fourth Amendment*, 28 U. Chi. L. Rev. 664 (1961); Kaplan, *Search and Seizure: A No-Man's Land in the Criminal Law*, 49 Calif. L. Rev. 474 (1961); Paulsen, *Safeguards in the Law of Search and Seizure*, 52 Nw.U.L. Rev. 65 (1957). The problems arising from the application of the Fourth Amendment to State action through the Fourteenth Amendment have been dealt with in a notable series of articles by Professor Francis A. Allen: *The Wolf Case: Search and Seizure, Federalism, and Civil Liberties*, 45 Ill. L. Rev. 1 (1950); *The Supreme Court, Federalism, and State Systems of Criminal Justice*, 8 U. Chi. L. S. Rec. 3 (Supp. Autumn 1958); *Federalism and the Fourth Amendment: A Requiem for Wolf*, [1961] Supreme Court Review 1. Another extremely valuable article is Kamisar, *Wolf and Lustig Ten Years Later: Illegal State Evidence in State and Federal Courts*, 43 Minn. L. Rev. 1083 (1959).

[104] See Barrett, *supra* note 11.

[105] The difference between the law of arrests and that of search and seizure may be explainable by the obviously greater difficulty in apprehending suspects than in searching houses. A warrant requirement for arrests would permit the escape of many guilty persons. The severe penalties in earlier centuries for what today would be regarded as minor offenses and the lack of effective communication un-

course, did not mean that arrest warrants were never used, nor was it true that all searches and seizures were based on warrants. Exceptions to the requirement of a search warrant existed from an early time and were drawn into our constitutional jurisprudence. The significant trend, from the viewpoint of one concerned with the protection of privacy, is that the Supreme Court has broadened the exceptions to the general rule that a warrant must be obtained before a search can be undertaken. The exception permitting search of the person at the time of arrest and allowing seizure of instruments or fruits of crime in open view and under control of the arrested person has grown so that in many situations it is now possible to say that a legal arrest, with or without warrant, makes possible a search that would not have been justified by a search warrant.[106]

The early application of this doctrine did not suggest its potentiality for growth. In *Marron v. United States*[107] seizure of a ledger and bills on a closet shelf in defendant's speak-easy was upheld. Later decisions refused to extend the doctrine and stressed that the articles seized in *Marron* were readily accessible and visible and had not been discovered by an exploratory search.[108] But in *Harris v. United States*[109] the Court allowed a detailed search of a four-room apartment as an incident to arrest with warrant. Justice Frankfurter, with the concurrence of Justices Murphy and Rutledge, and Justices Murphy and Jackson separately, wrote dissenting opinions protesting the enlargement of this exception to the general rule requiring search warrants. Frankfurter's opinion is a masterful survey of the historical background, rationale, and application of the Fourth Amendment. Murphy's conclusion was essentially that reached by Frankfurter:[110] "The result is that a warrant for arrest

---

doubtedly encouraged suspects to flee. See 3 HOLDSWORTH, HISTORY OF ENGLISH LAW 597–607 (3d ed. 1923), for a brief discussion of the development of arrest procedures.

106 The search-warrant requirements are set forth in Fed. Rules Crim. Proc. Rule 41(c). Essentially, the applicant must show probable cause that specified items, stolen or embezzled, or used or intended to be used as means of committing crime, will be found in a specific place.

107 275 U.S. 192 (1927).

108 Go-Bart Importing Co. v. United States, 282 U.S. 344 (1931); United States v. Lefkowitz, 285 U.S. 452 (1932).

109 331 U.S. 145 (1947).

110 *Id.* at 191.

is the equivalent of a general search warrant or writ of assistance. . . . As to those placed under arrest, the restrictions of the Fourth Amendment on searches are now words without meaning or effect."

Having veered toward a policy of widening the exception, the Court then took the opposite tack. In *Trupiano v. United States*,[111] in 1948, a majority of five sought to narrow the exception by requiring a search warrant in all cases where there was an adequate opportunity to obtain one. The facts of the case made the occasion less than ideal for announcing a new doctrine. Federal agents, apprised by the owner of a New Jersey farm that lessees appeared to be planning to construct and operate an illegal liquor still, planted one of their number as an employee of the lessee. Information supplied by the agent allowed detailed surveillance and finally led to a raid. Members of the raiding party could smell the mash and hear the motor of the operating still as they approached. One, looking through an open door, saw a still and a boiler. They entered the building, arrested one of the still operators, and seized the illicit alcohol and manufacturing equipment. In spite of the reasonableness of the agents' behavior, the majority, speaking through Justice Murphy, found the arrest legal but invalidated the seizure because the government had not procured a search warrant in spite of ample opportunity to do so. The dissenting opinion of Chief Justice Vinson found the majority opinion faulty in every respect. He thought the new rule would "confound confusion in a field already replete with complexities."[112] But the reconstitution of the Court after the deaths of Justices Murphy and Rutledge made possible a new alignment and a new rule in cases of search incident to arrest.

In 1950, in *United States v. Rabinowitz*,[113] the Court abandoned the *Trupiano* doctrine and permitted a detailed search of a one-room place of business incident to the arrest of the owner pursuant to a warrant. The owner was a stamp dealer charged with fraudulent overprinting of postage stamps. The fact that government agents had time to procure a warrant was deemed of no significance. Later decisions have not changed the rule laid down in *Rabinowitz*. The Court has not, however, approved all searches incident to an arrest. If, for example, it appears that the purpose of

111 334 U.S. 699 (1948).

112 *Id.* at 716.

113 339 U.S. 56 (1950).

entering a house is to search rather than to make an arrest, a search followed by an arrest is illegal.[114] The Court also has refused to uphold a seizure of the entire contents of a cabin in which a lawful arrest was made.[115] But the basic rule persists and, since in most instances no warrant is necessary for arrest, the judgment of a law-enforcement official, rather than of a magistrate, is sufficient to justify searches and seizures so long as the arrestee can be found in the place to be searched. The irony of the situation was noted by the late Judge Learned Hand, who commented that "it is small consolation to know that one's papers are safe only so long as one is not at home."[116]

While widening the scope of search incident to an arrest, the Court eased or seemed to soften the requirement of "probable cause" for making an arrest. In *Grau v. United States*,[117] where the Court had found a search warrant lacking in essential elements, it said: "A search warrant may issue only upon evidence which would be competent in the trial of the offense before a jury. . . ." But in *Brinegar v. United States*,[118] where there was a search of an automobile without warrant and seizure of illegal liquor, the Court rejected this test and stated that evidence of a lower quality than would be required at trial would justify search or arrest.[119] This doctrine, that inadmissible or less convincing evidence would support an arrest, was adhered to in *Draper v. United States*.[120] The arrest without warrant was held lawful because "hearsay" evidence was deemed sufficient to support a warrant, especially since the informer's phone call telling the arresting officer that the described suspect would get off a specified train carrying narcotics proved correct. The lone dissenter, Justice Douglas, asserted that decisions

---

114 Jones v. United States, 357 U.S. 493 (1958).

115 Kremen v. United States, 353 U.S. 346 (1957).

116 United States v. Kirchenblatt, 16 F. 2d 202, 203 (2d Cir. 1926).

117 287 U.S. 124, 128 (1932).

118 338 U.S. 160 (1949).

119 There was a strong dissenting opinion by Justice Jackson, with the concurrence of Justices Frankfurter and Murphy, expressing the view that the arrest and search had been found lawful on the basis of what the search revealed. The only facts showing probable cause were the officer's knowledge that the arrestee had been apprehended for a liquor violation on an earlier occasion and reputedly was a runner of illegal liquor. *Id.* at 180.

120 358 U.S. 307 (1959). Chief Justice Warren and Justice Frankfurter did not participate.

under the Fourth Amendment "taken in the long view, have not given the protection to the citizen which the letter and spirit of the Amendment would seem to require. . . . Wherever a culprit is caught red-handed, as in leading Fourth Amendment cases, it is difficult to adopt and enforce a rule that would turn him loose. A rule protective of law-abiding citizens is not apt to flourish where its advocates are usually criminals."[121]

The importance of the Court's more generous approach to the requirements for arrest was heightened by the Court's apparent unwillingness in *Chapman v. United States*[122] to allow similar opportunities where the officers undertook a search without warrant.[123] When a Georgia landlord invited the police to search a house in the absence of tenants who operated a still in the living room, the Court held the search invalid. It is not clear from Justice Whittaker's opinion whether the search was invalid because "probable cause" can never justify search of a house without warrant or because the police had abundant time to procure a warrant or because the "exceptional circumstances" in which "a magistrate's warrant for search may be dispensed with" did not exist.

Some may question whether the expansion of the exception to the search-warrant requirement adversely affects the right to privacy. It can be argued that the breach of personal privacy arising from the lawful arrest within the home or office is so substantial that an incidental search of the premises is hardly a significant additional interference with the privacy of the arrestee or, if it is recognized as an interference with a separate interest, it is justified by the existence of strong reasons why the affected individual should submit. For one thing, the individual whose premises are searched has, by definition, lost his status as an ordinary innocent citizen, because he has been lawfully arrested. It can also be argued that, in many jurisdictions, requiring a search warrant after a lawful arrest would be meaningless formality, since virtually all magistrates would find probable cause in those circumstances.[124] To insist on this step would simply add to police burdens, with a possibility of

---

121 *Id.* at 314.

122 365 U.S. 610, 615 (1961).

123 For a thoughtful treatment of the contrasts between the law of arrest and that of search and seizure, see Barrett, *supra* note 11.

124 It would depend on the breadth of the search permitted by statute and the kind of knowledge required of the officer obtaining it.

loss of seizable evidence, and with no compensating protection of the individual who, by the time the search takes place, has been deprived of his liberty.

The counterargument, so well expressed by Justice Frankfurter, is that historically the Fourth Amendment was intended to protect one's home, effects, and papers, as well as one's person.[125] These are distinguishable elements, or aspects, of the individual personality, and a legal interference with one element should not automatically carry the right to infringe others. It is also argued that the main purpose of many arrests on the premises is to make possible a search for which a warrant could not be obtained.[126] If nothing is revealed by the search, the arrestee is released and the matter dropped. If evidence is found, the arrest, viewed retrospectively, will usually appear lawful.

Perhaps the most fundamental difference between the protagonists of each position lies in their respective views of the effect on society of permitting an extensive search as an incident of arrest. The late Chief Justice Vinson, or Justice Clark on the present Court, would stress the difficulty of apprehending and convicting criminals and the care with which the police avoid interference with the privacy of innocent people.[127] The late Justice Murphy, or Justice Frankfurter, would emphasize that constitutional safeguards are designed to protect the innocent and guilty alike and that certain procedures and decisions should not be intrusted solely to law-enforcement officials.[128] Behind this argument are the fear of

---

[125] See especially his dissenting opinions in Harris v. United States, 331 U.S. 145, 155 (1947), and United States v. Rabinowitz, 339 U.S. 56, 68 (1950).

[126] If it is suggested that the statutory requirements for obtaining a warrant are unrealistically severe, the proper answer is that the law of warrants should be changed, not that the scope of search incident to arrest should be enlarged.

[127] On Chief Justice Vinson's views, see Allen, *Chief Justice Vinson and the Theory of Constitutional Government: A Tentative Appraisal,* 49 Nw.U.L. Rev. 3, 12–14 (1952). A good expression of his approach is his dissenting opinion in Trupiano v. United States, 334 U.S. 699, 710 (1948). Justice Clark's lone dissent in Chapman v. United States, 365 U.S. 616, 619 (1961), gives, in a few paragraphs, the flavor of his "no nonsense" attitude toward these problems.

[128] For a brief analysis of Murphy's attitude, see Marshall, *Mr. Justice Murphy and Civil Rights,* 48 Mich. L. Rev. 745 (1950). Jacobs, *op. cit. supra* note 70, at ch. 7, is a useful summary of Frankfurter's position with respect to procedural guaranties in federal cases.

official abuse of procedure to achieve political objectives and the knowledge that police may abuse their powers in acting against unpopular individuals or minority groups, without arousing sufficient public outcry to force the police to desist.

As shown by some of the earlier cases, a search without warrant of an automobile, ship, or other movable vehicle may be sustained, although a search of a house with the same information would require a warrant. The basic rule, laid down by Chief Justice Taft in *Carroll v. United States*,[129] is that where probable cause exists for believing that a vehicle contains articles legally subject to seizure, no warrant is necessary. It was pointed out that a statute of 1790 had given government officials power to enter and search, without warrant, ships suspected of evading customs duties; that a distinction between a search of permanent structures and vehicles, whose movement could defeat officers placed under a duty to obtain a warrant before searching, was reasonable under the Fourth Amendment. The rule has been followed, although difficult questions may arise as to whether probable cause exists at the time a vehicle is halted.[130] If the driver is lawfully arrested, a search of the vehicle is then possible as an incident to a lawful arrest, but if the arrest is not lawful, and probable cause for the search did not exist at the time of the stopping of the vehicle, the discovery of seizable objects cannot be used to justify the arrest or the search.[131] The real-life situations that are likely to give rise to this legal issue occur rather frequently, since police will have numerous occasions to stop a vehicle or approach a parked car where the appearance or action of the driver or other occupants arouses suspicion. The police do not regard these investigatory questionings as arrests, and at least one lower federal court has held stopping automobiles and questioning its occupants to be within the police power.[132] An arrest is a sufficiently damaging action against an individual that it would be

---

[129] 267 U.S. 132 (1925).

[130] Brinegar v. United States, 338 U.S. 160 (1949).

[131] Henry v. United States, 361 U.S. 98 (1959); Rios v. United States, 364 U.S. 253 (1960).

[132] United States v. Bonanno, 180 F. Supp. 71 (S.D.N.Y. 1960).

unfair to him, as well as to the officer, to insist that every stopping and questioning should be treated as an arrest.[133]

That the sanctioning of the practice of halting automobiles and questioning occupants can lead to serious abuses is evident. Obviously an occasional law violator may be turned up in any sustained police roadblock operation, but a serious invasion of the privacy of many innocent people results. Rallying to the defense of constitutional rights, automobile clubs have denounced excessive police actions against motorists. Their action, combined with strong individual protests, deters the police from resorting habitually to the "dragnet" method of solving crimes.

V. Privacy and the Administrative Search

A variant of the search accompanying a lawful arrest is the use of an administrative warrant, that is, one issued by authority of an administrative official. In *Abel v. United States*,[134] a conviction for conspiracy to commit espionage was upheld against the claim that seized articles were inadmissible because the arrest was made on the basis of a warrant for the purpose of deportation. The majority of five, speaking through Justice Frankfurter, who has vigorously supported a broad interpretation of the Fourth Amendment and has been consistent in upholding claimants who invoke the Amendment against the federal government, rejected the claim that the government had resorted to the administrative warrant only because there had been insufficient evidence to permit the issuance of either an arrest warrant or a search warrant on the criminal charge. Since the arrest was lawful, the search might be as extensive as those incidental to police arrests. The dissenting opinion of Justice Douglas, with the concurrence of Justice Black, stated that the initiative had been taken by FBI agents, who induced the Immigration and Naturalization Service officials to use the administrative warrants to make possible the search for evidence of crime. Justice Brennan, with the concurrence of Justices Black, Douglas, and Chief Justice Warren, also dissented. He saw the vice of the action

133 See Remington, *The Law Relating to "On the Street" Detention, Questioning and Frisking of Suspected Persons and Police Arrest Privileges in General*, 51 J. Crim. L. 386 (1960).

134 362 U.S. 217 (1960)

in the lack of any procedure by which the arrestee could challenge what was done and rejected the suggestion of the majority that the power of search might be greater where related to a civil proceeding such as deportation. This was in reply to Justice Frankfurter's statement:[135] "If anything, we ought to be more vigilant, not less, to protect individuals and their property from warrantless searches made for the purpose of turning up proof to convict than we are to protect them from searches for matter bearing on deportability." Stressing the distinction between a search for evidence of crime and searches for other purposes that he had set forth in the earlier case of *Frank v. Maryland*,[136] Frankfurter argued: "Searches for evidence of crime present situations demanding the greatest, not the least, restraint upon the Government's intrusion into privacy; although its protection is not limited to them, it was at these searches which the Fourth Amendment was primarily directed."[137]

In this, as in the more typical Supreme Court decisions discussed heretofore, the Court dealt with procedural issues involving persons initially suspected of criminal conduct and subsequently convicted of crime. The argument repeated in all these cases was that the safeguard had to be extended to the guilty if the constitutional principle limiting official action was to have any effectiveness in protecting the innocent. A contrary view, it was argued, would allow law-enforcement officials to determine for whom, and under what circumstances, constitutional guaranties were meaningful. But in two cases, where the Court was faced with the question whether health inspectors could insist upon entrance to a home without a warrant, the State governments imposed on innocent, if recalcitrant, homeowners. In *Frank v. Maryland* the Court's spokesman was Justice Frankfurter, who would not apply the federal exclusionary rule to the States and hence has been less likely to support the claimant in State search-and-seizure cases. For a majority of five, he upheld the power of a health official acting on a complaint but without a warrant to demand admission to a home at a reasonable hour in order to carry out his duties. The fact that there had been statutory authority for this action by health and other inspection officers for a long period of time helped the Court reach its conclusion. The main point of Frankfurter's opinion is

[135] *Id.* at 237.

[136] 359 U.S. 360 (1959).

[137] 362 U.S. at 237.

that there are two rights protected by the Fourth Amendment. One is the right to privacy; the second, and more important in his view, is the right of an individual to protection against a search for incriminating evidence. Only the former right—that of privacy—was involved here. And the State's interest in health was sufficient to overbalance the householder's insistence that the inspector must be armed with a warrant. The four dissenters, speaking through Justice Douglas, presented a strong argument that neither history nor precedent supported Frankfurter's restriction of the Fourth Amendment's protection primarily to cases involving search for evidence in criminal cases. As they pointed out, some of the classic abuses in English experience were the result of searches for political dissenters and in aid of customs regulations. The safeguarding of privacy of the innocent and guilty alike is the purpose of the Fourth Amendment, Douglas argued, and requiring a health inspector to obtain a search warrant was a modest price to pay for insuring the achievement of that purpose.[138]

In a similar State case, *Ohio ex rel. Eaton v. Price*,[139] where the only distinguishing fact was that no complaint had been cited to justify what appeared to be a random health inspection, the Court divided four to four, Justice Stewart not participating, with the effect of affirming the State-court decision. While the decision in *Eaton* was per curiam, the four Justices who earlier had dissented in *Frank v. Maryland* took the unusual step of giving their reasons for thinking that the factual differences between *Eaton* and *Frank* deserved full opinion. They justified their action by recalling that

---

[138] The analysis of Justice Frankfurter in the *Frank* case should be compared with that of Judge Prettyman in District of Columbia v. Little, 178 F. 2d 13 (D.C. Cir. 1949), where the power of a District of Colombia health inspector to inspect without a warrant was denied. The dissenting opinion in *Little*, written by Judge Holtzoff, contains many of the arguments used by the majority in *Frank*. The decision in *Little* was affirmed on other grounds by the Supreme Court. 339 U.S. 1 (1950). The flavor of Judge Prettyman's argument is suggested by the following: "The basic premise of the prohibition against searches was not protection against self-incrimination; it was the common-law right of a man to privacy in his home, a right which is one of the indispensable ultimate essentials of our concept of civilization." 178 F. 2d at 16–17. And again: "To say that a man suspected of crime has a right to protection against search of his home without a warrant, but that a man not suspected of crime has no such protection, is a fantastic absurdity." *Id.* at 17.

[139] 364 U.S. 263 (1960).

the four Justices voting for affirmance had expressed their view that this case was controlled by *Frank* at the time of noting probable jurisdiction in the *Eaton* case.[140] The distinction between the cases offered by Brennan was the existence of a complaint and unsanitary conditions outside the house in *Frank* and the absence of any showing why the inspectors sought entrance in *Eaton*. But the conclusion of the dissenters is that a search warrant should issue whenever a householder does not wish inspection.[141]

The most disturbing aspect of the *Frank* and *Eaton* decisions is the rationale of Justice Frankfurter that the Fourth Amendment means less when invoked to protect privacy than it does when used to restrict official searches for evidence. One justification for the application of the Fourth that he has set forth on numerous occasions is that sheltering the guilty in many cases provides the only effective way of protecting the innocent. But when the privacy of the innocent is invaded, the Court found the right to be insignificant.[142] The possibility of abuse of administrative search authorized by these decisions is great. Harassment of unpopular minorities, political dissenters, and party opponents can occur with few, if any, means of protecting the individual. Many police departments will find it useful to set up close working relations with health inspectors, to be utilized where there is insufficient evidence to justify arrest or search and seizure.[143] Obviously the capacity for abuse

---

140 360 U.S. 246 (1959).

141 For administrative experience in other urban areas as well as an excellent critique of *Frank*, see Comment, *supra* note 6. For other comments adversely critical of the rationale of the decisions, see 28 U. Cinc. L. Rev. 478 (1959); 1959 Ill. L. Forum 661 (1949); 43 Marq. L. Rev. 256 (1959); 27 Tenn. L. Rev. 406 (1960); 10 Hastings L. J. 430 (1959); 20 Md. L. Rev. 345 (1960). For favorable reactions, see 10 W. Res. L. Rev. 304 (1959); 26 Brooklyn L. Rev. 265 (1959).

142 Justice Douglas in his dissent in *Frank* had noted that a warrant is required for health inspections in Great Britain where the householder objects. For an English view that this requirement is, unfortunately, not imposed generally in Britain, see Waters, *Rights of Entry in Administrative Officers*, 27 U. Chi. L. Rev. 79 (1959).

143 See the reference in Douglas' dissenting opinion in Abel v. United States, 362 U.S. at 242–43, to an example of police-health department collusion in Baltimore. Although the action did not pass judicial scrutiny in the case he cited, it suggests that less blatant forms of co-operation could be highly successful in the same way that wire tapping in many instances furnishes leads that cannot be traced to the tap. And see references in Comment, *supra* note 6, at 519, n. 23, to evidence of a few cases of "co-operation" in Minneapolis and St. Paul.

under a particular ruling is not itself a convincing argument against it. When that potential is coupled with the novelty of the distinction drawn in *Frank*, however, the need for re-examination of the issue seems clear. If the theory of the two-fold purpose of the Fourth Amendment expounded by Frankfurter in *Frank* continues to command the support of a majority of the Court, the secondary interest—personal privacy—will certainly receive less protection than it deserves. This would make it desirable to view the right of privacy as a distinct right subsumed under "liberty" in the Fifth and Fourteenth Amendments in order to permit fuller consideration of the factors operating for and against its recognition in a specific case.

VI. Is Privacy Part of "Liberty"?

The discussion thus far has dealt with privacy as protected by the Fourth Amendment and the self-incrimination clause of the Fifth Amendment. It can be argued that privacy is part of the liberty or "property" protected against the federal government by the Due Process Clauses. This suggestion was made by Judge Washington of the District of Columbia Court of Appeals in his dissent in *Silverman v. United States.*[144] He thought the physical trespass issue on which the majority opinion concentrated was irrelevant. He was quite willing to concede that, in the light of the precedents, eavesdropping by a spike microphone "may be held not to abridge any Fourth Amendment right." What was violated, in his view, was "our fundamental concept of ordered liberty, as embodied in the due process clause of the Fifth and Fourteenth Amendments."[145] He cited *Irvine v. California*[146] and *Palko v. Connecticut*[147] as authority. In elaborating this view, he continued:[148] "Under a governmental system of constitutional or limited

144 275 F. 2d 173, 178 (1960). See text *supra,* at notes 95 *et seq.*

145 *Id.* at 179.

146 347 U.S. 128 (1954).

147 302 U.S. 319 (1937). Of course neither *Irvine* nor *Palko* is of any value as a factual precedent. In the former the Supreme Court upheld a State conviction where evidence was obtained by the most flagrant physical and electronic intrusions; in *Palko* the Court refused to invalidate State appeals in criminal cases on the ground of double jeopardy.

148 274 F. 2d at 179.

exercise of public power, ordered liberty requires that the police, like other public officials take action against a citizen only pursuant to duly-conferred authority." He regarded electronic eavesdropping as even more dangerous than wire tapping, since, as shown in *Silverman,* the police had overheard everything that was said in the entire house over a period of nine days.

While this proposal of Judge Washington's is unlikely to be readily adopted by the Supreme Court, it is worth pursuing. In the famous *Palko* case Cardozo attempted to set forth a rationalizing principle that would justify the inclusion of some, and the exclusion of other, rights in determining the meaning and content of the "liberty" protected against State action by the Due Process Clause of the Fourteenth Amendment. The majority of cases presented to the Court have involved specific rights of the first eight amendments, such as freedom of speech, press, or religion, but *Rochin v. California*[149] did not turn on that kind of analysis. The stomach pumping was regarded as a denial of due process because "shocking to the conscience" and violative of well-established principles of justice. Due process, in other words, includes rights that may not be specified in the Bill of Rights. The Fourth Amendment, it will be recalled, was at least partially read into the Fourteenth Amendment in *Wolf v. Colorado.*[150] In his opinion for the Court in that case, Frankfurter, after discussing the meaning of due process as it had been developed in a line of cases, observed:[151] "The security of one's privacy against arbitrary intrusion by the police—which is at the core of the Fourth Amendment—is basic to a free society. It is therefore implicit in 'the concept of ordered liberty'. . . ."

What Judge Washington seems to be suggesting, then, is that rather than continue efforts to protect privacy against State or federal action by invoking "the core of the Fourth Amendment," with all the exceptions and limitations that have been engrafted on search-and-seizure law, it is preferable to view the right to privacy as an

149 342 U.S. 165 (1952).

150 338 U.S. 25 (1949). While Mapp v. Ohio, 367 U.S. 643 (1961), has made the exclusionary rule effective in State cases, it does not follow that the Fourteenth Amendment is to be applied in exactly the same terms as is the Fourth Amendment against the federal government.

151 338 U.S. at 27.

essential liberty that deserves protection under the Fourteenth Amendment. By similar reasoning, the Due Process Clause in the Fifth Amendment would furnish protection against the federal government. Although the justification for this bold step was not spelled out, it would presumably take a form similar to that sketched by Professor Nutting who, after examining the reasons why the claims of witnesses before legislative investigating committees to a right to silence or to privacy had not received protection under the First Amendment or the self-incrimination clause of the Fifth Amendment, concluded that "neither [of the amendments] was intended to deal with the situation."[152] He went on to argue:[153] "The way to protect privacy [of witnesses] is to recognize the interest for what it is. . . . It is an interest which should receive protection as a 'liberty' which cannot be taken away without due process of law." In essence, he would place the government under a duty to justify any demand for disclosure of private matters by giving a reason to support their demand.

Whatever the difficulties faced by the Courts in attempting to impose such a restraint on congressional investigating committees, the line of thought is clear. If, in the process of making an analysis of interests requiring protection against government action, one is found that does not fit a specified category in the Bill of Rights, it can certainly be placed in the category of a "liberty." It can be argued that if free speech, free press, and freedom of religion can all be found implicit in the term "liberty" in the Fourteenth Amendment, little more is needed to add the right to privacy to that list. On the other hand, it is true that by including the meaning of First Amendment rights in the Fourteenth Amendment a court has the guidance furnished by First Amendment cases, whereas Judge Washington's proposal would leave the Court in the position of creating a new right without such guidance. But this is not a novelty. In *Kent v. Dulles*,[154] the Court, in the course of examining the power of the federal government to refuse to issue passports, stated that the right to travel is a part of the "liberty" of which the citizen cannot be deprived without due process of law under the Fifth

---

[152] Nutting, *The Fifth Amendment and Privacy*, 18 U. PITT. L. REV. 533, 543 (1957).

[153] *Ibid.*

[154] 357 U.S. 116 (1958).

Amendment, a conclusion with which the Solicitor General agreed.[155] It is only a short step, then, to assert that the right to privacy, like the right to travel, is essential to a free society and that interference with that right is an intrusion on the "liberty" of the person affected. While it may be readily conceded that the same result might be reached by returning to the broad interpretation of the Fourth and Fifth Amendments set forth by Brandeis in *Olmstead*, a more logical definition of the substance and scope of the right to privacy is possible if the courts are freed from the meandering and confusing precedents of search-and-seizure law.

Finally, there has been an argument, unaccepted by the Court, that a "right of silence" exists as one form of freedom of speech. Justice Douglas has expressed this view, chiefly with respect to those asked to subscribe to official oaths and to witnesses before legislative investigating committees who choose to resist questions that touch on the beliefs of the witness or his friends.[156] It should be recognized that the problem involves more than oath-taking or congressional investigating committees. It can arise in connection with the use of census questionnaires or other interrogations directed at the citizen by various government agencies, with or without specific statutory authorization. The difficulty in considering a right to silence or privacy as an aspect of freedom of speech is that it injects a "freedom from" claim into a concept that has always signified "freedom to do." The difficulties in interpreting the right to freedom of speech are sufficiently taxing to make a court reluctant to recognize an interest in privacy as part of that right. An interesting argument that reaches a different conclusion is that the First Amendment's freedom of expression is violated by wire tapping and electronic eavesdropping.[157] The chief difficulty with this approach is its subtlety. It raises difficult questions. Could a plainclothes police representative attend meetings of political groups without running afoul of the First Amendment? And is it not true that speech will be inhibited only if speakers suspect that they are,

155 *Id.* at 125.

156 "One great right protected by the First Amendment is the right of silence." DOUGLAS, *op. cit. supra* note 10, at 134.

157 King, *Wire Tapping and Electronic Surveillance: A Neglected Constitutional Consideration*, 66 DICK. L. REV. 17 (1961).

or are likely to be, overheard? In most cases the persons under surveillance would have no reasons for suspicion and would speak freely, as in *Olmstead* and *Goldman*.

It seems to me to be more feasible to work out a right to privacy based on the "liberty" concept in the Fifth and Fourteenth Amendments. It might be said in opposition to this proposal that any process of reading new meaning into "liberty" is undesirable if it appears to call upon judges to read natural-law concepts into the Constitution in the manner of the post-1890 decades. The charge is plausible. But what is sought here is a systematic development by the Court of a right that has always been thought to be part of the constitutional heritage of every American—the right to be free from unjustified intrusion by government—but one which has received less protection than seems desirable. The inadequacy of the Fourth Amendment suggests that other constitutional sources of protection for the right need cultivation. For, if the right is to have no more than the rhetorical function it now possesses, its employment in constitutional cases should be abandoned.

The remedies needed to make a right to privacy effective would be a tort remedy against the government and the individual officer. In certain instances, the exclusionary rule would be effective, and, of course, successful invocation of the right should provide an adequate defense to any action brought to recover a fine or to impose another penalty. But perhaps the immediate objective should be to define the right, without so much initial concern for the remedy. The lesson provided by the narrowing of the Fourth Amendment after the adoption of the exclusionary rule should not be forgotten.

VII. Conclusion

It is submitted that, to date, the Fourth Amendment protects the right to privacy only insofar as one can subsume official action under the heading "search and seizure." It appears that the generous interpretation exemplified by *Boyd* and *Gouled* has been replaced by the niggardly construction of *Olmstead* and *Goldman*, which rejects any broad notion of privacy as protected by the Fourth Amendment. The Court has weakened the protection of privacy supposedly furnished by the requirement of warrants, especially by taking a generous view of the power of police to search as an incident of legal arrest and of the kind and quantum of evidence needed to justify arrest. The validation of administrative searches without warrant has further diminished the area protected. In short, the right to privacy now means nothing more than a diminishing protection against unreasonable searches and seizures. The Fourth Amendment, combined with the protection against self-incrimination in the Fifth Amendment, furnishes only modest protection of the right to privacy.

It has been suggested that the Due Process Clauses of the Fifth and Fourteenth Amendments, or the provisions of the First Amendment, might provide a basis for developing adequate protection of the right to privacy. But of the various statements on the constitutional right to privacy contained in the Court's opinions to date, one might say:

> And be these juggling fiends no more believed,
> That palter with us in a double sense;
> That keep the word of promise to our ear,
> And break it to our hope.

PHIL C. NEAL

BAKER v. CARR: POLITICS IN SEARCH OF LAW

In the century since the Civil War it has become a firm belief that the Constitution has proved to be what Chief Justice Marshall in 1819 could only hopefully describe as the ideal of its framers, a plan intended "to be adapted to the various crises of human affairs."[1] A necessary condition of adaptation to crisis has been a potent and respected Supreme Court, wise enough to rework old principles to fit new problems and new conditions. That such a Court is also a sufficient condition for surmounting crisis has perhaps almost come to be taken for granted too, despite occasional resort to the amending process, but is a proposition which until recently had not been put to severe test since the unhappy effort in the *Dred Scott* case[2] to settle the sectional crisis over slavery. Our most trying judicial ordeal since then, that of the mid-thirties, posed the question whether the Court was to be an obstacle to adaptation, not whether it was to be the lever of change. But twice in the present decade the federal judiciary has been put to a different kind of test of its power, a test still going on. In these instances, the courts have been called upon to act as prime movers in effecting great reforms in areas where political and legislative processes have failed. The novel and acute

---

Phil C. Neal is Professor of Law, The University of Chicago.

1 McCulloch v. Maryland, 4 Wheat. 316, 415 (1819).

2 Dred Scott v. Sanford, 19 How. 393 (1857).

stress which they have placed on the judiciary is one element that links the school segregation cases[3] and the reapportionment cases, marking them as among the most important in decades. But there are differences. In the segregation cases, a unanimous Court exercised a judgment from which it could hardly escape, announced a principle whose inevitability had been made apparent in a series of prior decisions, and granted relief which in the exercise of conventional judicial powers could not be denied. The new test of judicial strength which has been initiated by last Term's decision in *Baker v. Carr*[4] starts from a more precarious base—a fragmented Court, an abrupt reversal of position, unexplored and debatable substantive principles, and the contemplation of remedies as novel as they are drastic.

As would surely have been appropriate in these circumstances, the Court's opinion in *Baker v. Carr* may have been no more than an invitation to the lower courts to give full consideration to the problem untroubled by doubts about the "justiciability" of the claims, not in any significant sense a decision "on the merits" and still less a command to proceed with reapportionment even "with all deliberate speed." Yet it has not been so read, and the few months since the decision was handed down have seen action by the lower courts swifter and more far-reaching than any that has occurred in implementing the school segregation decision in the seven years since it was announced. Whether the Court will ratify this incipient judicial reformation of our political structure and, if so, what principles will be formulated to justify it are questions on which *Baker v. Carr* itself sheds little light. All that is certain is that the Court will have to face them in the immediate future. If the Court does confirm the trend, it will be for a longer future to answer whether courts can successfully supply one conspicuous deficiency in the mechanism of our constitutional arrangements: a means of adapting the distribution of political power to new circumstances.

---

[3] Brown v. Board of Education, 347 U.S. 438 (1954); Bolling v. Sharpe, 347 U.S. 497 (1954); Brown v. Board of Education, 349 U.S. 294 (1955); Cooper v. Aaron, 358 U.S. 1 (1958).

[4] 369 U.S. 186 (1962).

I. Baker v. Carr: The Decision

The constitution of the State of Tennessee directs that there shall be an apportionment of the representatives and senators in the State's general assembly each ten years, following a census of the qualified voters in the State.[5] The ninety-nine representatives are to be apportioned among "counties or districts" according to the number of qualified voters in each, except that any county having two-thirds of the "ratio" shall have a representative. The thirty-three senators are likewise to be apportioned among counties or districts according to the number of qualified voters in each, except that no county is to be divided in forming a district, districts composed of two or more counties shall consist of adjoining counties, and in apportioning the senate "the fraction that may be lost by any county" in apportioning the house of representatives "shall be made up to such county . . . in the senate as near as may be practicable." Despite these requirements there had been, up to the time *Baker v. Carr* was decided by the Supreme Court,[6] no apportionment of the Tennessee legislature since the Act of 1901.[7] In the meantime great changes in the distribution of the population had occurred, producing extreme disparities in the number of voters in different districts. For example, Moore County with 2,340 voters elected one representative while Shelby County with 312,345 elected only seven.[8] There were senatorial districts with as few as 30,000 voters while others had as many as 130,000.[9] In the aggregate, these disparities permitted the voters in districts having only 40 per cent of the voting population to elect 63 of the 99 representatives and voters in districts having only 37 per cent of the voting population to elect 30 of the 33 senators.[10] These disparities between voting population and representation would have been greatly reduced, though not eliminated, by any reapportionment made in reasonable conformity with the somewhat vague prescriptions of the Tennessee constitution. The Tennessee legislature, however, had repeatedly rejected

---

5 Tenn. Const., art. II, §§ 4, 5, and 6 (1870).

6 For subsequent developments, see text *infra,* at notes 137–49.

7 Tenn. Laws 1901, ch. 122, Tenn. Code Ann. §§ 3-101 to 3-109.

8 Jurisdictional Statement, Appendix F, pp. 41–42.

9 *Id.*, Appendix L, pp. 55–56.

10 Brief for Appellants, pp. 11–12.

measures aimed at reapportionment.[11] The Supreme Court of Tennessee had held that this failure of the legislature to carry out the plan of the State constitution could not be remedied by the State courts.[12]

In turning to the federal court for relief and attempting to frame a case based on the Fourteenth Amendment and federal civil rights legislation, the voters who were plaintiffs in *Baker v. Carr* were challenging a formidable accumulation of recent Supreme Court precedents.[13] Beginning with *Colegrove v. Green* in 1946, in which the Court dismissed "for want of equity" a suit in a federal court to invalidate the Illinois statute prescribing congressional districts,[14] the Court successively had dismissed, as not presenting a substantial federal question, an appeal from the dismissal of a suit in a federal court to invalidate the Illinois legislative apportionment statute on grounds substantially identical with those subsequently asserted in *Baker v. Carr*;[15] rejected on the merits a Fourteenth Amendment challenge to an Illinois nominating procedure which permitted voters in counties having only 13 per cent of the State's population

---

11 *Id.* at pp. 14–15.

12 Kidd v. McCanless, 200 Tenn. 278, 282 (1956), appeal dism. 352 U.S. 920 (1956).

13 The cases are summarized and dissected in Lucas, *Dragon in the Thicket: A Perusal of Gomillion v. Lightfoot*, [1961] SUPREME COURT REVIEW 194, 215–31.

14 328 U.S. 549. An opinion by Mr. Justice Frankfurter, joined by Justices Reed and Burton, characterized the claim as one "not meet for judicial determination" and "beyond [the] competence" of the Court to grant. *Id.* at 552. Mr. Justice Rutledge, concurring in the result, wished to rely exclusively on "discretion" in finding a want of "equity jurisdiction." *Id.* at 564, 565–66. Mr. Justice Black dissented, joined by Justices Douglas and Murphy. Mr. Justice Jackson, being absent from the Court, took no part. Chief Justice Stone's death had occurred two months before the decision and his place had not been filled. At the following Term, motions for rehearing and for reargument before the full bench were successively denied, 329 U.S. 825, 828, Chief Justice Vinson and Mr. Justice Jackson noting their non-participation in each instance. Contemporaneously the Court dismissed, apparently on the ground of mootness, appeals from two district court decisions refusing, in reliance on *Colegrove v. Green*, to invalidate the Georgia county-unit voting system. See notes 17, 19, and 24 *infra*. Cook v. Fortson, Turman v. Duckworth, 329 U.S. 675 (1946). Mr. Justice Rutledge would have postponed jurisdiction to hearing on the merits and wrote an opinion further explaining his position in *Colegrove v. Green* and urging that rehearing be granted in that case.

15 Colegrove v. Barrett, 330 U.S. 804 (1947). Justices Black, Douglas, and Murphy voted to note probable jurisdiction. Mr. Justice Rutledge acquiesced in dismissal because of the Court's previous action in *Colgrove v. Green*, *Fortson*, and *Duckworth*.

to block the nomination of candidates for State offices;[16] affirmed, on the ground that federal courts "consistently refuse to exercise their equity powers" in such cases, the dismissal of a similar challenge to Georgia's county-unit method of weighing votes in a manner adverse to voters in populous counties;[17] dismissed for want of a substantial federal question an appeal from a Louisiana State court decision rejecting federal constitutional claims in an attack on unequal city districting;[18] dismissed for want of a substantial federal question a Georgia Supreme Court decision rejecting federal constitutional claims in an action at law attacking the county-unit system;[19] dismissed summarily on the authority of several of the preceding cases an appeal from a California Supreme Court decision rejecting a Fourteenth Amendment attack on California statutes apportioning the State assembly and the State's congressional districts;[20] similarly dismissed an appeal from the Tennessee Supreme Court decision refusing relief against the Tennessee apportionment statute involved in *Baker v. Carr*;[21] and summarily affirmed a federal district court decision dismissing, on the authority of the prior Supreme Court cases, a challenge to the apportionment of the Oklahoma legislature substantially identical with that later made in *Baker v. Carr.*[22]

The complaint in *Baker v. Carr*, asserting that the inequality in voting districts caused by the failure of the Tennessee legislature to obey the commands of the Tennessee constitution resulted in a denial to plaintiffs of rights guaranteed by the Fourteenth Amendment, presented neither a novel electoral situation nor any legal

---

16 MacDougall v. Green, 335 U.S. 281 (1948). The opinion of the Court was per curiam. Mr. Justice Rutledge concurred in the result, on grounds similar to the ones relied on by him in *Colegrove v. Green*. Mr. Justice Douglas dissented, joined by Justices Black and Murphy.

17 South v. Peters, 339 U.S. 276 (1950). The opinion of the Court was per curiam. Mr. Justice Douglas dissented in an opinion joined by Mr. Justice Black.

18 Tedesco v. Board of Supervisors, 339 U.S. 940 (1950).

19 Cox v. Peters, 342 U.S. 936 (1952). Justices Black and Douglas voted to note probable jurisdiction.

20 Anderson v. Jordan, 343 U.S. 913 (1952). Justices Black and Douglas dissented.

21 Kidd v. McCanless, 352 U.S. 920 (1956).

22 Radford v. Gary, 352 U.S. 991 (1957).

theory which had not been urged unsuccessfully in the prior cases. The new suit might well have been regarded as quixotic but for two circumstances. One was the change in the Supreme Court's personnel. Of the Justices who had participated in *Colegrove v. Green, MacDougall v. Green,* and *South v. Peters,* the only cases in the series decided after argument and with opinion, only four remained when *Baker v. Carr* was filed in May, 1959, and two of these, Justices Black and Douglas, had dissented in those cases and in other memorandum dispositions.[23] They had recently been joined by two of the newcomers in another memorandum dissent which possibly implied a revival of their earlier resistance to the Court's position.[24] The other circumstance was that, while the Court's prior rejection of claims like those advanced in *Baker v. Carr* was clear, it had never agreed upon a full-dress statement of the reasons for such rejection. So far as the prior decisions might have rested upon "want of equity" (a ground which could hardly explain the disposition of cases coming from the State courts) it had never been explained why such a defect must inhere in every reapportionment case. So far as they might have rested upon rejection of the substantive basis of the claims advanced, no majority opinion had dignified the Fourteenth Amendment contentions with extended analysis.[25] And so far as they might have rested upon the view that the questions raised were political questions "beyond judicial competence," the decisions gave currency to a position expressly avowed only once, in an opinion speaking for only three members of the Court.[26] There was

---

[23] See notes 14–20 *supra.* The other two were Justice Frankfurter, who was with the majority in all three of the cases mentioned, and Justice Clark, who had been a member of the Court only when *South v. Peters* was decided and was with the majority there.

[24] Hartsfield v. Sloan, 357 U.S. 916 (1958). Chief Justice Warren and Justice Brennan joined Justices Black and Douglas in dissenting from denial of leave to file a petition for mandamus to compel the convening of a three-judge court. The suit was another attack on the Georgia county-unit voting system.

[25] The most explicit consideration has been in one paragraph of the three-page per curiam opinion in *MacDougall v. Green.* The dissents of Mr. Justice Douglas in that case and *South v. Peters,* and of Mr. Justice Black in *Colegrove v. Green,* had relied on the Equal Protection Clause. For the evidence that the Fourteenth Amendment arguments had been considered and rejected in the earlier case of *Wood v. Broom,* 287 U.S. 1 (1932), see Lucas, *supra* note 13, at 218–22.

[26] Colegrove v. Green, *supra* note 14.

reason to hope, then, that repeated litigation of the questions might eventually be rewarded either by a reversal of the Court's position or, if not, by a clarification of the grounds on which it rested.

Conceding the possibility that the prior Supreme Court decisions had "conclusively settled" the issues against Baker and his fellow plaintiffs, District Judge Miller nevertheless declined to dismiss the complaint as "obviously without merit" without convening a three-judge court.[27] Though his opinion was guarded in tone, the plaintiffs may have found intimations of success in its somewhat ambiguous declaration that a court of equity should hesitate to dismiss such actions summarily and should be willing to re-evaluate the problem of remedy from time to time, "especially where a violation of individual constitutional rights is clearly established"[28]—perhaps a reference to the undoubted violation of the Tennessee constitution, perhaps an expression of opinion on the Fourteenth Amendment issues, or perhaps only a hypothetical assertion. Whatever comfort the remark gave, the plaintiffs were to enjoy it only until the three-judge court ruled on the motion to dismiss. In a per curiam opinion the court dismissed the complaint on the grounds:[29] "(1) that the Court lacks jurisdiction of the subject matter, and (2) that the complaint fails to state a claim upon which relief can be granted." The opinion made two main points. The first was that the Supreme Court had unmistakably decreed non-intervention by the federal courts in reapportionment matters, "whether from a lack of jurisdiction or from the inappropriateness of the subject matter for judicial consideration." The second was that the soundness of the Supreme Court's position was "strikingly pointed up" by the problem of finding an appropriate judicial remedy. The plaintiffs had asked the court to direct either (1) an election at large or (2) an election by districts prescribed by the court, complying with the Tennessee constitution's requirements and using the federal census of 1950 as the basis. The court found what it called insuperable objections, both practical and legal, to each remedy. As to the substantive merit of the plaintiffs' federal constitutional claim, the opinion confined itself to this cryptic statement:[30]

---

[27] 175 F. Supp. 649 (M.D. Tenn. 1959).

[28] *Id.* at 653.

[29] Record, p. 220.

[30] 179 F. Supp. 824, 828 (M.D. Tenn. 1959). (Emphasis added.)

> It is strenuously argued by the plaintiffs that the case alleged in the complaint is one involving a clear violation of their individual rights guaranteed by the Fourteenth Amendment. . . . With the plaintiffs' argument that the legislature of Tennessee is guilty of a clear violation of the *state* constitution and of the rights of the plaintiffs the Court entirely agrees. . . . But even so the remedy in this situation clearly does not lie with the courts. It has long been recognized and is accepted doctrine that there are indeed some rights guaranteed by the Constitution for the violation of which the courts cannot give redress.

Solicitor General Cox subsequently stated to the Supreme Court, correctly it would seem, that the district court did not decide the federal question on the merits but held only that the court was without jurisdiction to consider the merits.

On November 21, 1960, the Supreme Court noted probable jurisdiction of the plaintiffs' appeal, indicating for the first time in a decade its willingness to give plenary consideration to such a case.[31] The crucial event, perhaps, had been the decision a week earlier in *Gomillion v. Lightfoot.*[32] That decision established that the drawing of political district boundaries may be judicially determined to be an abridgment of Negro voting rights protected by the Fifteenth Amendment, and while Mr. Justice Frankfurter's opinion for the Court carefully distinguished the reapportionment cases it was foreseeable that other members of the Court might treat *Gomillion* as a steppingstone to re-examination of *Colegrove v. Green* and its progeny.[33] *Baker v. Carr* was argued on April 19 and 20, 1961, on May 1 was ordered reargued,[34] was reargued the following Term on October 9, and was decided on March 26, 1962. One further intervening event deserves notice.

It is ironic that *Baker v. Carr* should have become the vehicle for examining whether the Fourteenth Amendment obligates the States to provide equality of representation, for at the outset the appellant voters emphatically repudiated that issue. Their case, as put to the Supreme Court in the appeal papers, was much narrower: they

31 364 U.S. 898.

32 364 U.S. 339 (1960).

33 Mr. Justice Douglas specifically noted his adherence to the dissenting opinions in *Colegrove v. Green* and *South v. Peters. Id.* at 348.

34 366 U.S. 907 (1961).

asserted that the Tennessee apportionment plan violated the Fourteenth Amendment only because it violated the Tennessee constitution.[35] Having deliberately limited their position on appeal to this ground, appellants provided a basis for affirming the judgment below which conventional practice required the Court to accept if it failed to find this ground meritorious.[36] Nevertheless, the entire Court acquiesced in treating the case as presenting the broader federal claims which could have been read into the complaint. An important factor in this reshaping of the case was undoubtedly the entry into the case of the Solicitor General of the United States as amicus curiae on the side of the appellants. Ignoring the appellants' theory of their own case, the Solicitor General placed before the Court a more plausible, as well as more sweeping, version of the Fourteenth Amendment issue. His theory thereafter dominated the case. On the second round of briefing, after the case was ordered reargued, the appellants retreated from their own theory.

The eight members of the Supreme Court participating[37] in the decision in *Baker v. Carr* announced their views in six opinions. Mr. Justice Brennan delivered an opinion, designated as the opinion of the Court, which also spoke for the Chief Justice and Mr. Justice Black, the only two who wrote no opinions of their own. The Brennan opinion was also "joined" by Justices Douglas, Clark, and Stewart, each of whom, however, found it necessary to write his own gloss on the opinion. These revealed contradictory notions of the meaning of the Brennan opinion and of what was actually decided by the majority of the Court. As Mr. Justice Clark said, "One emerging from the rash of opinions with their accompanying clash-

---

35 "The Attorney General of Tennessee (for the Appellees) purports to make argument on behalf of the complaining voters (Appellants) of which they want no part. The complaining voters are not charging inequality of representation under the Fourteenth Amendment (Statement in Op., p. 5, 8). On the contrary, they claim equality in voting rights as provided by the Constitution of Tennessee, and charge that the legislative attempt (successful so far) to deny that equality results in a violation of the equal protection of the laws. This is an important distinction . . ." (Reply to Statement in Opposition, pp. 1–2).

36 See ROBERTSON & KIRKHAM, JURISDICTION OF THE SUPREME COURT § 418 (Wolfson & Kurland ed. 1951). For the Court's treatment of the appellants' argument, see discussion in text *infra*, at notes 104–35.

37 Mr. Justice Whittaker did not participate.

ing of views may w... himself suffering a mental blindness." And Mr. Justice Stew... concerned that the dissenting and other concurring opinions mig... convey "a distressingly inaccurate impression of what the Court decides," criticized Mr. Justice Harlan, one of the dissenters, for suggesting that the majority opinion implied a proposition which Mr. Justice Douglas, another of the concurring Justices, also seemed to treat the majority as holding and which Mr. Justice Clark, the third of the concurring Justices, stated that the majority "appears to hold, at least *sub silentio*." Mr. Justice Frankfurter and Mr. Justice Harlan dissented, each writing his own opinion and joining in that of the other.

The opinion of Mr. Justice Brennan explicitly settles only four propositions pertinent to the decision of *Baker v. Carr*, but two of which are interesting: (1) that apart from the "political question" problem the complaint brings the case within the subject-matter jurisdiction of the federal courts, a proposition that could hardly have been doubted by the district court or anyone else; (2) that *Colegrove v. Green* and the line of memorandum decisions subsequently entered had not authoritatively established that the issues in reapportionment cases are "political questions," a conclusion almost as self-evident; (3) that on a fresh examination of the matter the Court rejects the argument that such issues, at least in apportionment of State legislatures as distinguished from congressional districts, are "political questions" and therefore beyond the competence of courts; and (4) that individual voters have standing to raise the issues, in order to vindicate "an interest of their own, and of those similarly situated." On these propositions all six of the majority Justices were apparently in agreement.

The propositions just stated were sufficient to require reversal of the district court on the first ground it had given for dismissal, namely, "that the court lacks jurisdiction of the subject matter." And insofar as the district court's second ground, "that the complaint fails to state a claim upon which relief can be granted," was merely an alternative mode of stating the legal effect of the same considerations, these propositions also removed that much support from the second ground of dismissal. What was at issue in the Supreme Court, however, was not the validity of the district court's reasoning, stated or implied, but the correctness of its disposition of the case. Was it or was it not error to dismiss the complaint "for failure to state a claim upon which relief can be granted"?

There were at least two other grounds, in addition to those disposed of by the Brennan opinion, on which dismissal of the complaint might have been correct. One was "want of equity," the ground agreed on by a weighty minority in the leading case of *Wood v. Broom*[38] and by the controlling majority in *Colegrove v. Green*,[39] the ground relied upon by Mr. Justice Rutledge in special concurrences in that and several later decisions, and the ground most strongly suggested by the opinion of the three-judge district court in *Baker v. Carr* itself, which dwelt heavily upon the inadequacy and inappropriateness of any available remedy. The seriousness of this problem, whether viewed in the light of the earlier reapportionment cases or from the standpoint of the lower court's decision in this very case, is suggested by the elaborate attention given the point in the briefs of the parties and the United States as amicus curiae. The Brennan opinion disposed of it as follows:[40]

> Beyond noting that we have no cause at this stage to doubt the District Court will be able to fashion relief if violations of constitutional rights are found, it is improper now to consider what remedy would be most appropriate if appellants prevail at the trial.

The issue, of course, was not what remedy would be "most appropriate" but whether any remedy at all lay within the power of a federal court of equity acting within its discretion, an issue which it could hardly have been "improper" to consider in advance of trial. For the Court to remove that issue from the case, if that was its meaning, by asserting that it had "no cause . . . to doubt" was little less than an expression of contempt for the views of numerous other responsible judges.

The second ground on which the dismissal of the complaint might arguably have been correct was that the core of the plaintiffs' federal claim, that the Fourteenth Amendment invalidates a State legislative apportionment under the circumstances alleged in the complaint, was without legal foundation. This alleged defect was

---

38 287 U.S. 1 (1932), Brandeis, Stone, Roberts, and Cardozo, JJ., concurring. For discussion of the case, see Lucas, *supra* note 13, at 216–20.

39 See *supra* note 14.

40 369 U.S. at 198.

appropriately raised by the defendants' motion to dismiss, was distinctly asserted by them in their brief to the Supreme Court, and finds support in *Wood v. Broom*, in lower court decisions interpreting *Wood v. Broom*, in the opinion of three of the four-man majority in *Colegrove v. Green*, and explicitly in the majority opinion in *MacDougall v. Green*, not to mention arguable support in some of the memorandum dispositions of other apportionment cases.[41] Although the district court in *Baker v. Carr* apparently did not rule upon this issue, as we have seen, the Supreme Court could properly have done so. Whether it did so or not is the vexing ambiguity in the opinion of Mr. Justice Brennan that accounts for the discordant interpretative accompaniment in the other opinions.

Since this important substantive issue had not been explored by the district court, the Supreme Court might reasonably have accepted the suggestion of the Solicitor General at the first argument that it should decline to decide the question at this stage and remand to the three-judge court for "a full and detailed examination" of it.[42] That this is what the Court in fact intended may be indicated both by the absence of any captioned discussion of the issue in Mr. Justice Brennan's otherwise liberally captioned opinion and by its declaration that "we hold today only" that there was jurisdiction of the subject matter, that plaintiffs have standing, and "that a justiciable cause of action is stated upon which appellants would be entitled to appropriate relief."[43] There are certain ambiguities here, to be sure. Is a "justiciable cause of action" a cause of action or only a possible cause of action? Has it already survived or must it still face a conventional motion to dismiss for failure to state a claim sufficient in law? What is the "if" implied by Mr. Justice Brennan's curiously dangling subjunctive, "would be entitled to relief?" The seeds of doubt found here are not easily attributed to the unruliness of language; it would have been easy enough to make clear that the order sustaining the motion to dismiss was being vacated and the case remanded for further consideration of the questions of substantive law it raised. But doubt becomes strong suspicion that a broader

---

41 See Lucas, *supra* note 13, at 218–28.

42 Brief for the United States as Amicus Curiae in No. 103, O.T. 1960, p. 60.

43 369 U.S. at 197–98.

ruling was intended, a ruling reaching the substantive issues, when other fragments in the opinion are considered. Tucked away in a footnote, for example, is this statement referring to certain allegations in the complaint which invoked the Due Process Clause:[44] "[W]e need not rely upon them to support *our holding that the complaint states a federal constitutional claim of violation of the Equal Protection Clause*." Further on, in the midst of a discussion purportedly concerned with the "justiciability" of the issues raised by the complaint, the entire substantive issue seems to be disposed of with a flick of the pen:[45] "Judicial standards under the Equal Protection Clause are well developed and familiar, and it has been open to courts since the enactment of the Fourteenth Amendment to determine, if on the particular facts they must, that a discrimination reflects *no* policy, but simply arbitrary and capricious action." Finally, one goes back to reread another of the numerous statements of what it is "we hold" and finds at the very beginning:[46] "We hold that the dismissal was error, and remand the cause to the District Court *for trial* and further proceedings consistent with this opinion." Lest this be thought inadvertent, the penultimate paragraph reiterates that the complaint presents "a justiciable constitutional cause of action upon which appellants are *entitled to a trial* and a decision."[47] Since the defendants had not even answered the complaint, let alone controverted its allegations of fact (and in all probability could not do so), it is something of a mystery why the Court felt called upon to declare the plaintiffs' "right" to a trial. But unless the opinion uses language in a way which would be regarded as inexcusable in a first-year law student after his third week of study, its remanding "for trial" implies that the facts alleged in the complaint, if proved, entitle the plaintiffs to judgment in their favor.

But the concurring opinions must also be considered, since the votes of at least two of the concurring Justices were necessary for a majority. Mr. Justice Clark understands the holding to be "that the appellants have alleged a cause of action" and, being of the view that the facts "are undisputed," he takes the majority to task for

---

[44] *Id.* at 195, n. 15. (Emphasis added.)

[45] *Id.* at 226. (Emphasis in original.)

[46] *Id.* at 188. (Emphasis added.)

[47] *Id.* at 237. (Emphasis added.)

failing to award relief.[48] He endeavors to supply what is undoubtedly a serious omission in the Brennan opinion if Mr. Justice Clark's understanding of the holding is correct, namely, a statement of the reasons why the Tennessee apportionment is "without any rational foundation" and therefore, as he sees it, violates the Equal Protection Clause.[49] Next, he suggests the kind of remedy he would approve, consisting of a judicial rearrangement of the existing districts. Then, in perplexing self-contradiction, he declares it "unfortunate that a decision is not reached on the merits" after all the attention the Court has given the problem. But he qualifies this conclusion by noting that "the majority [which Justices are included in this 'majority' is not specified but the inference is that Justice Clark is not included] appears to hold, at least *sub silentio*, that an invidious discrimination is present, but it remands to the three-judge court for it to make what is certain to be that formal determination."[50] He concludes with a remarkably succinct diagnosis (or confession) of judicial pregnancy: "In my view the *ultimate* decision *today* is in the greatest tradition of this Court."[51]

Mr. Justice Douglas' concurring opinion is addressed mainly to the "political question" issue and indicates that he would confine the doctrine of political questions even more narrowly than does the opinion of the Court. On the question whether the majority have decided the merits of the case, however, he associates himself with Mr. Justice Clark in what may be intended as a sardonic commentary on the scope of the Brennan opinion:[52] "While I join the opinion of the Court and, *like the Court, do not reach the merits*, a word of explanation is necessary. . . . [T]he question is, may a State weight the vote of one county or one district more heavily than it weights the vote in another? . . . I agree with my Brother Clark that *if the allegations in the complaint can be sustained a case for relief is etsablished*."

There is, finally, the valiant effort of Mr. Justice Stewart to establish the true view of the majority holding. Reiterating the holding of *MacDougall v. Green* that the Equal Protection Clause does not

48 *Id.* at 251.

49 *Id.* at 253–58.

50 *Id.* at 261.

51 *Id.* at 262. (Emphasis added.)

52 *Id.* at 241, 244, 245. (Emphasis added.)

forbid a State the power to assure "a proper diffusion of political initiative" as between rural and urban areas, and recalling that "in case after case" the Court has held not only that the Fourteenth Amendment permits the States wide discretion in treating some groups of citizens differently than others but that the burden of establishing the unconstitutionality of a statute is on the challenger, Mr. Justice Stewart asserts:[53] "Today's decision does not turn its back on these settled precedents." He repudiates any suggestion that the majority have held either that there must be approximate equality in the weighing of every voter's voice or that the Tennessee apportionment must fall simply because it has not been shown to conform to any rational plan. The complaint asserts, he says, that the apportionment is utterly arbitrary. But "the District Court did not reach the merits of that claim, and this Court quite properly expresses no view on the subject." In restating the holding of the Court, however, first in the words of Mr. Justice Brennan's opinion and then in his own words, Mr. Justice Stewart understandably introduces a slight but significant variation: "[T]he Court today decides only . . . (2) that the complaint presents a justiciable controversy [not "cause of action"]." Understandably, too, he equivocates on the crucial procedural question whether the motion to dismiss for failure to state a claim is to be treated as overruled, observing merely that "the proper place for the trial is in the trial court, not here."[54]

Baker v. Carr thus presents its own special problems of vote-weighing for one who would attempt to state its holding. If the meaning of Mr. Justice Brennan's opinion hangs in the balance, whose vote is entitled to control its interpretation, that of Mr. Justice Stewart or that of the two concurring Justices who pull in the opposite direction? Should the opinion be taken as covering only the ground common to all six who "joined" it, thereby permitting Mr. Justice Stewart to define its limits, or should Mr. Justice Stewart's vote, being an unnecessary sixth vote, be treated as surplus and his opinion disregarded? Of course there is no solution to this problem. What the opinions reveal is a Court much divided despite the nominal concurrence of six of its members—a Court no longer closely divided over "justiciability," as in *Colegrove*, but unable to

---

[53] *Id.* at 266.

[54] *Ibid.*

muster a majority who are agreed upon the basic substantive principles that are at stake. Perhaps this is inaccurate, and it is only Mr. Justice Stewart and the dissenters who do not find it easy to say that the facts of Tennessee's apportionment constitute a violation of the Equal Protection Clause. But if this is so, it is hard to understand why Mr. Justice Brennan's opinion was written, as it surely was, with a careful eye on holding Mr. Justice Stewart's vote. There must have been at least one other member of the Court unwilling to go along with a forthright adjudication of the merits in favor of the plaintiffs. On the other hand, if Mr. Justice Brennan, for example, genuinely shared Mr. Justice Stewart's desire to postpone commitment on those issues, what would have been lost by making that position crystal clear, as Mr. Justice Stewart did, once the ambiguities of the opinion had been revealed by the other opinions that were circulated? No adequate answer suggests itself, save the possibility that the Court would then have found itself without an opinion that could be even spuriously labeled as the "opinion of the Court."

Without minimizing the difficulty of the Court's task one may think that this performance of the "majority" reveals an intolerable tolerance for fuzziness. To find judges divided on the answers to the profound questions they face, or taking different routes to arrive at the same answer, is neither surprising nor dismaying. Nor is it to be expected that the reasoning behind the collective or even individual answers will always come through with penetrating clarity or will do more than dispel the shadows for a short distance ahead. The disturbing aspect of *Baker v. Carr* is that a majority should have been content to make what purported to be a great pronouncement without agreement even on what the questions were that were to be answered: not the philosophical questions, but the elementary procedural questions which it is the business of litigation to formulate precisely and indisputably, so that one may know what it is that is disposed of by a decision. This failure is what, on the record, supports Mr. Justice Harlan's charge that the majority have committed themselves to "an adventure in judicial experimentation" rather than discharging the Court's responsibility to adjudicate.[55]

Mr. Justice Frankfurter's dissenting opinion is a reiteration of the

[55] *Id.* at 339.

position, expressed in his opinion in *Colegrove v. Green,* that the nature of the issues raised by the complaint places the controversy outside judicial competence and cognizance. He analyzes, more fully than in his earlier opinion, the classes of cases or issues previously treated by the Court as "political questions." On his reading of these cases, all of the various considerations that underlay them converge in the line of decisions uniformly holding that claims under the Guarantee Clause are non-justiciable. The Guarantee Clause cases are not merely relevant but decisive, he concludes, because the substance of the complaint in *Baker v. Carr* is indistinguishable from a charge that Tennessee's government is not "republican in form." It is "a Guarantee Clause claim masquerading under a different label."[56] For Mr. Justice Frankfurter the inquiry might properly have ended here, resulting in dismissal "for want of jurisdiction" without further consideration of the legal foundation for the complaint. Nevertheless, Mr. Justice Frankfurter permitted himself to examine at length the validity of what he took to be the plaintiffs' major premise, namely, that representation in proportion to population is the fundamental standard commanded by the Constitution. His opinion on this point amounts to a detailed exposition of the historical case for concluding that this proposition "is, to put it bluntly, not true."[57]

The dissent of Mr. Justice Harlan approaches the problem from the other end. Observing that if there is no cause of action it is not necessary to deal with the somewhat elusive concept of "justiciability," he proceeds directly to the question whether the complaint stated a cause of action if the facts pleaded were taken as true and concludes that it did not. In this respect there is a welcome clarity and hardness about Mr. Justice Harlan's position; it poses sharply the issue "on the merits" which, it must be hoped, the Court as a whole will deal with explicitly at its next opportunity. If despite this forthright approach Mr. Justice Harlan's opinion is a less satisfying discussion of the "merits" than Mr. Justice Frankfurter's, it is perhaps because Mr. Justice Harlan regards the answer as almost too obvious for argument and therefore is content to rest upon general and almost formal propositions concerning the respect to be accorded the legislative judgment. "[T]here is nothing in the Federal

[56] *Id.* at 297.

[57] *Id.* at 301.

Constitution to prevent a State, acting not irrationally, from choosing any electoral legislative structure it thinks best suited to the interests, temper, and customs of its people."[58] In apportionment as in taxation, regulation, and other matters, he says, the Court must give the usual presumptive validity to the legislative judgment; the statute must be upheld if there is a conceivable rational basis for it; the burden of showing unconstitutionality is on the plaintiffs; and they have failed to demonstrate that the Tennessee apportionment rests on an arbitrary, capricious, or otherwise impermissible policy. It has been one of the difficulties of the constitutional controversy over reapportionment that both sides have tended to treat their positions as self-evident and the discourse has often not risen much above the level of dogmatic assertion of conclusions. Whether there is more to be said on the issue, on either side, is one of the challenges of the problem. Mr. Justice Frankfurter's historical analysis is one response. Mr. Justice Harlan attempts another by noting a variety of considerations which a reasonable legislature might conceivably take into account in framing an apportionment plan and suggesting that some conceivable combination of these factors could rationally explain the Tennessee pattern. There is an air of unreality about this line of argument as applied to the Tennessee situation, however, in view of the fact that most of the disparities complained of were concededly attributable to population changes since the last action of the legislature.[59] And Mr. Justice Harlan does not really deal, except by peremptory rejection, with the major premise that equal protection means per capita equality of voting weight.

---

58 369 U.S. at 334.

59 In a side debate with Mr. Justice Clark, Mr. Justice Harlan exposed the difficulties with the former's attempted statistical demonstration that the Tennessee apportionment was inescapably arbitrary. Their lively exchange seems to have been a draw, but it illustrates the elusiveness of the entire problem. The point in issue between them may be stated thus: Counties *A* and *B* have a population of 10,000 each, County *C* has 2,000. Each is entitled to one representative and, in addition, the three together constitute a district for the election of one more. Should County *C*'s "total representation" be considered as 1 and $\frac{1}{3}$ representative (which might make it "overrepresented" in relation to some other small county) or as only 1 and $^1/_{10}$? Mr. Justice Clark said the former, Mr. Justice Harlan the latter. Both figures, it would seem, are meaningless because the base of representation is different for the three-county representative than for the single-district representative; different "things" are being represented.

A second reapportionment case decided by the Supreme Court during the 1961 Term was *Scholle v. Hare*. The case originated as a petition for mandamus in the Supreme Court of Michigan to prevent the holding of an election for State senators under the districting provisions of the Michigan constitution. The petitioner urged that the inequalities in population among districts rendered the State constitutional provision invalid under the Fourteenth Amendment. Three members of the Michigan court agreed with this contention.[60] Their position, in substance, was that the Fourteenth Amendment requires approximate equality in the distribution of voting strength. They treated *Colegrove v. Green* and its successors as stating only a doctrine limiting the remedial powers of federal courts and hence as presenting no obstacle to the enforcement of such a Fourteenth Amendment right by a State court. (The Michigan court had previously deemed itself entitled to invalidate statutory apportionments violating an earlier State constitutional provision that expressly required apportionment by population.[61]) Four members of the court, however, joined in an opinion which held that the Supreme Court decisions had definitely rejected the Fourteenth Amendment claims advanced by the petitioner.[62] In addition to analyzing the Supreme Court decisions the opinion went on to examine historic and contemporary practice with respect to inequality of apportionment and concluded that it was impossible to characterize Michigan's provisions as arbitrary or irrational. This opinion cannot be read other than as an adjudication on the merits, relying strongly on the line of Supreme Court decisions. It thus presented squarely, although with possibly significant variations from *Baker v. Carr*, the substantive issue which the Court professed not to decide in *Baker*. A fifth member of the Michigan court joined the majority of four but did so under protest.[63] He regarded *Colegrove* and the other cases as controlling but thought that they should be overruled.

The appeal in *Scholle v. Hare* was filed December 12, 1960,[64] but

---

60 Scholle v. Secretary of State, 360 Mich. 1, 3, 42 (1960).

61 Giddings v. Secretary of State, 93 Mich. 1 (1892); Williams v. Secretary of State, 145 Mich. 447 (1906).

62 360 Mich. at 85, 124.

63 *Id.* at 110.

64 See 30 U.S. LAW WEEK 3010.

no action was taken by the Supreme Court until April 23, 1962, one month after the decision in *Baker v. Carr*. On that date the Court vacated the judgment below and remanded the case to the Michigan court "for further consideration in the light of *Baker v. Carr*."[65] Mr. Justice Harlan, in what amounted to a postscript to his *Baker* dissent, noted with obvious justification that the decision in *Baker*, taken at its word, was not a source of light on the only issue decided by the Supreme Court of Michigan. Accordingly, he said, the Court's obligation was either to note jurisdiction and hear the case on its merits or dismiss for want of a substantial federal question in line with the earlier precedents. The suggestion constrained Justices Clark and Stewart to explain in a separate opinion that they read the State court opinions as resting on non-justiciability, a forced if not wholly inaccurate reading. The explanation was, of course, quite unnecessary. In reversing the district court in *Baker v. Carr* and holding that the Fourteenth Amendment claims were "justiciable," the Court could not help but cast doubt on the authority of *Colegrove* and the other prior decisions as precedents on the merits of the Fourteenth Amendment issues. The action in *Baker* necessarily implied that those questions were now, at the very least, open questions. It was therefore appropriate to give the Michigan court an opportunity to consider the questions anew, getting whatever light it could from the action in *Baker*.

Similarly the Court on June 11, 1962, vacated the judgment of a three-judge district court which had dismissed on the merits a suit attacking the constitutionality of statutory and State constitutional provisions governing the apportionment of both houses of the New York legislature. It remanded that case too, "for further consideration in the light of *Baker v. Carr*."[66]

II. The Substantive Issue

A. THE NATURE OF THE INTERESTS

Some of the difficulties of the reapportionment problem would be exposed by closer attention to the problem of standing

---

65 369 U.S. 429 (1962). Mr. Justice Frankfurter did not participate.

66 W.M.C.A., Inc. v. Simon, 202 F. Supp. 741 (S.D.N.Y. 1962), vacated and remanded, 369 U.S. 186 (1962). On August 16, 1962, the district court reaffirmed its

than the Court has given it. Mr. Justice Brennan was correct in stating that prior decisions supported the standing of the plaintiffs as citizens or voters to challenge the constitutionality of an apportionment statute.[67] As he acknowledged, however, the issue had not been carefully canvassed in the prior cases. If standing is to be recognized, there is much to be said for facing the problem squarely in terms of allowing citizen suits in the federal courts for the purpose of vindicating public interests, as State courts have done with increasing frequency.[68] Certainly it seems inaccurate to describe the plaintiffs in the reapportionment suits as representing interests "of their own," with the implication that these are individual interests. If the interests are individual they would be vindicated by a decree that gave individual relief, a theoretical if not a practical possibility. But a decree that gave Mr. Baker and the other plaintiffs in *Baker v. Carr* votes equal in weight to the weightiest vote in Tennessee would not be merely inadequate relief from their standpoint; it would be no relief at all. It should be perfectly clear, therefore, that the interest sought to be vindicated is either that of the public at large (Tennessee "as a polity," as Mr. Justice Frankfurter put it in *Colegrove v. Green*) or at least that of a loose, indeterminate, and very numerous group. It is doubtful if any other case can be pointed to in which the Court has accorded protection to collective interests of such a group, absent separable, identifiable individual harm. The difficulty of identifying any individual interest is emphasized by the Court's need to rely on the ballot-box stuffing and false-count cases in oblique support of its conclusion that plaintiffs assert a

---

previous decision and ordered the complaint dismissed. An appeal to the Supreme Court was filed September 26, 1962. No. 460, O.T. 1962.

[67] Koenig v. Flynn, 285 U.S. 375 (1932); Smiley v. Holm, 285 U.S. 355 (1932); Colegrove v. Green, 328 U.S. 549 (1946); *cf.* Wood v. Broom, 287 U.S. 1 (1932); Coleman v. Miller, 307 U.S. 433 (1939).

[68] With his usual insight and balance, Professor Jaffe has stated the case for recognizing the "public action" and the difficulties of setting appropriate limits on its use. Jaffe, *Standing To Secure Judicial Review: Public Actions,* 74 HARV. L. REV. 1265, 1282–1307 (1961). He suggests that the case may be at its strongest where protection of the franchise is at stake. *Id.* at 1297–98. The development in the States is summarized. *Id.* at 1275–80.

private right.[69] Those were criminal cases, in which the interests vindicated were represented by the public prosecutor.[70]

The Court also suggests that plaintiffs seek to protect interests "of those similarly situated." If the action is a class action, as this suggests, whom do the plaintiffs in fact represent? Not, presumably, the voters in rural districts, even those whose votes may be "undervalued." But even in the cities there are voters who approve of legislative frugality, who dislike freeways, or who believe that urban redevelopment should be left to private initiative. If these and other voters are more nearly content with the existing distribution of political power than any likely to result from the lawsuit, are the plaintiffs to be deemed their representatives? If the answer is that such interests must be considered as represented by the defendants, the answer is not adequate. The defendants in these cases are usually officials having merely nominal or ministerial responsibilities in the conduct of elections. An official interest in upholding the law is presumed to make such persons adequate representatives of the "public" interest, but if the interest asserted by the plaintiffs in these cases is not merely the "public" interest, neither are the interests on the other side. The inadequacy of the official defendants as representatives of these diverse opposing interests is especially conspicuous when it comes to problems of relief. What interests will determine their position when the question is whether one plan of reapportionment is better than another? A realistic view of the situation must also take account of the fact that responsibility for representing the official defendants normally devolves on the executive branch of the State government, which typically is more responsive to the interests represented by the plaintiffs than is the legislature whose composition is under attack.[71]

---

69 United States v. Saylor, 322 U.S. 385 (1944); United States v. Classic, 313 U.S. 299 (1941); United States v. Mosley, 238 U.S. 383 (1915); Ex parte Siebold, 100 U.S. 371 (1880).

70 The criminal statutes involved in these cases presuppose deprivation of rights secured by the Constitution to a person or citizen and in enforcing them the Court has necessarily characterized the dilution of one's vote as the deprivation of a personal right. But resort to the criminal process is necessary, among other reasons, precisely because of the difficulty of establishing private, individual harm.

71 In a number of the cases decided since *Baker v. Carr*, the official defendants have declined to defend the reapportionment laws under attack or have even joined

These problems are cause for doubt that a court is a suitable forum for resolving such a many-sided contest. But they also have a bearing on the substantive principles involved because they focus attention on the real interests that seek recognition and help clarify the nature of the claim advanced. What is at stake in the reapportionment cases is not, except in the most abstract sense, an individual concern with equality, the interest of man in being treated like fellow man. In this respect the cases differ from those that have been the traditional concern of the Equal Protection Clause. Denial, or dilution, of the vote of a particular racial group, for example, offends the Fourteenth or Fifteenth Amendment not primarily if at all because it weakens the legislative influence of the voter as an individual or even of all the affected class as a group. Such a discrimination harms the individual directly by singling him out for different treatment on grounds that are offensive and that degrade him. No comparable personal injustice or injury can be asserted by a city voter who enters the polling booth knowing that his vote will weigh less than that of a country cousin.

The "discrimination" that hurts in the reapportionment cases lies in such things as the way the legislature levies taxes and spends money.[72] The legal injury, if any, is that the plaintiffs as a group have too little control over these decisions. Specifically, as all commentary on the reapportionment cases assumes and as the identity of the parties and much of their argument demonstrate, the issue is whether "urban" interests have as much power in the legislatures as the Constitution guarantees them. What is needed, and what is difficult, is to find a principle that says how much that power should be.

---

in the plaintiffs' prayer for invalidation. In some, but not all, of such cases the defense has been undertaken by intervenors. See, *e.g.*, Moss v. Burkhart, 207 F. Supp. 885 (W.D. Okla. 1962), note 191 *infra*.

[72] Plaintiffs in *Baker v. Carr* alleged discrimination in the distribution of various State tax revenues by the use of grant-in-aid formulas favoring the less populated counties, especially with respect to schools and highways. See Brief for Appellants, pp. 12–14; Jurisdictional Statement, p. 7; and Appendices D, E, G, H, and I. The Court declined to say whether such "taxation arguments and exhibits as now presented add anything, or whether they could add anything however presented," leaving that for the district court to decide. 369 U.S. at 195, n. 15.

B. THE EQUAL-REPRESENTATION PRINCIPLE

The strongest case for the plaintiffs, ably urged by the Solicitor General in *Baker v. Carr,* takes its stand on the principle that representation must be based primarily on equality of voting strength, *i.e.*, representation apportioned to population. This requirement is said to stem directly from the Fourteenth Amendment (and not derivatively by way of State constitutional requirements, as the argument originally advanced by the plaintiffs themselves would have had it). For reasons that will appear, the Solicitor General's argument avoids identifying either the Equal Protection Clause or the Due Process Clause as the exclusive source of the requirement, but it is clear that the dominant appeal is to the Equal Protection Clause and it is that clause to which Mr. Justice Brennan looks in asserting the existence of "well developed and familiar" standards which make the claim justiciable. As a matter of advocacy the power of the suggested principle is apparent. It cloaks the problem with an appearance of determinateness and commensurability, suggesting the availability of arithmetic as a major aid to solution. It invokes a clause of the Constitution that has been applied with rigor in a series of recent cases to strike down legislation without apparent need for deference to legislative judgment or for delicate exercises of judicial judgment. It makes applicable the special rhetoric of equal protection—"discriminatory," "invidious," "arbitrary classification," etc. And, more substantially, it appeals to an ideal that has unquestionably been influential in democratic thought and practice.

It is an important issue, however, not yet adequately posed in briefs and not faced in the majority or concurring opinions, whether the suggested principle is not too gross an oversimplification of the problem of fair representation to serve as the controlling constitutional rule, the fundamental benchmark by which to measure State representation plans. This is an issue that would exist even if one were to put aside the absence of support for the suggested principle in the language of the Constitution, in prior judicial decisions, or in the past understanding of the Fourteenth Amendment, and even if one were to ignore the imposing case against the principle found in historic and contemporary practice as detailed by Mr. Justice Frankfurter. There are, in short, doubts to be explored even for a

Court which might be prepared—whatever its warrant for doing so—to act as if it were a wise draftsman revising the Fourteenth Amendment.

Fair representation clearly depends on more than the weight of individual votes in voting for legislative representatives, relevant as that factor is. The equality theme is useful to the plaintiffs in *Baker v. Carr* and other current cases because, in addition to invoking a thriving and expanding clause of the Constitution, it would under present circumstances probably work in a direction beneficial to the urban position. But it is not clear that it suggests a principle which even the interests represented by the urban plaintiffs could consider satisfactory under all circumstances, and even less clear that it is a principle which assures fair treatment to other interests equally entitled to fair treatment.

The principle of equal weight for each vote would be fully satisfied by a system under which all representatives were elected at large, a method which plaintiffs in *Baker v. Carr* and other cases have urged should be judicially decreed, at least as an interim method. It needs no reflection to see that such a plan, while giving a theoretically equal voice in government to every voter, may completely deprive important interests of all effective participation. It is not certain that the underrepresented interests which now urge reapportionment would indefinitely fare well under such a system, at least in the absence of other supporting arrangements such as the domination of parties by city political organizations. Urban population, while a majority in the United States by the census classification that includes in the term all persons living in places of over 2,500 inhabitants, is a minor fraction if only persons living in large cities with their distinctive and financially burdensome problems are included.[73] Even within these areas, it can safely be predicted that as the problems of congestion and rehabilitation in the "central city" mount, the interests of voters in the newer and outlying sections will tend to diverge more and more, accentuating the conflict between "urban" and "suburban" interests.

Straight majority rule, however consonant with equality of

---

[73] See STATISTICAL ABSTRACT OF THE UNITED STATES 23 (1961). 9.8 per cent of the population live in places of 1,000,000 or more, 28.5 per cent in places of 100,000 or more.

voting rights, might leave city voters worse off than now. More compelling examples are not hard to imagine. One need look no further than our southern States, where the clash between white and Negro interests is presently the overriding political cleavage. However successful the movement to give the Negro the vote may be, a system of Statewide election of legislatures could leave the Negro largely without effective political participation unless Negro voters became a majority.

These possibilities do not demonstrate the invalidity of the equal-vote principle but only its insufficiency. This is an important point, however, for its advocates have tended to speak as though all other factors entering into a representation formula are departures—tolerable, perhaps, but only within limits—from the one true principle of equally weighted votes, rather than as reflecting equally important principles with which the assumed principle of equality may have to be accommodated.

As the foregoing examples suggest, another fundamental of fair representation is the principle of districting. Districting serves various purposes but important among them is giving representation to interests which would be submerged by majorities in larger groupings of voters. It is one aspect of the federal principle—a principle that, no less than the principle of popular rule, has been central to our whole governmental system from the beginning, not only at the nation-State level but down to the lowliest level of local government. Like the dispersion of governmental powers among a variety of governmental units, each differently based—national, State, and local—the principle of districting within each such unit reflects our conviction that the general interest, and the innumerable separate interests of which it is composed, will be better expressed in a medley of voices from minor fractions of the population than by any monolithic majority.

The districting problem bears on the equal-protection argument in two ways. First, it suggests how relatively little control over the adequacy of a representation plan is provided by a constitutional principle that all votes must have approximately equal weight. On the one hand, no constitutional principle has been suggested by which courts could require that representatives be elected by districts at all. Thus in a State where Negroes comprised 25 per cent of the population an at-large system which resulted in no Negroes being elected to the legislature would be constitutional whereas an apportionment involving unequal districts that gave sparsely populated, predominantly Negro districts 40 per cent of the legislative seats would presumably be unconstitutional. On the other hand, no constitutional principle has been suggested by which courts can control the drawing of district lines so that even districts of approximately equal population cannot be used to achieve results similar to those produced by unequal districts. The problem of apportionment cannot be divorced from the problem of the gerrymander. Is it possible that the Equal Protection Clause can be read not only as requiring districts equal in population but also as prescribing "compactness," "contiguity," or other criteria to limit the ingenuity of legislators in manipulating boundary lines? It is significant that one of the most influential recent statements of the case for Supreme Court intervention in the apportionment problem carefully sets to one side the entire problem of malapportionment through drawing of district boundaries.[74] Yet the principle of apportionment-by-population may be of only marginal significance unless all other factors in the equation can be made to remain constant. An asserted constitutional principle that may not be much more useful than one half of a pair of pliers ought to be viewed with some skepticism.[75]

---

[74] See Lewis, *Legislative Apportionment and the Federal Courts*, 71 HARV. L. REV. 1057, 1059–60 (1958).

[75] A striking instance of the problem, apparently, is the recent redrawing of New York's congressional districts. On January 23, 1962, the *New York Times* made the following statement in an editorial:

"A letter on this page by George M. Shapiro, a distinguished Republican lawyer, defends New York's recent realignment of Congressional districts by virtually ignoring the gerrymandering and pointing to the one respect in which proper standards did rule—relative equality of population.

"Representative government requires more than this. It presumes that those entrusted with lawmaking powers are reasonably representative of the interests, thinking and aspirations of the people in whose name they legislate. The Republican Legislature violated this principle in fixing lines for many of the twenty-two districts outside New York City. These were so drawn that Republican candidates are now favored in twenty districts and Democrats in only two, even though the Democrats ordinarily poll 40 to 45 per cent of the Congressional vote in these areas. Not only do the new lines thus fail to meet the test of fairness in party balance, but a number also ignore the desirability of creating districts in such a way that

The districting problem helps test the equal-protection argument in a second and deeper way because it invites reflection about the extent to which minority interests can constitutionally be given effective political representation. The pervasive use of the districting device in our system shows that it is permissible to give such interests not only a vote at the polls but a voice in the legislature; the Constitution does not ordain absolute majoritarian rule. The question is, "How much of a voice?" Implicit in the contentions of the plaintiffs in the reapportionment cases seems to be the proposition that no "interest" should be given more weight in the legislature than its proportion of the population.

Even on this premise it would not follow that there is overrepresentation because "rural" districts have more seats than the proportion of "rural" population. The argument overlooks the fact that representatives from "rural" districts also serve as spokesmen for some voters in "urban" districts who cast their votes for unsuccessful candidates in their own districts and whose interests would otherwise go unrepresented. This, too, is an important function of districting, and one would need a marshaling of voters and representatives in terms of "interests," not merely in terms of districts, before concluding that any given interest had more than its proportionate voice in the legislature. The argument assumes a homogeneity of voters in "urban" or "rural" districts that is contrary to fact—contrary to fact with respect to any single issue that may come before the legislature and absurdly at variance with the facts when extended to the whole range of issues with which a legislature must deal.

Paradoxically, the homogeneity of districts necessary to validate this assumption could be promoted only by drawing district lines so as to segregate the population by major interest groupings as

---

the voters represented have major interests in common, as in a river basin or a natural marketing area."

The letter referred to stated that New York is the only State with four or more congressional seats that has voluntarily met the population standards for congressional reapportionment recommended by the American Academy of Political Science, *i.e.*, that no district shall vary more than 15 per cent in population from the average population per district in the State.

The *New York Times* detailed the "violence to proper standards of apportionment" in a series of editorials. See N.Y. Times, editorial page, January 23, 24, 25, 26, 1962.

nearly as possible. This is precisely the technique condemned in *Gomillion v. Lightfoot*,[76] a decision by which the reapportionment plaintiffs set great store. While *Gomillion* involved the use of district lines to exclude Negroes from the vote, the technique would presumably be just as invalid if used to improve their position by "equalizing" or "proportionalizing" the Negro vote, as Mr. Justice Whittaker's concurring opinion, relying on the Fourteenth Amendment and treating the case as a "segregation" problem, implied.[77] It is also true that such "segregation" of voters on Negro-white lines might be forbidden without condemning similar segregation on rural-urban or some other classification, but the plaintiffs themselves have urged in the reapportionment cases that such classifications are "invidious" in the same sense as racial classification.[78] Doubtful as that proposition is, it is certainly true that one of the important values of districting on geographic lines is that, in contrast with political structures that explicitly reflect economic, occupational, religious, or other interest groupings, it tends to mute and blend rather than to accentuate the clashes of different interest groups. Homogeneity of districts would thus be a goal of doubtful wisdom even if there were not practical and possibly constitutional objections to its realization.

But the premise that would limit "minority" interests to proportional representation is itself difficult to accept, even as an ideal. The aims of government are too complex to be achieved by proportional distribution of its burdens or benefits; the same may well be true of the distribution of political power that allocates those benefits and burdens. The same reasons that favor giving a minority interest some political expression may also support giving it enough to deflect the action of "the majority." It is rational to believe that a more stable, harmonious, productive, healthy, or interesting society will be produced by a particular "unproportional" balance of interests than by a proportional one. One may, for example, believe

---

[76] 364 U.S. 339 (1960).

[77] *Id.* at 349. On the permissibility of racial classification for the ostensible benefit of a minority, see Bittker, *The Case of the Checker-Board Ordinance: An Experiment in Race Relations*, 71 YALE L.J. 1387 (1962).

[78] Brief for Appellants, p. 30; Brief for the United States as Amicus Curiae on Reargument, pp. 22–23, 48. See Douglas, J., concurring, 369 U.S. at 244–45.

that the general interest will be served by keeping open the possibility of public expenditures for farmers or for farm families out of proportion to their number—rural electrification, irrigation projects, education and health services that cost more per capita, etc.—or of similarly disproportionate benefits for poorer and less populous sections of nation or State. Believing this, one might also think it desirable to safeguard the possibility by building into the political structure effective strength for those likely to be the beneficiaries of such expenditures rather than trusting to the momentary perception of the general interest held by transitory majorities representing the more populous districts. In one dimension the issue is how long-run a view of their own or of the general welfare may be taken by the people when they frame a government.

Stated otherwise, the question is whether it is permissible to insist that legislative action be based on a broader consensus than a bare majority. Every device that limits the power of a majority is, in effect, a means of giving disproportionate representation to the minority. A constitutional principle that puts unequal districting in doubt also calls into question, by necessary implication, provisions requiring special majorities for particular kinds of legislation, such as approval of bond issues in municipal referenda or adoption of proposed constitutional amendments by legislatures or passage of legislation over an executive veto. Why should it not reach, as well, other procedural rules or devices that give obstructive power to minorities, such as the filibuster or the seniority system for choosing committee chairmen?

If it is permissible to arrange a State government so that broader consensus than a bare majority is required, the statistics pressed upon the courts in *Baker v. Carr* and other cases may appear less compelling. To say, for example, that 40 per cent of the voters elect 63 members of the legislature while 60 per cent elect only 36 suggests tyranny by a minority. But the suggestion implies an identity and solidity of interests among the 40 per cent and the 60 per cent, respectively, that is not demonstrated and may be quite contrary to fact. It is relevant to inquire not only whether these arithmetic abstractions correspond to real alignments in the State but, if so, how large a fraction of the 40 per cent must be won over by the "other" bloc in order to get the 12 additional votes needed for a majority on particular issues or many issues. Working merely with numbers it is obviously possible to assemble on paper some or many combinations of districts comprising somewhat over 50 per cent of the voters and able to elect somewhat over 50 per cent of the legislature, but this would not demonstrate the fairness of the representation plan any more than the plaintiffs' figures demonstrate its unfairness. The question is what kinds of effective coalitions the representation plan permits and how wide a consensus they require. Again, it should not be overlooked that even if "minority rule" were deemed the evil to be avoided, the principle of equal representation no more protects against that evil than against the opposite one of majority tyranny. It is perfectly possible in an equally districted State for a bare majority of the voters in each of a bare majority of the districts—approximately one-fourth of the total voting population, in short—to control the legislature.[79]

The theory of proportional representation has also to be reconciled with that branch of the federal principle which has to do with the allocation and limitation of governmental powers. "Urban" interests in obtaining a larger slice of the State pie can be defeated not only by the distribution of political power in the State legislature but also by the allocation of sources of revenue and spheres of power as between State government and local units. If the framers of a State constitution have seen fit, for example, to withhold from the State government the power to levy an income tax and if such a tax is essential before State government can shoulder emergent problems of the city, is the Fourteenth Amendment violated because the State's constitution-amending processes enable a minority to block such reform?

Still another difficulty is raised by the facts of *Baker v. Carr* itself, though not by all reapportionment cases. The malapportionment complained of in Tennessee resulted not from action of the legislature but from its inaction. Although feeble argument was

---

[79] In view of the assumption sometimes made that in the national government the Senate is the only serious departure from majoritarian principles, it is worth noting that if the election of the President should fall to the House of Representatives, pursuant to the Twelfth Amendment, a President could theoretically be chosen by the combined votes of representatives elected by slightly more than one-fourth of the voters in each of the 26 smallest states, or about 5 per cent of the population of voting age in 1960. (Based on STATISTICAL ABSTRACT OF THE UNITED STATES 360 [1961].) This would be true even if the House of Representatives were perfectly apportioned by districts of equal population.

made that the Act of 1901 was invalid when adopted,[80] it is clear that most of the inequality in population among districts was the product of population growth and shift since 1901. Thus the principle asserted is not merely that the Equal Protection Clause sets limits on the way a State may apportion when it reapportions, but that it imposes an affirmative duty to reapportion. It is possible, of course, to say that a statute valid when enacted may become invalid, and therefore unenforceable, because of the passage of time and change of circumstances. But this does not dispose of the difficulty. Time itself is a dimension of the problem with which the asserted principle of equal representation must reckon. Stability of structure and permanence for great and difficult compromises are rational objectives in the framing of governments.[81] It is worth recalling that the one provision of the national Constitution that is explicitly placed beyond reach of the amending process is the provision which governs representation in the Senate.[82] Can the Fourteenth Amendment be read as outlawing such a principle if adopted or practiced by a State or, even more drastically, as prescribing a maximum time limit for an apportionment to remain in effect?

For Mr. Justice Harlan this aspect of *Baker v. Carr* provided one clear and easy route to rejecting the complaint. The problem, he suggested, was whether the Court could treat as irrational a judgment of the legislature that redistribution of seats should be deferred.[83] The suggestion is not wholly convincing, perhaps, in view of the ephemeral quality of any supposed "legislative judgment" that is attributed to legislative inaction. Nor is it wholly satisfying

---

[80] Brief for Appellants, p. 25.

[81] "That the people have an original right to establish, for their future government, such principles as, in their opinion, shall most conduce to their own happiness is the basis on which the whole American fabric has been erected. The exercise of this original right is a very great exertion; nor can it, nor ought it, to be frequently repeated." Marshall, C. J., in Marbury v. Madison, 1 Cranch 137, 176 (1803).

[82] U.S. Const., art. V.

[83] "But is not this matter one that involves a classic legislative judgment? Surely it lies within the province of a state legislature to conclude that an existing allocation of senators and representatives constitutes a desirable balance of geographical and demographical representation, or that in the interest of stability of government it would be best to defer for some further time the redistribution of seats in the state legislature." 369 U.S. at 336.

to give the normal deference to a legislative judgment so readily explainable in terms of the desire of the entrenched forces to retain their power, despite the traditional doctrine that courts will not look to legislators' motives. But the question remains, "Whose judgment or what rule is to determine how often a State legislative apportionment must be revised?" and if this question is not satisfactorily answered by Mr. Justice Harlan, neither is it satisfactorily answered elsewhere.

What has been said is enough to show that equality of voting weight is scarcely any guide to the reasonableness or fairness of a State's representation plan. As a standard of performance it is about as adequate an instrument as would be a ruler for judging a work of sculpture or a metronome a symphony orchestra. "It is as if you were to turn harmony into mere unison, or to reduce a theme to a single beat."[84] Recognition of the inadequacy of this measure gives a different perspective on the reapportionment problem than the majority opinions in *Baker v. Carr* afford. It suggests difficulties that affect both the substantive issues and the question of "justiciability." If the test of equality goes so short a distance in guiding judicial judgment, it remains uncertain not only what the other determinants are but whether any exist which will enable a court to claim more for its conclusion than that it is a political judgment–probably more disinterested, and conceivably wiser, than that of a legislature but still essentially a political rather than a legal judgment. When the magnitude of the unknowns is appreciated, it becomes difficult indeed to share Mr. Justice Brennan's easy optimism that "well developed and familiar" judicial standards are available to resolve the constitutional issues in reapportionment cases.

To return to the Solicitor General's arguments, it must be said that his brief reveals awareness that the problem of fair representation has many dimensions and that statistical equality of voting weight cannot be the exclusive test. His insistence is only that per capita equality of representation must be "the starting point";[85] other factors, such as representation of subordinate government units, protection for minority interests, recognition of a district's share of the costs of government, shifts in population since the last appor-

---

84 Barker, The Politics of Aristotle 51 (1948).

85 Brief for the United States as Amicus Curiae on Reargument, p. 26.

tionment, and the availability of non-judicial avenues to reform, are entitled to consideration as justifying departures from the standard of equality.[86] The fundamental issue, as he puts it, is whether the State law "arbitrarily and unreasonably apportions its legislature so as to deny the real meaning of the right to vote, *i.e.*, effective participation in democratic government."[87] In this view the problem is not to be referred solely to the Equal Protection Clause but is a matter of due process as well as of equal protection,[88] a concession that understandably finds no counterpart in the majority opinions in *Baker v. Carr*. For a court allergic to substantive due process[89] it would cause discomfort, one may surmise, to acknowledge that reapportionment cases cannot be decided without resort to the general warrant of the Due Process Clause. But the Court's preference for the rhetoric of equal protection cannot permanently obscure the fact that the kind of discretion called upon is wholly different in its breadth from that involved in the racial equal protection cases, or even in the free-speech and other Bill of Rights cases, and is more nearly comparable to the broad claims of higher wisdom that brought an earlier Court, invoking the Due Process Clause, under such sharp attack.

Realistic as the Solicitor General's statement of the problem is, solution of the problem is not advanced very much by identifying a "starting point" and enumerating a host of other "factors to be considered." Presumably this means that a given degree of departure from the per capita standard will be acceptable under some circumstances and not under others. The problem is not merely to identify relevant factors but to find principles that relate them to each other and point in the direction of a judgment in the particular

---

86 *Id.* at 28–34.

87 *Id.* at 25.

88 *Id.* at 10, 11, 23, 24, 25.

89 ". . . I deem this application of 'cruel and unusual punishment' so novel that I suspect the Court was hard put to find a way to ascribe to the Framers of the Constitution the result reached today rather than to its own notions of ordered liberty. If this case involved economic regulation, the present Court's allergy to substantive due process would surely save the statute and prevent the Court from imposing its own philosophical predilections upon state legislatures or Congress. I fail to see why the Court deems it more appropriate to write into the Constitution its own abstract notions of how best to handle the narcotics problem. . . ." White, J., dissenting, in Robinson v. California, 370 U.S. 660, 689 (1962).

case. The search for such principles, if it leads anywhere, seems in danger of leading toward quite arbitrary rules. To take one example, the Solicitor General suggests that departure from the population principle will be easier to defend in one house of a bicameral legislature than in both.[90] Why this should be so is far from clear. Assuming that the two houses have equal roles in the legislative process, as is almost invariably true, it would seem apparent that a combination of per capita representation in one house and per county representation in the other is the equivalent of a *pro tanto* dilution of the population principle in the former. One may wonder why from the standpoint of constitutional principle there is virtue in achieving the dilution by the combination of two differently constructed houses rather than by two similarly diluted ones. On the other hand, if the Fourteenth Amendment really commands representation according to population, it is difficult to see on what principle it could be said to make such a command for one house of the legislature and not for both. The suggestion recalls Pascal's observation about the validity of the supposed law of physics that nature abhors a vacuum, following his experiment with the mercury tube: "One cannot well say that nature abhors a vacuum more at the foot of the mountain than at its summit."

For purposes of the Tennessee case, however, the Solicitor General deemed it unnecessary to probe very far the difficulties of articulating meaningful and rational principles. Having carried the argument far enough to expose the complexity of the problem, his brief then proposed a sudden detour around the looming intellectual trap. The suggested escape is attractive and convenient; it seems likely to figure prominently in subsequent judicial discourse on the reapportionment problem. It is a solution that may dispose of cases without the need for formulating principles. In its own way, however, it is scarcely less arbitrary than would be an outright adoption of a requirement that all apportionment must be based on per capita equality of representation.

C. THE RATIONAL-PLAN PRINCIPLE

The alternative argument advanced by the Solicitor General consists essentially of shifting the burden to the defenders of the

---

[90] Brief for the United States as Amicus Curiae on Reargument, p. 31.

challenged apportionment statute. On this argument, disparities in the population of districts do not necessarily invalidate the apportionment but they do require, at least where the disparities are "gross," that "rational" justification for the plan be offered.[91] "If the State can point to neither rhyme nor reason for a discriminatory apportionment, save that it is an anachronism, the apportionment should be held to violate the Fourteenth Amendment."[92] It is this argument that the Brennan opinion appears to accept when it states that "it has been open to courts since the enactment of the Fourteenth Amendment to determine, if on the particular facts they must, that a discrimination reflects *no* policy . . ." (a proposition for which, incidentally, the opinion points to no authority).[93] It is clearly the argument that Mr. Justice Clark accepts in his concurring opinion condemning the Tennessee statute. Stating that he takes the law of the case from *MacDougall v. Green*, a decision which many would suppose to be squarely against the claims advanced by plaintiffs in *Baker v. Carr*, Mr. Justice Clark reads that case as imposing a requirement that statutes dealing with voting rights must reflect "a rational state policy."[94] The requirement was satisfied in that case, he notes, by the principle of assuring "proper diffusion of political initiative as between . . . thinly populated counties and those having concentrated masses. . . ."[95] No such principle can be attributed to the Tennessee statute, on the other hand, because it is "a crazy quilt," it is "loco," it "cannot be made to fit the pattern cut" by the Tennessee constitution or any other discernible pattern, including variant statistical measures of "total representation" advanced by himself and Mr. Justice Harlan.[96] Therefore the statute is invalid, for "certainly there must be some rational design to a State's districting."[97]

While this may not be an example of winning without actually cheating, it seems too easy a victory to carry conviction. As applied

---

91 Brief for the United States as Amicus Curiae on Reargument, pp. 28, 45–47.

92 *Id.* at 28.

93 369 U.S. at 226. (Emphasis in original.)

94 *Id.* at 251–52.

95 MacDougall v. Green, 335 U.S. 281, 284 (1948).

96 369 U.S. at 254, 257, 258.

97 *Id.* at 258.

to a situation like that in Tennessee, where most of the disparities in voting strength resulted from population changes, the argument must always prevail. It would be a bold defendant who would try to show that population shifts in his State had followed a "rational pattern." To reverse the usual presumption of constitutionality under these circumstances is simply a disguised way of saying that reapportionment has been delayed too long. It leaves unexplained the principle which determines how often a State must reapportion.

Shifting the burden on the constitutional issue is a technique which would really decide the issue, not only in the time-lag cases like Tennessee's, but in most apportionment cases. What is meant by the requirement that an apportionment must be shown to have a rational basis? Apparently it is not enough, at least on Mr. Justice Clark's interpretation, merely to point to the variety of factors that might reasonably have entered into the composite legislative decision. What is necessary is to show that the apportionment in fact resulted, or could have resulted, from the logical or systematic application of identified principles. If this is indeed Mr. Justice Clark's meaning, it leads to some paradoxes that might well give the Court pause. Not the least of them is that it puts the Court in the position of demanding of the legislature a standard of "rationality" in enacting apportionment statutes that has yet to be demonstrated by the judiciary in testing their constitutionality; one would suppose that if adherence to definable principle was to be expected from one branch rather than the other it would be from the courts. Another is that Mr. Justice Clark's notion of a rational plan would apparently be satisfied by any principle of districting which served to explain in consistent fashion all the discrepancies in voting-weight as between districts.[98] This condition would be fulfilled by an apportionment consisting of a grid of uniform-sized squares, each having one representative. Such geometric precision could not be described as "a topsy-turvical of gigantic proportions"[99] and would surely be above the suspicion that it was the product of sinister

[98] The requirement in *MacDougall v. Green*, which Mr. Justice Clark describes as a rational plan, was that a nominating petition have two hundred signatures from each of fifty counties, regardless of population. Mr. Justice Douglas, dissenting in that case, characterized the requirement as "a rigid, arbitrary formula." 335 U.S. 281, 289.

[99] 369 U.S. at 254.

legislative motives; it might also be, from the standpoint of wise statecraft, highly unreasonable if not irrational.

In the attempt to throw the burden of justification on the defendants, the argument on behalf of the plaintiffs professed to find a parallel in *Gomillion v. Lightfoot.*[100] In *Gomillion* the complaint had alleged that the purpose of the statute was to exclude Negroes from the city of Tuskegee. Of this allegation the Court had observed that "respondents have never suggested, either in their brief or in oral argument, any countervailing municipal function which Act 140 is designed to serve,"[101] an observation perhaps unnecessary to enable the Court to sustain the complaint against a motion to dismiss but which served to emphasize that the case was not one requiring extrinsic examination into legislators' motives. The parallel sought to be drawn in *Baker* was that since the complaint had alleged "gross geographic discrimination" it fell to the defendants to show what "countervailing purpose" the Tennesseee apportionment was designed to achieve.[102] The fallacy, of course, is that "gross geographic discrimination" cannot be equated with the allegations of deliberate racial classification made in *Gomillion.* No matter how often the phrase "geographic discrimination" is repeated it remains true that nothing in the Fourteenth and Fifteenth Amendments forbids geographic distinctions as such, whereas they do, as now and historically understood, specifically condemn racial distinctions. To speak of geographic "discrimination" is to beg the entire question that is at issue in *Baker v. Carr,* and the defect is hardly cured by adding the adjective "gross." Indeed, the adjective implicitly concedes the weakness of the analogy: It implies, as must be true, that the Constitution permits at least some geographic discrimination. Is racial discrimination also a matter of degree?

In these efforts to resolve the dilemma of the reapportionment cases by reversing the presumption of constitutionality there is much that is mere sophistry. But there is also an issue of substance that is close to the heart of the problem. Taken seriously, the suggestion that apportionment must conform to "a rational plan" is

---

100 364 U.S. 339 (1960). See generally Lucas, *supra* note 13; TAPER, GOMILLION VERSUS LIGHTFOOT (1961).

101 364 U.S. at 342.

102 Brief for the United States as Amicus Curiae on Reargument, pp. 47–48.

really a refusal to recognize or accept as legitimate the process by which reapportionment or unsuccessful efforts to reapportion have characteristically been carried out. That process is compromise. To any legislator who has participated in a legislative struggle over districting, Mr. Justice Clark's sense of outrage at the vagaries of the Tennessee apportionment must appear ludicrous or feigned. To ask for explanation of all the apparent "inconsistencies" or "discrepancies" in such a legislative act is to demand reconstruction of the details of a complex political battle; to look for "principled" explanations is to expect the impossible. Such a test of the validity of an apportionment statute analogizes the legislative process to the determination of an administrative agency, bound to decide in accordance with stated principles of law and to give a reasoned explanation for its conclusions. A more realistic analogy would be arbitration or collective bargaining, processes of adjustment of conflict not usually thought of as irrational.

This is not to say that alternative methods are unavailable. It is possible for a State's constitution to prescribe detailed rules for the apportionment of its legislature and to make conformity with these requirements a matter of judicial scrutiny. It is possible even to commit responsibility for reapportionment not to the legislature but to an administrative body, or to reduce the operation to a ministerial level by freezing districts and apportioning representatives among them by mathematical formula, as in the case of the apportionment of members of the House of Representatives to the States.[103] Some States follow such methods. To some extent, no doubt, they divert into other channels some of the accommodation and compromise that might otherwise occur in the reapportionment process; perhaps also by taking some of the play out of the joints they increase the strain on the fabric of government at some points and times. Whether the strictness of these methods or the flexibility of legislative compromise or some combination of the two approaches is best would seem to be one of the most subtle and complex questions of political wisdom. But it is certainly possible in theory for a State to have a constitution that makes apportionment a principled process and not a political process, and it is possible that the Supreme Court is saying or will say that that is what a

[103] 55 Stat. 761 (1941), 2 U.S.C. § 2*a*(*a*) and (*b*) (1958).

State must do under the compulsion of the Fourteenth Amendment.

If this is the conclusion toward which the "rational plan" principle leads, the argument takes another interesting turn. For it would then appear that the requirements of the Fourteenth Amendment would be satisfied whenever it could be shown that a State's apportionment was in accordance with requirements of the State constitution, provided only that those requirements were stated in the form of general principles rather than mere description of districts. The special interest of this possibility lies in comparing it with the initial, and apparently rejected, constitutional argument of the plaintiffs' own counsel in *Baker v. Carr.*

D. VIOLATION OF STATE LAW AS DENIAL OF EQUAL PROTECTION

Whereas the Solicitor General's argument might make of State constitutional principles a shield against federally imposed apportionment requirements, the argument originally advanced by plaintiff's own counsel in *Baker v. Carr* sought to use State constitutional provisions as the blade of a Fourteenth Amendment sword which would cut down the State apportionment statute. Their view of the Fourteenth Amendment was this: "It does not in itself decree equality in voting rights. It says that if the state policy is to afford equal voting rights (expressed here by the people of Tennessee in their organic law), the attempt by state officers, under color of law, to deny such equality to some of the citizens is a denial of equal protection."[104]

As a solution to the substantive problems of the reapportionment cases the theory has considerable appeal. By treating the Fourteenth Amendment as incorporating State constitutional requirements, courts would be spared the painful if not impossible task of finding adequate standards in the Amendment itself. From the standpoint of federal-State relationships, the theory would reduce the gravity of federal interference with State autonomy; there would be a sense in which it could be said that the court was not disturbing the State's "frame of government" but only enforcing a commitment by the State to the nation as to what its frame of government would be. The theory would allow more room for a variety of representa-

---

[104] Reply to Appellees' Statement in Opposition and Motion To Dismiss, p. 2. See also Jurisdictional Statement, pp. 3, 9, 12–13, 14–15; Brief for Appellants, pp. 4, 23–26.

tion plans and for accommodation to local desires than is likely to result from any set of independent federal standards of representation. And it would mitigate the force of the objection that in erecting standards of representation courts are undertaking enforcement of the Guarantee Clause.

The Solicitor General did not take up this argument on behalf of the plaintiffs and in his second brief expressly disclaimed it.[105] The plaintiffs themselves seem not to have pressed it strongly after the first oral argument, although their supplemental brief did maintain the position that the provisions of the Tennessee constitution somehow made the case easier to decide than it would be without them. By reason of those provisions, they suggested, voting rights in Tennessee "have taken on a measured meaning"; they "provide the courts with a yardstick which save [*sic*] the courts the more difficult judgment of determining in the case of this state (as distinct from cases which might arise in other states) how much of a departure from mathematical equality the Fourteenth Amendment permits, and what is a suitable standard for compliance in judging remedial action to be taken by the state."[106]

Only the dissenting opinion of Mr. Justice Frankfurter went into this aspect of the case.[107] Mr. Justice Harlan noted that the plaintiff's contention was "manifestly untenable" for the reasons given by Mr. Justice Frankfurter.[108] The opinion of Mr. Justice Brennan observed in a footnote that, in view of the majority holding "resting in no degree" on the Tennessee Constitution, it was unnecessary to "consider, let alone enforce, rights under a State Constitution which go further than the protections of the Fourteenth Amendment."[109]

As an abstract proposition the theory of absorption of State law into the Equal Protection Clause is not without plausibility. The command of the Fourteenth Amendment that "No State shall . . . deny to any person within its jurisdiction the equal protection of the laws" seems to be an injunction requiring even-handed admin-

---

105 Brief for the United States as Amicus Curiae on Reargument, p. 45.

106 Supplemental Memorandum for Appellants, pp. 3–4.

107 369 U.S. at 325–27.

108 *Id.* at 332.

109 *Id.* at 195, n. 15.

istration of whatever laws a State has and not merely a requirement that its laws meet some independent federal test of "equality." The equality ordained is a Statewide equality, encompassing the persons "within its jurisdiction," and not a nationwide or external equality; the implication seems to be that all persons within the State are entitled to the benefit of such classifications as the State has established for itself, not some different classification which the State would be free to adopt if it chose to do so. From this it might be thought to follow that any departure from the settled legal norms of a State whereby some person within its jurisdiction is denied the benefits promised by those norms is *ipso facto* a denial of equal protection in the federal sense, at least if the departure is permitted by the State to go unremedied.

In *Snowden v. Hughes*[110] an unsuccessful candidate for a State political office sought damages under the Civil Rights Act against State election officials, asserting a deprivation of the equal protection of the laws. The alleged deprivation of a federal right consisted in the refusal of the election officials, contrary to State law, to certify plaintiff as having been nominated in the primary election. The Court held that these facts did not constitute a denial of equal protection and, in an opinion by Mr. Chief Justice Stone, went far toward total rejection of the theory that denial of equal protection can ever be predicated on violation of State law as such. The most sweeping proposition announced was that the action of the defendant officials was "subject to constitutional infirmity to the same but no greater extent than if the action were taken by the state legislature. Its illegality under the state statute can neither add to nor subtract from its constitutional validity."[111] But other passages in the opinion appear more equivocal. Thus the opinion repeatedly emphasized elements in the complaint which were lacking, without clearly stating that the complaint would be insufficient unless it alleged "discrimination" of a kind that would be unconstitutional if embodied in a State statute. What was lacking, said the Court, was any allegation of intentional or purposeful discrimination. Where official action "purports to be in conformity to the statutory classification, an erroneous or mistaken performance of the statutory duty, although a violation of the statute, is not *without*

---

[110] 321 U.S. 1 (1944).

[111] *Id.* at 11.

more a denial of the equal protection of the laws."[112] The "unlawful administration" of a statute, "resulting in its unequal application to those who are entitled to be treated alike, is not a denial of equal protection *unless there is shown to be present in it an element of intentional or purposeful discrimination*."[113] The opinion noted that "so far as appears the Board's failure to certify petitioner was unaffected by and unrelated to the certification of any other nominee."[114] A possible inference from these and other statements in the opinion is that under some circumstances departure from a State's own laws might constitute a denial of equal protection even though the resulting "discrimination" reflected a constitutionally permissible classification. The issue is hard to isolate, however, since purposeful abuse of powers by administrative officials seems likely in the nature of things to result in "classifications" arbitrary by any standard. The most that can be said of *Snowden v. Hughes* is that the opinion taken as a whole manifests reluctance to close the door entirely on the possibility that State law may be the measure of a "discrimination" that violates the Equal Protection Clause. It leaves uncertain what the requisite elements of such "discrimination" might be.[115]

Mr. Justice Frankfurter concurred specially in *Snowden v. Hughes*. On the "discrimination" question his opinion, too, left the crucial issue somewhat in limbo but came close to asserting that deliberate departure from State law denies equal protection. The thrust of Mr. Justice Frankfurter's objection to the majority opinion was elsewhere; his point was that mistreatment need not be "systematic" to be discriminatory, as the majority opinion possibly implied. But it is hard to avoid the impression that the discrimination he had

---

112 *Id.* at 8. (Emphasis added.)

113 *Ibid.* (Emphasis added.)

114 *Id.* at 10.

115 Judge Learned Hand thought it clear that in *Snowden v. Hughes* "had the complaint . . . read a little differently, the majority would have held that a case had been made out, based upon a denial of the equal protection of the laws," and thus read the decision as settling that "if a complaint charges a state officer, not only with deliberately misinterpreting a statute against the plaintiff, but also with purposely singling out him alone for that misinterpretation, it is good against demurrer." Burt v. City of New York, 156 F. 2d 791, 792 (2d Cir. 1946). Of course, "singling out him alone" may well be arbitrary by any standard, hence Judge Hand's statement also fails to shed light on the issue of immediate interest.

in mind was departure from a State norm, not violation of some external federal standard. Conceding that the Constitution does not assure "uniformity of decisions or immunity from merely erroneous action" by State officials, he nevertheless asserted that "the Fourteenth Amendment does not permit a State to deny the equal protection of *its* laws because such denial is not wholesale."[116] Talk in other cases about systematic discrimination means only that "in order to give rise to a constitutional grievance a *departure from a norm* must be rooted in design and not derived merely from error or fallible judgment."[117]

It was easier for Mr. Justice Frankfurter than for the majority to accept the implications of a holding that the complaint in *Snowden v. Hughes* sufficiently alleged "discrimination" because he was willing, as the majority were not, to rest dismissal on the debatable doctrine of *Barney v. City of New York*.[118] Under that doctrine the action of the defendants, being assertedly contrary to State law, could not be deemed action of the State and therefore fell outside the injunction of the Fourteenth Amendment. Acceptance of this view would have meant that denial of equal protection could not be established at least until the highest court of the State had refused to correct the alleged departure from State law, a conclusion that might reduce the "discrimination" problem to the vanishing point. But acceptance of such a view would also have kept the federal courts out of front-line action to enforce the Fourteenth Amendment in a much larger class of cases, namely, those in which official misconduct was alleged to violate not only State law but an independent federal standard. The *Barney* case had been severely restricted even before *Snowden v. Hughes*[119] and its "fluctuating history"[120] has since ended in substantial rejection,[121] a development in which Mr. Justice Frankfurter eventually acquiesced.[122]

---

116 321 U.S. at 15. (Emphasis added.)

117 *Ibid.* (Emphasis added.)

118 193 U.S. 430 (1904).

119 Home Telephone & Telegraph Co. v. City of Los Angeles, 227 U.S. 278 (1913).

120 The phrase is Mr. Justice Frankfurter's. Snowden v. Hughes, 321 U.S. 1, 16 (1944); Screws v. United States, 325 U.S. 91, 148 (1945).

121 Screws v. United States, 325 U.S. 91 (1945); Monroe v. Pape, 365 U.S. 167 (1961).

122 See United States v. Raines, 362 U.S. 17, 28 (1960); *but* cf. Frankfurter, J., dissenting in Monroe v. Pape, 365 U.S. 167, 212, n. 16 (1961).

It is interesting, in the context of *Baker v. Carr*, that Mr. Justice Frankfurter's concurring opinion in *Snowden v. Hughes* made no mention of his own earlier opinion for the Court in *Nashville, C. & St. L. Ry. v. Browning*,[123] despite important reliance on that decision in the majority opinion in *Snowden*. In the *Nashville* case a railroad complained that its property was valued by the State tax authorities at actual value while the property of all other taxpayers was assessed at two-thirds of actual value, and that this was in the teeth of a statute requiring all property to be assessed at actual value and of a State constitutional provision requiring uniformity. The State court denied relief, professing itself unable to make a finding, essential to the railroad's claim of mistreatment, that the "State Board intentionally and systematically refused to equalize assessments" as was its duty.[124] The Supreme Court held that there was no denial of equal protection. The Court declined to rest solely on the State court's view of the evidence. Instead it went on to say that if the discrimination complained of had been the result of a formal classification written into the State's statutes it would be unobjectionable (because railroad property may be taxed differently from other property) and that under the circumstances the case must be treated as if that were the situation. The circumstances were that:[125]

> Here, according to petitioner's own claim, all the organs of the state are conforming to a practice, systematic, unbroken for more than forty years, and now questioned for the first time. . . . Settled state practice cannot supplant constitutional guarantees, but it can establish what is state law. . . . [I]f the state supreme court chooses to cover up under a formal veneer of uniformity the established system of differentiation between two classes of property, an exposure of the fiction is not enough to establish its unconstitutionality.

In other words, Tennessee had not denied the railroad the equal protection of its laws because the differential treatment the railroad received *was* Tennessee's law. In *Snowden v. Hughes*, however, the holding of the *Nashville* case was converted by Mr. Chief

---

123 310 U.S. 362 (1940).

124 Nashville, C. & St. L. Ry. v. Browning, 176 Tenn. 245, 260 (1940).

125 310 U.S. at 369.

Justice Stone into the proposition that "state action, *even though illegal under state law*, can be no more and no less constitutional under the Fourteenth Amendment than if it were sanctioned by the state legislature."[126]

Was the plaintiffs' claim in *Baker v. Carr* clearly foreclosed by the *Snowden* and *Nashville* cases or either of them? If Mr. Chief Justice Stone's concept of "discrimination" is important, the action of the Tennessee legislature seems to come closer to fitting that notion than the action of the election board in *Snowden v. Hughes*. In perpetuating the apportionment of 1901 the legislature was not only violating the mandate of the Tennessee constitution and thereby giving some citizens less, and others more, participation in government than the constitution seemed to assure, but this "discrimination" was widespread, persistent, and in some sense purposeful. If, on the other hand, the crucial question is whether the discrimination was "the law" of Tennessee, there would appear to be at least some relevant circumstances differentiating the case from *Nashville v. Browning*. It seems difficult to claim significance for the fact that the legislature has "conformed to" the situation when the basic charge is that the legislature has violated its own duty, has done so to perpetuate its own power, and has been for practical purposes beyond the reach of political processes as structured by the State constitution. Nor is it easy to say that action by the Supreme Court of Tennessee has, as in the *Nashville* case, made the existing situation the authentic expression of Tennessee law when that court's failure to provide a remedy rested so plainly on the belief that it was powerless to do so or that any remedy it attempted might only make matters worse.[127]

Despite these possible distinctions, Mr. Justice Frankfurter dismissed the plaintiffs' theory as one that would not bear analysis. For him the claim was fully refuted by the principle of the *Nashville* case, a principle now restated by him in terms approximating the

---

126 321 U.S. at 11. (Emphasis added.)

127 Kidd v. McCanless, 200 Tenn. 273 (1956). The Court held that it was without power to compel the legislative or the executive department "to perform the duties committed exclusively to their respective domains by the fundamental law" and that it could not declare the existing statute unconstitutional because thereafter the legislature elected under it would not be a *de facto* legislature, hence such relief would "ultimately bring about the destruction of the State itself." *Id.* at 279, 282.

proposition announced by Mr. Chief Justice Stone in *Snowden*:[128] "It is settled that whatever federal consequences may derive from a discrimination worked by a state statute must be the same as if the same discrimination were written into the State's fundamental law."

As thus restated Mr. Justice Frankfurter's position comes down to the view that one has no "rights" under State law except to the extent that State courts will provide a remedy. On this view it automatically follows that a litigant who pursues his remedies to the highest court of a State has received the full protection of the State's laws, except in the remote event, suggested by Mr. Justice Frankfurter in *Snowden*, that "the highest court of a state should candidly deny to one litigant a rule of law which it concededly would apply to all other litigants in similar situations. . . ."[129]

It is possible, however, to conceive of State "law" and one's "rights" under that law as defined by the State's authorized institutions and processes for declaring substantive law, independent of its remedial law. Suppose voting officials persistently refused to register as voters all persons in a particular county who had been resident in the State less than a year although State law entitled them to vote after six months' residence, and that the State court held such violation of State law to be a basis for an action for damages but consistently refused injunctive or other effective relief.[130] Is it clear that in such circumstances the remedial powers of the federal court ought not to be available or, if they ought to be available, that the Court should be entitled to intervene only if it were willing to declare that not even the State legislature or the State constitution could have provided for such differential treatment of the county's residents? Is unremedied flouting of State norms always to be treated as establishing new norms, the authentic command of the State? And if so, can this be said to be according persons within the State's jurisdiction the full measure of "equal protection of the laws"? Perhaps Mr. Justice Frankfurter meant to assert the proposition only with respect to action by the State legislature as distinguished from action by subordinate bodies or executive officials. If so, it is a way of saying that legislatures, unlike others who act

---

128 369 U.S. at 325–26.

129 321 U.S. at 16.

130 As to the potential importance of federal remedies for official misconduct that violates State law, see Harlan, J., concurring, in Monroe v. Pape, 365 U.S. at 196–98.

under color of law, can never be lawless. In a legal system as fully committed to the principle of *Marbury v. Madison* as ours has been, at the State level no less than at the federal, this proposition, too, is hard to accept.

Nevertheless, even if the Equal Protection Clause could ever be said to import a federal standard of remedial law for enforcement of State norms, the reapportionment cases would be a strange place to invoke such a doctrine. All the reasons which might lead a State court to deny a remedy, or deem itself powerless to provide a remedy, should apply with even greater force to a federal court. Beyond this, however, the implications of such a doctrine outside the reapportionment field, with respect to the relations between federal and State law, seem too far-reaching to permit its serious consideration. Barring curtailment by Congress of the scope of existing civil rights statutes[131] and jurisdictional grants,[132] acceptance of such a doctrine would go far toward substituting federal for State courts in the administration of all State law involving official action. Even where enforcement of independent federal constitutional norms is involved it was not without difficulty that the Court adopted interpretations of the Civil Rights Acts which have made it the business of federal courts to correct actions of police and other local officials that is also "lawless" under State law.[133] The same statutory provisions, now read so that all official action is action "under color of law,"[134] would be available for the enforcement of equal protection claims founded on departure from State norms alone. This would indeed make of the Fourteenth Amendment's guaranty a federal law "to regulate the quotidian

131 *E.g.*, 42 U.S. C. §§ 1983, 1985 (1958); 18 U.S. C. § 242.

132 Especially 28 U.S. C. § 1343 (3), the basis of jurisdiction in *Baker v. Carr:* "The district courts shall have original jurisdiction of any civil action authorized by law to be commenced by any person: . . . (3) To redress the deprivation, under color of any State law, statute, ordinance, regulation, custom or usage, or any right, privilege or immunity secured by the Constitution of the United States or by any Act of Congress providing for equal rights of citizens or of all persons within the jurisdiction of the United States." See Hague v. C.I.O., 307 U.S. 496 (1939).

133 Screws v. United States, 325 U.S. 91 (1945) (see dissenting opinion of Roberts, Frankfurter, and Jackson, JJ.); Monroe v. Pape, 365 U.S. 167 (1961).

134 Screws v. United States, *supra* note 133, construing 18 U.S. C. § 242; Monroe v. Pape, *supra* note 133, construing 42 U.S. C. § 1983.

business of every traffic policeman, every registrar of elections, every city inspector or investigator, every clerk in every municipal licensing bureau in this country."[135]

Reapportionment decisions since *Baker v. Carr* have, understandably, reflected a strongly felt need of lower courts to draw upon State constitutional provisions. Thus far, however, they have failed to reveal any satisfactory rationale for such reliance.

III. The Quest for Standards

If the Court's purpose in *Baker v. Carr* was to open the reapportionment problem to development through trial and error, the decision has already been successful. Courts in which litigation was pending at the time of the decision or was commenced as a result of the decision have moved energetically in reapportionment matters.[136] Their pronouncements have already provided substantial

---

[135] Frankfurter, J., dissenting, 365 U.S. at 242. *Cf.* Cobb v. City of Malden, 202 F. 2d 701 (1st Cir. 1953); Glicker v. Michigan Liquor Control Commission, 160 F. 2d 96 (6th Cir. 1947); Burt v. City of New York, 156 F. 2d 791 (2d Cir. 1946).

[136] In addition to the cases discussed in this article, the following *partial* list of reapportionment decisions since *Baker v. Carr* gives an indication of the volume of the litigation:

California: Silver v. Jordan (Los Angeles Superior Ct., No. 794987) (suit dismissed); *Colorado:* Stein v. General Assembly, 374 P. 2d 66 (jurisdiction retained for reapportionment if legislature does not act); *Idaho:* Caesar v. Williams, 371 P. 2d 241 (apportionment statute not invalid); *Indiana:* State ex rel. Grills v. Welsh (Indiana Supreme Court, No. 30253) (lower court restrained from proceeding further); *Maryland:* Maryland Committee for Fair Representation v. Tawes, 180 A. 2d 656 (remanded for hearing on merits); *id.* (Circ. Ct. Arundel County, May 24, 1962, Equity No. 13, 920) (apportionment of lower house unconstitutional); *id.* (June 28, 1962) (apportionment of State senate constitutional); *id.* 182 A. 2d 877 (Maryland Sup. Ct.) (circuit court judgment affirmed); *Mississippi:* Fortner v. Barnette (Chancery Ct. Harrison County, No. 43,076) (apportionment unconstitutional, jurisdiction retained to allow legislature to reapportion); *New Hampshire:* Levitt v. Maynard, 182 A. 2d 897 (State constitutional provisions as to senate held valid); *Pennsylvania:* Butcher v. Trimarchi (Ct. of Common Pleas, Dauphin County, Equity Nos. 2531, 2533, 2536) (jurisdiction retained to give legislature opportunity to reapportion); *Rhode Island:* Sweeney v. Notte, 183 A. 2d 296 (State constitutional provisions as to lower house unconstitutional); *Vermont:* Mikell v. Rousseau, 183 A. 2d 817 (apportionment of State senate unconstitutional).

Federal: Lisco v. McNichols (D. Colo., No. 7501) (injunction denied but cause continued until after November elections); Sobel v. Adams (S.D. Fla.) (constitutional amendment proposed by legislature approved by court, jurisdiction retained pending vote on amendment); State ex rel. Lien v. Sathre (D.N.D.) (jurisdiction retained to give legislature opportunity to reapportion itself at next session); Thig-

light on the reception of the Supreme Court decision and on the ability of courts to derive meaningful standards from the Fourteenth Amendment. The discussion that follows considers a substantial sample—by no means a full review—of the results to date.

A. BAKER V. CARR

Upon the remand of *Baker v. Carr,* the defendants themselves apparently accepted the decision as a ruling on the merits invalidating the Tennessee statute, for they declined to make further defense of it.[137] This was also the view of the three-judge district court. It later said:[138] "There can be no doubt that the majority of the Supreme Court ruled in this case . . . that invidious discriminations were present in the 1901 reapportionment statute and that it fell far short of the standards of the equal protection clause."

But this did not end the problem. Following the Supreme Court decision the governor had decided to convene a special session of the legislature to consider reapportionment and the litigation was stayed to await its action. The legislature met on May 29; bills reapportioning both houses were passed on June 6, and the governor approved them the next day. The pleadings in *Baker v. Carr* were amended to put in issue the validity of the new statutes and a motion for summary judgment followed.[139] On June 22 the court delivered an opinion. In the perspective of the entire reapportionment problem, it is significant that this opinion seems to be a pure example of an advisory opinion as distinguished from a declaratory judgment;[140] it is not clear how such a pronouncement can be reconciled with settled limitations on the use of federal judicial authority.[141]

---

pen v. Meyers (W.D. Wash.) (interlocutory injunction denied; motion to dismiss denied; and case set for hearing on merits November 27, 1962); Wisconsin v. Zimmerman 205 F. Supp. 673 (W.D. Wisc. 1962) (State has no standing to maintain the suit); *id.*, Opinion of Special Master, August 6, 1962 (legislative apportionment and congressional districting held valid and dismissal of action recommended); *id.*, Order of August 14, 1962 (*semble*, case dismissed or continued indefinitely for failure of plaintiffs to make required deposit to cover costs).

137 Baker v. Carr, 206 F. Supp. 341, 345 (M.D. Tenn. 1962).

138 *Ibid.*

139 *Id.* at 344.

140 See text *infra,* at note 148.

141 Coffman v. Breeze Corporations, 323 U.S. 316 (1945). See generally HART & WECHSLER, THE FEDERAL COURTS AND THE FEDERAL SYSTEM 75–81; 135–38 (1953).

The court set forth its "views with respect to each Act" and the "steps to be taken to correct the deficiencies."[142] These were: (1) The new apportionment of the House of Representatives, considered independently, was on the whole constitutional but contained "discrepancies and inequities" which "should be pointed out." The legislature had observed the requirement of the Tennessee constitution that each county having two-thirds of a "ratio" receive one representative; it had applied the same principle, although without constitutional command or authority, in creating "floterial" districts.[143] This was a rational plan, consistent with the Fourteenth Amendment despite the resultant weighting of the legislature in favor of less populous areas. The two-thirds principle, however, would not account for certain disparities, consisting of two specified counties which appeared underrepresented when compared in various ways with some six other named counties.[144] (Whether these deficiencies would be fatal to the plan as a whole the court did not indicate.) (2) The new apportionment of the Senate, considered independently, was clearly invalid because devoid of a discernible underlying rational plan. The thirty-three senatorial districts it created fitted no pattern based on population, area, number of counties per district, or representation of subordinate government units.[145] (3) Even if the Senate apportionment were revised to re-

---

142 206 F. Supp. at 344.

143 *I.e.*, districts consisting of two or more counties. See Clark, J., concurring, in Baker v. Carr, 369 U.S. at 256; Harlan, J., dissenting, *id.* at 341.

144 It had been argued that discrepancies in favor of two of the counties could be explained on the basis that these counties qualified under the two-thirds rule if population rather than voting population was considered. The court rejected this as a justification because these were the only counties where population rather than voting population was taken into account. The argument, however, was that these were the only counties which would qualify for a representative on the basis of total population but not on the basis of voting population. Thus the court's view seems to have been that a single formula must be applied uniformly, regardless of exceptional circumstances in particular counties. 206 F. Supp. at 246, n. 7.

145 The court's analysis suggested that there may have been a rough pattern of differentiation in density of districts as between the eastern, middle, and western sections of the State. It implicitly rejected such regional differentiation as a "rational" basis, but did not discuss the question. 206 F. Supp. at 347. Compare the opinion of Clark, J., in *Baker v. Carr*, which seems to admit the possibility that maintenance of a balance between rural and urban areas might be a permissible ground for inequality of representation. 369 U.S. at 256.

flect a rational plan, it would be invalid when considered with the new apportionment of the House unless the Senate plan were based on population alone. Apportionment in at least one house must be based exclusively on numbers of qualified voters, "without regard to any other factor." (4) To achieve "minimal standards" the Tennessee legislature must either (i) reapportion the Senate on a pure population basis or (ii) reapportion the Senate on some rational basis and reapportion the House on a pure population basis, discarding the two-thirds rule.

In reaching these conclusions the court said that it found in the Supreme Court's opinion "certain guidelines" though not "exact standards." The substance of the "test to be applied" was that "if a state legislative classification for apportionment purposes is wholly irrational and arbitrary, supported neither by the standard of the state nor by any other standard, it is outside the permissible limits of the Fourteenth Amendment."[146] The court apparently regarded this test as an adequate support for its first two conclusions. For its requirement that at least one House must conform to population alone, however, it relied heavily on the apportionment provisions of the Tennessee constitution.[147] Thus its conclusions seem to be a mixture, in uncertain proportions, of federal and State constitutional ingredients.

Despite these views the three-judge court deemed that it should "expressly withhold final judgment on all issues, *including a decla-*

---

[146] 206 F. Supp. at 344.

[147] "Considering that the Constitution of Tennessee, with the exception of the two-thirds principle applicable to the House of Representatives, provides for the distribution of legislative strength in both Houses on the basis of qualified voters; that apportionment in both houses of the legislative branch on the basis of numbers of persons has been a part of the organic law of the State of Tennessee under each of its three Constitutions since it was admitted to the Union in 1796; that this basic principle or standard of state law has been systematically and persistently disregarded and ignored by the legislature since 1901, notwithstanding substantial changes and shifts in population as set forth in the opinion of the Supreme Court in the present case; that the less populous areas and communities of the state have an important place in the political and governmental life of Tennessee; and considering all other relevant and pertinent facets of the problem, we are of the opinion that if the two-thirds principle should be applied and used in apportioning seats in the House of Representatives, either by applying it to counties or floterial districts, or to both, then it would follow that the Senate would have to be apportioned on the basis alone of numbers of qualified voters." 206 F. Supp. at 349.

ration of invalidity, the issuance of an injunction, or otherwise"[148] until the legislature elected under the new laws could have a chance to reform itself at its 1963 session. The purpose of this disingenuous disclaimer was to avoid a possible pitfall of State law. The Tennessee Supreme Court had declared that by Tennessee law a legislature elected under an invalid apportionment statute would be no legislature at all, not even a "de facto" one.[149] This doctrine, reasoned the federal court, rested on the absence of "good faith" of such a legislature; the "de facto" principle would apply if the legislature could be spared the "knowledge" of its lack of authority that would come from a judicial declaration of invalidity.

With this waving of the judicial wand the new legislature presumably may forget for the moment that it was conceived in sin and thus become a *de facto* federal princess, but it is warned that on the stroke of adjournment in 1963 it will find itself only a *de jure* Tennessee waif. The court retained jurisdiction and continued the cause to that date.

B. SCHOLLE V. HARE

Following the Supreme Court's decision on April 23 remanding *Scholle v. Hare* for further consideration,[150] the Michigan Supreme Court on June 5 ordered the cause resubmitted for decision on the plaintiff's motion for summary judgment. On July 18, by a 4–3 vote and with six opinions, the Michigan court reversed its previous position.[151] It declared the provisions of the Michigan constitution apportioning the State senate invalid under the Fourteenth Amendment and enjoined the holding of the Senate primary election scheduled for August 7. The result was only partly and in a sense accidentally attributable to the decision in *Baker v. Carr*; a crucial fact was the change in composition of the Michigan court that had occurred between its first and second decisions. Of four members of the court who had joined in rejecting the plaintiff's case on the merits in the first decision, the surviving three found nothing in *Baker v. Carr* to require a change of position. The fourth

148 *Id.* at 350.

149 Kidd v. McCanless, 200 Tenn. 273, 281 (1956).

150 369 U.S. 429 (1962). See text *supra*, at notes 60–65.

151 Scholle v. Hare, 116 N.W. 2d 350 (Mich. 1962).

had meanwhile resigned and been replaced by the former attorney general of the State, who disqualified himself. A fifth member, Black, J., had also previously voted against the plaintiff but only under compulsion of the Supreme Court precedents and with a plea that the Supreme Court "loan the Fourteenth Amendment" to the State courts for reapportionment purposes.[152] Considering that the Court had made such a "loan" in *Baker v. Carr*,[153] he added what was now the decisive vote to the previous dissenting position. The other votes in the new majority were those of Justices Kavanagh and Souris, who adhered to their previous position, and Justice Otis Smith who replaced Justice Talbot Smith in vote as well as in name. The four in the majority are said to be Democrats, and the three dissenters, Republicans.[154] In the circumstances it is understandable why at least one member should have thought that a good reason for prompt if not hasty decision was the fact that within nine months elections for four of the seats on the court were to take place.[155]

The majority judges plainly considered *Baker v. Carr* decisive of the merits as well as the justiciability of the plaintiff's claim. Their three opinions add little by way of rationale, relying instead on tireless reiteration of the familiar chain of phrases—"invidiously unequal," "arbitrary, discriminatory and without reasonable or just relation or relevance to the electoral process," "well developed and familiar judicial standards under the equality clause," and "wide disparity" in the population of voting districts. The opinion of Mr. Justice Souris recognizes the possibility that deliberate dilution of voting strength in some districts as a means of assuring "the effective representation of all its people" may be a legitimate objective of

---

152 Scholle v. Secretary of State, 360 Mich. 1, 120 (1960).

153 116 N.W. 2d at 388.

154 See N.Y. Times, July 28, 1962, p. 9, col. 5.

155 116 N.W. 2d at 387. On the question whether *Baker v. Carr* creates judicial responsibilities that are likely to strain judicial detachment, skeptics should read the opinions of the Michigan court in full, especially that of Black, J. And *compare* the dissenting opinions of Riley, J., in Jones v. Freeman, 193 Okla. 554, 564 (1944), and Latting v. Cordell, 197 Okla. 369, 374 (1946), *with* Riley v. Cordell, 200 Okla. 390 (1948) (mandamus petition by Riley, J., to compel secretary of state to place his name on ballot as candidate for nomination for United States Senator after filing for nomination for re-election as justice of supreme court at same election; writ granted, on the ground that later declaration for Senate candidacy, being presumably filed in good faith, extinguished candidacy for re-election as justice).

State policy. He seems to concede that this was the purpose of the constitutional amendments in issue. For him it is decisive, however, that the resulting disparity in population ratios between the most and least populous districts is "wide" not "minor" and that "the arrangement of the districts was made without any discernible or conceivable basis, let alone upon any rational basis. . . ."[156]

The constitutional provisions invalidated by the Michigan court were part of a reapportionment plan that was placed on the ballot as an initiative measure and adopted by the voters of Michigan in 1952.[157] The Senate provisions created 34 permanent senatorial districts, described in the constitutional provision itself, each of which was entitled to elect one senator. The provisions as to the House of Representatives, which were not in issue in *Scholle v. Hare*, prescribed periodic reapportionment on the basis of equal-population districts but subject to various qualifications, including the allowance of one representative for any district having one-half a "ratio." Provision was also made for reapportionment by the State board of canvassers upon the failure of the legislature promptly to carry out its duty of reapportionment each tenth year. Thus the new plan sought to cure the problem of legislative failure to apportion either House or Senate over many years by making the Senate apportionment permanent and the House apportionment automatic on a basis reflecting changes of population. The amendments were adopted by a majority of approximately 300,000 votes in an election *in which all voters in Michigan cast equal votes*. Simultaneously, the same electorate rejected by a majority of approximately 500,000 votes an alternative proposal requiring that members of both houses be selected on the basis of a legislative apportionment in accordance with population.[158]

The decision of the Supreme Court of Michigan, if carried out, would give the State a Senate apportioned according to the provi-

---

[156] 116 N.W. 2d at 381.

[157] Mich. Laws 1953, p. 438, amending Mich. Const., art. V, §§ 2, 3, and 4.

[158] 116 N.W. 2d at 357, 376. See GLAZER, REJECTED AMENDMENTS TO THE MICHIGAN CONSTITUTION 1910–1961 23 (Mich. Constitutional Convention Studies, 1961); GARFINKEL, THE CONSTITUTION AND THE LEGISLATURE 17 (Mich. Constitutional Convention Studies, 1961): "Not only did a majority of all the voters approve the present apportionment provision, but even in the most densely-populated counties there was considerable support registered for the current system."

sions of the constitution of 1908 and a House apportioned according to the provisions of the 1952 amendments, a result apparently approximating the rejected constitutional proposals of 1952. The court avoided the problem of compelling a new constituent act by the people of Michigan by declaring the resurrection of the dead provisions of the Michigan constitution respecting apportionment of the Senate. These authorize reapportionment by the legislature. Then, being free to fashion its own law of *de facto* powers, as the district court in Tennessee was not, the court determined that the present Senate may function as a *de facto* Senate until December 13, 1962, notwithstanding the erasure from the constitution not only of the districting provisions but along with them the provision under which the present 34-member Senate was created. It advised the governor and legislature that new legislation was urgently required because as a result of its decision no provision now existed under which State senators could validly be elected for the term beginning January 1, 1963. Looking at earlier decisions of the Michigan court enforcing the apportionment provisions of the old constitution, and at the dissenting opinion of three members of the Supreme Court in *MacDougall v. Green*,[159] the court derived a standard to guide the legislature:[160] "When a legislative apportionment provides districts having more than double the population of others, the constitutional range of discretion is violated. This is not to say that less than such 2 to 1 ratio is constitutionally good. It is to say only that peril ends and disaster occurs when that line is crossed." Finally, the court in-

---

[159] The court quoted the following from the dissenting opinion of Mr. Justice Douglas (Black and Murphy, JJ., concurring): "None would deny that a state law giving some citizens twice the vote of other citizens in either the primary or general election would lack that equality which the Fourteenth Amendment guarantees." 335 U.S. 281, 288. It is not readily apparent why the proposition, if valid, would not be equally so if some other number (such as one-and-a-half or one-and-a-quarter) were substituted for "twice." Yet no one thus far, including all the majority Justices in *Baker v. Carr,* has suggested that the Fourteenth Amendment requires more than approximate equality, or not too much inequality, in legislative apportionment. It must be that Mr. Justice Douglas' proposition is either not so relevant or not so self-evident as is suggested.

[160] 116 N.W. 2d at 355. The court noted that the disparity in voting weights (presumably between largest and smallest districts) under the existing senatorial apportionment was 7 to 1 by the 1950 census and 12 to 1 by the 1960 census. The comparable figure for the United States Senate, based on the 1960 census, is approximately 89 to 1. See Statistical Abstract of the United States 360 (1961).

structed the secretary of state that if the *de facto* legislature did not adopt a valid reapportionment of the Senate by August 20, 1962, he was to apply to the court for directions to conduct a special election at large for 32 senators on September 11, 1962.

On July 27th Mr. Justice Stewart stayed the Michigan court's order, pending application to the Supreme Court for a writ of certiorari.[161]

The Michigan decision thus crystallizes some problems that were not sharply posed in the first *Baker v. Carr* situation, problems similar to the ones that have emerged in the district court's new *Baker v. Carr* decision. Specifically, it presents the questions whether the equal-protection principle, whatever it may be, is the same for both houses of a bicameral State legislature as for one; and, if not, what justification can be advanced for a difference in federal constitutional treatment that does not impeach the principle as applied to one house alone. If the answer to these questions is that the appraisal of a State's representation scheme must be a composite appraisal that looks at both houses together, this conclusion must surely drive reliance on arithmetic further into the background and force a rational and not arbitrary Court to come to closer grips with the difficulties of articulating a meaningful constitutional principle.

Beyond this, however, the Michigan situation has grave difficulties of its own, difficulties that might cause the Supreme Court to treat it as a special case but which in truth merely provide still further grounds for doubting the validity of all that seems to be implicit in *Baker v. Carr*. The Solicitor General's brief suggested that one important consideration "relevant" to the constitutionality of an apportionment is the availability of "other methods of expressing the popular will."[162] The Michigan situation is one where such a method, constitutional amendment by popular initiative and ma-

---

[161] See N.Y. Times, July 28, 1962, p. 9, col. 5. Mr. Justice Stewart was quoted as saying, "It is very clear the issues decided by the Michigan Supreme Court are new issues; ones that were not decided in Baker v. Carr." The effect of the stay was to reinstate the primary election previously scheduled for August 7, 1962.

[162] Brief for the United States as Amicus Curiae on Reargument, pp. 31–32. Referring to legislation by initiative and referendum, the brief suggests that such a device may offset malapportionment either by permitting reform of the legislature or by permitting enactment of ordinary legislation directly by a majority, or both. How a court is to appraise the practical utility of such alternatives is not discussed. More puzzling, however, is the suggestion that even such a remedy would be insufficient "if a minority of the people were seriously underrepresented."

jority vote, not only was available and is still available but has been exercised. If this is "relevant," what is its significance? Is it merely another "factor" to be stirred into the stew, or does it have some definable bearing on the problem? If it should turn out that it is not merely relevant but decisive, what becomes of the asserted principle that an apportionment plan must be "rational" in the artificial sense that it must reflect some arithmetic formula or architectural symmetry? Would it then be true that the people themselves may act "irrationally" by adopting a compromise that a majority deem to be in their own or the State's best interest but that they may not delegate such compromising power to their elected representatives? Does a plan that is rational when approved by a referendum become irrational when voted by a legislature? If, on the other hand, the Michigan senatorial apportionment is to be upset despite its approval by Michigan's voters, even more curious anomalies appear. It might then follow that the electorate may not exercise the most fundamental of its constituent powers, the power to determine the frame of government, and that the provisions of the Michigan constitution permitting popular amendment of the basis of apportionment are themselves unconstitutional. Or it might follow that the Fourteenth Amendment permits the electorate to act, indeed in a situation like that in *Scholle v. Hare* may force it to act, but forbids it to act in what is really the only way it can act, by seeking a satisfactory accommodation of conflicting interests. At this point, surely, the perversity of the "rational plan" slogan must be evident. If the voters, voting equally, conclude that they are better off under a "crazy quilt" than under a neatly crocheted one such as Mr. Justice Clark's grandmother may have made, how can Supreme Court Justices justify imposing a different preference upon them?[163]

C. SIMS V. FRINK

In a suit like that in Tennessee, Alabama voters asked a three-judge federal court for a "declaration of their rights" concerning

163 Of course action does not become constitutional merely because it is taken by a majority of the voters rather than by the legislature. Approval by even 99 per cent of the voters would not validate racial qualifications for voting, even if members of the disqualified race themselves supported it overwhelmingly. If inequality of apportionment is like racial discrimination a referendum cannot make it good. But in that event such "other methods of expressing the popular will" are not merely inconclusive, they are irrelevant.

apportionment of the Alabama legislature and for "such relief as may be proper" to assure them such rights. Following the Supreme Court's action in *Baker v. Carr*, the district court on April 14 denied an application for interlocutory injunction to restrain the holding of impending elections under the existing apportionment.[164] It indicated, however, that the existing apportionment was unconstitutional and that unless the legislature changed it by July 16 further judicial action would be forthcoming. As in Tennessee, the alleged malapportionment in Alabama had resulted from the failure of the legislature, since the turn of the century, to reapportion the State as required by its constitution.

In an opinion filed July 21 the court summarily disposed of the question of the constitutionality of the existing apportionment.[165] It noted that "it has been generally conceded throughout this litigation by all the parties that the present apportionment of both Houses of the Legislature of the State of Alabama constitutes 'invidious discrimination' in violation of the Equal Protection Clause of the Fourteenth Amendment." The "invidiousness" of the situation was demonstrated, the court added, by appendices to its opinion. The appendices referred to consisted of a list of the counties and senatorial districts in the State, their respective populations, and the number of representatives and senators allocated to each.[166]

Meanwhile the governor had summoned the legislature into special session with an irate plea to "beat the Federals to the draw" and reapportion the State before the date of the district court's "shotgun ultimatum."[167] Two measures were shortly forthcoming. One was a proposed constitutional amendment, to be submitted to the voters in November, which provided for a new system of apportionment beginning with the legislature to be elected in 1966.[168] The other was a statute prescribing a revised apportionment within the framework of existing constitutional provisions, to take effect in the event

164 Sims v. Frink, 205 F. Supp. 245 (M.D. Ala. 1962).

165 Sims v. Frink, Civil No. 1744-N (M.D. Ala. July 21, 1962).

166 Opinion of July 21, 1962, Appendices D and E.

167 N.Y. Times, June 13, 1962, p. 44, col. 1.

168 Act 93, July 13, 1962. The amendment, referred to by the district court as the "67-Senator Amendment," appears as Appendix B to the district court's opinion of July 21, 1962.

the proposed constitutional amendment was not approved by the voters.[169]

The constitutional amendment proposed to substitute for the present Senate, consisting of 35 members from senatorial districts drawn by the legislature, a Senate of 67 members consisting of one from each county. As to the House of Representatives, it retained the present size of 106 members and provided that in 1971 and decennially thereafter the House should be automatically reapportioned to counties according to population, "by the method known as the method of equal proportions," except that no county should have less than one representative. In sum, the amendment provided a permanent plan of representation for Alabama identical in principle with that which now determines the composition of Congress. Pending the 1971 reapportionment, the amendment prescribed the apportionment of the House, apparently in accordance with the permanent formula. Under this apportionment representatives would be shifted from some of the less populous counties to the more populous ones, reducing the existing disparity of representation. For example, the two most populous counties would receive 17 and 8 representatives, respectively, as compared with their present 7 and 3.

The alternative statutory reapportionment rearranged the 35 senatorial districts. In the House it redistributed the 39 excess representatives over the 67 needed to give one to each county, providing somewhat greater representation for the more populous counties than under the old apportionment but less than under the proposed constitutional amendment. For example, the two most populous counties would receive 12 and 6 representatives, respectively, as compared with their present 7 and 3.

In its opinion of July 21 the three-judge court declared both the proposed constitutional amendment and the alternative apportionment statute unconstitutional. It found both to be "so obviously discriminatory, arbitrary and irrational that it becomes unnecessary to pursue a detailed development of each of the relevant factors of the test."

---

169 Act 91, July 12, 1962. The statute, referred to by the district court as the Crawford-Webb Act, appears as Appendix C to the district court's opinion of July 21, 1962.

In holding the constitutional amendment invalid the court concentrated its attention on the Senate provisions. These, it said, would make the discrimination in the Senate "even more invidious" than at present, reducing from 25 per cent to 19 per cent the proportion of the population represented by the number of senators necessary to control the Senate. Observing that the "only conceivable rationalization" for the plan was the use of subordinate political units as the basis of representation, it dismissed as obviously inapplicable the analogy to the United States Senate.[170] Counties are mere creatures of the State, it said; also, the analogy "cannot survive the most superficial examination into the history of the requirement of the Federal Constitution and the diametrically opposing history of the requirement of the Alabama Constitution that representation shall be based on population."[171] Moreover, if representation in the House of

---

[170] The comparable figures in the case of the United States Senate are that the 26 least populous states, having approximately 17 per cent of the population of voting age, elect 52 per cent of the membership of the Senate, while the 9 most populous states, having over 50 per cent of the population of voting age, elect only 18 per cent of the membership of the Senate. The district court also noted that senators elected by 14 per cent of the population could prevent the submission of proposed constitutional amendments. The comparable figure in the United States Senate is about 6.5 per cent of the voting population, that of the 17 least populous states, electing 34 senators. (Figures as to United States Senate based on population data in STATISTICAL ABSTRACT OF THE UNITED STATES 360 [1961].)

[171] The provision of the Alabama constitution referred to is the last sentence of § 284. Section 284 prescribes the mode of amending the constitution. The last sentence provides: "Representation in the legislature shall be based upon population, and such basis of representation shall not be changed by constitutional amendments." Ala. Code § 284 (1958).

Article IX of the Alabama constitution, §§ 197–203, prescribes the composition of the Alabama legislature. Section 197 fixes the size of the Senate at not less than one-fourth nor more than one-third of the number of representatives. Section 198 limits the size of the House of Representatives to 105, plus one for each new county, and provides for decennial reapportionment "among the several counties of the state, according to the number of inhabitants in them, respectively." Section 199 provides that each county shall be entitled to at least one representative. Section 200 provides that the legislature shall determine senatorial districts "as nearly equal to each other in the number of inhabitants as may be," that each district shall elect one senator, and that no county shall be divided between two districts. Section 202 prescribed the initial allocation of representatives and Section 203 determined the initial groupings of counties into senatorial districts. These original apportionments of Senate and House have continued in effect until the present.

If § 284 is taken literally there is obvious incompatibility between it and Article IX. However, all the provisions were adopted simultaneously in the constitution of 1901. In an advisory opinion the Supreme Court of Alabama held that a proposed consti-

Representatives must depart substantially from the population standard, as the Alabama constitutional provisions require,[172] then "it may well be" that representation according to population must "to some extent" be reflected in both Houses. Whether this latter requirement was thought to follow solely from the Fourteenth Amendment the court did not make clear, although that appears to have been its view; here and throughout the opinion, however, there was a confusing interweaving of State and federal constitutional arguments. Indeed it is not clear whether the court meant to advance as an independent ground for invalidating the proposed constitutional amendment that under State law the State constitution was not amendable in the manner proposed.[173]

In holding the statutory reapportionment invalid the court chose the House of Representatives provisions as the chief target of its criticism. The Senate provisions were "a step in the right direction" though "an extremely short step." They eliminated a few of the more glaring disparities but left control of the Senate in 27.6 per cent of the people, "an improvement of only 2.6 per cent over the present control of 25.1 per cent," and they also left wide disparities

---

tutional amendment providing for allotment of representatives on a bracket system, with a maximum of 12 representatives for the largest counties and a minimum of one for counties with less than 38,500 population each, was consistent with § 284. It also held that a proposal for giving one senator to each county under 650,000 population and two to each county over that number was not consistent with § 284, but that its adoption would be lawful and would impliedly repeal § 284. Opinion of the Justices, 263 Ala. 158 (1955). The district court's repeated reference to § 284 as the "controlling or dominant provision" of the Alabama constitution is difficult to understand.

172 What the court apparently regarded as a substantial departure from the "population standard" would necessarily result, under either the present or the proposed constitutional provisions, from the limit on the size of the House of Representatives in combination with the requirement that each county have at least one representative. While the principle here is the same as that which determines the federal House of Representatives, the resulting disparities in any particular State may of course be greater than in the case of Congress.

173 Despite the Alabama Supreme Court opinion referred to in note 171, *supra,* the district court expressed doubt that it would be followed in view of the fact that the Alabama court had divided 4–3 on the question and that two of the majority, but none of the dissenters, had since been replaced. The district court said: "The manifest uncertainty of the legality of the proposed constitutional amendment . . . forces this Court to the conclusion that the Legislature may not have complied with the State Constitution in the passage of such an Act."

existing in the weights of individual votes as between the most populous and least populous groups of districts. The House of Representatives provisions, however, were "totally unacceptable" because "no rational reapportionment plan was followed." This characterization is difficult to follow. What the legislature obviously did was distribute among the larger counties the 39 representatives remaining after giving each county one, allowing a maximum of 12 to Jefferson, the largest county, and allowing proportionate extra representation to the others. Thus Jefferson County with 634,000 population was given 12 representatives, Mobile with 314,000 received 6, Tuscaloosa with 109,000 received 3, and so on. Disparities within the "brackets" which were allotted extra representatives do not appear great; for example, the largest 3-representative county has a population of 117,000 and the smallest 95,000. That the court should consider this not a "rational" plan is incomprehensible, unless it meant that a mathematical formula, or some particular mathematical formula, must be employed. The latter inference is suggested by the court's contrasting endorsement of the "equal proportions method," adopted in the proposed constitutional amendment, as a "known and accepted" standard of apportionment.

As a further reason for invalidating the reapportionment statute the court observed that it would not go into effect until the election of 1966 and that there was no good reason why the plaintiffs should be thus postponed in the enjoyment of their rights. It deserves note, however, that the members of both houses of the Alabama legislature are elected for four-year terms.[174] If the legislature considered that the interval between July 12 and the date of the general election in November was too short to permit reasonable opportunity for selecting candidates and holding campaigns in the newly constituted districts, the election of 1966 was the earliest next date which could have been chosen. It was also, of course, the earliest date at which an election under the proposed constitutional amendment could be held since approval of the amendment at a general election was a prerequisite. The court considered only the latter factor and deemed it eliminated by the ruling invalidating the proposed amendment.

On July 25 the court entered a decree enjoining all election officials in Alabama from taking any steps in connection with the

[174] Ala. Const., art. IV, § 46.

holding of elections for members of the State legislature "except and in accordance with the apportionment of the Alabama Legislature as hereinafter specifically set out."[175] It then decreed the number of representatives each county should have, adopting in this respect the apportionment prescribed in the proposed constitutional amendment, and it specified the composition of the 35 senatorial districts, adopting in this respect the apportionment prescribed in the invalidated new statute. It ordered officials of the State Democratic and Republican Committees, together with certain State officers, to take the necessary steps to nominate candidates for an election of the new legislature in November, and it decreed that the new apportionment should remain in effect until the legislature reapportions itself "in accordance with the equal protection provisions of the Fourteenth Amendment."

In adopting this apportionment the court made clear that it did not regard it as meeting the constitutional standard permanently required but that it preferred taking parts of legislation already passed by the legislature to imposing a wholly new apportionment of the court's own devising. It expressed the hope that the revisions ordered would "break the stranglehold" on the legislature and enable it to reapportion itself constitutionally.

On August 25 Mr. Justice Black denied a stay.[176]

D. THE GEORGIA CASES

1. *The county-unit case.* Within hours after *Baker v. Carr* was announced, the attack on the so-called county-unit system of voting for Statewide offices was renewed. In *Sanders v. Gray*[177] a voter in Fulton County, Georgia's most populous county, sought a declaration of the invalidity of the Neill Primary Act,[178] the county-unit statute, and an injunction against the holding of any primary under

175 Decree, Sims v. Frink, Civil Action No. 1744-N (M.D. Ala.), filed July 25, 1962.

176 N.Y. Times, August 26, 1962, p. 42, col. 3. The reapportionment problem may have reached its apex of irony in the statement attributed to Mr. Justice Black in denying the stay: "All preparations for this primary appear to have been made. No facts are alleged or shown which in my judgment would support a stay that would so drastically disrupt the state's primary plan."

177 203 F. Supp. 158 (N.D. Ga. 1962).

178 Ga. Laws 1917, p. 183 *et seq.*, as amended by Ga. Laws 1950, p. 79, GA. CODE ANN. §§ 34-3213 to 34-3218.

its terms. The governor, not waiting for action by a court, called a special session of the legislature shortly afterward[179] and on April 27 a new county-unit statute was enacted.[180] On April 28 the federal district court heard and granted the plaintiff's application for what the court termed a "temporary" injunction. The court's order entered the same day enjoined the defendants, State and Democratic party officials, from conducting any primary election under the amended statute or according to any unit method not conforming to standards laid down in the court's opinion, and was to be effective "until the further order of this Court."[181]

The Neill Primary Act, in force in Georgia since 1917, prescribes rules to be followed by any political party which holds a primary election to select candidates for any of various State offices, including governor, and for United States senator. Among the rules is that a candidate receiving the majority of the popular vote in a county shall receive "the full vote of such county on the county unit basis" and the candidate receiving the majority of county unit votes shall be the nominee of the party, a result up to now the equivalent of election in the case of Democratic nominees. Prior to the recent amendment, each county's "unit vote" was twice the number of its representatives in the State House of Representatives, or six each for the eight most populous counties, four each for the thirty next largest, and two each for the remainder.[182] The amended statute of April 27 established a bracket system for distributing unit votes, ranging from 2 votes for counties with population under 15,000 to 50 votes for counties with population over 690,000. From 30,000 up the bracket system assigned an additional unit vote for each 15,000 of population; between 15,000 and 30,000 it assigned additional votes at intervals of 5,000 and 10,000 respectively.

The district court acknowledged that, in order to apply the Four-

---

179 Proclamation, April 5, 1962, Ga. Laws 1962, p. 1214.

180 Ga. Laws 1962, p. 1217.

181 Order, Civil Action No. 7872 (N.D. Ga.), entered April 28, 1962.

182 This was the system which Mr. Justice Clark in *Baker v. Carr* characterized as based on a rational policy. "Georgia based its election system on a consistent combination of political units and population, giving six unit votes to the eight most populous counties, four unit votes to the 30 counties next in population, and two unit votes to each of the remaining counties." 369 U.S. at 253, n. 4. See also his opinion at 256, n. 8.

teenth Amendment to the statute, a "test for invidiousness must be formulated,"[183] and that the problem was different from "per se invidiousness" resulting from discriminations based on race, creed, or color. The test must be based, it said, on consideration of "all relevant factors" including "rationality of state policy." Citing *MacDougall v. Green*,[184] it conceded the rationality of diffusing political strength throughout the State. It also noted that the county-unit system had a fair purpose in the beginning, and an historical basis in the State; its lengthy review of the history of the system as applied to primaries showed that the system was a direct outgrowth of the method of voting long used in party conventions in the State, corresponding to the representation of counties in the legislature. The court compared the unit system with the federal Electoral College and suggested that despite the special circumstances surrounding the formation of the Union it "could hardly be said that such a system used in a state among its counties, assuming rationality and absence of arbitrariness in end result, could be termed invidious."[185] Relevant also was the availability of a political remedy; the court thought there was no substantial likelihood of such relief, although it observed that plaintiff was complaining of treatment received from other members of his own party under a statute sponsored by a governor of his party and passed by a legislature predominantly of the same party.

Having recited these various "factors," the court announced its conclusion: that the statute must be held invalid "because of discrimination so excessive as to be invidious." What was at fault, it said, was not the unit system as such but this particular version of it, which failed to give plaintiff's unit "a reasonable proportion of the whole" and failed to give units representing a majority of the population "a reasonable proportion of the whole."[186] A footnote drew attention to the fact that when Fulton, the largest county, was compared to each of the four smallest counties the ratio of its population-per-unit-vote to theirs was 14 to 1, 11 to 1, 10 to 1, and 8 to 1, respectively. The footnote also pointed out that counties aggregating one-third of the population of the State had been allotted a majority of the unit votes.

---

[183] 203 F. Supp. at 168.

[184] See text *supra*, at notes 16, 25, 53, 95, 98.

[185] 203 F. Supp. at 169.

[186] *Id.* at 170.

The court did not stop here, however. It ventured to formulate a more precise standard to justify its conclusion and guide further revision. The standard was as follows:[187]

> [W]e . . . hold that a unit system for use in a party primary is invidiously discriminatory if any unit has less than its share to the nearest whole number proportionate to population, or to the whole of the vote in a recent party gubernatorial primary, or to the whole vote for electors of the party in a recent presidential election; provided no discrimination is deemed to be invidious under the system if the disparity against any county is not in excess of the disparity that exists against any state in the most recent electoral college allocation, or under the equal proportions formula for representation of the several states in the Congress, and provided it is adjusted to accord with changes in the basis at least once each ten years.

This, said the court, is "a 'judicially manageable standard' contemplated in *Baker v. Carr.*"

What this extraordinary formulation of constitutional principle suggests, of course, is that the problem "How much inequality is unequal?" is scarcely manageable except in terms of the kind of fiat that only a legislature or a constitutional convention is entitled to prescribe. The court's standard may be "judicially manageable" but that does not make it appropriate for judicial declaration; legislatures, too, furnish judicially manageable standards, but not everything a legislature can do is for a court to do. The court's formula appears to be legislative because it merely draws a bright line unrelated to a principle, let alone a principle that can be extracted from the Fourteenth Amendment. Even assuming that the Electoral College is a relevant or controlling datum, for example, one would suppose that it is the principle underlying the Electoral College that should be relevant rather than the precise numbers prevailing at a given moment. The court's formula says in effect that Georgia's electoral system shall be determined by the rate of change in the population of Alaska. This may be judicially convenient, but can it be a constitutional principle?

This difficulty aside, it is questionable how significant a standard the court has announced. The formula simulates exactness ("its share to the nearest whole number") while allowing a latitude of disparity that makes this precision inconsequential. The limiting

---

187 *Ibid.*

factor in the test, quite evidently, is the Electoral College comparison; what the test really says is that a State's system is not "invidious" if the disparity against any county is not in excess of the disparity against any State in the Electoral College. As of 1960, this would permit a disparity of 6 to 1, the disparity in population per electoral college vote between New York and Alaska.[188] Since the disparity is only 8 to 1 between Fulton County and the fourth smallest Georgia county, it appears likely that very slight modification of the new Georgia plan would bring it within the limits of tolerance employed by the court. More important, the formula says nothing whatever about the number of counties in which the permitted disparity may exist. In the Electoral College only Alaska enjoys so disproportionate a voting weight; under the court's suggested constitutional standard Georgia could make Alaskas of all its rural counties.

Finally, there is the question of the standard's rationality as applied to representation in the legislature. As a constitutional principle it must apply to all aspects of a State's electoral processes if it applies to any. At least it does not appear likely that cogent reasons can be found for employing a different *measure* of "invidiousness" in, say, the legislature than in an election for governor or in the Senate than in the House of Representatives of the State legislature. Leaving aside the great difficulties of finding the appropriate fraction to test "disparity of representation" in some representation plans,[189] the suggested test seems incompatible with allowing even in one house a plan analogous to that of the United States Senate and many present State senates.

2. *The legislative-apportionment case.* In *Toombs v. Fortson*,[190] a second Georgia suit filed immediately after the decision in *Baker v. Carr*, plaintiffs sought invalidation of the State's constitutional and statutory provisions apportioning both houses of the Georgia legislature. On May 25, after adjournment of the special session of the legislature without action on the governor's request for reapportionment, the three-judge district court declared that the composi-

---

188 See STATISTICAL ABSTRACT OF THE UNITED STATES 352, 360 (1961).

189 Compare Clark, J., concurring, in Baker v. Carr, 369 U.S. at 255–58, with Harlan, J., dissenting, 369 U.S. at 342–44; see note 59 *supra*.

190 205 F. Supp. 248 (N.D. Ga. 1962).

tion of the Georgia legislature, considered as a whole, violated the requirements of the Fourteenth Amendment. It ruled that the legislature would continue to be in violation of the federal Constitution until at least one house should be reapportioned on the basis of population. Affirmative relief was withheld, however, in order to give further opportunity for the legislature (either the existing legislature or the new one scheduled to be elected in November) to take action in special session to correct the situation prior to the convening of the next regular session in January, 1963. The court did not discuss the *de facto* doctrine or the question of the legislature's legal authority to enact new laws on apportionment or on any other matters prior to a valid reapportionment. In a supplemental opinion, from which one judge dissented, it disclaimed having intended to rule in its opinion of May 25 that no legally constituted legislature would be in existence after January 1, 1963, if reapportionment had not occurred by that date.[191]

---

191 "We have not reached that point. It would be a drastic intrusion into the affairs of the State—the most drastic of the remedies available to the Court." Memorandum Opinion (per Bell, C. J., and Morgan, D. J.), Civil Action No. 7883 (N.D. Ga.), filed July 18, 1962. Judge Tuttle, who filed a dissenting memorandum, made it clear that he considered that his colleagues had retreated from their initial position. The original opinion, written by Judge Tuttle, had stated: "We have concluded that we should postpone any further proceedings in this matter until the State has had a reasonable opportunity to reconstitute the Legislature so as to meet the constitutional standards here laid down prior to the January, 1963, session. If it appears that the Legislature has taken such action as brings the composition of the General Assembly within such constitutional standards, then this Court need take no further action. If, on the other hand, the Legislature does not act, or if its action does not meet constitutional standards, then we will be under a clear duty to take such action as is necessary and feasible to accord plaintiffs their rights." 205 F. Supp. at 259.

Cf. Moss v. Burkhart, 207 F. Supp. 885 (W.D. Okla. 1962). On June 19, 1962, the court held unconstitutional the apportionment of both houses of the Oklahoma legislature and entered a decree declaring the pertinent Oklahoma statutes and constitutional provisions to be "prospectively null and void, and inoperative for all future elections." *Id.* at 898. It continued the cause to July 31 for "appropriate relief and final judgment," stating in its accompanying opinion that ample time remained for the governor to call the present legislature into special session and enact a new apportionment prior to the 1963 general session, and that if such a session had been called by July 31 the court would grant a further continuance to September 10th. On August 3 the court entered a supplemental order admonishing the legislature that it must reapportion itself at its next general session or be judicially reapportioned, supplying detailed directions as to how the reapportionment must be effected, and continuing the case until March 8, 1963. *Id.* at 898–99. The order stated that the "forthcoming November 6, 1962 election is not a 'future election' within the

The Georgia constitution, adopted in 1945, provides for a Senate of fifty-four members, one to be elected from each of fifty-four senatorial districts as specified by the legislature but comprised of counties.[192] The legislature redefined senatorial districts in 1946.[193] With two exceptions, the districts consist of three counties each, which are contiguous. Fulton, the most populous county, is a single district, and Chatham, the second most populous at the time the apportionment was made, is a district with one other county.[194] The constitution provides for a House of Representatives consisting of three representatives from each of the eight most populous counties, two from each of the thirty next most populous counties, and one from each of the other counties.[195] It calls for reapportionment after each federal census.[196] The legislature reapportioned the House on the basis of this formula in 1961.[197] In Georgia, therefore, there was no question of failure to carry out the State's constitutional provisions. The apportionment of the House of Representatives conforms to a formula using the county as the basic unit of representation but with some weighting on a population basis. The apportionment of the Senate, though not based on a stated formula,

meaning of said Interlocutory Decree, but is an election under way and in being at the time said order was entered, the same having started with the filing period in February, 1962." The court explained that it was withholding judicial reapportionment "on the solemn word of the intervening legislators that once their constitutional duty is unequivocally and unescapably clear, they will discharge it with befitting honor and fidelity." *Ibid.* Rizley, D. J., filed a vehement dissent, insisting that the majority were retreating from their previous position; that under Oklahoma law the court had no power to give any prospective validity to the statutory and constitutional provisions it had declared invalid or to confer *de facto* powers on the Oklahoma legislature; that there was no reason to believe the legislature would pass a valid apportionment law; and that the court's duty was to reapportion the legislature forthwith. *Id.* at 899–904.

192 Ga. Const., art. III, § II, GA. CODE ANN. § 2-1401: "The Senate shall consist of not more than fifty-four members and there shall be not more than fifty-four Senatorial Districts with one Senator from each District as now constituted, or as hereafter created. The various Senatorial Districts shall be comprised of the Counties as now provided, and the General Assembly shall have authority to create, rearrange and change these Districts within the limitations herein stated."

193 Ga. Laws 1946, p. 42; GA. CODE ANN. § 47-102.

194 205 F. Supp. at 250.

195 Ga. Const., art. III, § III, par. I, GA. CODE ANN. § 2-1501.

196 *Id.*, par. II, GA. CODE ANN. § 1-1502.

197 Ga. Laws 1961, p. 111.

is similar except that three counties is the basic unit and the modification in respect of population is very slight.

The district court concluded that the apportionment reflected "invidious discrimination." Although it reiterated the statement made in *Sanders v. Gray* that "a test for invidiousness must be formulated," it made no use of or reference to the mathematical test enunciated in that case, but simply characterized the disparity in representation between counties as "gross." Its recital of facts noted, among other figures, that senatorial districts containing only 21.4 per cent of the population elected 54 members of the Senate, a majority, while districts containing 55 per cent of the population elected only 12 members, or 22 per cent of the Senate; and that in the House of Representatives counties containing only 22.5 per cent of the population elected a majority of the 205 members while counties aggregating 41 per cent of the population could elect only 11.7 per cent of the members.[198] It said that no "factual evidence" had been presented from which it could conclude that this disparity rested on a rational State policy and hence it must conclude that "there is no policy but simply a reluctance of those with grossly disproportionate power over the legislative process to surrender such power." "Another test," it said, "is whether or not the system is arbitrary. Having concluded that the gross disparities here . . . can not be related to a rational policy, we also conclude that the system is arbitrary in any sense of that term."[199] Continuing with its examination of "important factors" the court reviewed the "historical basis" of the Georgia representation plan but dismissed the consistent historical pattern as a possible justification because "the passage of time and changing living habits of the people have distorted it into something entirely different from what it was at its genesis."[200] By this the court meant, apparently, that the plan, initially "to some degree adjusted to population," had become less so. The court also referred to the absence under the State constitution of any provision for initiative or referendum to amend the constitution or statutes. The sum of all the factors considered, the opinion concluded, was that Georgia's plan "offends what are found to be fundamental political concepts inherent in a republican form of

---

198 205 F. Supp. at 251.

199 *Id.* at 254.

200 *Id.* at 255.

government"[201]—an invocation of the language of the Guarantee Clause that is of interest in the light of the statement in *Baker v. Carr*[202] that reliance on the Guarantee Clause would "of course" be futile.[203]

3. *The congressional districting case.* The third of the Georgia cases, brought like the other two by voters in Fulton county, was an attack on the Georgia statute prescribing the districts from which Georgia's ten representatives in Congress are to be elected. The suit, *Wesberry v. Vandiver*,[204] thus revived issues not considered by the Supreme Court since *Colegrove v. Green.* With one judge dissenting, the district court dismissed the complaint.

Attempting to give due respect to both *Baker v. Carr* and *Colegrove v. Green,* the opinion took a somewhat halting and meandering course. The Fifth Congressional District, in which Fulton county lies, is greatly disproportionate in population to the other districts, the court observed, due mainly to its exceptional growth in population since 1931 when the districts were drawn. It "dramatically exceeds" the 15 per cent maximum-variation-from-average suggested by plaintiffs as an appropriate standard. But such a standard is not acceptable; indeed, there is no basis here for an exact or mathematical standard, despite the fact that one was found in the unit-vote case. The problem is essentially legislative in nature, since correction of the Fifth District's disparity in size will require adjustments in other districts and could set off a "chain reaction." Comparable disparities exist in many congressional districts through-

---

201 *Id.* at 256.

202 369 U.S. at 227.

203 The district court also held unconstitutional the Georgia statutory provisions, GA. CODE ANN. §§ 47-102 and 47-102.1, providing that in multi-county senatorial districts the candidates for senator shall be "furnished" by each county in rotation, and restricting the vote at a primary election for senator to the voters of the county "furnishing" the candidate in that year. 205 F. Supp. at 257. This rotation system, it noted, placed effective control of the senate in the hands of an even smaller proportion of Georgia's population. 205 F. Supp. at 251. On the assumption that nomination in a Democratic primary is the practical equivalent of election, the court's conclusion was factually correct. Its implications are far-reaching, however, since it suggests that any nominating procedure effectively controlled by less than the entire electorate in a constituency may be unconstitutional, including, perhaps, nominating conventions.

204 206 F. Supp. 276 (N.D. Ga. 1962) (per Bell, C. J., Morgan, D. J., concurring; Tuttle, C. J., concurring in part and dissenting in part).

out the country. To be actionable such unequal treatment must reach the point of "invidiousness." The issue must be treated as justiciable, however, in the light of *Baker v. Carr*. The statute when enacted was rational because it reasonably reflected population. But it has now become arbitrary when considered in the light of the present population of the Fifth District, "as measured by any conceivable reasonable standard."[205] But a "judicially manageable standard" requires that normal State governmental processes be allowed to run their course where there is a substantial chance of relief. Such a chance now exists, by reason of the decision in *Toombs v. Fortson* requiring reapportionment of the State legislature. Therefore, "we do not now find proscribed invidiousness," under either the Fourteenth Amendment or under Article I, Section 2. It would be appropriate to retain jurisdiction and await action by the legislature. But *Colegrove v. Green* must be considered. That decision was not overruled in *Baker v. Carr* but was distinguished. The rationale of *Baker v. Carr* "goes no further than to open the doors of the courts . . . where no question is concerned involving a coequal political branch of the government."[206] That does not mean, however, that *Colegrove* is a precedent for dismissal "based on the nonjusticiability of a political question involving the Congress as here." Rather it is an authority requiring dismissal for "want of equity" in a case such as this which involves "a political question involving a coordinate branch of the federal government; a political question posing a delicate problem difficult of solution without depriving others of the right to vote by district, unless we are to redistrict for the state; relief may be forthcoming from a properly apportioned state legislature; and relief may be afforded by the Congress." Therefore the court is persuaded "of a want of equity in the position of plaintiffs to the extent that no cognizable constitutional claim is presented."[207]

The dissenting judge agreed that as a matter of discretion an injunction should be withheld in order to afford a reconstructed Georgia legislature the opportunity to reconstruct the congressional districts. He objected to dismissal of the action and to intimations that the case lay outside the court's competence. In his view the opinion in *Baker v. Carr* had removed any room for doubt based on

---

[205] *Id.* at 282.

[206] *Id.* at 285.

[207] *Id.* at 285, 286.

Colegrove v. Green. The reference in *Baker* to questions "decided, or to be decided, by a political branch of government co-equal with this Court" meant only that interference with the prerogatives or powers of Congress was to be avoided. In a congressional districting case no such interference is necessary because relief can be granted by action directed against the State authorities.

Whatever the other uncertainties of *Baker v. Carr,* on this point the dissenting judge seems to have interpreted it correctly. The majority who joined in Mr. Justice Brennan's opinion were evidently prepared to hold that congressional districting as well as State apportionment was within federal judicial control. It is true that Mr. Justice Brennan initially offered as the overriding reason why the political question doctrine was no barrier in *Baker v. Carr* the fact that no co-ordinate branch of the federal government was involved.[208] Throughout much of his discussion of "political questions" he sought to shape the doctrine as one concerned exclusively with separation of powers on the federal level. That view, if correct, was enough to remove the doctrine as an obstacle in *Baker,* distinguish *Colegrove v. Green,* and leave the question of congressional districting to another day. But Mr. Justice Brennan felt impelled to go on to distinguish *Colegrove* (and with it the other cases, including State apportionment cases, tracing their authority to it) on the quite different ground that it did not rest on "political question" considerations at all.[209] For this conclusion he pointed to the acceptance by four of the seven Justices in *Colegrove* (willing acceptance on the part of the three dissenters, reluctant on the part of Mr. Justice Rutledge) of the precedents in *Smiley v. Holm* and related cases.[210] Those cases, which held that under Article I, Section 4, a State's congressional districting law must be enacted in the same manner as other legislation, were indeed authority that not every question touching on congressional districting is exclusively committed to Congress. However, in stressing that their authority was untarnished by *Colegrove,* Mr. Justice Brennan's treatment of *Colegrove* was ignoring the quite different version of the political question doctrine implicit in the three-man opinion on the majority

---

208 369 U.S. at 210.

209 *Id.* at 232–34.

210 Smiley v. Holm, 285 U.S. 355 (1932); Koenig v. Flynn, 285 U.S. 375 (1932); Carroll v. Becker, 285 U.S. 380 (1932).

side. That opinion had emphasized the unsuitability of the question of apportionment for judicial determination. In this respect, however, *Colegrove* was tacitly repudiated in those passages of Mr. Justice Brennan's opinion which, without direct reference to *Colegrove*, proclaimed the availability of accepted and familiar judicial standards for passing on claims of discriminatory apportionment. Presumably it is as easy or as difficult for courts to decide when "invidious discrimination" exists in the case of congressional districts as in the case of State legislative districts. The upshot is that the majority opinion in *Baker v. Carr* leaves standing no generally applicable objection to the federal judicial intervention in congressional districting cases.

IV. Conclusion

The opinions and orders in the reapportionment cases since *Baker v. Carr* must speak for themselves. No doubt they will be received with varying degrees of indulgence by observers who differ in their enthusiasm for the results or who appraise differently the necessity or wisdom of distorting judicial institutions for the sake of correcting distortions in legislative ones. But several points seem to emerge beyond reasonable contradiction. First, there has been a striking absence of disposition to take seriously the difficult substantive issue ostensibly left open in *Baker v. Carr;* in the cases examined here the assumption that the Fourteenth Amendment confers a right to equality in representation has passed practically without scrutiny. So far as the lower courts are concerned, the turbid pronouncement of the Supreme Court has succeeded in moving the asserted right from the realm of non-justiciability to the realm of unquestioned law, without intervening exposure to serious examination. Second, the opinions give little reason for thinking that the assumed right can be formulated in terms of principle. All they have provided, and perhaps all that can be provided, is a series of *ex cathedra* judgments that a particular disparity in constituencies is "gross" or that a given apportionment plan is "irrational." These judgments have been offered with only negligible effort to identify the competing considerations that go into the scales of judgment, indeed almost without recognition that such an exercise might be necessary or appropriate. Third, the mere declaration of invalidity of apportionment laws, or injunctions against their enforcement, will seldom be seen as an adequate remedy. To avoid repeated litigation or a prolonged gap in the framework of government, courts have been drawn into providing detailed prescriptions of the legislative action to be taken, into threatening judicial reapportionment if such action is not promptly forthcoming, and into actually decreeing reapportionment. Fourth, despite the obviously serious questions raised by such use of judicial power—questions of constitutional authority, of propriety, and of enforceability—these courts have granted such relief with an almost complete lack of concern about the foundations of their authority and without manifest hesitation except for some expressions of reluctance to act before giving the legislature an opportunity for self-correction. The problems of remedy are beyond the scope of this discussion and deserve separate study, but the fact is that in all the federal court opinions examined above there is no discussion of a single precedent bearing on the scope of a federal court's remedial powers, let alone any dealing with the question of a federal court's power to order affirmative action by State officials in an area committed to State legislative authority. The courts have simply assumed that, having entered the field of reapportionment, they have unlimited authority to bring about reformation of the State legislatures.

It has been said that the decision in *Baker v. Carr* is "a great example of the rule of law in our society."[211] As a prediction that legislatures will bow to judicial decrees the statement may be prophetic. If it means more than that it must be disputed. Law makes demands on courts as well as on legislatures. Until the Supreme Court can provide a more satisfying explanation of the authority and principles by which courts decree reapportionment than it or the lower courts have yet given, the case will serve better as an example of the role of fiat in the exercise of judicial power.

---

[211] Katzenbach, *Some Reflections on Baker v. Carr*, 15 VAND. L. REV. 829, 836 (1962). But the most devastating comment on *Baker v. Carr* is surely Mr. Katzenbach's: "The Supreme Court has not attempted to define what are the inequities of representation or to prescribe remedies. *It has issued merely a call for action.*" *Id.* at 832. (Emphasis added.)

PRINTED IN U.S.A.